WILKES COMMUNITY
LEARNING RESOURCE
WILKESBORO, NC 2

D0563983

Costs of Occupational Injuries and Illnesses

Costs of Occupational Injuries and Illnesses

J. Paul Leigh, Ph.D.

Steven Markowitz, M.D.

Marianne Fahs, Ph.D., M.P.H.

Philip Landrigan, M.D.

Ann Arbor

THE UNIVERSITY OF MICHIGAN PRESS

Copyright © by the University of Michigan 2000
All rights reserved
Published in the United States of America by
The University of Michigan Press
Manufactured in the United States of America
∞ Printed on acid-free paper

2003   2002   2001   2000   4   3   2   1

No part of this publication may be reproduced, stored in a
retrieval system, or transmitted in any form or by any means,
electronic, mechanical, or otherwise, without the written
permission of the publisher.

A CIP catalog record for this book is available from the British Library.

Library of Congress Cataloging-in-Publication Data

Costs of occupational injuries and illnesses / J. Paul Leigh . . . [et al.].
       p.   cm.
   Includes bibliographical references and index.
   ISBN 0-472-11081-0 (alk. paper)
   1. Industrial accidents — United States — Costs.   2. Occupational
diseases — United States — Costs.   3. Industrial safety — Economic
aspects — United States.   4. Industrial hygiene — Economic aspects —
United States.   5. Costs, Industrial — United States.   I. Leigh, J. Paul.

HD7262.5.U6 C67   2000
363.11′0973 — dc21

                                                                                  99-87029

To my wife, Maria, for her wisdom, and my children, Wesley, Angelina, and John-Paul, for their joy.

— J. Paul Leigh

To Milton and Selma Markowitz, who showed me how to combine public health and medicine, and to Mary, Jonah, and Nathaniel for their patience and encouragement.

— Steven B. Markowitz

Acknowledgments

Lawrence Mishel suggested the idea for this book and arranged for funding in the first year. Jared Bernstein made many helpful comments on early drafts. Roxanne Leary provided excellent programming and editorial assistance.

Steven Markowitz carried out the research and wrote the chapter on number of illnesses. Marianne Fahs contributed virtually all of the data, methods, and analysis in the chapter on costs of illnesses. Philip Landrigan provided valuable comments and suggestions, especially for the disease chapters.

I am grateful to each of these people for adding their time and talent.

I am also grateful to the National Institute for Occupational Safety and Health for providing partial funds for the first year of research.

—J. P. Leigh

Contents

CHAPTER 1

Introduction and Summary

I. Introduction

Most of us between the ages of 22 and 65 spend 40 to 50 percent of our waking hours at work. Every year millions of us suffer injuries, diseases, and deaths in our workplaces. Yet little effort has been made to estimate either the extent of these injuries, deaths, and diseases or their cost to the economy. Thus, important questions about workplace safety and the economic resources expended due to workplace health problems remain unanswered. In this study, we address these questions by presenting estimates of the incidence, prevalence, and costs of workplace-related injuries, illnesses, and deaths for the entire civilian workforce of the United States in 1992. We also consider controversies surrounding cost methodologies, estimate how these costs are distributed across occupations, consider who pays the costs, and address some policy issues.

Our major findings are as follows.

Roughly 6,371 job-related injury deaths, 13.3 million nonfatal injuries, 60,300 disease deaths, and 1,184,000 illnesses occurred in the U.S. workplace in 1992 (see table 1.1).

The total direct and indirect costs associated with these injuries and illnesses were estimated to be $155.5 billion, or nearly 3 percent of gross domestic product (GDP).

Direct costs included medical expenses for hospitals, physicians, and drugs, as well as health insurance administration costs, and were estimated to be $51.8 billion.

The indirect costs included loss of wages, costs of fringe benefits, and loss of home production (e.g., child care provided by parent and home repairs), as well as employer retraining and workplace disruption costs, and were estimated to be $103.7 billion.

Injuries generated roughly 85 percent whereas diseases generated 15 percent of all costs.

These costs are large when compared to those for other diseases. The costs are roughly five times the costs for AIDS, three times the costs for Alzheimer's disease, more than the costs of arthritis, nearly as great as the costs for cancer, and roughly 82 percent of the costs of all circulatory (heart and stroke) diseases.

Workers' compensation covered roughly 27 percent of all costs. Taxpayers paid approximately 18 percent of these costs through contributions to Medicare, Medicaid, and Social Security.

Costs were borne by injured workers and their families, by all other workers through lower wages, by firms through lower profits, and by consumers through higher prices.

Our study appears to be the first to use national data to produce estimates on costs for occupational injuries and illnesses. Prior studies have underestimated costs by ignoring nondisabling injuries, deaths, and workplace violence, by taking inadequate account of diseases, and, most importantly, by relying on only one or two sources of data.

The Annual Survey of the Bureau of Labor Statistics (BLS) provides the most reliable and comprehensive data on nonfatal injuries. However, it misses roughly 53 percent of job-related injuries. This omission, in part, is due to the exclusion of government employees and the self-employed and also, in part, due to illegal underreporting by private firms.

Contrary to Annual Survey data, we find small firms have exceptionally high injury rates.

Occupations contributing the most to costs included truck drivers, laborers, janitors, nursing orderlies, assemblers, and carpenters. On a per capita basis, lumberjacks, laborers, millwrights, prison guards, and meatcutters contributed the most to costs.

TABLE 1.1.   Number and Costs of Injuries and Illnesses in 1992

| Category | Number | Costs (in $billions) | | |
		Total[a]	Direct	Indirect
Injuries	13,343,000	132.8	38.4	94.3
Deaths	6,371	3.9	0.2	3.7
Nonfatal	13,337,000	128.9	38.2	90.6
Illnesses[b]		22.8	13.4	9.4
Deaths	60,290	15.1	8.8	6.3
Morbidity	1,184,000	7.7	4.6	3.1

Source: Current study.

[a]May not sum due to rounding.

[b]The number of deaths and morbidity for illnesses cannot be summed precisely.

Occupations at highest risk for carpal tunnel syndrome include dental hygienists, meatcutters, sewing machine operators, and assemblers. Among well-paid professions, dentists face the highest risks.

Any of the major sources of data, such as the Bureau of Labor Statistics, National Institute for Occupational Safety and Health, workers' compensation systems, or National Health Interview Survey, by themselves underestimate the numbers of injuries and illnesses.

Greater efforts need to be directed toward gathering data on job-related injuries and illnesses. The United States needs a comprehensive data bank for fatal and nonfatal injuries and all illnesses. Future researchers should not have to investigate the over 20 sources of primary data and 300 sources of secondary data that we investigated.

These costs are great, but the reason for their size is no mystery. Roughly 120 million of us worked in 1992. Every job carries some risks (Leigh 1995a). Many of us are exposed to job-related safety risks of traffic accidents, falls, murder, electrocution, fire, being struck by objects, explosion, heat, cold, animal attacks, and airplane crashes, as well as health risks from radiation, asbestos, silica, benzene, coal dust, tuberculosis, secondhand smoke, carbon monoxide, pesticides, benzidine, arsenic, lead, chromium, and stress.

The estimates are the result of an exhaustive compilation of data from a variety of sources. Chapters 2 through 6 present a detailed account of our methodology and estimates. In developing the estimates, we most frequently selected conservative rather than generous assumptions. The assumptions with greatest consequences are listed in appendix B for chapter 10. Here, we mention four. First, with 7.4 percent of the workforce unemployed, 1992 was a high unemployment year. When fewer people are employed, fewer job-related injuries and diseases occur. Second, we did not account for health effects of occupational injuries and illnesses on the relatives of victims or, more importantly, for the cost of caregivers' time and energy (Arno, Levine, and Memmott 1999). After a serious injury or disease, someone in the family frequently provides care. Third, we restricted *job-related* circulatory disease deaths to people under 65 years old. It could be argued that jobs have a cumulative effect on circulatory disease that becomes evident only during retirement. Finally, our Human Capital method of estimating costs ignored costs of pain and suffering. These costs would add at least an additional $350 billion to our overall $155.5 billion estimate.

Ten sections follow this one, each corresponding to one of the chapters. Within each section we first present the major findings and, second, discuss methods and limitations.

II. Number of Injuries

Major general findings are listed in the following.

> We estimated that 6,371 deaths and 13.34 million new nonfatal injuries occurred in 1992.
> Disabling injuries accounted for 5.326 million of these injuries, and nondisabling injuries accounted for 8.011 million. Disabling means that the injury resulted in at least one day of work loss, whereas nondisabling means no full days of work loss.
> Within the disabling category, there are several subcategories. We relied on the workers' compensation (WC) categories: Permanent Total (PT), Permanent Partial (PP), and Temporary Total and Partial (TTP). We estimated 12,124 PTs, 741,000 PPs, and 1,947,000 TTPs.
> No one source of data is sufficient to estimate deaths or nonfatal injuries. The National Safety Council omitted violent acts. The Rand study by Hensler et al. (1991) omitted deaths. The National Traumatic Occupational Fatality Study relied solely on death certificates. The Census of Fatal Occupational Injuries (CFOI) may have resulted in an undercount because of the strict two source requirement. The BLS's Annual Survey underestimated injuries from small firms. All other sources had additional problems.
> Econometric time-series models using the National Health Interview Survey (NHIS) data as well as NHIS data on black/white injury rates suggest that the NHIS data may not be as reliable as is commonly believed.
> Workers' compensation records underestimate the number of injuries by 55 percent.

The most important findings involving socioeconomic and geographic characteristics are listed in the following.

> Disabling injuries are strongly correlated with job experience. New employees, regardless of age, experience a high and disproportionate number of injuries.
> Men are more likely than women to sustain a work injury. This is especially true for an injury resulting in death. The nonfatal in-

jury ratio for men to women is nearly 2:1, whereas the fatal injury ratio is about 11:1.

Blacks and Hispanics experience greater injury rates than non-Hispanic whites.

In 1992, the CFOI and the NHIS underestimate injuries experienced by blacks.

The self-employed, persons employed in small firms, and persons over age 65 are at high risk for sustaining an injury death.

Laborers, truck drivers, and taxi drivers generate among the highest death rates of all occupations.

Mining, farming, and construction are the industries with the highest rates of fatal and nonfatal injuries.

Murder is the most likely cause of death for business executives and sales workers.

Operators and laborers generate the greatest numbers of deaths and nonfatal injuries among all broad occupation groups.

Laborers, truck drivers, nursing aides, janitors, assemblers, stock handlers, and cashiers generate the most disabling injuries among detailed occupations.

Being at work is not safer than being at home. People who work are more likely to be injured at work than at home. This is especially true for men. Moreover, work-related injuries are more likely to result in hospitalizations than injuries originating outside of work.

The most important findings pertaining to types of injuries are listed in the following.

Injuries to the back generate the highest frequency of disabling injuries.

Recall bias on questions asking for incidents dating back 12 months may result in a serious undercount of nondisabling injuries.

Transportation accidents involving highway vehicles, industrial vehicles, and aircraft boats and railroads contribute to 40 percent of injury deaths. Transportation accidents have frequently been ignored by the Occupational Safety and Health Administration (OSHA).

Assaults and violent acts contribute another 20 percent of injury deaths. These, too, have frequently been ignored by OSHA.

Transportation accidents, assaults, and violent acts comprise a smaller share of nonfatal injuries than fatal injuries. Assaults and violent acts are more likely to be fatal than most other injuries at work.

The numbers of deaths and nonfatal injuries were estimated after considering five primary sources and four secondary sources. The primary sources included the BLS Census of Fatal Occupational Injuries (CFOI), the BLS Annual Survey of Occupational Injuries and Illnesses (Annual Survey), the Ultimate Reports of the National Council on Compensation Insurance (NCCI), the National Health Interview Survey (NHIS), the National Traumatic Occupational Fatalities Study (NTOF), and the BLS's Supplementary Data System. Secondary sources included studies by Hensler et al. (1991), Rossman, Miller, and Douglas (1991), Miller (1994), and the National Safety Council (1992, 1993). These data have strengths and weaknesses. The BLS's CFOI and Annual Survey data were regarded as the best data, and our estimates were ultimately derived only from them.

III. Number of Illnesses

For deaths, we estimate 41,367 from cancer, 7,638 from heart disease and stroke, 9,154 from chronic obstructive pulmonary disease (COPD), 1,136 from pneumoconioses, 538 from nervous system disorders, and 460 from renal disorder, for a total of 60,293 deaths.

For new cases of chronic disease in 1992, we estimate 89,050 for cancer, 64,475 for heart disease and stroke, and 150,000 for COPD. These sum to 303,525.

Among new cases for acute and/or nonfatal conditions, we estimate a total of 880,172, which includes an estimate of 14,250 for poisoning from lead.

Illnesses that are responsible for the greatest numbers of days away from work as reported by private firms to the BLS include the following: nervous system diseases, musculoskeletal disorders, rheumatism, carpal tunnel syndrome, and digestive disorders.

Whereas reported cases of injuries appear to be slowly increasing over time, reported cases of diseases and conditions are rising rapidly. In some cases, such as for repeated trauma disorders (which include carpal tunnel syndrome), that increase has been especially steep.

Cases of occupational illnesses are likely to be seriously undercounted since many physicians are not properly trained to look for them.

We have good evidence for some job-related causal agents and risk factors for some diseases. Exposure to asbestos can cause lung cancer.

Lead, carbon monoxide, and solvent exposures as well as psychosocial stress have been linked to cardiovascular and cerebrovascular disease. Occupational exposures to coal, silica, grain dust, and cadmium have been linked to chronic respiratory diseases. Job-related exposures to lead, mercury, glycol ethers, some solvents, and pesticides have been linked to renal disorders and nervous system disorders. However, there is little evidence for a definite number of cancers, circulatory diseases, and so on, that would be job related. We therefore assigned percentages to the overall numbers of cancers, circulatory diseases, and so on. The percentages we assigned were these: 6–10 percent for cancer; 5–10 percent for circulatory disease; 10 percent for COPD; and 1–3 percent for renal and nervous disorders. We restricted attention to persons over age 24 and, for the circulatory diseases, to persons also under age 65 and to only roughly two-thirds of all circulatory diseases. These restrictions on circulatory disease resulted in an effective range of 0.6 to 1.1 percent for all circulatory diseases rather than a 5–10 percent range. The death estimates were based on data from the National Center for Health Statistics.

Estimates for acute and nonfatal diseases are drawn from the BLS's Annual Survey after adjustments are made for the well-known undercounts involving self-employed persons, workers in small firms, and the economic incentive to underreport. Estimates on lead poisoning are drawn from the Adult Blood Lead Epidemiology and Surveillance program.

IV. Two Methods for Measuring Costs

A crude Willingness-to-Pay estimate for all occupational injuries and illnesses would range between $533 and $905 billion.

Economic studies of compensating wage differentials are seriously flawed by not properly accounting for broad interindustry differences in pay.

Economists have developed two methods for estimating the costs of injuries and illnesses: the Human Capital cost method and the Willingness-to-Pay (WTP) method. The Human Capital method is the most widely used method in legal and medical settings. It is practical, intuitive, and easy to implement (i.e., numbers are available). The WTP method is more widely used in the U.S. economics literature. Many, but not all, economists believe it is theoretically more compelling than the Human Capital method. All economists agree, however, that the WTP method is difficult to implement.

Direct costs are a major component of the Human Capital method. Direct costs represent actual dollars spent or anticipated to be spent on providing medical care to an injured or ill person and administrative costs for insurance companies. Medical care costs include doctors' and nurses' services, hospital charges, drug costs, rehabilitation services, ambulance fees, and payments for medical equipment and supplies. Indirect costs are a second component. They include lost wages while the workers cannot work.

The WTP method attempts to put prices on injuries and illnesses that are generated in private market transactions. The presumption behind WTP is that individual workers themselves are in the best position to evaluate the true value of medical costs, lost earnings, family hardship, pain and suffering, and so on, rather than researchers analyzing statistical data. These prices, theoretically, may be observed through market transactions, for example, buying safe or dangerous cars. We used the WTP estimates in Viscusi 1993 to price our deaths, injuries, and illnesses.

We prefer the estimates based upon the Human Capital method for a variety of reasons but most importantly (1) so that we can compare our estimates with those of other diseases such as AIDS, arthritis, and cancer that were estimated with the Human Capital method and (2) to estimate medical costs, the category of spending that commands the most public attention.

V. Costs of Injuries

Direct costs comprise 29 percent, and indirect costs 71 percent, of total injury costs.

Within the direct cost category, medical only costs are roughly $26 billion (68 percent), medical insurance administration costs are $5.5 billion (14 percent), and indemnity insurance administration costs are $6.8 billion (18 percent).

Within the indirect cost category, lost earnings summed to $67 billion (71 percent); fringe benefits, $15.7 billion (17 percent); home production, $9.3 billion (10 percent); and workplace training, restaffing, and disruption, $2.2 billion (2 percent).

Fatality costs comprised only roughly 3 percent of the total. Sensitivity analysis that would have altered interest rates for present value calculations would not have appreciably affected our results.

Insurance administration costs have frequently been omitted from prior cost studies. This is a mistake. Insurance administration costs (for both medical and indemnity insurance) are significant, comprising 32 percent of direct costs.

Estimation of the costs of injuries required multiplying the number of injuries in each category by the average costs of such injuries. Direct average costs for medical care were drawn from the National Council on Compensation Insurance Ultimate Reports. Lifetime medical costs (1992 dollars) for deaths were valued at $17,226; for Permanent Total at $113,372; for Permanent Partial at $15,342; for Temporary Total and Partial at $2,782; and for no work loss at $294. The medical expenses were drawn from workers' compensation accounts and did not require adjustment for charges versus payments since workers' compensation paid virtually 100 percent of medical bills in 1992; that is, very few co-payments or deductibles were charged to clients.

The calculation of the indirect costs was based on a variety of sources, including National Council's indemnity data and federal government data on employment, earnings, and mortality. Home production costs, as well as hiring, training, and workplace disruption costs, were priced in accord with estimates in the literature. Indirect costs for fatalities required a present value calculation. We assumed that persons who died would have earned what others of the same age and gender earned. The distribution of deaths by age and sex was estimated with information from the CFOI. These age and sex data were combined with information on wages and on probabilities of survival to age 75, as well as on the employment within those categories.

The National Council figures also provided us with indemnity benefits that were used to estimate wage loss. The indemnity benefits themselves were not added to wage losses. The indemnity benefits were adjusted assuming workers' compensation paid to clients the following rates: 40 percent of pretax wages for Permanent Total conditions; 50 percent for Permanent Partial conditions; and 60 percent for Temporary Total and Partial conditions. Fringe benefits were assumed to be 23 percent of the pretax wages for men and women combined.

Insurance administration costs were assumed to be 31 percent for workers' compensation and 15 percent for all others.

VI. Costs of Disease

Roughly 66 percent of these costs were attributed to direct costs, while 34 percent were attributed to indirect costs.

Within direct costs, $11 billion (85 percent) went for medical care,

$1.6 billion (12 percent) went for insurance administration on medical care, and $.7 billion (3 percent) went for insurance administration on indemnity.

Within indirect costs, $6.9 billion (73 percent) went for lost earnings, $1.6 billion (17 percent) went for fringe benefits, and $.9 billion (10 percent) went for home production.

Disease contributions to costs were as follows: cancer, 48 percent; circulatory diseases, 16 percent; pneumoconioses, 2 percent; nervous system disorders, <1 percent; renal disorders, <1 percent; and all others, including hearing loss, carpal tunnel syndrome, skin diseases, chronic respiratory disease, and so on, 33 percent.

Using the National Hospital Discharge Survey, we calculated the total number of days spent in the hospital by patients with a primary diagnosis for one of the following six deadly diseases, five of which were estimated with the attributable percentages from chapter 3: cancer, circulatory, chronic respiratory, nervous system, and renal disorders. Total days of hospitalization by disease group were transformed to obtain standardized proportions of national hospital utilization attributable to occupational disease. We applied these disease-specific proportions to the national health expenditure accounts, estimated by disease category by the Health Care Financing Agency, to obtain an estimate of medical costs.

Indirect costs were estimated using age-specific and sex-specific mortality data from the same sources identified earlier in the discussion of indirect costs of deaths caused by injury. By applying the occupational attributable proportions for deaths caused by disease, the present value of the indirect costs of premature mortality attributable to occupational disease was estimated for the base year 1992. Morbidity costs for persons who survived the six deadly diseases were calculated by applying to our estimates highly regarded ratios of morbidity costs to direct costs.

We investigated the medical costs of nonfatal occupational diseases, including skin diseases, using prices per disease from the literature. Wage rates were applied to lost work time to obtain an estimate of indirect costs.

VII. Workers' Compensation Costs across Occupations

The public is frequently misinformed about job hazards. Most of the high cost per person jobs, such as production helpers, laborers, janitors, nursing orderlies, sales workers who drive on the job, truck drivers, polishing machine operators, kitchen machine operators, assemblers, and others, are not generally regarded as dangerous by the public.

Many of the most costly occupations are not well described by U.S. Census categories but appear to occupy the lowest status categories, for example, laborers, miscellaneous machine operators, freight handlers (not elsewhere classified), production helpers, construction helpers, and miscellaneous food preparation occupations.

The cost per person lists reinforce the view that the most hazardous jobs enjoy the least pay. Occupations within the laborer and operative categories receive the lowest pay of all occupation groups but generate among the highest costs.

Jobs that are high on both the total and per person cost lists include truck drivers, laborers (inside and outside of construction), janitors and cleaners, nursing aides, assemblers, carpenters, miscellaneous food preparation occupations, timber cutters, electricians, welders, bus drivers, police officers, and firefighters. Jobs that are high on both lists should be candidates for greater attention from occupational safety and health regulators and researchers.

This chapter uses exclusively workers' compensation (WC) data to rank occupations by costs. Data were drawn from a large national representative BLS data set — the Supplementary Data System. Information was obtained on occupations and WC category of injury and illness and was then matched to information on costs. Six broad occupations were ranked by total costs. Six broad and 223 specific occupations were ranked by costs per person (average costs). Unlike cost data in all other analyses of the book, these rankings applied to 1985 and 1986, not 1992.

VIII. Who Pays?

Using the nominal payment method, we found that injured or ill workers and their families absorbed about 44 percent of the costs. Medicare, Medicaid, Social Security, and other government accounts contributed 18 percent, or roughly $28.5 billion.

Using the incidence payment method, we found employers absorbing some noninjury costs in terms of lower profits, consumers absorbing some in terms of higher prices, and all workers absorbing some in terms of lower wages.

There are two methods for assessing who pays, the nominal method and the incidence method. The nominal method considers who writes the check. The incidence method uses economic theory to assess the burden. For example, the business owner writes the WC premium payment check to the insurance company. But the owner may try to pass on the cost of that premium to the consumer in terms of higher prices. There is considerable controversy surrounding how much employers, consumers, and workers pay in the incidence method, however. We therefore prefer the nominal over the incidence method for assessing the cost burden of job-related injuries and illnesses.

IX. Policy and Cost Comparisons

One policy option would be to provide more information to workers pertaining to the hazards of their jobs. A report card could be prepared by the BLS that would rank and compare occupations and industries across the United States. The report card could be attached to every job application form.

We suggest that a general occupational injury and illness tax be levied on all employers to pay for the substantial amount of costs that is currently being shifted to taxpayers and the general public. This tax could be modeled on the Federal Black Lung Trust fund that taxes all coal companies on a per tonnage amount to pay for the medical costs of pneumoconioses. Taxes would vary by industry based upon that industry's contribution to circulatory diseases, cancer, and so on.

We argue for more and heavier fines on firms that willfully underreport injuries to the BLS.

The effect generous WC benefits has had on encouraging injuries is likely to be small.

Small firms are treated gingerly by OSHA. They should not be since they have the highest injury and illness rates of all firms.

The methods introduced in this chapter pertain to the economic laws of diminishing returns and increasing opportunity costs. Put simply, the last, say, 5 percent of heart disease spending could be reallocated to occupational injury and illness spending with the result being a substantial net gain in lives saved and illnesses and injuries prevented.

X. Limitations and Assumptions

The dollar amount of fraudulent WC claims submitted by workers pales in comparison to the amount for claims never filed and, more importantly, the overall small amount of total costs paid by

WC systems. Moreover, fraud committed by insurance companies at workers' expense is likely to be significant.

We list 31 critical assumptions: 25 result in a smaller estimate than
otherwise would obtain; two result in a higher estimate; the bias
on the remaining four is unknown.

Human Capital costs can be viewed as measuring overall health and
are strongly proportional to quality-adjusted life years (QALYs).

Many episodes of occupational injuries also involved innocent bystanders. For example, a single pilot death may be associated
with scores of deaths to passengers. We estimated 218 deaths and
68,000 nonfatal injuries to innocent bystanders in 1992. The total
costs of deaths and injuries to bystanders were $2.9132 billion.

XI. Conclusion

Our study attempted to estimate the total costs of occupational injuries
and illnesses to the United States in 1992. This study appears to be the first
to use national data to estimate these costs.[1] We find that the costs of
occupational injuries and illnesses are considerable, surpassing those of
AIDS and nearly as great as those of cancer and heart disease. Potential
victims include any one of the roughly 120 million Americans who work
for a living. Since the injuries and illnesses occur at places of business,
some of their costs are spread to consumers in the form of higher prices
throughout the economy, all workers in the form of lower wages, and
taxpayers. But despite the size of these costs and the fact that so many
people pay them, occupational injuries and illnesses do not receive the
attention they deserve (Rosenstock 1981). By almost any measure,
AIDS, arthritis, Alzheimer's disease, cancer, and heart disease receive
far more attention than occupational injuries and illnesses.[2] In the course
of four years of medical training, the typical U.S. doctor receives six hours
of instruction in occupational safety and health. The national debate on
medical care rarely addresses occupational safety and health issues. This
is unfortunate. The potential for cost savings from prevention of occupational injuries and illnesses appears to be significant.

CHAPTER 2

Number of Injuries

I. Introduction

In 1966, Secretary of Labor Willard Wirtz offered the following testimony to Congress (Lemen et al. 1989):

> Mr. Chairman, and members of the Committee, while we sit here talking, from now until noon, seventeen American men and women will be killed on their jobs. Every minute we talk, 18 to 20 people will be hurt severely enough to have to leave their jobs — some of them never to work again. In the time these two sentences have taken, another 20 people — one every second — have been injured on the job — less seriously, but in most cases needlessly. Today's industrial casualty list — like yesterday's — and tomorrow's — and every working day's in each week, after month, after year — will be 55 dead, 8,500 disabled, over 27,200 hurt. The figures for the year will be 14,000 to 15,000 dead, over 2 million disabled, over 7 million hurt.

More recently, an analysis of the Office of Technology Assessment (OTA) of Congress concluded that at least 4,650 and as many as 13,200 workers died each year between 1979 and 1983 as a result of job-related injuries (Office of Technology Assessment 1985). In 1985, the U.S. Congress estimated that job-related deaths due to injuries were 13,000 per year (Lemen et al. 1989). As we will see, what is surprising about the Wirtz quote and the OTA and congressional conclusions are that the numbers from 1966, 1979, 1983, and 1985 are not terribly different from those today. From these early years of recording injuries, the number of fatal injuries has declined, while the number of nonfatal injuries has increased.

The first purpose of this chapter is to update these estimates to 1992. The second purpose is to identify the merits and limitations of the most widely used data sets containing job-related injury information. The third purpose is to provide some descriptive analyses of the demographic, occupational, industrial, and geographic characteristics of job-

14

related injuries. The fourth purpose is to analyze the kinds of injuries that occur.

This chapter is split into nine sections, some with several subsections, as well as two appendixes. The first section is this introduction. Section II provides our definition of job-related injury. Sections III and IV present national estimates for the numbers and rates of fatal and nonfatal injuries. Within the fatal injuries section (III), five primary data sources are discussed. The two most popular primary sources include (1) the Census of Fatal Occupational Injuries (CFOI) by the Bureau of Labor Statistics (BLS) and (2) the National Traumatic Occupational Fatalities (NTOF) study by the National Institute for Occupational Safety and Health (NIOSH).

Section IV — Nonfatal Injuries — is also split into subsections based upon primary data sources. The popular primary sources are the BLS's Annual Survey and the National Health Interview Survey (NHIS). A lesser-known primary source is the workers' compensation (WC) data from the National Council on Compensation Insurance (NCCI).

Section V presents a summary of our estimates and a classification scheme.

Section VI presents a literature review and discussion of secondary sources (i.e., someone else's interpretation of primary data). The secondary sources include the following: (1) Marquis 1992, for which the data were drawn from the Hensler et al. 1991 study at the Rand Institute for Civil Justice; (2) Rossman, Miller, and Douglas 1991; (3) Miller 1995; and (4) the National Safety Council 1993.

Section VII addresses the demographic, occupational, industrial, and geographical characteristics of victims. The CFOI, the NTOF, BLS's Annual Survey, and the 1988 NHIS data are especially rich in their detail on the characteristics of victims.

Section VIII investigates the nature, source, and type of injuries. The CFOI and the NTOF have extensive information on the characteristics of deaths, and the Annual Survey and the NHIS have considerable information on the characteristics of nonfatal injuries.

The conclusion is presented in section IX.

This chapter also has two appendixes. Appendix A contains discussions of the primary data sets. These discussions describe and critique the primary data. As indicated earlier, we believe the detailed discussions are important. One of the contributions of our book is to indicate how existing data sources could be improved to better count all job-related injuries. Appendix B contains tables describing the demographic characteristics of those injured as well as the types of injuries that most frequently occur.

II. Definitions of Job-Related Injuries

Our definitions of job-related injury deaths and job-related nonfatal injuries are the conventional ones. We adopt the definition from the Bureau of Labor Statistics' Census of Fatal Occupational Injuries (CFOI) as our general definition of a *job-related injury*. First, the *injury* is any unintentional or intentional wound or damage to the body resulting from acute exposure to energy — such as heat or electricity or kinetic energy from a crash — or from the absence of such essentials as heat or oxygen caused by a specific event, incident, or series of events within a single workday or shift (U.S. Bureau of Labor Statistics 1995b, 1301). Second, the injury is *job related* if an event or exposure (1) occurs either on the employer's premises when the person was there to work, or (2) occurs off the employer's premises when the person was there to work, or (3) was related to the person's work or status as an employee.[1]

Next we consider the specific definitions of *death* and *nonfatal* injuries. A *death* occurs when the job-related injury conditions are met and the person dies as a result of the injury. A *nonfatal* injury occurs when the conditions are met, the person does not die, and one of the following applies: loss of consciousness involving days away from work, restriction of work, transfer to another job, or medical treatment beyond first aid (U.S. Bureau of Labor Statistics 1995a). Examples of injuries include cuts, fractures, sprains, and amputations. We will not count trivial injuries such as those that can be accommodated with first aid.

We measure injuries in *episodes,* not persons or diagnoses. The same person might experience two different job-related injuries in 1992: one in January and another in December. Our episode count would be 2. A person count would be 1. A car crash might involve a concussion and a lacerated finger to the same person. Our episode count would be 1. A medical-diagnoses count would be 2.

We define a *disabling* nonfatal injury as any that results in one or more full days of work lost at the usual activity level. By "full" day we mean the loss of all work hours generally worked in a 24-hour day by that individual. For some, that might mean 4 hours; for others, over 10. By "usual" we mean the typical daily tasks. If a person shows up to work after the injury but is assigned less difficult tasks or no tasks at all, we count that as a disabling injury.

Our definitions of *injury, job related, fatal, nonfatal, episode,* and *disability* are drawn from the BLS's Census of Fatal Occupational Injury and the BLS's Annual Survey. The *injury* definitions are virtually identical to the definitions (regardless whether on or off the job) in the National Health Interview Surveys (NHIS) (Benson and Marano 1994) and federal government reports on injuries (Fingerhut and Warner 1997), as well as those used by leading researchers in the field (Baker et al. 1992; Rice et al. 1989a; Miller 1995). The NHIS defines an episode of injury as an event that results in injury that either prompts medical attention or at least a half day of restricted activity. Our *job-related* definitions are similar to all other studies that attempt to count all job-related injuries of which we are aware. As we will see, some studies do not attempt to count all injuries but rather rely exclusively on death certificates or workers' compensation records.[2] Counting *episodes* rather than persons or diagnoses is consistent with the lion's share of studies on injuries (U.S. Bureau of Labor Statistics 1995a; Miller 1995; Marquis 1992; Baker et al 1992; National Safety Council 1992).

Carpal tunnel syndrome (CTS) and other repetitive trauma disorders have aspects of injury, but we (as well as the Bureau of Labor Statistics [BLS]) treat them as illnesses; hence, they are not discussed in this chapter. We, as well as the BLS, *do* regard back pain as resulting from a back injury and thus include these conditions in this chapter.

Finally, our count of injuries is an incidence, not a prevalence, count.

As we will see, a problem will arise in this study, as in any study on nonfatal injuries, concerning the many ways to classify nonfatal injuries. Our classification scheme allows for some of the most popular categories. We include the NHIS and BLS definitions of disabling and nondisabling; the workers' compensation (WC) definitions of Permanent, Temporary, Partial, and Total disability; and the Rice et al. 1989a scheme involving hospitalizations or lack thereof. Category schemes involving body parts will receive scant attention. Our emphasis on disabling injuries, WC categories, and injuries causing hospitalizations matches the medical and indirect costs data available on injuries more closely than the body part schemes. The medical and indirect cost data for WC categories are especially rich. Moreover, many accidents result in more than one body part being hurt. The same hospitalization cost could cover two body part injuries. If we assigned this hospitalization cost to body parts separately, we would be double counting costs.

III. Fatalities

Five primary sources — the Census of Fatal Occupational Injuries (CFOI), National Traumatic Occupational Fatality Study (NTOF), Annual Survey, National Council on Compensation Insurance (NCCI), and

Supplementary Data System (SDS)—are introduced in this section. A summary discussion that includes our estimates of fatalities is also presented.

III.A. Primary Sources

III.A.1. Census of Fatal Occupational Injuries (CFOI)

The CFOI is one of the most current and arguably the most reliable of all the data sets we will examine. The CFOI was initiated by the BLS in response to an expert panel from the National Academy of Sciences (National Research Council 1987) that "found it rather startling that an agreed upon method has not been devised to estimate a phenomenon as basic as traumatic death in the workplace." The CFOI was designed to be a true census, or complete count, of job-related injury deaths. There were no limitations imposed such as relying on only workers' compensation (WC) records, only OSHA records, only death certificates, and so on. Stout and Bell (1991) and Jack and Zak (1993) have shown that no single private, state, or national system, such as workers' compensation (WC), or OSHA's Form 200 data sets, or the BLS's Annual Surveys of Occupational Injuries and Illnesses, or NIOSH's National Traumatic Occupational Fatality Study, or the National Council on Compensation Insurance (NCCI) reports, provides a complete count. This is a key finding of our study: few data sets are available that can provide credible estimates of the total numbers of fatal and nonfatal injuries.

Table 2.1 indicates the sources used to compile the CFOI for 1992. Table 2.1 is drawn from Jack and Zak 1993. Before we explore each of these sources, however, we want to emphasize the most important findings in table 2.1. Most prior studies of fatal (and nonfatal) injuries have relied on only one of the sources in table 2.1. But none of the sources are complete. Subsequently, we detail the reasons for the lack of completeness. Here it will suffice for us to underscore that death certificates missed 28 percent, WC reports missed 60 percent, and OSHA Form 200 reports missed 63 percent of the deaths.

The CFOI initially counted 6,083 job-related deaths for 1992.[3] The majority (72 percent) of the deaths in table 2.1 were located or corroborated with death certificates marked "at work." An additional 1,274 deaths had certificates but were not marked "at work." The fact that death certificates cannot be relied on for 100 percent coverage is an important finding and has been supported in several studies. Other estimates of underreporting of job-related fatalities due to incorrect marking of "injury at work" have ranged from 12 percent to 83 percent (Colorado Department of Health 1988; Davis, Honchar, and Suarez 1987; Karlson and Baker 1978; Baker et al. 1982; Ruble 1993, 17 percent missed; Stout and Bell 1991, 19 percent missed; Murphy, Seltzer, and Yesalis 1990, 20 percent missed). In California, Kraus et al. (1990) found that 83 percent of job-related deaths among persons over age 64 were not recorded as an "injury at work" on the death certificate. We consider reasons for these undercounts in our section on the National Traumatic Occupational Fatality Study.

The CFOI researchers require that two independent sources confirm a death. The requirement of two substantiating sources was designed to improve the reliability of the CFOI data. No other data set we considered in our injury analysis had this requirement. The minimum of two substantiating sources could be criticized, however, as resulting in an undercount. Some employers may not want to acknowledge that a death was job related. Some employees and their families might be poorly informed concerning reports or workers' compensation claims that should have been filed after a job-related death.

A troubling race finding emerged from the CFOI 1992 data. There was virtually no difference in the fatality rates for whites (4.938 per

TABLE 2.1. Source Documents Used to Compile the Census of Fatal Occupational Injuries, 1992

	Fatalities	
Source Document	Number	Percentage
Total	6,083[a] (or 5,929)[b]	100
Death certificates	4,359 (or 5,633)[b]	72 (or 93)[b]
State WC reports	2,434	40
Coroner, medical examiner	3,768	61
OSHA reports	1,926	32
News media	2,077	34
Follow-up questionnaires	1,504	25
State motor vehicle reports	485	8
Other federal reports (e.g., MSHA)	328	5
Other reports (e.g., local police)	2,033	33

Source: U.S. Bureau of Labor Statistics, Census of Fatal Occupational Injuries.

[a]The 6,083 also includes 154 deaths among persons in the armed forces residing in the United States. We exclude these 154 military deaths in our final CFOI estimate. We will include the 134 deaths improperly omitted from the first 1992 CFOI report.

[b]The number and percentage of death certificates in parentheses include 1,274 certificates initially *not* marked "at work."

100,000) and blacks (4.962 per 100,000). This finding stands in contrast to almost all other occupational studies and general studies on death rates for injuries that investigated black/white differences. It also stands in contrast to more recent (1993) CFOI data showing a higher rate for non-Hispanic blacks, especially non-Hispanic black men, than non-Hispanic whites (Ruser 1996). The NIOSH National Traumatic Occupational Fatality Study (NTOF) found a black rate of 6.5 per 100,000 and a white rate of 5.8 per 100,000. Cone et al. (1991), in studying data from California, found blacks had job-related injury deaths roughly 20 percent higher than whites and Hispanics.[4]

The CFOI counted 508 Hispanic deaths, which yielded a rate of 5.589. This exceeds the 4.938 rate for whites. A higher rate for Hispanics than non-Hispanic whites has been found by Robinson (1991) using data on nonfatal injuries and by Ruser (1996) using 1993 CFOI data for men. But the 5.589 Hispanic rate may also be an underestimate. Robinson's data suggest Hispanics have a rate 79 percent higher than whites. Ruser's data suggest a 60 percent higher rate for male Hispanics.

The fact that the CFOI estimated white and black fatality rates were virtually identical in 1992 is, therefore, disquieting, as is the slight difference between the CFOI's Hispanic and non-Hispanic rates. There may be an undiscovered flaw in the CFOI methods, at least for the 1992 estimates.[5]

The CFOI estimate can be adjusted upward to reflect the undercount of non-Hispanic blacks and Hispanics.[6] We estimate 98 more black deaths and 210 more Hispanic deaths than were counted in the CFOI. Summing the two adds 308 more deaths to the CFOI total of 6,063 (6,083 − 154 military deaths + 134 late deaths).[7] We, therefore, estimate 6,371 (6,063 + 308 = 6,371) "race- and ethnic-adjusted" job-related deaths based on the CFOI data for 1992.

This estimate of 6,371 assumes that the only problem in the CFOI is an undercount of blacks and Hispanics. No adjustment was made for the undercounts associated with (1) heavy reliance on death certificates (see app. A, the CFOI section); (2) improperly recorded "heart attacks" (see app. A, the CFOI section); (3) the strict two source corroborating requirement; or (4) the general problems suggested by the questionable lack of rate differences for blacks and whites and the modest rate differences between whites and Hispanics. That is, the race and ethnic problems suggest a larger problem of counting people in low-paying jobs such as farm or construction laborers. We do not adjust for any underreporting of deaths in low-paying jobs.[8]

Finally, although the CFOI was prevalence based, we assume our 6,371 number is incidence based.[9]

III.A.2. National Traumatic Occupational Fatality
Study (NTOF)

The NTOF, unlike the BLS's CFOI, began in the 1980s. The 50 states,
Washington, DC, and New York City were contacted and asked to supply death certificates beginning with 1980. The certificates must have
been marked "injury at work," the decedents must have been 16 years of
age or over, and an external cause of death must have been noted (ICD-
9, E800–E999).[10]

The NTOF deaths were recorded in the year of the death, not the
injury. The NTOF, like the CFOI, is a prevalence study.

Bell et al. (1990) present an analysis of the NTOF for the years 1980
through 1985. The 1980 to 1989 data are analyzed in a publication available from NIOSH in Morgantown (National Institute for Occupational
Safety and Health 1993).

Exclusive reliance on death certificates results in a serious undercount. The CFOI (table 2.1) indicated that exclusive reliance on
certificates marked "at work" would have resulted in a 28 percent undercount of the deaths, ignoring our race and ethnicity adjustments.
Using our "race-adjusted" CFOI estimate would imply a 32 percent
undercount. In other studies the undercounts of job-related deaths due
to exclusive reliance on death certificates ranged from 12 percent to 83
percent as identified in section III.A.1.

One explanation for the omissions resulting from reliance on death
certificates could be due to the fact that motor vehicle crashes are
the most frequent cause of job-related deaths. Motor vehicle crashes
have frequently not been regarded as job related by the public or by
some Occupational Safety and Health (OSH) researchers (Baker et al.
1982, 114–15; National Safety Council 1993, 39). The original OSHA
legislation, for example, did not extend any regulations to operating
motor vehicles. Only in the 1990s has OSHA propagated rules to gov-
ern vehicles and drivers (Rolle 1993). An example will illustrate the
point. A self-employed real estate agent may have been killed in a car
accident at 8:00 pm. while traveling to meet a client. Since the self-
employed are frequently excluded from WC coverage, the only official
report would be a police accident report or coroner's information on a
death certificate. Police reports of crashes may be defective, however.
In Washington State, there is no code or identifier on the police traffic
collision reports to indicate the decedent was working at the time of
the accident (Rolle 1993). CFOI investigators, in fact, acknowledge
that "traffic accident reports usually cannot be used to verify work
relationship because they do not contain information on the purpose of

the trip" (Toscano and Windau 1993). Moreover, a coroner, who has no knowledge of the purpose of the trip, may not check the "at work" box on a death certificate. Runyan, Loomis, and Butts (1994) present evidence that coroners have difficulty determining whether many crashes were job related. It is therefore likely that the real estate agent's death would not be reported on any report or certificate as job related. Additional problems are noted in Davis 1988 and Russell and Conroy 1991.

There are other problems with the NTOF as indicated in Bell et al. 1990 and NIOSH 1993. For example, in the early years (1980–85) of the NTOF, some states and New York City coroners and certifiers did not regard any homicide or suicide as job related. The policy was changed in 1986.

Nevertheless, the NTOF was an exceptional effort, collecting information on 82,696 civilian and military deceased workers from 1980 through 1993. Of the total, 98 percent were civilian and 2 percent were military deaths. NTOF continues to generate many studies (Fosbroke, Kisner, and Myers 1997; Kisner and Pratt 1997). NTOF researchers counted 4,803 deaths in 1992 (personal communication with Susan Kisner, September 20, 1997).

Perhaps the most important cause of the NTOF's undercount is its exclusive reliance on death certificates. Assume that 28 percent of deaths were missed by death certificates. The 1992 NTOF number must therefore be divided by 0.72. The result is 6,671. Had we assumed a 32 percent undercount, our adjusted NTOF number would be 7,063.

These numbers—6,671 and 7,063 deaths—compare favorably with both the CFOI unadjusted number—6,063—and the "race- and ethnic-adjusted" number, 6,371. The data were collected *independently* in the same years by different federal agencies—one headquartered in Washington, DC, and the others in Morgantown and Cincinnati. The proximity of the NTOF estimate to the CFOI count and "race-adjusted" estimate attests to the credibility of both.

The NTOF, unlike the CFOI, is useful in analyzing a historical record. As we will see, an analysis of the historical NTOF record will be useful in assessing the credibility of data sets we have yet to consider (see app. A, the NTOF section).

III.A.3. BLS's Annual Survey of Occupational
Injuries and Illnesses

The OSH Act of 1970 requires that almost all private sector employers with 11 or more employees keep a log of occupational injuries and illnesses and submit the data to the BLS once a year. The BLS then assembles the data and publishes the results in its Annual Survey of Occupational Injuries and Illnesses in the U.S. by Industry — what we will refer to as the Annual Survey (U.S. Department of Labor 1992, chap. 14). The Annual Survey contains aggregated data on roughly 250,000 private firms. The Annual Survey data suffer a number of weaknesses, as the BLS acknowledges. First, in general, the Annual Survey covers firms regulated by the OSH Act. Railroads and mines, for example, are covered under separate federal legislation.[11] There are other much larger exclusions than these, however. The self-employed are excluded, as are government employees at all levels — federal, state, and local. Private household workers and farmers are also excluded. Finally, all firms with fewer than 11 employees are excluded from the fatality data, and some farms with fewer than 11 employees are excluded from the nonfatal injury data.

As a result of the BLS efforts on the CFOI, the BLS no longer relies on fatality data in the Annual Survey.[12] The BLS continues to place great reliance on the Annual Survey for nonfatal injuries, however. As a result, we will do so also; hence a complete discussion of the strengths and weaknesses of the Annual Survey with regard to nonfatal injuries appears in section IV.A.1 and in appendix A.

Nevertheless, some discussion of the deaths counted by the Annual Survey will be useful in our analysis of the nonfatal cases counted (and not counted) by the Annual Survey. Our discussion will compare two death estimates from the Annual Survey with the CFOI estimate for 1992.

In the 1991 Annual Survey Bulletin No. 2424 (U.S. Bureau of Labor Statistics 1993), the fatalities and rates were as follows: 2,900 and 4.3 for 1990; and 2,800 and 4.3 for 1991. These rates were per 100,000 employees. Assuming 10 percent of all BLS Annual Survey fatalities were due to diseases,[13] we estimate that the Annual Survey counted 2,610 injury fatalities in 1990 and 2,520 injury fatalities in 1991.

A second comparison can be made simply by referring to table 2.1. The lion's share of Annual Survey deaths was likely drawn from OSHA Form 200 reports by firms submitting data to the BLS. Those reports ("OSHA reports" in table 2.1) accounted for only 32 percent of the unadjusted civilian CFOI number (and 30 percent of the race- and ethnic-adjusted number). We estimate that the Annual Survey would have counted 2,430 injury deaths in 1992. This 2,430 suggests the Annual Survey counted only roughly 38 percent to 40 percent of the deaths.[14] We conclude that the Annual Survey deaths would have ignored some 60 to 70 percent of all injury deaths in 1992.

III.A.4. National Council on Compensation
Insurance (NCCI)

The NCCI, a private enterprise, collects data from public and private
workers' compensation insurers from 41 states and the District of Columbia. The NCCI helps establish insurance rates for WC insurers in
most states. The data are provided to the NCCI by private WC insurers
and some competitive state funds. The NCCI does not collect data
from (generally large) firms that self-insure, the six states with exclusive state funds (Nevada, North Dakota, Ohio, Washington, West
Virginia, and Wyoming), some competitive state funds, and all public
and private insurers in three states (California, Minnesota, and New
York). The most serious drawback is that the NCCI relies exclusively
on WC data.

The NCCI publishes a number of reports using the data. The NCCI
sent us what they refer to as Ultimate Reports: one from May 1992 and
another from May 1993 (National Council on Compensation Insurance
1992, 1993). The Ultimate Reports contain information on claims originating in prior years, deaths and nonfatal injuries, costs in the claims-
originating years, and expected costs in future years. Monthly data available on these Ultimate Reports can be used to estimate the number of
national deaths in 1992: 8,306 (Leigh et al. 1996). But this estimate
requires that a number of assumptions be made. For example, we assumed that 19.15 percent of deaths would be accounted for by self-
insured firms and 0.85 percent by some competitive state funds. We
assumed that the nine excluded states would have contributed another
28 percent to total injuries. Because of the tenuous nature of some of
these assumptions, we will not include this 8,306 number as part of our
ultimate estimate of job-related injury deaths in 1992.

On the other hand, the NCCI data are useful in generating *relative*
differences in magnitudes among workers' compensation injury categories. As a result, we will revisit the NCCI data in the nonfatal section
IV.A.3.

III.A.5. Supplementary Data System (SDS)

The SDS was organized by the Bureau of Labor Statistics (BLS) in 1976
in an attempt to gain national information on the nature, source, and
type of occupational injuries and illnesses nationwide (U.S. Department of Labor 1992, chap. 14). The SDS, in turn, drew data from the
reports of injuries and illnesses that employers, employees, and physi-

cians submitted to workers' compensation (WC) insurers or agencies within 11 states (Arkansas, Colorado, Delaware, Idaho, Iowa, Montana, New York, North Carolina, Oregon, Virginia, and Wisconsin). A detailed description of the SDS is available (Leigh 1995a). Useful information on familiar WC categories for nonfatal injuries (Permanent Total, Permanent Partial, Temporary Total, and Partial and Medical Only) ended in 1986.

The SDS data have been used in numerous BLS analyses. Perhaps the best introduction to the data is provided by Root and Sebastian 1981. Root and Sebastian (1981) pointed out that railroad, maritime, farming, and private household service occupations were underrepresented in the SDS because these occupations were excluded from workers' compensation insurance coverage in a number of states. Root and Sebastian (1981), nevertheless, concluded that "our observations and tests, and the geographic and industrial diversity of the states included in this study, support our thesis that these data are representative of the national experience" (27).

Leigh 1995a provides an annual estimate of 4,985 for injury deaths for the mid-1980s. After accounting for the WC undercount and using the NTOF time series model (app. A), we (Leigh et al. 1996) generated a 1992 estimate of nearly 7,000 deaths. Again, heroic assumptions were made to arrive at this estimate. As a result, we will not use the 7,000 figure in our ultimate estimate of deaths.

III.B. Our Fatality Estimate

Our best point estimate for fatalities will be the civilian CFOI count adjusted for the African American and Hispanic undercount: 6,371.[15] Our lower bound estimate will be the civilian CFOI count: 6,063. We take this as a lower bound because the CFOI requires at least two independent documents to verify a job-related injury death occurred. It is unlikely that the true number is less than 6,063. Our upper bound estimate is the NTOF count, assuming a 32 percent undercount due to the NTOF's exclusive reliance on death certificates — 7,063.

IV. Nonfatal Injuries

The fourth section of this chapter investigates nonfatal injuries. Our primary sources include the BLS's Annual Survey, the NCCI data, and the National Health Interview Survey (NHIS) data. This section closes with a summary of our estimates.

IV.A. Primary Sources

IV.A.1. BLS's Annual Survey of Occupational
Injuries and Illnesses

The BLS's Annual Survey of Occupational Injuries and Illnesses was briefly mentioned earlier and is extensively discussed in appendix A. The Annual Survey is more thorough in its investigation of nonfatal than of fatal injuries. Moreover, the number of firms reporting nonfatal injuries is greater than that reporting fatalities. All firms with fewer than 11 employees (not just farms) are exempt from reporting fatalities. However, nonfarm firms with fewer than 11 employees who are selected into the sample report nonfatal injuries (and illnesses). We believe the BLS's Annual Surveys, despite their limitations, present the best current data available and the most historically consistent data available on nonfatal injuries.

According to the Annual Survey (U.S. Bureau of Labor Statistics 1994a), private industry workers experienced roughly 6.342 million new nonfatal job-related injuries during 1992.[16] These numbers represent new injuries. We are, therefore, appropriately counting the incidence rather than the prevalence of injuries with these BLS numbers.

To arrive at a 1992 estimate of the total number of job-related injuries among all U.S. workers, we must first account for the well-known undercount of nonfatal injuries mentioned earlier, involving government employees, self-employed persons, household workers (e.g., domestics), and all farms with fewer than 11 employees that are excluded. Second, we must account for the economic incentives to underreport.

There are two ways to estimate the number of nonfatal injuries for all U.S. workers. The first would assume that the undercount percentage of nonfatal injuries is at least as great as the undercount percentage for fatal injuries. This approach yields two estimates: (1) 16.63 million using the published 2,800 and 2,900 figures from 1990 and 1991; (2) 20.725 million using the "OSHA reports" percentage in table 2.1, assuming the 32 percent death undercount applies to the nonfatal Annual Survey undercount.[17]

But the 20.725 million figure may be high. The Annual Survey death estimates did not exclusively rely on OSHA reports. Some adjustments were made using MSHA reports, railroad reports, and so on. We prefer the 16.69 million estimate. But this 16.69 million estimate may also be criticized. The BLS Annual Survey injury and illness fatality estimates (2,800 and 2,900) ignored all firms with fewer than 11 employees, and OSHA reports also are incomplete on small firms. The BLS

Annual Survey nonfatal estimate, on the other hand, included nonfarm firms with fewer than 11 employees. Moreover, a higher percentage of injury deaths may have been undercounted than nonfatal injuries. This is because motor vehicle crashes have high fatality rates and also high rates of exclusion from job-related injury data sets.

A second approach would make use of the injury rates for reporting firms. Our rate-based estimate, not adjusting for willful or negligent underreporting, involves the following calculation:

$$(8.3/100) \times (38.8/40.0) \times 117{,}598{,}000 = 9{,}467{,}814,$$

where 8.3/100 is the Annual Survey's estimate of the rate per 100 full-time equivalent workers for firms reporting to the BLS; 38.8 is the ratio of average hours worked per week in 1992 for full- *and* part-time workers (U.S. Bureau of the Census 1993a); 40 is the number of hours per week assumed for "full-time equivalent worker" by the BLS; and 117,598,000 is the number of civilians employed full- and part-time in 1992.

The 9,467,814 estimate accounts for the Annual Survey's lack of coverage of small farms, government employees, and household workers. The 9,467,814 assumes that the omitted groups have the same rate as the included workers. This is likely to be roughly correct. Whereas the self-employed and workers on small farms are known to have significantly higher than average rates, government workers have roughly the same or a little lower than average rates.

The 9,467,814 ignores willful and negligent underreporting. This underreporting might be due to an employer desiring to minimize workers' compensation premiums or the threat of an OSHA inspection. Alternatively, it might be the result of workers deliberately hiding an injury so as to maximize the chance of a promotion. We are aware of only two studies that attempted to measure the undercount. Glazner et al. (1998) found at least a 20 percent undercount for disabling injuries and a 35 percent undercount for nondisabling ones. Biddle et al. (1998) found roughly a 55 to 91 percent undercount for disabling injuries and illnesses that would have qualified for WC benefits to the workers.

Our analysis of Ruser's (1994) data from the Annual Survey (app. A) indicates a 135 percent undercount. This undercount is likely to be especially serious for small firms.

None of these studies is without fault. Our preferred estimate will rely on the Glazner et al. 1998 study because it was expressly designed to measure the magnitude of the BLS undercount.

As Glazner et al. (1998) suggest, the underreporting is higher for nondisabling than disabling injuries. From 1987 through 1992, the BLS Annual Survey reported roughly 46 percent to 47 percent of injury cases resulted in at least one day away from work. Miller (1995) estimated that 46.56 percent of all work injuries resulted in one or more days of work loss in 1989. In 1992, the BLS Annual Survey estimated roughly 44 percent resulted in work loss. We will assume a 45 percent rate. As we will see, this is an important assumption. Disabling injuries are more costly than nondisabling ones.

Assuming that 45 percent of injuries are disabling and 55 percent are not then our preferred rate-based estimate would be

$$[9,467,814 \times 0.45 \times (1(1 - 0.20))] + [9,467,814 \times 0.55 \times (1(1 - 0.35))] = 5,325,645 + 8,011,227 = 13,336,871,$$

where 9,467,814 is our rate-based estimate unadjusted for undercounting; 0.45 and 0.55 are the assumed percentages for disabling and nondisabling injuries; and 0.20 and 0.35 are the percentage estimates of the undercounts for disabling and nondisabling injuries.

Our best point estimate is 13,336,871. Our lower bound estimate is 9,467,814. Our upper bound is 16,690,000, the lower of the two estimates based upon the undercount of deaths in the Annual Survey and the count of deaths in the CFOI.

Table 2.2 summarizes our estimates.

Finally, one clarification needs to be made. These 13.34 million are new injuries in 1992. The 13.34 million is an incidence, not a prevalence, number. It does not take into account that, in any given year, there will be workers away from work due to job-related injuries that occurred in prior years. The prevalence of injury would undoubtedly be higher than 13.34 million. In chapter 5, "Costs of Injuries," we account for the fact

TABLE 2.2.   Estimates of Nonfatal Injuries Based upon the BLS's Annual Survey

	Point Estimate	Range[a]
Total	13,336,871	9,467,814–16,690,000
Disabling	5,325,645	3,781,210–6,664,607
Nondisabling	8,011,227	5,687,971–10,025,249

[a]Assumes same percentage range applies to disabling and nondisabling as applies to total, i.e., 0.71 for lower bound and 1.214 for upper bound as the ratio of point estimate to lower bound (0.71) and point estimate to upper bound (1.2514).

that some of these 1992 injuries will disable people and generate costs beyond 1992.

IV.A.2. The National Health Interview Survey (NHIS)

The NHIS is conducted annually by the National Center for Health Statistics. The NHIS is intended to provide national incidence and prevalence estimates for a number of diseases as well as injuries. The NHIS provides relatively consistent data on many conditions, including injuries dating back to 1975. Injury data generally come from roughly 9,000 people in any given year.

The NHIS injury data suffer a number of defects as appendix A (the NHIS section) illustrates. First, only employed people age 18 or older are asked about job injuries. Persons under age 18 who experience a job injury are not included. Second, persons not employed due to serious job-related injuries are not included. Third, the NHIS questions on the questionnaire use the term *accident* in referring to an injury. Terms such as *assault, violence, attempted murder, rape,* and so on, are not used. As a result, it is likely that nonaccidental (intentional) injuries are undercounted. Fourth, the time series of NHIS job-related injuries does not appear to be reliable (see app. A, the NHIS section). NHIS job-related injuries do not correlate with unemployment or the passage of time. This stands in contrast with other time-series analyses of job-related injury data. Fifth, some persons may not want to confess to a government interviewer that the injury occurred on the job, especially if they have made a decision to hide the injury from their employer.

Finally, and perhaps most incriminating for the NHIS, the 1992 estimate is 7.806 million. This is over one and a half million less than the Annual Survey lower bound estimate (9.47 million), which, as we have seen, does not allow for any "willful" underreporting by firms or for the higher injury rates in small firms and farms. We therefore do not use the NHIS estimate in our calculations for the number of nonfatal injuries.

IV.A.3. National Council on Compensation Insurance

Table 2.3 summarizes some of the data available in the two NCCI Ultimate Reports. The WC categories are in the first column. These categories include the following: Permanent Total; Permanent Partial Major; Permanent Partial Minor; Temporary Total and Partial; Medical Only, no indemnity. Permanent Total injuries are the most serious. An injury rendering a construction laborer a paraplegic would likely qualify as

Permanent Total. The injured worker cannot work at the old job. WC generally encourages him or her to seek training in a new field. The least serious injuries are Medical Only, no indemnity. A manager sustaining a broken ankle might return to work the following day with the ankle in a cast. All medical expenses would be paid by WC, but no lost wages would be covered. Most WC claims are not for permanent disabilities. Only roughly 7 percent of all cases in table 2.3 are permanent cases. In data from Washington State, Cheadle et al. (1994) found roughly 55 percent of all injured persons exit WC within one month; 70 percent exit within two months; 80 percent exit within four months. Cheadle et al. (1994) also found that over 90 percent of all WC cases last no more than 12 months. Hashemi et al. (1997) found 93 percent of all low back pain claims last no more than 12 months.[18]

The next two columns (2 and 3) correspond to the May 1992 NCCI Ultimate Report (1987–89) and the May 1993 NCCI Ultimate Report (1988–90). The notes for table 2.3 (a through d) indicate states not

TABLE 2.3.   Number of Cases per Year in Policy Years Covering 1987 through 1990

(1) Category of Nonfatal Injury and Illness	(2) 1987–89 39 or 41 States plus DC	(3) 1988–90 38 or 40 States plus DC
Permanent Total	5,523[a]	4,795[c]
Permanent Partial Major	120,458[a]	103,280[c]
Permanent Partial Minor	210,414[a]	196,927[c]
Temporary Total and Partial	870,392[a]	788,230[c]
Medical Only, no indemnity	3,510,961[b]	3,269,227[d]
Total	4,717,748	4,362,459

Source: NCCI Ultimate Reports and current study.

[a]Excludes California, Minnesota, Nevada, New York, North Dakota, Ohio, Washington, West Virginia, and Wyoming. In 1988, these states contributed 28.38% of U.S. employment. In 1989, they contributed 28.54% of U.S. employment (U.S. Bureau of the Census 1992).

[b]Excludes all states in note a plus Delaware and Pennsylvania for a total of 11 states excluded. These 11 states contributed 33.03% of U.S. employment in 1988 and 33.19% in 1989.

[c]Excludes all states in note a plus Texas. These 10 states contributed 35.24% of U.S. employment in 1989.

[d]Excludes all states in note b plus Texas. These 12 states contributed 40.12% of U.S. employment in 1989.

included in the NCCI reports. The data in table 2.3 can be used to generate an estimate of nonfatal injuries in 1992 (Leigh et al. 1996). That estimate is 17.21 million. But, again, a number of assumptions were made to generate that estimate, including assumptions about WC injury contributions from self-insuring firms and state-run monopoly firms. We chose not to use this 17.21 million estimate in our overall injury estimate because of these heroic assumptions. The NCCI data, however, are useful in describing the likely *relative* distribution of all injuries among the WC categories.

One important finding emerged in our attempt to generate a national estimate (17.21 million) based on these NCCI WC data. We estimated that WC missed at least 55 percent of all job-related injuries. As the section on the NCCI in appendix A will show, seven studies were reviewed and several explanations were offered to arrive at this estimate of a 55 percent undercount by the WC system. The studies and the estimated undercounts were these: Toscano and Windau 1993, 60 percent; Cone et al. 1991, 55.9 percent; Stout and Bell 1991, 45 percent; Parker et al. 1994, 67 percent; NHIS-OSH 1992, 58 percent; Hensler et al. 1991, 58 percent; Marquis 1992, 72.5 percent. The average of these is 60 percent. We selected 55 percent for our calculations, however, because the high estimates are less credible in applying to all injuries. That is, the Parker et al. study applied only to teenagers, and the Marquis study applied to costs, not the *number,* of injuries.

IV.B. Our Nonfatal Estimate

We use our BLS Annual Survey estimates to produce our overall global estimate. The BLS Annual Survey numbers are frequently cited in the literature. The NHIS numbers also receive considerable favorable mention by researchers investigating non-job-related injuries (Baker et al. 1992). Nevertheless, we judged the NHIS job-related injuries estimate to be unreliable. Rarely are the NCCI data used to estimate the national burden of occupational injuries. Our nonfatal estimates are summarized in table 2.2.

V. Our Fatal and Nonfatal Estimates and Classification Scheme

In this section we present a summary of our estimates for fatal and nonfatal injuries. Table 2.4 shows these estimates as well as our classification scheme and our estimates for each category of injury.

The categories of injuries we selected were those that lent themselves to straightforward cost calculations. Cost data were readily available for categories involving disabling and nondisabling distributions as well as those involving workers' compensation classifications. Cost data were not readily available for the medically diagnosed job-related injuries or for classification schemes involving parts of the body.

First, we need to allocate these 5.326 million disabling injuries among the familiar WC categories: Permanent Total (PT), Permanent Partial (PP), and Temporary Total and Partial (TTP). This will require some assumptions since at least three days would be required before WC indemnity benefits are paid in some states. That is, not all of these 5.326 million injuries would qualify for WC indemnity benefits. We assume 50.7 percent would, theoretically, qualify for some WC indemnity and 49.3 percent would not. These 50.7 and 49.3 percentages are derived by using ratios of numbers of PTs, PPs, and TTPs to deaths in the NCCI data[19] (table 2.3). Multiplying 50.7 percent times 5.326 million injuries yields 2.700 million injuries. These 2.700 million injuries can be allocated into the WC categories by assuming our estimated percentages of the TPs, PPs, and TTPs will be the same as the actual PT, PP, and TTP percentages in the NCCI data (table 2.3). These percentages are .449 percent for PTs, 27.438 percent for PPs, and 72.1134 percent for TTPs. Multiplying these numbers by 2.700 million yields 12,124 for PTs, 740,881 for the PPs, and 1,947,206 for TTPs.

TABLE 2.4.   Estimates of Injury Deaths and Nonfatal Injuries

		Lower and Upper Bound for Deaths and Total Nonfatal Injuries
Deaths	6,371[a]	6,083[a] to 7,063[a]
Total nonfatal injuries	13.337 million	9.468 to 16.690 million
Nondisabling	8.011 million	
Disabling	5.326 million	
Permanent Total	12,124[a]	
Permanent Partial	0.741 million	
Temporary Total and Partial	1.947 million	
One to seven days lost	2.626 million	
Hospitalizations (5.4% of total)	0.720 million	

Source: Current study.

[a]Deaths and Permanent Totals are *not* expressed in millions.

Finally, we consider hospitalizations. We assume 5.4 percent of the total nonfatal injuries result in hospitalization.[20]

Table 2.4 summarizes our nonfatal estimates.

VI. Secondary Sources, Literature Review

VI.A. Hensler et al. 1991 and Marquis 1992

The Rand Institute for Civil Justice conducted a study of the costs of all nonfatal injuries—whether on or off the job—in the late 1980s. The results were published in 1991 (Hensler et al. 1991). An updated version of the study applying only to job-related injuries was prepared for congressional testimony in 1992 (Marquis 1992). The original and updated versions of the study were based on a large survey conducted by Rand between August 1988 and May 1989.

The Rand authors were careful to point out that their unit of analysis was not an injury or an accident or a person but a "person-incident." An accident could have injured more than one person. A person could have sustained more than one medically diagnosed injury during a given accident (e.g., a fractured leg and a concussion would be two separate medically diagnosed injuries). Their *person-incident* term refers to a person who was injured in a specific accident. This is consistent with our term *episode* of injury as well as the definitions in the BLS Annual Survey and the NHIS.

Rand contacted roughly 26,000 people and obtained injury information on 2,770, all of whom had sustained at least one injury over the prior 12 months. The 26,000 were selected as a random sample of the continental United States. However, after all the data were collected, a reanalysis revealed that their sample underrepresented single-person households, older persons, blacks and Hispanics.

In analyzing their data, the Rand investigators first compared their results with the NHIS from 1981. (It was unclear why 1981 was chosen.) They concluded that their Rand study missed many minor injuries but compared favorably to the NHIS on serious injuries. They attributed part of this disparity to the 12-month recall bias. The Rand investigators asked respondents to report on injuries sustained during the prior 12 months. The "12-month" aspect of the Rand question insures that many minor injuries will not be reported (Landen and Hendricks 1992).

In addition to the recall bias, the Hensler et al. 1991 study contains other limitations. Deaths were ignored. Institutionalized persons (i.e., persons currently in the hospital) were excluded. The questions they asked respondents did not specifically mention assault or attempted murder or suicide or rape; hence, injuries resulting from violence would likely be underestimated.

Although the Rand study was of all injuries, special attention was directed toward job-related injuries. Apart from their estimate of the injury rates and their costs, a number of other findings emerged: (1) Despite the fact that job-related injuries comprised only 21 percent of all injuries, job-related injury costs *totaled nearly half of all injury costs.* Work injuries appeared to be more serious than nonwork injuries. (2) Adult injuries were roughly divided between work and nonwork. (3) Adult males were much more likely to be injured on the job than anywhere else. (4) Low-income men were more likely than women or any other income group to be injured on the job. As a result of job injuries being more serious than others, low-income men were more likely than other groups to require significant and expensive treatment. (5) They found WC was paid in less than 60 percent of all job-related injury cases and no more than 55 percent of all job-related injury hospitalizations. Given that the Rand investigators believed they had a better count of serious than nonserious injuries, one would have hoped for a higher rate of WC coverage.

The Hensler et al. 1991 Rand study provided information on the injury rate per 100 workers. They did not attempt to estimate the overall number of injuries. Marquis (1992), however, did attempt to estimate the *number of people affected,* not "person-incident" or episode. Marquis's (1992) incidence estimate was 7 million *persons,* while her prevalence estimate was 11 million *persons* for 1989 for job-related injuries requiring medical treatment or resulting in lost work time.[21] Marquis's study has been widely cited. But, what is frequently missing from the citation is that her study, together with the original Rand injury study on all injuries whether on or off the job, ignored fatalities, undercounted minorities, and was plagued by serious recall bias.

VI.B. Rossman, Miller, and Douglas 1991

Rossman, Miller, and Douglas (1991) estimated the incidence and costs of workplace injury and illness for 1989. The study was commissioned by NIOSH and is available in manuscript form from NIOSH. A substantial part of their study was based on the Detailed Claims Information (DCI) data maintained by the National Council of Compensation Insurance (NCCI). The DCI data covered 450,000 generated WC claims (i.e., claims that resulted in some WC payment). The Rossman, Miller, and Douglas 1991 study and the Miller and Galbraith 1995 and Miller 1995 studies mentioned subsequently are the only ones to analyze the rich data available in the DCI. Rossman, Miller, and Douglas also analyzed data from the BLS's Annual Survey, the Social Security Administration studies of WC by Nelson (1992, 1993), and the Rice et al. 1989a study on the costs of all injuries. They presented a useful summary of their findings.

> [W]e estimate the incidence of workplace injuries (in 1989) at 11 million. As such, workplace injuries account for roughly 19% of the annual 57 million injuries due to all causes reported by Rice et al. (1989a). Of the 11 million workplace injuries, approximately 11,000 resulted in fatalities (in 1989).

Out of 11 million annual injuries, Rossman, Miller, and Douglas (1991) estimated that WC provided indemnity payments to 1.93 million. Roughly 82 percent of all injuries were, therefore, not compensated with indemnity payments by WC. They also estimated 1.675 million injuries involving some work loss were not covered by WC.

The DCI/NCCI data contain WC information from some 35 to 38 states, depending on the year. Rossman, Miller, and Douglas (1991) studied data from 1979 to 1988. The DCI sample was restricted by WC coverage. Therefore, many limitations — all recognized by the authors — were encountered. First, Rossman, Miller, and Douglas focused on "disabling" injuries using the WC definition of "disability." For an injury to be "disabling" for WC requires at least three and sometimes seven days of work loss, depending on the state law. Second, during the time of their study, roughly 12 percent to 14 percent of employees were not covered by WC. Third, most of the self-employed were excluded. Fourth, not all injuries were reported to WC, even if they qualified due to workers' fear of employers' recrimination. Fifth, WC mixes illnesses with injuries. Rossman, Miller, and Douglas, however, estimated that roughly 98 percent of claims were for injuries and 2 percent were for illnesses. This stands in contrast to the higher percentage of WC *death* claims (11 percent) attributed to illnesses (Leigh 1995a).[22]

VI.C. Miller 1995

Ted Miller (1995) of the National Public Services Research Institute provided estimates of the number of job-related injury fatalities. Miller produced five estimates for 1985 and two for 1990. The first estimates in 1985 and 1990 were the same as those provided by the National Safety Council (NSC). (Miller was hired by the NSC to revise their estimates.) He added to the NSC estimate, however, an additional 1,500 to account for homicides. He did not account for suicides. His 1985 NSC-adjusted estimate was 13,000. His 1990 estimate unadjusted for homicides was 10,500. His second estimate (1985 only) used the NTOF estimate adjusted for homicides. Again, he added 1,500. NIOSH admitted missing some homicides during the early 1980s. NIOSH attempted to correct the homicide undercount in the late 1980s (National Institute for Occupational Safety and Health 1993). His NTOF estimate was 9,450 for 1985. His third 1985 estimate was derived from the BLS's Annual Surveys. He adjusted the Annual Survey numbers upward to account for the well-known undercounts mentioned previously. He also added his estimate of homicides not reported to the BLS to arrive at a 1985 estimate of 7,400.

Miller's fourth 1985 estimate was derived from the NCCI data for 1985. He took the original NCCI number — 3,084 — and multiplied by 2.484. The reciprocal of the last number — .4026 — indicates that Miller estimated that the NCCI counted only 40.26 percent of all job-related deaths in 1985. The product (3,084 × 2.484) yields 7,661. To this 7,661, Miller added another 1,239 for the undercount of homicides, bringing his total 1985 estimate based on the NCCI to 8,900.

Miller's fifth 1985 estimate and second 1989 estimate were the most useful for us since his first four relied on data we have analyzed in the preceding. His last estimate was derived from data on auto deaths — the Fatal Accident Report System (FARS) — that have been established at the National Highway Traffic Safety Administration. Miller assumed that 6.85 percent of all traffic deaths were job related and that *all* job-related injury deaths were 3.355 times the number of job-related motor vehicle crash deaths. He then added 1,500 homicides. These calculations allowed him to estimate 9,900 job-related deaths using the FARS data in 1985 and 11,600 in 1989. Miller prefers the FARS estimate and thus concludes with 11,600 job-related injury deaths in 1989.

Miller's 1995 study drew heavily upon the analyses in Rossman, Miller, and Douglas 1991, as well as several sources to estimate the number of job-related nonfatal injuries in 1989. The first was the NHIS for 1989. The NHIS estimate was 10,947,000. This represented approximately 18.8 percent of all injuries (whether on or off the job) for 1989 identified in the NHIS. This 18.8 percent estimate is similar to the 21 percent estimate in the Hensler et al. study (1991) from Rand and the 19 percent estimate in Rossman, Miller, and Douglas 1991 for the same year — 1989. These NHIS injuries resulted in contact with a medical provider or restricted activity for at least one-half day.

The second source was the BLS's Annual Survey for 1989. Miller (1995) assumed that the BLS *rate* estimates — 8.2 per 100 full-time workers — would apply to the 117.3 million civilian full- and part-time employees and self-employed in 1989. He, thus, estimated 9.6 million worker injuries in 1989 with the Annual Survey. He did not make any of the adjustments we made to the Annual Survey data involving full-time/part-time work-hour differences, employer or employee "willful" underreporting, and so on.

Miller argued that the NHIS 10,947,000 number was more credible than the BLS's Annual Survey number in part because the NHIS resulted from a national survey. Miller did not address the biases associated with the NHIS that we mentioned earlier.

Miller encountered the same problem we have in classifying injuries. His solution was to classify according to whether there was work loss or hospitalization. Using the NHIS 10,947,000 injuries number, Miller estimated that there were 5,094,000 lost workday injuries and 5,853,000 lesser injuries. He estimated, in other words, that 46.53 percent of all injuries resulted in work loss.[23] Miller (1995) also provided an estimate for the number of hospitalized workplace injuries: 614,000 in 1989.[24]

VI.D. National Safety Council (NSC)

The NSC is a private, nonprofit public service organization. Their funding derives primarily from corporate donations. Each year, the NSC publishes *Accident Facts,* a paperback book filled with statistics covering injuries and accidents of all kinds. Some are provocative. For example, bees, wasps, and hornets killed three times as many people as snakes, lizards, and spiders (38 versus 11) in 1992 (National Safety Council 1993, 10). Some NSC statistics are drawn directly from government reports. For example, entire tables from the BLS's Annual Survey are reproduced in *Accident Facts.* Other statistics are estimates derived from government reports, academic studies, internal NSC studies, data submitted to the NSC by a number of corporations, and analyses of time trends. The NSC is the largest organization of its kind. There is no single federal government agency or federal health institute dealing only with injuries. The U.S. government's efforts on the collection of data on injuries are split among the National Highway Traffic Safety Administration, Injury Surveillance Departments at NIOSH and OSHA, the Centers for Disease Control and Prevention, BLS's Office of Compensation and Working Conditions, and the Federal Aviation Administration.

The NSC has been providing estimates for job-related fatal injuries for over 20 years. They estimated 8,500 deaths in 1992. The NSC estimates for job-related deaths rely on death certificate data from the National Center for Health Statistics (NCHS). The NCHS data were

TABLE 2.5. Estimated Number of Job-Related Injury Deaths and Death Rates

Source	1980	1981	1982	1983	1984	1985	1986	1987	1988	1989	1990	1991	1992	Death Rate[a] per 100,000, 1992
CFOI actual													6,063	5.20
Our CFOI estimate													6,371	5.42
NTOF actual	7,405	7,136	6,459	5,856	6,162	6,250	5,672	5,884	5,751	5,714	5,384	5,191	4,803	4.10
Our NTOF adjusted													7,063	
Annual Survey actual including diseases											2,900	2,800		
Our Annual Survey estimate injury only											2,610	2,520		
NCCI actual including diseases									3,306	2,768				
Our NCCI estimate injury only									2,975	2,491				
Our SDS estimate including diseases				5,601										
Our SDS estimate injury only				5,041										
NSC actual	13,200					11,500	11,100	11,300	11,000	10,700	10,100	9,300	8,500	7.1
Miller's estimate										11,900				
Best point estimate:													6,371	
Lower and upper bound:													6,063 to 7,063	

Source: Current study.

[a]Death rate: 6,083/117,598,000 = 5.2; 6,371/117,598,000 = 5.42; and so on. The 117,598,000 comes from Toscano and Windau 1993.

readjusted by historical benchmark "allocative factors" as described in Brand and Hoskin 1993.

Problems associated with death certificates have been noted in the preceding discussions on the CFOI and the NTOF. There are also a number of limitations associated with using percentage allocation factors—some dating back over 30 years—as indicated in Brand and Hoskin 1993.

Another drawback to the NSC estimates is the explicit omission of homicides and suicides. The NSC wanted to count nonintentional injuries; hence violent deaths are excluded.

The NSC draws on the NHIS and internal NSC records and methods to estimate the number of nonfatal injuries. The NSC estimated number of nonfatal injuries in 1992 was 7,806,000, which is drawn directly from the NHIS. We will not use the NSC 7,806,000 estimate, since it is merely the NHIS estimate for that year. The NSC did, however, provide their own estimates for the number of disabling injuries (3.3 million).

VI.E. Summary Tables of Primary and Secondary Sources

Table 2.5 summarizes the estimates for all sources considered here. Most prior studies estimated deaths in the 1980s. The sources are listed down the left-hand side. Years appear across the top.

Our preferred estimate is from the CFOI, adjusted for a race-ethnic undercount: 6,371. Our lower bound is the actual CFOI (6,063), and the upper bound is from the NTOF adjusted estimate (7,063).

We turn now to summarizing the nonfatal data in the BLS Annual Survey; NHIS; Marquis 1992; Rossman, Miller, and Douglas 1991; and Miller 1995. Table 2.6 provides the summary. On the left-hand side are the data sources and studies. On the right-hand side is the estimate. The top third of the table presents the estimates from the two primary sources—Annual Survey and NHIS. The middle third of the table presents information from the secondary sources. The bottom third provides our point estimate and range.

VII. Demographic, Occupational, Industrial, and Regional Characteristics of Injuries

Discussions in this section of the chapter are based upon tables provided in appendix B and analyses in the NIOSH report (Leigh et al. 1996). These tables contain a great amount of information from a variety of data sets. Our discussion here merely highlights the important findings in these tables and analyses.

VII.A. Demographics

VII.A.1. Age and Experience

Table B2.1 (app. B), panels A through E, presents the age results on fatalities and nonfatal injuries from the CFOI, NTOF, SDS, WC, Annual Survey, and NHIS-OSH.

There are some similar patterns across the three *death* studies (the CFOI by Toscano and Windau [1993]; NTOF by Jenkins et al. [1993]; and the SDS/WC by Leigh [1995a]; all summarized in table B2.1, app. B). The smallest percentage contributors of *total* deaths are those in age brackets under 20 and 65 and older. This is understandable given the high percentage of young persons in school (not working) and the high percentage of seniors who are retired (not working). The lowest death *rates* apply to those persons under 20 years old. The highest *rates*

TABLE 2.6.   Estimates of Nonfatal Injuries, 1992

Data Source or Study	Estimate (in millions)	
BLS's Annual Survey		
Without adjustment	6.34	(1992)
With adjustment	13.34	(1992)
National Health Interview	8.78	(1991)
Survey	7.80	(1992)
Marquis 1992	7.0	(1989)
Rossman, Miller, and Douglas 1991 and Miller 1995	10.8	(1989)
National Safety Council		
Disabling	3.3[a]	(1992)
All injuries	7.8[b]	(1992)
Our preferred point estimate	13.34	(1992)
Our range (low and high estimates are adjusted Annual Survey numbers)	9.47 to 16.69	(1992)

[a]This is an NSC estimate.
[b]This number is drawn directly from the NHIS estimate for 1992.

apply to those 65 and over. From age 21 to 44 the rates do not change appreciably. The rates begin to rise for the 45 to 54 age group, and again for the 55 to 64 year old group.[25] These results are consistent with an in-depth study of the NTOF (Kisner and Pratt 1997) and other data (Mitchell 1988).

The death rates by age conform to death rates for persons aged 25 and beyond for all accidents whether on or off the job (National Safety Council 1993). As age increases, especially beyond age 64, death rates for all accidents accelerate at an increasing rate (National Safety Council 1993).

Sections D and E of table B2.1 (app. B) present data for nonfatal injuries drawn from the BLS Annual Survey and from the NHIS's Occupational Health and Safety Supplement Survey (NHIS-OSH). Beginning with the 1992 data, the BLS revised its collection procedures and data presentation. For example, prior to the 1992 data, very little demographic data were available. The new Annual Survey demographic data pertained only to disabling injuries, however. The Annual Survey from 1992 presents only injuries and illnesses resulting in at least one day away from work. Unfortunately, these published BLS Annual Survey numbers confuse injuries with illnesses.[26]

The NHIS-OSH was a special 1988 supplement to the NHIS pertaining to occupational safety and health data. The *rate* data from the NHIS-OSH on nonfatal injuries display a pattern different from the death *rate* data.[27] As people grow older, their chances of sustaining a nonfatal injury decrease. The BLS Annual Survey nonfatal data also support this conclusion. The highest percentage of injuries occurs in the middle years (25 to 44). As people age, they may take fewer risks. It could also be that the same injury is more likely to kill an older than a younger worker. The results on the nonfatal injuries are consistent with the view that work experience reduces nonfatal injury rates; that is, experienced workers have greater knowledge about how to complete a job safely.

A literature has emerged concerning child and adolescent work-related injuries (Belville et al. 1994). Castillo, Landen, and Layne (1994) used the NTOF data to estimate a death rate of 5.1 per 100,000 full-time equivalent civilian workers aged 16 and 17. These young workers appeared to be at greater risks than adults for dying of electrocution, suffocation, drowning, and poisoning. Layne et al. (1994) used data from a nationally representative sample of emergency rooms — the National Electronic Injury Surveillance System (NEISS) — to find that adolescents aged 14 through 17 experienced roughly 37,405 injuries nationwide for a 7.0 per 100 full-time worker rate for males and a 4.4 rate for females. The highest percentage of injuries occurred in retail trades, especially restaurants and taverns. Finally, Parker et al. (1994) studied 534 work-related injuries among adolescents in Minnesota. The most serious injuries involved backs and burns.

A characteristic similar to age is length of time on the job. There is substantial evidence that new employees experience a disproportionate share of injuries. A state of California study (Division of Labor Statistics and Research 1985) of 338,866 work-related disabling injuries in 1983 and 1984 discovered that 42 percent of all injured workers had been with their employer for less than one year. Moreover, even within the first year of employment, the first month was associated with the greatest number of injuries. It could be argued that job mobility explains this result; that is, most people at most jobs are relatively new. But this was not the case. In 1983 (the time of the California study), a national survey showed that only 27 percent of employees had been on the job for less than 12 months (Sehgal 1984).

Finally, the state of California study showed that, whereas nearly 10 percent of employees had been with their employer for 20 years or more, only 2.6 percent of injured workers had been with their employers that long. We conclude that inexperience is an important predictor of who is likely to experience an injury.

VII.A.2. Gender

Table B2.2 (app. B) presents results on gender differences in death and nonfatal injury rates. The ratio of male to female deaths was 11:1 in the CFOI, 12:1 in the NTOF, and 18 to 1 in the SDS/WC data. The male to female ratio for nonfatal incidents was roughly 2:1 in the Annual Survey. Again, because illnesses were so few, this ratio is likely to apply to injuries. This is a provocative finding. Virtually all studies on dangerous jobs have found males at greater risk than females (Zwerling et al. 1993). But our study appears to be the first to show such a sharp distinction between fatal and nonfatal rates.

The two NHIS data sets on nonfatal injuries—one from the 1988 OSH supplement and the other from 1980–81—are consistent with each other. Females contributed 30 percent of job-related injuries in 1980–81 and 35 percent in 1988. The male to female job-related injury ratio was 1.8 to 1 in 1988 and 2.3 to 1 in 1980–81. This increase in female injuries from 1980–81 to 1988 could reflect the increasing numbers of women in dangerous jobs over time.

Sexual assault of women at work is receiving increasing attention. Alexander, Franklin, and Wolf (1994) used WC claims data in Washington State and found that sexual assault was especially high for taxicab drivers, job training instructors, radio and TV retail stores salespersons, gasoline service station attendants, truck drivers, and hotel workers.

Seligman et al. (1987) reviewed 21 WC claims for sexual assault in Ohio, from 1983 to 1985. They found a rate of 7.0 per 1,000,000 females employed in convenience stores compared to 0.3 per 1,000,000 for all employed females. Historically, sexual assault was not viewed as work related. It could be that many of these incidents still go unreported as work related even while the police reports are complete on all other details of the assault. These statistics exclude incidences of sexual harassment. Historically, harassment has been treated as a personnel matter. This may change in the future, especially if harassment can be shown to result in psychological damage.

VII.A.3. Race and Ethnic Differences

Table B2.3 (app. B) presents the race and Hispanic characteristics of the samples. A curious and troubling result appears in the CFOI and NHIS data. There is virtually no difference in the rates for whites (4.938) and blacks (4.962) in the CFOI data. Both NHIS studies (NHIS-OSH and Collins 1985) show a higher rate for whites than blacks. These findings stand in contrast to all other occupational studies and general studies on death rates for injuries that investigated black/white differences with which we are familiar. For example, the NIOSH study — NTOF — found a black death rate of 6.5 per 100,000 and a white (including Hispanics) rate of 5.8 per 100,000. If Hispanics had been excluded, the white rate would have been lower. Of those reporting to the Annual Survey, black non-Hispanics contributed 13.2 percent of the black and white total. Yet blacks accounted for less than 11 percent of total non-Hispanic employment in 1992 (U.S. Bureau of the Census 1993a).

In our preceding discussion of the CFOI (sec. III.A.1), we cited a number of studies indicating that the black rate exceeded the white rate (Cone et al. 1991; Copeland 1985; Baker et al. 1982; Robinson 1991). We note here that the social science literature on racial differences in employment in safe white-collar and dangerous blue-collar jobs supports the same pattern (Gill 1994). We conclude that the CFOI likely underestimates black deaths for several reasons, including long-standing patterns of discrimination.

Regarding the NHIS, it could be that African Americans are reluctant to admit health or injury problems to an interviewer, especially a white interviewer. Bauman and Emmett (1994) found that blacks significantly underreported their cigarette use when compared to whites. Mensch and Kandel (1988) found a similar result for drug use.

Hispanics as a group are difficult to analyze because researchers and the government have changed definitions of *Hispanic* over time. In the 1970s, they were frequently placed in the "other race" category. In the 1980s, a separate category was created, but the separate category continued the "race" confusion. Many Hispanics are black or Asian. Only in the 1990s have Hispanics been treated as an ethnic rather than a race category in most government documents and private studies.

Few studies have considered Hispanic job injuries. In one of the few, Robinson (1991) found Hispanics with a higher rate than white non-Hispanics. The CFOI counted 508 Hispanic deaths, which resulted in a rate of 5.589, a higher rate than for white non-Hispanics.

VII.A.4. Self-Employment and Small Firms

The CFOI appears to be the only source that considered whether there were injury differences between the self-employed and all other employees. An astonishing result emerged. The self-employed, including paid and unpaid family members, comprised 20 percent of all fatalities. Yet, the self-employed comprised only roughly 9 percent to 10 percent of all employed people in the United States in 1992. Many of the self-employed work on family farms, and farming is known to be exceedingly hazardous (Goodman et al. 1985; Purschwitz and Field 1985; Rossignol and Pineault 1993). But small farms comprise only roughly 13 percent of all the self-employed (Becker 1984). Small businesses, in general, have much higher fatality and nonfatal injury rates than medium and large firms. A 10-year (1977–86) analysis of OSHA investigations by firm size showed that firms with fewer than 20 employees had the highest kill ratios: 10 per 100,000 compared to less than 5 per 100,000 for firms with 20–99 workers and 3 or less per 100,000 for firms with 100 or more employees (Marsh 1994). A Colorado study found much higher fatality rates for small than large firms (Marine et al. 1990). Mendeloff and Kagey (1990) found the same pattern in Pennsylvania. Small mining companies have the highest injury rates of all mining companies (Bennett and Passmore 1984). A study of trucking firms found the highest vehicle crash rate among the smallest firms and the lowest among the largest firms (Moses and Savage 1994). The same pattern was found in construction (McVittie, Banikin, and Brocklebank 1997).

This disparity in rates by firm size might be partially attributed to OSHA enforcement policies. Many small firms are exempt from OSHA regulations, and they are also exempt from WC coverage. The disparity may also be the result of the greater ability of large firms to purchase safe equipment and pay for safety training. Finally, Oleinick, Gluck, and

Guire (1995) suggest that the disparity may be the result of substantial underreporting by small firms. Seligman et al. (1988) found that OSHA record keeping was the worst for small firms and the best for large firms.

In any case, the CFOI finding is significant and suggests that greater research and perhaps OSHA regulatory attention be devoted to small firms.

VII.B. Occupations and Industries

Some occupations have generated more deaths and injuries and have higher kill ratios and injury rates than others (Leigh 1987a). Variations are also apparent across industries. In this section, we consider occupations and industries with some of the highest and lowest numbers and rates. Unlike the previous section, this section is organized around data since definitions of occupations and industries differ across these data sets and each data set has unique information not available in the other sets.

VII.B.1. Census of Fatal Occupational Injuries

Table B2.4 (app. B) presents the numbers and percentage distribution of fatal occupational injuries in the CFOI by occupation in 1992. There is a sharp split between white-collar and blue-collar, with the blue-collar jobs having rates three to six times larger than those for the white-collar. Moreover, the number of deaths was also much greater among blue- than white-collar workers. The lowest death rates were for managers, professionals, technical, sales, and administrative support. The highest rates were for lumberjacks, taxi drivers, constructions laborers, and truck drivers.

These rates and rankings are supported in the literature (Leigh 1995a and 1987a; Bell et al. 1990; Robinson 1991; Thaler and Rosen 1976; Meng 1991; Cone et al. 1991). Using SDS/WC data, Leigh (1995a) also found lumberjacks, taxi drivers, construction laborers, and truck drivers to have excessively high death rates.

Table B2.5 (app. B) presents the number and percentage distribution of fatal occupational injuries by industry in 1992. The denominators for the rates (available in Toscano and Windau 1993) were calculated from Current Population Surveys. The greater *number* of fatalities occurred, in order, in construction (903); transportation (884); manufacturing (751); services (725); retail trade (710); government (699); wholesale trade (244); mining (182); and finance, insurance, and real estate (118). The high *rates* were in mining (27), agriculture (24), construction (14), and transportation (13), and the low *rates* were in the trades (5 and 4), manu-facturing (4), government (4), services (2) and finance (2). This sharp contrast between the industries with the high and low rates has been noted before (NIOSH, NTOF 1993; Cotter and Macon 1987; Leigh 1995b).

The NIOSH report on the National Traumatic Occupational Fatali-ties (NTOF) found that the four industries with the highest rates contrib-uted over 50 percent of all injury deaths yet accounted for less than 20 percent of employment in the economy (Baker et al. 1992, 349).

VII.B.2. National Traumatic Occupational Fatality Study

Table B2.6 (app. B) presents the number and rate data by broad occupa-tion division from the NTOF. A familiar pattern emerges: crafts, trans-port, labor, and farming, fishing, and forestry occupations account for 63 percent of all deaths and produce the highest death rates. Occupa-tions that contribute the remainder include managers, service workers, sales representatives, machine operators, professionals, technicians, and clerks. Except for machine operators, this occupational pattern of deaths follows traditional blue-collar and white-collar lines.

Figures and data in the NIOSH publication describing NTOF (Jen-kins et al. 1993) present numbers and rates by industry division. The same pattern seen in the CFOI is again evident in the NTOF. The largest number of fatalities occurred in the construction, transportation, com-munication, public utilities, manufacturing, agriculture, forestry, and fishing industry divisions. The mining industry had the highest average annual fatality rate per 100,000 workers (31.9), followed by construction (25.76), transportation, communication, and public utilities (23.3), fol-lowed by agriculture, forestry, and fishing (18.3).

Tables B2.7 and B2.8 (app. B) present the leading causes of injury deaths within each occupation and industry division from the NTOF. A few provocative results emerge. Among executives, sales workers, and service workers (table B2.7), murder was the leading cause of death. The leading cause of death among technical support was aircraft crash (these include helicopter crashes). Craft workers most frequently died from falls. Among industries, murder led the list for retail trade; fi-nance, insurance, and real estate; and services.

Castillo and Jenkins (1994) present additional data on occupations at high risk for murder. These included taxicab drivers, sheriffs, police officers, hotel clerks, gas station attendants, guards, stock baggers, bar-bers, bartenders, and prison guards. Finally, Toscano (1997) compares and contrasts occupations with CFOI and Annual Survey data. Toscano finds fishers to have the highest fatality rates.

VII.B.3. BLS's Annual Survey of Occupational
Injuries and Illnesses

A BLS Annual Survey (U.S. Bureau of Labor Statistics 1993) presents information on the number of deaths within eight broad industry divisions. The same report also indicates the cause of the death, within the broad industry division. Since the CFOI and NTOF present much more reliable data for fatal injuries, cause of deaths, and industry division, the BLS's Annual Survey detailed information on these subjects is omitted. But brief points should be made. First, the same general patterns in the CFOI and NTOF emerged in the Annual Survey death data. For example, three industries — agriculture, construction, and transportation — contributed the largest share of deaths and generated the highest rates. Moreover, vehicle crashes caused the most deaths, consistent with both the CFOI and the NTOF. Second, the Annual Survey data did not place homicide nearly as high in the cause of death list as either the CFOI or the NTOF. This underscores the continuing problem associated with convincing industry executives, WC officials, and the public that homicide is a risk in many jobs.

Third, the Annual Survey shows the importance of one occupational illness — heart disease. In the 1980s, 9 percent of all Annual Survey deaths were attributed to heart attacks. These cases were ignored by the CFOI and NTOF (Leigh and Miller 1998b).

The BLS's Annual Survey is useful in presenting nonfatal injury data for industries. The information reported here pertains to lost workday cases. This would be equivalent to our definition of disabling injuries. The data at the one-digit level are similar to those on death rates appearing earlier in our discussion of the CFOI and the NTOF. The ranking from highest to lowest for lost workday injury incidence rates is as follows: construction; transportation and public utilities; mining; agriculture, forestry, and fishing; manufacturing; wholesale and retail trade; services; finance, insurance, and real estate.

The BLS's Annual Survey contains information by four-digit industry and three-digit occupation. Table B2.9 (app. B) presents information by four-digit industry. Rates for injuries only are presented. *Rates* are a measure of the injury risks faced by the typical employee. They do not necessarily measure the overall magnitude of the contribution of a particular industry to the national volume of occupational injuries. For example, an industry such as raw cane sugar employs few people but has a high rate.

Table B2.9 (app. B) presents the top 30 industries with the highest lost workday injury rates for 1992. These industries include household appliances, raw cane sugar, shipbuilding and ship repairing, cottonseed oil mills, bottled and canned soft drinks, structural wood members, wood pallets and skids, creamery butter, and malt.

The 1992 BLS Annual Survey *News* report (U.S. Bureau of Labor Statistics 1994a) provided information for three-digit occupations. Table B2.10 (app. B) shows the rankings according to the contribution of each occupation to the overall worker injuries *and* illnesses involving days away from work. Again, illnesses comprised roughly 7 percent of the total. The numbers are not rates but rather are the actual number of recorded cases. Obviously, the greater the employment in any occupation, the greater its contribution to total injuries is likely to be. Nevertheless, the ranking is useful as a measure of the overall contribution of an occupation to total injuries, unlike the per worker (rate) ranking of industries in table B2.9.

The top three are nonconstruction laborers, truck drivers, and nursing aides and orderlies. The kinds of injuries experienced by laborers and drivers are well known (Leigh 1995a). Injuries can occur among aides and orderlies who must frequently move patients — some quite heavy — from bed to chairs and back again. Additional high-ranking occupations include janitors, construction laborers, assemblers, stock handlers, cashiers, food preparers, cooks, carpenters, registered nurses, maids, welders, sales supervisors, and automobile mechanics.

Finally, table B2.11 (app. B) presents data by broad occupation divisions. Operators, fabricators, and laborers contributed by far the largest percentage — 40.8.

VII.B.4. Supplementary Data System

Root and Sebastian (1981) used the SDS to develop a job hazard index for roughly 60 occupations and 180 occupation and industry combinations. The index was created by accounting for the percentage of total injuries contributed by a particular occupation or occupation-industry cell and dividing by the expected percentage for that occupation or cell. Occupations with the highest indexes were, in order, warehouse laborers, all other laborers, structural metal crafts workers (ironworkers), roofers, sheet metal workers and apprentices, construction laborers, freight handlers, millwrights, and truck drivers.

VII.C. Geography, NTOF, States

Only the NTOF presents a comprehensive analysis of state differences in injury rates. Jenkins et al. (1993) present the NTOF death rates by state. The greatest *number* of fatalities occurred in Texas (6,664), California

(16,623), Florida (3,681), Illinois (2,853), and Pennsylvania (2,564). The states with the highest annual *rates* were Alaska (34.8), Wyoming (29.0), Montana (20.9), Idaho (16.7), and West Virginia (15.7). States with low rates, less than 2.9 per 100,000 per year, included New York, Connecticut, and Massachusetts.

VIII. Causes of Death and Injury

VIII.A. Deaths

Table B2.12 (app. B) presents information on the number and percentage distribution of fatal injuries by cause of death from the CFOI. At the top of the list, with 40 percent of all injuries, are transportation accidents, including highway and nonhighway accidents, aircraft crashes, pedestrian accidents, boating accidents, and railway accidents.

Today, most OSH researchers and a large percentage of the public recognize that transportation accidents are the leading cause of job-related injury deaths. It was not always that way, however. Moreover, it could be that, even now, the majority of working people in the United States are not aware that transportation injuries are the leading cause of job-related injury deaths. As indicated in the preceding, the OSH Act virtually ignored vehicle collisions. Only in the last few years has OSHA considered regulations governing job-related travel in vehicles. Moreover, the recent standard governing truck drivers and the number of hours per day they are allowed to drive was promulgated by the National Highway Traffic Safety Agency, not OSHA. The fact that most researchers, and perhaps much of the public, now recognize the importance of vehicle collisions in job-related deaths is testimony to the influence of studies by Baker et al. (1982), Bell et al. (1990), Kraus (1985), Leigh (1987a), Toscano and Windau (1993), and others over the past 15 years, and equally as important are the popular press's reports on these studies.

Transportation accidents also involve aircraft. These include airline crashes but also, perhaps more importantly, any aircraft. Helicopter pilots, crop dusters, pilots hauling advertising banners above beaches, corporate pilots in small jets, and so on, are at high risk (Leigh 1995a).

The second leading cause of death involves violence, either homicide or suicide (Davis 1987; Fox and Levin 1994; Bachman 1996; Kraus 1987; Honchar and Suarez 1986; Richardson 1993). The murders in the CFOI (as well as in WC records) must be job related. They cannot be, for example, the result of a husband and wife quarrel. The victim must have been killed during a robbery or job-related dispute (i.e., a supervisor-subordinate quarrel). The victim could, of course, have been a bystander who was simply performing his or her duties when the robbery or quarrel erupted. Contrary to public opinion, most murders involve attempted robbery and are not quarrels among employees and bosses (Castillo and Jenkins 1994).

Suicides must also have been judged to be job related by the CFOI (and the WC). These appear to be especially disturbing, sometimes involving disgruntled workers who shoot their bosses and then turn the gun on themselves (Fox and Levin 1994). Most cases, however, do not also involve attempted murders. A serious injury can leave a worker paralyzed for life. People in this condition have been known to take their own lives (Conroy 1989; Minter 1993).

The importance of murder and suicide should be emphasized. Together, they are the second leading cause of death, and they appear to be increasing in their percentage contribution. Moreover, they were ignored in the 1970 OSH Act and were subsequently not of great concern to OSH regulators in the 1970s and 1980s.

Murder on the job is receiving increasing media and legislature attention (Friedman 1994). One proposal to reduce the toll would be to require retail stores that operate at night to post armed guards on duty during evening hours.

The next four categories of causes of death—contact with objects, falls, exposures, and fires—are much more likely to be associated with job hazards in the public mind than most transportation accidents or violent acts. Ironworkers, for example, most frequently die from falls (Leigh 1995a). Blasters die in fires and explosions. A high percentage (60 percent) of hospitalized burn injuries among men in Massachusetts were found to be job related (Rossignol et al. 1986).

VIII.B. Types of Nonfatal Injuries

VIII.B.1 BLS's Annual Survey, Nonfatal Injuries

The BLS's Annual Survey report (U.S. Bureau of Labor Statistics 1994b) on characteristics of people and injury episodes contained a table on the percentage distribution of nonfatal occupational injuries and illnesses involving days away from work. Some of the data are reproduced here.

The categories with the highest percentages include overexertion (28.3 percent); contact with object or equipment (27.4 percent); fall on same level (10.3 percent); fall to lower level (5.0 percent); exposure to harmful substance (2.9 percent); repetitive motion (3.9 percent); slips, trips (3.5 percent); transportation accidents (2.9 percent); assault (1.0 percent); and fires and explosions (0.2 percent).

These rankings stand in contrast to those from the CFOI. There are a number of reasons for these contrasts. The CFOI was for fatalities only, while the Annual Survey was for nonfatal injuries only. Transportation accidents and assaults are more likely to be fatal than other accidents and exposures. But perhaps a more important reason is the nature of the two data sets. The CFOI was designed as a census, a comprehensive count. The Annual Survey used data provided by 250,000 firms. The Annual Survey data have been found to capture only 30 percent to 40 percent of all deaths (Toscano and Windau 1993). Hence, some of the discrepancies between the CFOI and the Annual Survey could be viewed as further evidence for the problems discussed in the Annual Survey section of appendix A.

VIII.B.2. NHIS-OSH

In 1988, the annual National Health Interview Survey (NHIS) collected supplemental data on 27,408 employed persons pertaining to job-related injuries and health (Park et al. 1993). The supplement to the NHIS is referred to as the Occupational Health Supplement to the NHIS (or NHIS-OSH).[28]

Park et al. (1993) found that 7.7 percent of the working population in 1988 had reported a job-related injury over the past 12 months. Of course, some could have been injured more than once. From 1987 to 1989, the simple "injury at work" information in the usual NHIS samples (not the OSH subsample) was used to calculate annual rates of 8.1, 8.7, and 9.3 per 100 persons working. But, the usual NHIS questions applied to the last two weeks whereas the NHIS-OSH applied to the last 12 months. Recall bias was found to be much greater over 12 months than two weeks (Landen and Hendricks 1992). With these caveats in mind, it is nevertheless useful to consider the Park et al. 1993 analysis of the NHIS-OSH.

Park et al. (1993) present data on the percentage of injuries by type (as opposed to nature or source) of injury as follows: strain or sprain (28.4 percent), other (22.3 percent), lacerations or punctures (20.5 percent), contusions or abrasions (12.5 percent), not stated (7.1 percent), fractures (6.8 percent), and burns (4.7 percent). Park et al. (1993) go on to analyze these data in the following way.

> The distribution is not substantially different from the percent distribution of types of injuries for all injuries to the total U.S. population (Collins 1990). There were more burns among the work-related injuries (4.7% as opposed to 2.7% reported in Collins (1990)) and fewer fractures (6.6% as opposed to 12.7% reported in Collins

(1990)). About 8% of the injured persons either changed employer, kind of work, or work activity as a result of the injury.

Park et al. (1993) present another table (their table D) indicating the nature of injury and body parts injured for disabling and nondisabling injuries combined. The greatest numbers of combined injuries occurred to hands, wrists, or fingers (624); backs (463); other (433); and feet, toes, and ankles (186). Park et al. (1993) indicate that more than half of workers who missed at least one-half day of work sustained an injury to their shoulder, back, foot, toe, or ankle.

Finally, the NHIS-OSH investigators asked one question that was especially helpful in our analysis. It pertained to whether or not the injured worker filed a WC claim. Roughly 52.7 percent did not file a claim. The NHIS-OSH investigators did not ask whether the claim was successful (i.e., whether WC paid any benefits). It is likely some people filed a claim but were denied because of a technical reason such as the worker was absent only six days rather than seven days. In this case, we would want to include the injury in our count of the number of injuries not covered by WC. On the other hand, we would not want to include a claim that was fraudulent and was denied WC benefits.[29]

VIII.B.3. NHIS, 1985–87

In 1988, the NHIS investigators constructed a table of data from 1985 through 1987 that allows a comparison between the type of injuries sustained by everyone whether on or off the job with the types of injuries sustained only by people on the job. Table B2.13 (app. B) was drawn from this NHIS table. National estimates are provided for all injuries and work-related injuries only. Most work injuries tend to be similar to all injuries. One exception, however, is for total sprains and strains, especially of the back. A much higher percentage of work injuries than all injuries resulted from back injuries. Other exceptions involve wounds and lacerations. The workplace generates a higher percentage of wounds to upper limbs but a lower percentage to heads, necks, and trunks than all classes of injuries. Finally, effects of "foreign body on eye" comprise a higher percentage among work injuries than all classes of injuries.

Rankings by type of injury from previous years, 1980 and 1981, are available (Collins 1986). Rankings by frequency of injury and education level are also available (Collins 1986, 1990). Persons with low levels of education report much higher injury rates than persons with high education levels. This pattern partially reflects the categories of jobs entered into by persons with low and high levels of education.

VIII.B.4. National Safety Council 1993; Rand; and Rossman et al. 1991; Division of Labor Statistics and Research 1985 and Leigh 1989

The NSC uses NHIS and WC data, as well as their own data provided by corporations, to assemble information on the parts of the body injured in work accidents and the WC costs associated with the injuries. These data are displayed in table B2.14 (app. B).

According to the NSC, disabling injuries most frequently occur to the back, legs, arms, and fingers. The WC costs follow a similar pattern with an interesting exception: injuries to the trunk are apparently more costly than injuries to the fingers (Hoskin et al. 1993).

The Rand study, by Hensler et al. (1991) and Marquis (1992), found the characteristics of work-related injuries and their contributions to the total of work-related injuries to be these: sprains and pulls (48 percent); cuts, lacerations, punctures (20 percent); fractures, broken bones, dislocations (16 percent); and bruises (13 percent). Body parts affected and corresponding percentages were as follows: back, spine (34 percent); hand, fingers, wrist (21 percent); foot, ankle, knee (15 percent); head, eyes, ears, face (13 percent); arm or elbow (12 percent); leg (8 percent); neck (6 percent); and chest, lung, and heart (5 percent).

In the Rossman, Miller, and Douglas 1991 study on the NCCI-DCI data, the following pattern was observed: sprains and strains accounted for 47 percent, followed by dislocation and fractures (12 percent), contusion (12 percent), and laceration (11 percent). The most frequent parts of the body to be injured included, in order, lower backs, followed by fingers and thumbs, followed by knees.

Most of the Rossman, Miller, and Douglas 1991 DCI cases resulting in days away from work (82 percent) involved a Temporary Total disability. Roughly 10.5 percent were Permanent Partial; 0.5 percent were Permanent Total; and 7 percent were Temporary Partial and "mixed patterns of Temporary and Permanent disabilities."

The state of California study (Division of Labor Statistics and Research 1985) of 374,000 disabling injuries reported the following injuries (and illnesses) by body part: back and spine (21 percent); lower extremities (leg, foot, ankle, toe) (19 percent); upper extremities (arm, wrist, hand, not fingers) (13 percent); finger (11 percent). The incidents in California were as follows: strains, sprains, dislocation, and hernias (41 percent); cuts and punctures (14 percent); fractures (10 percent); contusions and crushing injuries (8 percent).

Leigh (1989b) analyzed 1,511 respondents from the University of Michigan's 1977 Quality of Employment Survey (QES). The QES asked respondents whether they thought working conditions caused or worsened any injury or illness "during the past three years." Women most frequently mentioned strain injuries, back injuries, and colds or flu. Men most frequently mentioned back injuries, broken bones, and chemical burns.

IX. Conclusion

The first purpose of this chapter was to generate estimates of the number of fatal and nonfatal job-related injuries for 1992. These estimates appear in table 2.4. We estimate 6,371 fatalities and 13.34 million nonfatal injuries. The fatality estimate was based upon adjusted data from the BLS's CFOI and the nonfatal estimate from the BLS's Annual Survey.

This chapter contained a number of secondary purposes. We pointed out problems associated with primary and secondary sources of data. For example, we argued that the CFOI in 1992 likely undercounted minorities. We also argued that firms and workers likely significantly underreport nonfatal injuries to the BLS and that the Annual Survey likely undercounts assaults and rapes.

Other serious problems plague other sources of data. For example, WC reports likely underestimate the total number of injuries by 55 percent. Based upon an econometric forecasting model, the NHIS does not appear to have reliable estimates for on-the-job injuries.

Tertiary purposes of this chapter included analyses of socioeconomic and occupational differences in injuries as well as the kinds of injuries experienced. Men were found to be much more likely to experience a fatality but only somewhat more likely to experience a nonfatal injury than women. Small firms have especially high injury rates. Laborers, truck drivers, nursing aides, janitors, assemblers, stock handlers, and cashiers among others generated the most disabling injuries compared to other occupations. Injuries to the back generated the highest frequency of injuries.

In chapter 5, our estimates in table 2.4 will be multiplied by medical costs, indirect costs, and Willingness-to-Pay costs to arrive at an estimate of the total costs of occupational injuries in 1992.

CHAPTER 3

Number of Illnesses

by Steven Markowitz

I. Introduction

The goal of this chapter is to obtain a count of the number of workers who developed and/or died from occupational diseases in the United States in 1992. However modest this goal may seem, in fact, the task is difficult. Previous attempts to achieve this goal have been less than fully successful, because they rely on unsubstantiated data sources (President's Report on Occupational Safety and Health 1972) or on single data sources (U.S. Bureau of Labor Statistics 1994a) or represent extrapolations from the experience of a single state (Landrigan and Markowitz 1989). An expert committee convened by the National Research Council reached a similar conclusion (Pollack and Keimig 1987). There have been, however, recent gains in our ability to identify the extent of occupational disease in a comprehensive manner in the U.S. population. It is therefore worthwhile to evaluate current data sources in order to measure our progress in obtaining such a count.

Significant improvements in the surveillance of occupational diseases have been achieved in the past decade. Some of the limitations in the data gathered by the Department of Labor have been acknowledged and are being partly addressed in a redesigned Annual Survey (U.S. Bureau of Labor Statistics 1995a) and proposed initiatives of OSHA (U.S. Department of Labor 1994). A new national adult lead poisoning surveillance program coordinated by the National Institute for Occupational Safety and Health (NIOSH) demonstrates that such a national surveillance program is possible (Chowdhury et al. 1994; NIOSH 1997). The NIOSH program, Sentinel Event Notification System for Occupational Risks (SENSOR), initiated in the late 1980s, is leading to high-quality case finding and identification of selected occupational disorders in numerous states (Baker 1989). Both the quality and quantity of surveillance activities undertaken by state health departments, led by those in New Jersey, Michigan, California, New York, and others, have markedly improved (Rosenman, Trimbath, and Stanbury 1990; Windau et al. 1990).

Despite such gains, calculating how many workers are made ill and die by occupational causes each year remains a perilous task. The peril lies in the inescapable use of assumptions and estimations. While their use is hardly the unique province of occupational health, the degree of extrapolation from known data and the associated lack of consensus are especially problematic in occupational health.[1] As a result, we will generate estimates, subject to important qualifications. First, to better reflect the inherent uncertainty in the estimates obtained, we emphasize ranges of numbers around point estimates. Second, where data are less than optimal, we specify the limitations of the data. When assumptions are required, we make these assumptions explicit and provide a rationale for their use. Third, and finally, since the underlying goal is to estimate the costs of occupational illness, it is necessary to convert qualitative concerns into quantitative ones. This process involves some error but hopefully no more error than would be involved in ignoring these qualitative concerns altogether in an attempt to avoid uncertainty.

II. Approach to the Problem

II.A. Major Obstacles to the Recognition and Counting of Occupational Diseases

Numerous explanations for the difficulty in counting how many cases of illness and death result from occupational exposures have been offered.

One explanation for the underreporting of occupational illness is the inherent difficulty in diagnosing occupational diseases and in establishing cause and effect relationships. The link between occupation and disease is often elusive, because most occupational diseases are not clinically or pathologically distinct from chronic diseases associated with nonoccupational etiologies. For example, the lung cancer caused by asbestos is identical in its clinical and pathological presentation with that caused by cigarette smoking (Selikoff and Lee 1978). Indeed, synergism has been shown to exist between occupational and nonoccupational risk factors in the causation of cancer (Hammond, Selikoff, and Seidman 1979). Similarly, solvent-induced encephalopathy may easily be attributed to old age (Landrigan, Graham, and Thomas 1994) and lead-induced neuropathy to hypertension or diabetes (Landrigan et al. 1984). Only in rare instances, such as in the association between asbestos and malignant mesothelioma (Selikoff, Churg, and Hammond 1964) or in that between vinyl chloride monomer and angiosarcoma of the liver (Creech and Johnson 1974), is the causal association between occupational exposure and disease highly specific.

A second cause of the widespread underrecognition is that the majority of chemicals in commerce have never been fully evaluated with regard to their potential toxicity. A study by the National Research Council in the 1980s found no information available on the toxicity of approximately 80 percent of the 60,000 chemical substances in commercial use (National Research Council 1984). Even for those groups of substances that are most closely regulated and about which the most information is available — drugs and food additives — reasonably complete information on potential untoward effects is available for only a minority of agents.

This problem of insufficient toxicological data is compounded by the fact that premarket testing of the toxicity of newly developing chemical substances is inadequate. Premarket testing is the most effective means of assessing the toxicity of new chemical compounds. However, until the passage of the Toxic Substances Control Act (TSCA) in 1976, there was no legal mechanism in the United States for prospective evaluation of the toxicity of new industrial compounds. Even since passage of the TSCA, inadequacies in testing requirements remain. Many thousands of potentially toxic compounds whose introduction to commerce antedated passage of TSCA remain untested, and there are no requirements at present for routinely testing such compounds. Also, testing procedures for new industrial compounds have not been standardized, especially for measurement of reproductive, neurological, and immunological outcomes. Responsibility for deciding whether or not to test a new chemical and for the development of testing protocols is left almost entirely to the discretion of chemical manufacturers.

The long latency that typically elapses between occupational exposure and onset of illness is a third factor that may obscure the occupational etiology of chronic disease. For example, few occupational cancers appear within 10 or even 20 years of first exposure. Similarly, the chronic neurotoxic effects of solvents may become evident only after many decades of exposure (National Research Council 1992). A worker so affected may well have retired. In such a case, it is unlikely that the worker will be diagnosed as having a disease of occupational origin and even less likely that the employer will learn of this episode of occupational illness.

Lack of awareness among health practitioners about the hazards found at work is a fourth cause of underestimation of occupational disease. This lack of information reflects the fact that most physicians are not adequately trained to suspect work as a cause of disease (Burstein and Levy 1994). Very little time is devoted in most U.S. medical schools to teaching physicians to take a proper occupational history, to recognize the symptoms of common industrial toxins, or to recall the known associations between occupational exposure and disease. The average U.S. medical student receives only six hours of training in occupational medicine during the four years of medical school (Burstein and Levy 1994). In consequence of this lack of training, most physicians do not routinely obtain histories of occupational exposure from their patients. Surveys indicate that adequate occupational histories are recorded on fewer than 10 percent of hospital charts (Institute of Medicine 1988).

Compounding this lack of medical awareness is the limited ability of many workers to provide an accurate report of their toxic exposures. Workers may have had multiple toxic exposures in a variety of jobs over a working lifetime. Until recently, they have not been informed of the nature of the hazard of the material with which they have worked. Employers' reporting requirements remain limited even under the OSHA Hazard Communication Standard and under state and local right-to-know laws (Pollack and Keimig 1987). In many instances, an ill patient will simply not know about his or her past occupational exposures.

Finally, given the potential financial liability associated with the finding that a disease is of occupational origin, employers may be resistant to recognizing the work relatedness of a disorder, especially in cases where personal habits (such as cigarette smoking) or nonoccupational pursuits are possible contributory factors. Since employers are often in the best position to recognize causal associations between workplace exposures and disease, this unfortunate conflict of interest represents a major obstacle to obtaining accurate estimates of the burden of occupational illness.

II.B. Proportional Attributable Risk Model

Given our inability to delineate for nearly all causes of death which individual deaths were due to occupational causes acting alone or in conjunction with other causes, it is necessary to resort to estimating the proportions of diseases and deaths to which occupational exposures have contributed (Peto and Schneiderman 1981). The aim of this section, then, is to establish reasonable ranges of such proportions for major causes of death, while fully acknowledging the limitations of the approach.

Several issues underlie this approach to estimating occupational morbidity and mortality. First, since most disease is multifactorial in origin, to attribute a death to an occupational exposure does not exclude a causal role for another factor that is not occupational. Both causes may have actively contributed to a person's death. Indeed, most lung cancers in asbestos-exposed workers who smoke cigarettes occur as a result of the combined action of exposure to asbestos and cigarettes (Hammond, Selikoff, and Seidman 1979). It would be proper, therefore, to assign a lung cancer death in such a person simultaneously to an occupational cause and to a lifestyle factor. This will lead to double counting as long as categories of causes are considered mutually exclusive. In this chapter, we use the term *attributable proportion* with reference to an exposure to mean the proportion of disease that would have not occurred in the absence of that exposure.

A deeper problem exists, however. While it is likely that occupational causes frequently interact with nonoccupational causes to produce illness and death, the nature of this interaction is largely unknown and unquantified. It is, therefore, difficult to determine, for most occupational exposures, the relative importance of each factor, occupational and nonoccupational, acting alone and in concert.

Second, the proportion of disease due to occupational causes (or any other causes) can be expected to vary in time and place. This is due principally to (1) differing relative risks resulting from variation in type, intensity, and duration of exposures and (2) variation in the proportion of the populations exposed to various occupational toxins. An empirical demonstration of this variation and its sources is provided by the body of case control studies of lung cancer completed in the past 15 years (Correa et al. 1983; Pastorino et al. 1984; Kjuus, Langard, and Skjeerven 1986; Lerchen, Wiggens, and Samet 1987; Schoenberg et al. 1987; Benhamou, Benhamou, and Flamant 1988; Levin et al. 1988; Ronco et al. 1988; Vineis et al. 1988; Morabia et al. 1992).[2]

The occupational health research community is unlikely to command the resources in the foreseeable future to undertake the number and kinds of detailed studies that would provide the knowledge base allowing qualitatively better estimates of the occupational contribution to disease than we are able to complete at present. Our approach in this book is to use estimates of ranges of proportions of major categories of diseases that are consonant with current knowledge and thinking. Ranges of estimates of similar magnitudes have been used by numerous groups of occupational health researchers in various states, including New York, Connecticut, Texas, New Jersey, Pennsylvania, and Canada (Markowitz et al. 1989a, 1989b; Fahs et al. 1989; Occupational Health Working Group 1990; Rothstein and Cooper 1993; Pennsylvania Department of Health 1990; Kraut 1994). A summary of our estimates is provided in table 3.1.

II.B.1. Cancer

We estimate that 6 percent to 10 percent of all cancers among people aged 25 and older in the United States are caused by occupational exposures.

Previous estimates of the proportion of cancer due to occupational factors range from 4 percent to 38 percent. The former number was proposed as the best point estimate by Doll and Peto (1981) as part of a major review of the causes of cancer published in 1981. Their report was written in part in response to a 1978 consensus document written by numerous U.S. governmental agencies, estimating that 22 to 38 percent of all cancers in the United States were due to occupational carcinogens (Bridbord et al. 1978). The 1978 report was flawed inasmuch as relative risks derived from cohorts heavily exposed to occupational agents were applied to populations with a broad range of exposure to these agents, yielding an overestimate of the number of people likely to develop occupational cancer. On the other hand, a major industry-sponsored review of the 1978 report by Stallones and Downs (1978) only mildly criticized the governmental report and estimated that 10 percent to 33 percent of cancers in the United States were caused by occupational agents at that time.

Our estimate of 6 percent to 10 percent is grounded in part on a specific set of studies of selected cancers and in part on general trends in human and animal cancer research. There have been at least a dozen case control studies of lung cancer and occupation completed in the

TABLE 3.1.   Estimated Percentages of Selected Diseases Caused by Occupational Factors

Condition	ICD-9 Codes	Percentage Attributed to Occupation
Cancer	140–209	6–10
Coronary heart disease[a]	410–414,440	5–10
Cerebrovascular disease[a]	430–438	5–10
Chronic obstructive pulmonary disease	490–496	10
Renal disorders	580–589	1–3
Nervous system disorders	323.7, 331, 332, 349.82, 356, 357.7, 359.4	1–3

[a]Only includes new and recurrent cases of coronary heart disease and cerebrovascular disease among people between ages 25 and 64, inclusive.

United States and Europe since 1982. After controlling for cigarette smoking, they collectively show that 10 percent to 33 percent of all types of lung cancer in males are attributable to occupational exposures.[3] Applying a narrower range of point estimates, 15 percent to 20 percent, to the 91,405 deaths from lung cancer among males in the United States in 1992 yields a total of 13,711 to 18,281 deaths in males from lung cancer due to occupational agents. These lung cancer deaths represented 2.7 percent to 3.5 percent of all cancer deaths in the United States in 1992. A similar analysis of deaths from another well-documented occupational cancer, bladder cancer, provides an estimate that 21 percent to 27 percent of male bladder cancer deaths are due to occupation in the United States (Silverman et al. 1989a, 1989b). Since there were 7,123 deaths from bladder cancer among U.S. males in 1992, 1,496 to 1,923 bladder cancer deaths, or approximately 0.3 percent of all cancer deaths, were due to occupational agents. Together, bladder cancer and lung cancer among males alone accounted for approximately 3 percent to 4 percent of all cancer deaths in the United States in 1992.

The proportions of lung and bladder cancer among males that we attribute to occupation are consistent with other published analyses. Doll and Peto used a single point estimate of 15 percent of male lung cancer deaths as the proportion associated with occupational factors (Doll and Peto 1981). In 1991, Vineis and Simonato (1991) reviewed published studies and concluded that a range of at least 1 percent to 5 percent of lung cancer as the lower estimate (when considering only asbestos exposure) and 40 percent as an upper estimate of lung cancer was due to occupational exposures. They analyzed only case control studies and emphasized the heavy dependence of the proportion on the prevalence of exposure to lung carcinogens in the studied population.

More recently, Steenland et al. (1996) took an alternative approach to estimating the burden of occupationally related lung cancer. They used the results of published cohort studies to obtain summary relative risks for lung cancer and selected exposures and applied these to the estimated populations at risk in the 1980s in the United States. They performed this analysis for nine agents categorized by the International Agency for Research on Cancer as definite or probable lung carcinogens (cadmium, nickel, arsenic, chromium, diesel exhaust, silica, beryllium, radon, and asbestos). They concluded that approximately 10,000 male lung cancer cases occurred each year due to prior exposure to these occupational lung carcinogens. This represents 10 percent of male lung cancer cases in the United States. They emphasized that this estimate was likely to be conservative, because it did not include occupations that have been shown to have an excess risk of lung cancer but which do not have exposure to one of the nine lung carcinogens included in their analysis (Steenland et al. 1996).

Vineis and Simonato (1991) reviewed the existing case control studies on bladder cancer from Europe and North America and concluded that the range of percentages of bladder cancer due to occupation was 0 percent to 3 percent at the low end of the range to 16 percent to 24 percent at the high end of the range. We used the range of 21 percent to 27 percent that was obtained by Silverman et al. (1989a) at the National Cancer Institute because it was a broadly representative, population-based study that was recent, much larger than the other studies, and specific to the United States.

Obviously, there are cancers of organ sites other than bladder and lung that are caused by occupational exposures.[4]

Three sets of research findings in occupational cancer in the past 10 to 15 years support the proposition that the percentage of cancer due to occupation is significantly higher than the 3 percent to 4 percent specifically due to cancer of the lung and bladder. First, recent studies have provided data suggesting that a number of well-known toxins are human carcinogens. Included in this category are diesel exhaust and silica and lung cancer (Steenland et al. 1996; Goldsmith 1994); vinyl chloride and brain cancer (Wong et al. 1991); and orthotoluidine and bladder cancer (Ward et al. 1991; Sellers and Markowitz 1992). For other agents, limited evidence has accumulated to support, though has not yet established, an etiologic role in cancer. Among these agents are formaldehyde, 1,3-butadiene, and perchloroethylene (National Toxicology Program 1998). Whereas the carcinogenicity of some of these agents may be refuted as additional human evidence is accumulated, it is unlikely all will be exonerated as human carcinogens. Notably, industrial exposure to many of these agents is common, increasing the significance of even modest elevations in relative risk.

A second set of findings that is not addressed by the single agent approach to identifying occupational cancer is the large number of studies that demonstrate increased risks of cancer for specific occupations without clear identification of the suspect agents. Many occupations have multiple exposures, exposures of uncertain intensity, or no obvious exposures at all (Ward 1995). Yet, some of these occupations show consistent elevations on cancer risk. Examples include farmers and lymphoma (Pearce and Reif 1990; Blair et al. 1992) and firefighters and brain cancer (Demers, Heyer, and Rosenstock 1992; Demers et al. 1994; Vena and Fiedler 1987). Undoubtedly, some of these associations are not causal, but it is also likely that many are.

Third, toxicological assays in animals completed in the past two decades show that a significant number of chemicals tested to date show evidence of carcinogenicity. More than 600 chemical agents have been shown to be carcinogenic in at least one rodent species (Rall et al. 1987). In a review of the experience from the National Toxicology Program (NTP), 130, or one-third, of 404 experiments conducted by the NTP with 105 chemicals showed evidence of carcinogenicity (Rall et al. 1987). Among the more important agents that tested positive in the NTP experiments but for which epidemiologic research is incomplete are methylene chloride, perchloroethylene, and propylene oxide (Rall et al. 1987). Whereas there is considerable disagreement about the significance of the results of animal testing for human cancer (Huff and Rall 1992; Ames and Gold 1990), it is nonetheless considered prudent, given a paucity of human data, to regard chemicals that cause cancer in animal experiments as being reasonably likely to do so in humans as well (International Agency for Research on Cancer 1987). In the *Eighth Annual Report on Carcinogens,* the National Toxicology Program lists approximately 207 substances that, based primarily on the results of animal studies, are reasonably anticipated to be carcinogens (National Toxicology Program 1998). While the results of animal studies certainly do not contribute to the precision of the estimates of the fraction of human cancer attributable to occupational exposures, they nonetheless suggest that the problem of occupational cancer may be larger than is recognized when only established human carcinogens are considered.

Finally, incumbents in some occupations are more likely to smoke than in other occupations (Leigh 1996). Passive smoking can therefore be another factor.

Taken together, these lines of evidence — an increased number of epidemiologic studies tying individual agents to specific cancers; the body of literature relating specific occupations to selected cancers even in the absence of identified single agents; and the finding that a large proportion of chemicals causes malignancies in animals — exert an upward pressure on the estimates of the proportion of cancer attributable to occupational exposures. They support our assumption that no fewer than 6 percent of cancer deaths have an occupational cause and that the 6 percent to 10 percent range may be a conservative estimate of the occupational fraction of cancer deaths.

II.B.2. Cardiovascular and Cerebrovascular Disease

Despite the importance of heart and related large vessel disease as a cause of mortality in the United States, there has been little attention given to the overall burden of cardiovascular disease (CVD) caused by occupational risk factors. In contrast to the links demonstrated between chemicals and carcinogenesis, relatively few chemical agents have been shown to cause or promote heart disease and hypertension. Carbon disulfide and nitroglycerin have been demonstrated to cause or exacerbate ischemic heart disease. Carbon monoxide displaces oxygen from hemoglobin, reducing oxygen supply to the heart and worsening symptoms of coronary heart disease. It also appears to promote atherogenesis. Lead raises blood pressure, thereby contributing to the risk of hypertension and ischemic heart disease and stroke.

Lead and carbon monoxide are widespread hazards. According to the National Occupational Exposure Survey conducted by NIOSH in the early 1980s, there were 1.4 million people with potential occupational exposure to lead (NIOSH 1992). The number of people exposed to carbon monoxide is less well described but is large. The level of excess risk of cardiovascular and cerebrovascular disease experienced by the large numbers of workers exposed to these agents is not known. It is, therefore, not possible to calculate the fraction of CVD caused by these agents.

A large body of scientific literature exists linking a number of non-chemical occupational risk factors to heart disease and stroke or to the antecedent risk factors known to cause these diseases, such as high blood pressure, increased serum lipids, and others (Fine and Rosenstock 1993; Leigh 1988a). Occupational stress, noise (Talbott 1988), shift work, passive smoking, and the physical inactivity inherent in many occupations have been implicated in excessive rates of heart disease, stroke, and hypertension. It is beyond the scope of this chapter to examine in detail the dozens of studies that have addressed these issues, which have been reviewed elsewhere (Kristensen 1989; Olsen and Kristensen 1991; Schnall, Landbergis, and Baker 1994; Murphy 1991; Leigh 1986a).

Psychosocial stress in the workplace has been shown to be a probable cause of cardiovascular disease. Empirical support for this relationship is best developed when stress is formulated in the "job strain" model introduced by Karasek (1979). This model designates jobs involving high demands and low decision-making latitude as "high strain" jobs. A review evaluated 36 studies published between 1981 and 1993 addressing this issue, the majority of which showed a positive association between job strain and cardiovascular disease or known cardiovascular risk factors (Schnall, Landbergis, and Baker 1994). The findings were consistent across populations, study designs, and outcome measures. The authors concluded that available data "strongly suggest" that job strain causes cardiovascular disease. More recent studies further support the relationship between job strain and cardiovascular disease (Leigh 1991b; Marmot et al. 1997; Bosma et al. 1997; Lynch et al. 1997a, 1997b; Steenland, Johnson, and Nowland 1997; Karasek and Theorell 1990).

Finally, job strain may also induce persons to drink excessively (Leigh 1995c; Leigh and Jiang 1993; Seeman et al. 1988).

Olsen and Kristensen use these studies to obtain estimates of the etiologic fraction of cardiovascular disease that is caused by job strain and by other workplace factors in Denmark (Olsen and Kristensen 1991). They restrict their estimates to "premature" cardiovascular disease (i.e., such disease occurring in people under age 70). They estimate that 6 percent of men and 16 percent of women have high strain jobs. They use an average relative risk of two for cardiovascular disease associated with job strain to determine that 6 percent of CVD in men and 14 percent of CVD among women is due to job strain. The authors note the similarity between their results and those obtained in Sweden, that is, etiologic fractions of 3 percent to 7 percent for CVD in men and 9 percent to 13 percent for CVD in women (Olsen and Kristensen 1991).

By a similar method, Olsen and Kristensen obtain etiologic fractions of CVD ascribed to other nonchemical occupational risk factors: 7 percent of CVD in both sexes due to shift work; 2 percent of CVD in both sexes due to passive smoking; 1 percent of CVD in both sexes due to noise; and 42 percent of CVD in both sexes due to sedentary work. Excluding the risk attributable to sedentary work, the aggregate risk of CVD due to these nonchemical occupational risk factors was 16 percent in men and 22 percent in women.[5]

The age groups for inclusion in the estimates of occupational disease are of crucial importance for cardiovascular disease. Roughly 84 percent of all deaths due to cardiovascular diseases in the United States occur among people aged 65 and over (National Center for Health Statistics 1993a, 1993b). This skewed age distribution is less true for cancer. Roughly 69 percent of deaths from cancer in the United States occur among people aged 65 and over (National Center for Health Statistics 1993a, 1993b). For our estimates of the number of cancers caused by occupational factors, we apply a range of proportions to cancers in all age groups, because the well-known phenomenon of latency dictates that occupational exposures experienced during the later working years, ages 40 to 64, may not be expressed until well after retirement age. Whether such a latent period applies to the nonchemical occupational risk factors for CVD is not known. We, therefore, restrict our estimates of occupational cardiovascular disease to people aged 64 and below.[6]

We estimate that 5 percent to 10 percent of all ischemic and hypertensive heart disease and cerebrovascular disease among people below age 65 and above age 24 in the United States is due to occupational causes. We employ lower percentages than those cited earlier in an attempt to be conservative and in recognition of the uncertainty of the underlying data. Moreover, we restrict attention to only those diseases for which substantial evidence indicates an association: hypertension, ischemic heart disease, cerebrovascular disease, and arteriosclerosis. These assumptions about age and our inclusion of only certain specific diseases result in our attributing to occupation less than 1 percent of all circulatory diseases among all persons (0.836 percent as a point estimate and a range of 0.557 to 1.114 percent).

II.B.3. Chronic Obstructive Pulmonary Disease

Chronic obstructive pulmonary disease (COPD) is the principal occupational cause of nonmalignant respiratory mortality and morbidity other than the pneumoconioses. COPD also constitutes the primary cause of deaths due to chronic respiratory disease in the United States. Whereas cigarette smoking is undoubtedly the major cause of COPD at present, studies have demonstrated a role for occupational exposures in the etiology of COPD (Blanc 1987). The best quantitative data exist for a limited number of exposures, principally coal, silica, grain dust, cadmium, and others (U.S. Department of Health and Human Services 1985; Becklake 1992; Oxman et al. 1993). Other studies have related specific occupations to excess COPD mortality. The literature relating to this topic is extensive and has been reviewed elsewhere (Becklake 1992; Oxman et al. 1993).

Studies clearly support a role for occupational exposures in COPD mortality (Korn et al. 1987; Lebowitz 1977; Krzyzanowski and Kauffman 1988; Viegi et al. 1991; Xu et al. 1992). These large population-based studies consistently show that exposure to a wide variety of occupational dusts, and, to a lesser extent, gases and fumes, is associated with a 30 percent to 50 percent increase in symptoms and pulmonary function deficits characteristic of COPD. In order to recognize the likelihood that occupational exposures play a limited but definite role in the cause of death from COPD, we assign an estimate of 10 percent among persons age 25 and over to the proportion of COPD caused by occupational exposures.

II.B.4. Pneumoconioses

That all deaths and most illness caused by pneumoconioses are due to occupational exposures to pathogenic dusts is well known. Exposure to asbestos, coal, silica, and other dusts occurs outside of the workplace, especially in the homes of workers and in the neighborhoods of dust-producing facilities. However, the intensity of these nonoccupational exposures is unlikely to cause death.

A more important issue is the extent to which pneumoconioses may be underdiagnosed and, therefore, missing from death certificates. The most extensive analysis of the underdiagnosis of mortality from a pneumoconiosis was performed among insulators in the United States and Canada by Selikoff and Seidman (1991). Between 1977 and 1986, there were 123 insulator deaths ascribed to asbestosis on the death certificates in this cohort. After investigators reviewed medical records, chest radiographs, and tissue pathology when available ("best evidence"), they ascribed 259 insulator deaths occurring between 1977 and 1986 to asbestosis (Selikoff and Seidman 1991). Over one-half of pneumo-coniosis deaths were, thus, missed in this group well known to have heavy asbestos exposure. A more recent study of deaths between 1982 and 1991 among a subset of the same overall cohort of insulators continues to show a 50 percent underdiagnosis of pneumoconiosis on the death certificate (Markowitz et al. 1997). Unfortunately, there are not a sufficient number of other studies of the underdiagnosis of pneumoconioses on death certificates to allow a reliable correction of the mortality statistics available from the National Center for Health Statistics.

II.B.5. Renal and Neurologic Disease

The extent of research documenting the occupational causes of renal and neurologic disease is considerably less extensive than that supporting the relationships between occupational agents and cancer and chronic respiratory disease. Examples of exposure-response relationships for these outcomes abound, even if the accumulated research has not been sufficiently comprehensive or appropriately designed to support precise estimates of the occupational etiologic fraction. Both categories of disease can be caused by exposure to common occupational toxins. Renal toxicity has been associated with occupational exposure to lead and mercury, glycol ethers, and other organic solvents (Landrigan et al. 1984; Daniell 1994). Neurological disorders stemming from the workplace exposures have been caused by pesticides, heavy metals, many organic solvents, and other organic agents (National Research Council 1992; Office of Technology Assessment 1990). Because the exposure-response relationships have not been well characterized for these disease categories, estimates of the etiologic fraction due to occupation can only be crudely estimated. We employ a range of 1 percent to 3 percent.

A number of diseases are not considered due to lack of evidence or very small numbers. AIDS is included in that group (Center for Disease Control 1992).

III. Estimates of Morbidity and Mortality from Occupational Disease

III.A. Occupational Morbidity

III.A.1. Survey-Based Data

III.A.1.1. BLS's Annual Survey

Background. The federal Bureau of Labor Statistics has conducted the Annual Survey of Occupational Injuries and Illnesses (Annual Survey) since 1972 under a mandate established by the Occupational Safety and Health Act of 1970. The goal of the survey is to obtain the numbers and the rates of injuries and illnesses recorded by the employers as being occupational in origin. The 1992 survey reflects questionnaire data obtained from a stratified random sample of approximately 250,000 establishments in the private sector. The survey completed by the employer is principally a distillation of data that employers are required to maintain by OSHA (OSHA Form 200). The Annual Survey is discussed at length in appendix A to chapter 2. A number of limitations regarding injury data are noted in that appendix. In addition to those, occupational illness reporting has another limitation: the failure of the employee's physician to diagnose the illness as being work related. Occupational diseases occurring among retired workers are not subject to the BLS reporting requirement. Indeed, it is unlikely that the employer would be aware of the onset of a work-related illness in a retiree. Since many cases of chronic occupational illnesses with long latency, including cancer and lung disease, are likely to have their onset following retirement, a large proportion of such cases would not be included in the data collected by the BLS. These limitations are recognized by BLS.

Nonetheless, the BLS Annual Survey has important strengths. It has been conducted consistently over the past 20 years, and, therefore, time trends can be expected to be reasonably reliable. Furthermore, the illnesses recorded by employers as being work related would be generally accepted as being work related by physicians.

Results of the BLS Annual Survey, 1982 to 1992. In 1992, there were 457,400 occupational illnesses in private industry in the United States, according to the BLS Annual Survey (table 3.2). This is an increase of

89,100 cases, or 24 percent, over the 368,300 illnesses recorded in the 1991 Annual Survey. Expressed as rates, the incidence of new occupational illnesses was 49.0 per 10,000 full-time workers in 1991 and 59.8 per 10,000 such workers in 1992, a 22 percent increase.

Disorders associated with repeated trauma, such as carpal tunnel syndrome, tendinitis of the wrist and elbow, and hearing loss, dominate the occupational illnesses recorded in the Annual Survey and have done so since 1987 (table 3.2) (Bureau of Labor Statistics 1994b). In 1992, they accounted for 62 percent of all illness cases recorded on the Annual Survey. Other important categories of disease were skin disorders, pulmonary diseases, and disorders associated with physical trauma (table 3.2).

The time trend of occupational illnesses recorded in the Annual Survey since its inception is remarkable. Table 3.3 shows the numbers of occupational illnesses by disease category from 1973 to 1992. Recorded occupational illnesses decreased sharply through the 1970s and reached a nadir in 1982, when 105,600 such illnesses were reported in the private sector (fig. 3.1). The numbers of occupational illnesses increased thereafter, especially after 1986. The 1992 total, 457,400 cases, represents an increase of 333 percent, or 351,800 cases per year, compared to 1982. Indeed, most of this increase has occurred over a shorter time period (i.e., since 1986). Comparing 1986 and 1992, there has been an increase of 234 percent, or 320,600 occupational illness cases per year (table 3.4).

TABLE 3.2. Numbers of Occupational Illnesses in the United States, 1992 (BLS Annual Survey)

Category of Illness	Number of Cases	Percentage
Skin diseases	62,900	13.7
Dust diseases of the lungs	2,800	0.6
Respiratory conditions due to toxic agents	23,500	5.1
Poisonings	7,000	1.5
Disorders due to physical agents	22,200	4.9
Disorders associated with repeated trauma	281,800	61.6
All other occupational illnesses	57,300	12.5
Total	457,500	100.0

Source: Data from U.S. Bureau of Labor Statistics 1995a.

TABLE 3.3. Occupational Illnesses in the United States, 1973–92 (BLS Annual Survey)

Year	Dust Diseases of the Lungs	Respiratory Conditions Due to Toxic Agents	Poisonings	Skin Diseases or Disorders	Disorders Due to Physical Agents	Associated with Repeated Trauma	Other Occupational Illnesses	Total
1973	1,500	11,500	6,800	89,200	27,500	23,600	40,400	200,500
1974	1,700	12,700	7,400	89,400	27,100	24,600	37,400	200,400
1975	1,000	11,900	6,200	74,400	21,200	23,700	24,900	163,300
1976	1,200	13,100	6,100	71,600	24,200	23,000	28,800	167,900
1977	2,000	13,100	5,700	73,000	23,600	23,400	21,100	161,900
1978	1,600	13,600	5,600	65,900	16,700	20,200	19,600	143,500
1979	1,700	13,100	5,800	67,900	15,100	21,900	23,200	148,900
1980	2,300	11,400	4,700	56,100	13,200	23,100	19,200	130,200
1981	2,100	10,800	5,600	51,200	11,900	22,900	21,500	126,100
1982	2,000	8,800	3,400	41,900	8,300	22,600	18,600	105,600
1983	1,700	7,900	3,000	39,500	8,800	26,700	18,400	106,100
1984	1,800	10,600	4,500	42,500	9,000	34,700	21,400	124,800
1985	1,700	11,600	4,200	41,800	9,000	37,000	20,100	125,400
1986	3,200	12,300	4,300	41,900	9,200	46,000	20,400	136,800
1987	3,400	14,300	4,800	54,200	13,800	72,900	26,800	190,200
1988	2,900	16,100	5,500	57,900	17,300	115,400	25,600	240,700
1989	2,600	18,900	5,800	62,100	17,700	146,900	29,700	283,700
1990	3,000	20,500	6,100	60,900	18,200	185,400	37,300	331,600
1991	2,500	18,300	6,700	58,200	18,200	223,600	40,800	368,300
1992	2,800	23,500	7,000	62,900	22,200	281,800	57,300	457,400

Source: Data from U.S. Bureau of Labor Statistics 1993 and 1995a.

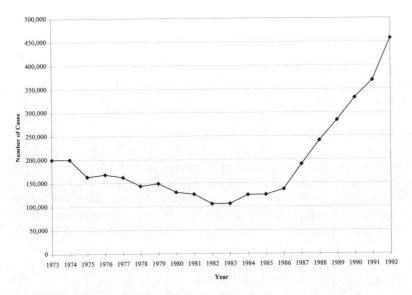

Fig. 3.1.   Illness cases over time

Table 3.4 compares the number of new cases of occupational illnesses and percentage changes according to the Annual Surveys for
selected years, 1982, 1986, and 1992. Table 3.5 shows the comparable
data by incidence rates for 1986 and 1992. Because the average annual
employment in the private sector rose only 23 percent between 1982 and
1992 and 9 percent between 1986 and 1992, the percentage changes in
the rates are only slightly less than the percentage changes in the numbers of new cases.

Disorders associated with repeated trauma clearly account for the
largest proportion of the increment in cases of occupational illness. This
rise is well known. Whereas repeated trauma disorders were associated
with 45,500 cases of occupational illness in 1986, or 33 percent of all
illnesses recorded by the BLS, they increased to 281,800 by 1992, or 62
percent of all BLS-recorded occupational illnesses. Of the 320,600 additional cases of all occupational illness that occurred in 1992 compared to
1986, 236,300, or 74 percent, were disorders associated with repeated
trauma (table 3.4).

An analysis of these data shows that occupations at most risk for
carpal tunnel syndrome include, in order, dental hygienists, meatcutters, sewing machine operators, machine feeders, assemblers, production helpers, punching press machine operators, hand packers, molding

machine operators, billing machine operators, upholsterers, food batch makers, packing machine operators, grinding machine operators, laborers outside construction, and slicing machine operators. Among professionals, dentists face the greatest risk for carpal tunnel syndrome (Leigh and Miller 1998b).

This epidemic rise in disorders associated with repeated trauma, however, cannot be allowed to obscure the significant increases that have occurred in other categories of occupational illness. Overall, there was an 80 percent increase in the recorded incidence in these occupational illnesses in the six years between 1986 and 1992 (table 3.5). Excluding disorders associated with repeated trauma, there were an additional 84,300 cases of occupational disease recorded in the Annual Survey in 1992 compared to 1986 (table 3.4). Indeed, the total number of reported occupational illnesses other than those due to repeated trauma in 1992, 175,600 cases, exceeds the *total* number of recorded occupational ill-

TABLE 3.4.   Number of New Cases of Occupational Illnesses by Category of Illness (BLS Annual Survey, 1982, 1986, and 1992)

Category of Illness	1982	1986	1992	Change 1982–92 (%)	Change 1986–92 (%)
Skin diseases	41,900	41,900	62,900	+50.1	+50.1
Dust diseases of the lungs	2,000	3,200	2,800	+40.0	−12.5
Respiratory conditions due to toxic agents	8,800	12,300	23,500	+167.0	+91.1
Poisonings	3,400	4,300	7,000	+105.9	+62.8
Disorders due to physical agents	8,300	9,200	22,200	+167.5	+141.3
Disorders associated with repeated trauma	22,600	45,500	281,800	+1,146.9	+519.3
All other occupational illnesses	18,600	20,400	57,300	+208.1	+180.9
Total	105,600	136,800	457,500	+333.2	+234.4
(Total excluding repeated trauma)	83,000	91,300	175,700	+111.7	+92.4
Average annual employment, private sector	73,729,000	83,291,200	90,459,600	+22.7	+8.6

Source: Data from U.S. Bureau of Labor Statistics 1993 and 1995a.

nesses (including those associated with repeated trauma) in 1986, when 136,800 cases of occupational illness were reported by employers. With the exception of dust diseases of the lungs, all other categories of occupational diseases experienced 50 percent to 181 percent increases in the numbers of cases and 40 percent to 160 percent increases in case rates. Of the specific categories, the category showing the greatest increase is that of disorders due to physical agents, which increased by 141 percent in cases between 1986 and 1992. The breadth of the increase is also shown by the 181 percent increase in the rate of diseases in the category of "all other occupational illnesses" between 1986 and 1992 (U.S. Bureau of Labor Statistics 1993, 1994b).

These increases in the numbers and rates of occupational diseases recorded by employers and reported to the BLS in recent years are remarkable. During the same time period, 1986 to 1992, the rate of occupational injuries per 100 full-time workers recorded by the BLS increased from 7.7 in 1986 to 8.3 in 1992, a 7.8 percent increase. The number of recorded fatalities in the workplace has likewise not increased dramatically in the past five years. This suggests that, if the increase in occupational diseases reflects an increase in the prevalence of workplace hazards, these hazards must be quite specific. Yet, the

TABLE 3.5.   Incidence of Occupational Illness (BLS Annual Survey, 1986 versus 1992, rate per 10,000 full-time workers)

Category of Illness	1986	1992	Change (%)
Skin diseases	5.9	8.2	+39.0
Dust diseases of the lung	0.5	0.3	−40.0
Respiratory conditions due to toxic agents	1.7	3.1	+82.4
Poisonings	0.6	0.9	+50.0
Disorders due to physical agents	1.3	2.9	+123.1
Disorders associated with repeated trauma	6.4	36.8	+475.0
All other occupational illnesses	2.9	7.5	+158.6
Total	19.3	59.7	+209.3
(Total excluding repeated trauma)	12.8	23.0	+79.7

Source: Data from U.S. Bureau of Labor Statistics 1993 and 1995a.

breadth of the categories of diseases showing an increase in rates of illness argues against such specificity.

The change in the recording of occupational illnesses may be due to a change in the underlying occurrence of disease or to a change in the recognition and reporting of these conditions. The latter may reflect increased awareness of occupational diseases among workers, improved diagnosis by physicians, improved reporting by workers to employers, enhanced recording of occupational illnesses by employers, or a combination of all of these factors. In the case of disorders associated with repeated trauma, it is likely that rapid changes in the workplace, including the introduction of personal computers, have altered the nature and prevalence of hazards leading to repeated trauma. Most of the increase in the disorders associated with repeated trauma between 1986 and 1992 would, therefore, represent a frank increase in the underlying incidence of disease. On the other hand, with respect to the other occupational illnesses, while one cannot rule out that workplace conditions in the private sector have changed between 1986 and 1992 such that the likelihood of occupational illness has increased, it is more likely that the recognition of occupational illnesses has significantly changed in this five-year time period. This would imply that workers, employers, and/or health care professionals have significantly improved their ability to recognize, report, and/or record occupational illnesses. Whereas this explanation is the most plausible one with respect to the occupational illnesses other than those involving repeated trauma, it is nonetheless striking that the recognition of occupational disease would change in such a short time period.

Revised BLS Annual Survey, 1992. In response to recommendations by the National Academy of Sciences (Pollack and Keimig 1987), the BLS redesigned its Annual Survey in the early 1990s (Bureau of Labor Statistics 1994a). In addition to previous information collected, the new survey includes specific information on workers with occupational illnesses and injuries that are considered serious (i.e., involve one or more lost workdays). Newly collected information includes occupation, age, gender, race, length of service, nature of illness/injury, part of body affected, event or exposure, and primary and secondary sources of illness and injury. This redesigned survey was first conducted in 1992.

In 1992, one-third (34 percent), or 2.33 million, of the 6.80 million occupational illnesses and injuries recorded in the 1992 BLS Annual Survey were of a serious nature. Of these 2.3 million serious occupational illnesses and injuries, 2.29 million were classified into either injuries or illnesses.

Occupational illnesses were more likely to be serious than occupational injuries. Occupational illnesses represented 6.7 percent (457,400) of the total 6.8 million occupational illnesses and injuries in 1992, yet they comprised 8.0 percent (182,862) of the 2.29 million serious occupational illnesses and injuries in 1992, an excess of 19 percent. Occupational illnesses also disproportionately accounted for the most serious cases (i.e., involving more than 30 days away from work). Nearly one-third (31 percent), or 56,883, of the 182,862 occupational illnesses led to greater than 30 lost workdays, compared to 19 percent (392,389) of the 2.1 million occupational injuries.

The redesign of the BLS Annual Survey in 1992 provides an unprecedented opportunity to examine the extent to which employers record specific chronic diseases as occupational in origin. Categories of disease used in previous BLS Annual Surveys were too broad and few to identify diseases of interest such as cancer and heart disease. Table 3.6 shows numbers of selected occupational illnesses in the BLS survey in 1992. For coronary heart disease, stroke, cancer, and chronic obstructive pulmonary disease combined, there were 1,485 cases, or 0.8 percent of all serious occupational illnesses. While the nature of nonserious

TABLE 3.6. Number of Occupational Illnesses Involving Days away from Work (BLS Annual Survey, 1992)

Systemic diseases and disorders	148,834
Nervous system and sense organs diseases	49,474
Carpal tunnel syndrome	33,042
Circulatory system diseases	1,462
Ischemic heart disease	591
Stroke	75
Respiratory system diseases	3,892
COPD	716
Asthma	272
Pneumoconioses	188
Digestive system disease and disorders	32,987
Musculoskeletal system and connective tissue disease and disorders	46,148
Rheumatism (including tendonitis, synovitis, ganglia, and others)	40,324
Skin diseases	13,845
Infectious diseases	3,237
Neoplasms	103
Symptoms, signs, and ill-defined conditions	21,274
Other conditions	6,992
Mental disorders or syndromes	6,765
Multiple disorders and conditions	2,385

Source: Data from U.S. Bureau of Labor Statistics 1995a.

occupational illnesses recorded in the BLS survey is unknown, they are unlikely to consist of a significant number of cases of coronary heart disease, stroke, cancer, and chronic respiratory disease, given the severity of morbidity that usually accompanies these diseases. Thus, even with the well-demonstrated increase in occupational diseases recorded by the BLS, especially from 1986 to 1992, including diseases other than those involving repeated trauma, the four leading causes of death and disease in the United States are still not recorded in large numbers by the occupational disease surveillance system of the Bureau of Labor Statistics.

III.A.1.2. Public Employees, Self-Employed, and All Others

The most important exclusion from the BLS Annual Survey for which data exist on occupational illnesses and injuries is the exclusion of workers in the public sector. In 1992, there were a total of 18,644,000 workers employed by public agencies, including 2,969,000 federal employees, 4,408,000 state employees, and 11,267,000 employees of local governments (Green and Becker 1994). There were 90,459,600 private sector workers covered by the BLS Annual Survey in 1992.

Data on occupational illnesses among federal employees are collected by the federal Occupational Workers' Compensation Program (OWCP). In 1993, there were 24,500 claims filed for occupational illnesses, and 15,500 of these claims were approved (Office of Workers' Compensation Program 1994). There were approximately 2.9 million federal employees in 1993, yielding a rate of 51.7 cases of occupational illnesses per 10,000 full-time workers. Data for 1991 and 1992 are not available from the OWCP. The OWCP does not categorize approved claims by category of illness. The 24,500 claims filed during 1993 have been so categorized, but 17,257 (70 percent) of these claims are categorized as "other occupational diseases," making the disease profile by category uninformative (Office of Workers' Compensation Program 1994).

Data on the rates and numbers of illnesses due to occupation among state and local employees are also available for selected states. A recent study of state and local employees in New Jersey documented 1,700 occupational illnesses among state and local employees in 1990, yielding an incidence of 50 per 10,000 public sector workers (Roche 1993). Similar rates were obtained for 1988 and 1989.[7]

The self-employed, farmworkers on farms with fewer than 11 employees, domestics, and others are either intentionally excluded or known to be seriously underrepresented on the Annual Survey. The self-employed and farmworkers are known to have high injury rates and are likely to have high illness rates as well (chap. 2). We nevertheless will assume all have the same rate as those in the Annual Survey.

All illness rates are expressed per 10,000 full-time employees. We must adjust for part-time workers and for work hours variations among full-time workers. We follow the same procedure outlined in chapter 2, whereby rates are adjusted for average weekly hours for all employees (38.8) divided by the full-time equivalent hours per week (40.0).

The rates of occupational disease among federal and nonfederal public workers are remarkably congruent with each other and with the rates of such illness among private sector workers as recorded in the Annual Survey. It is reasonable to apply an occupational illness rate of 59.8 per 10,000 full-time workers to the 18,644,000 federal, state, and local workers and the 8,495,000 self-employed, farmworkers, and others employed in 1992. This yields an estimate of 162,291 illnesses among public workers and others occurring in 1992. This total should be added to the number of occupational illnesses recorded in the Annual Survey (table 3.7).[8]

III.A.1.3. Heavy Metal Poisoning

Numerous states require that clinical laboratories report the results of selected categories of specimens to the state health department. Among the agents relevant to the occupational setting are lead, arsenic, cadmium, and mercury as well as measures reflecting pesticide exposure. Since 1992, NIOSH has compiled the results of adult blood lead testing in the Adult Blood Lead Epidemiology and Surveillance (ABLES) program (Chowdhury et al. 1994). By 1997, 27 states were reporting elevated blood lead levels to NIOSH, and an additional eight states were developing the capacity to collect and report blood lead data ((NIOSH 1997). In 1993, there were 11,240 individuals with blood lead levels that equaled or exceeded 25 micrograms per deciliter (μg/dl) of blood in the 20 states that reported at that time (Chowdhury et al. 1994) (table 3.8). These 20 states contain 60 percent of the U.S. population. Since among these states are the most heavily industrial states in the United States (e.g., California, Illinois, New Jersey, New York, Pennsylvania, and Michigan), it may be reasonably estimated that they contain 75 percent of all individuals in the United States who have elevated blood lead levels. Using this adjustment, it can be estimated that approximately 15,000 individuals had elevated blood lead levels in the entire United States in 1993.

Assuming that 95 percent of adults with elevated blood lead levels have an occupational source of lead exposure (Chowdhury et al. 1994), then an estimated 14,250 individuals had elevated blood lead values as a result of occupational lead exposure in 1993. This number well exceeds 7,000, the total number of poisonings that was reported by employers to BLS in the Annual Survey in 1992. The BLS category of poisonings includes illnesses with systemic effects due to heavy metals, solvents, pesticides, toxic gases, and other chemical agents. It should be noted that we assume that the numbers of adults with excessive occupational lead exposure in 1992 and in 1993 were not appreciably different. If 3,500, or one-half, of the 7,000 cases of poisonings reported by the BLS in 1992 were due to elevated body lead burden secondary to occupational exposure, then 10,750 adults with such workplace lead exposure were not reported to the BLS in the Annual Survey. This represents three-quarters of the estimated number of adults with excessive blood levels due to occupational exposure. Indeed, even if all of the 7,000 poisonings reported by employers to BLS in 1992 represented individu-

TABLE 3.7.   Numbers of Occupational Illnesses Based on Current Surveys and Proportional Attributable Risk Estimates (United States, 1992)

Survey-Based Data Source	Number of Occupational Illnesses (unadjusted)	Adjustment for Incentive to Undercount	Point Estimate Subtotal
BLS Annual Survey	452,415[a]	184,888	637,303
Adult blood lead surveillance program	14,250		14,250
Public employees, self-employed, and all others	162,291	66,328	228,614
Subtotal	563,660		880,167
Proportional Attributable Risk-Based Data			
Cancer			
Coronary heart disease			
Cerebral disease			
Chronic obstructive lung disease			
Subtotal (from table 3.10)	258,340–348,710		303,525
Total	1,138,512–1,228,882[a]		1,183,697[a]

[a]Total excludes estimated overlap among data sources. This includes 1,485 cases of cancer, heart disease, stroke, and COPD that were recorded in the 1992 BLS Annual Survey and an estimated 3,500 cases of elevated blood lead level that are included in the 1992 BLS Annual Survey.

als with excessive blood lead levels, over one-half (51 percent) of such individuals recorded by the NIOSH ABLES program would not have been reported by employers to BLS.[9]

III.A.1.4. Adjustment for Incentive to Undercount

If we subtract for the double counting of 1,485 BLS cases of cancer, circulatory disease, and COPD and subtract for the double counting of lead poisoning (3,500) we arrive at 452,415. Neither this 452,415 figure from the Annual Survey nor our 162,291 figure for government workers, the self-employed, and so on, accounts for the economic incentive to underreport. In chapter 2, we estimated this to be about a 40 percent factor. To account for this undercount, we therefore multiplied 452,415 and 162,291 by 1.40867 to arrive at 637,303 and 228,614. These figures appear in table 3.7.

III.A.1.5. National Health Interview Survey

The National Health Interview Survey (NHIS) is a household survey conducted by the National Center for Health Statistics in order to obtain estimates of the prevalence of health conditions from a representative sample of households reflecting the civilian noninstitutionalized population of the United States (see app. A for chap. 2). In 1988, an Occupational Health Supplement (NHIS-OHS) was included in order to obtain population-based estimates of the prevalence of selected conditions that may be associated with work (Centers for Disease Control and Prevention 1993). Approximately 50,000 households were sampled in 1988, and 27,408 currently employed individuals were interviewed. The results of the NHIS reflect the reporting of health problems by participating individuals. No medical or workplace verification of the reported information is performed. Despite this limitation, the NHIS Occupational Health Supplement is uniquely able to provide estimates of the perceptions of potentially work-related illnesses for the United States as a whole (Centers for Disease Control and Prevention 1993).

Among the health conditions addressed by the NHIS-OHS are work-related injuries; dermatologic conditions; cumulative trauma disorders; eye, nose, and throat irritation; hearing loss; and low back pain (Centers for Disease Control and Prevention 1993). NHIS-OHS data on injuries and low back pain are addressed in chapter 2. To date, the only other fully analyzed condition is carpal tunnel syndrome (Tanaka et al. 1995). Carpal tunnel syndrome, or entrapment of the median nerve in the wrist, is one of the cumulative trauma disorders of the upper extremity.

Tanaka and colleagues from NIOSH recently reported that, based on the 1988 NHIS-OHS data (Tanaka et al. 1995), 1.1 million people in the United States who have worked at least part of the past 12 months reported "prolonged hand discomfort" that they referred to as "carpal tunnel syndrome." "Prolonged hand discomfort" was defined as discomfort for seven consecutive days or 20 or more days in total during the previous 12 months. Of these 1.1 million people, 675,000 people also reported that their health care providers had told them that they had carpal tunnel syndrome. This corresponds to approximately one of every 200 workers who have worked at least part of the previous 12 months. Tanaka et al. report that, of the 675,000 people who report that their health care providers had diagnosed carpal tunnel syndrome, 52.8 percent also state that their health care provider has said that the carpal tunnel syndrome is work related (Tanaka et al. 1995). Thus, by this method, Tanaka et al. estimate that the national prevalence of work-related carpal tunnel syndrome in 1988 was 356,000 cases (Tanaka et al. 1995). This estimate does not include workers who had not worked in the 12 months prior to the survey and who may have been disabled due to work-related carpal tunnel syndrome.

Comparison between the results of the NHIS-OHS and the BLS Annual Survey are difficult, because the former measures prevalence of disease during a specified internal and the latter includes reports of new episodes of illness. In 1988, 115,000 individuals had disorders associated with repeated trauma, according to the BLS Annual Survey (Bureau of Labor Statistics 1993). The BLS includes in this category noise-induced hearing loss, Raynaud's phenomenon, tenosynovitis, and bursitis in addition to carpal tunnel syndrome. While it is not known what proportion of these 115,000 illnesses was carpal tunnel syndrome, it is unlikely to represent the most common diagnosis. In a recent study of workers' compensation claims in Ohio, Tanaka and NIOSH colleagues reported that less than 50 percent of cases with disorders associated with repeated trauma involved the wrist. The diagnosis in the majority of these cases was tenosynovitis of the wrist (Tanaka et al. 1988). The NHIS-OHS analysis completed to date suggests, however, that the BLS Annual Survey is underestimating the incidence of work-related carpal tunnel syndrome (356,000 in NHIS-OHS versus roughly 52,000 in the Annual Survey).

III.A.1.6. National Hospital Discharge Survey

A unique source of information about medical care utilization for occupationally specific diseases is provided by the National Hospital Discharge Survey maintained by the National Center for Health Statistics.

This database provides summary information about inpatient admissions at nonfederal hospitals in the United States, including primary and other diagnoses, patient gender and age, hospital charges, payment sources, and other variables. A full description of the database and its use is available elsewhere (Graves 1994).

A fundamental problem with the National Hospital Discharge Survey is that the unit of measurement is hospitalizations or discharges, not individuals. To the extent that individual patients have more than one hospitalization per year, the number of discharges will be discrepant from the number of people with a given diagnosis. It is, therefore, not possible to obtain a count of the number of unique individuals who are hospitalized per year for a particular health problem. In addition, since individuals hospitalized in any particular year will have been first diagnosed as having the disorder of interest during any of a number of years, including the year of hospitalization and preceding years, the incidence of disease for any specific year cannot be obtained. While prevalence of occupational disease is of interest, the focus of this chapter so far has been on incidence.[10]

Table 3.9 gives numbers of hospitalizations incurred as a result of diseases that are specific to occupational exposures (Graves 1994). For the primary diagnosis associated with the hospital stay, there were 2,360 hospitalizations for pneumoconioses, principally coal workers' pneumoconiosis (1,646 hospitalizations) and asbestosis (479 hospitalizations), and 857 hospitalizations for malignant neoplasm of the pleura, most of which are malignant mesothelioma of the pleura.

Table 3.9 also provides the numbers of hospitalizations for which pneumoconioses and malignancy of the pleura were not the primary diagnoses but were among the multiple diagnoses listed for hospitalizations in the National Hospital Discharge Survey (Graves 1994).[11]

TABLE 3.8. Numbers of Adults with Elevated Blood Lead Levels (20 States, 1993)

Blood Lead Level (μg/dl)	Number of Persons	Percentage
25–39	8,041	71.5
40–49	2,293	20.4
50–59	627	5.6
$\geq$60	279	2.5
Total	11,240	100.0

Source: National Adult Blood Lead Epidemiology and Surveillance, NIOSH. Adapted from *Morbidity and Mortality Weekly Report* 43:26, July 8, 1994.

TABLE 3.9.   Numbers of Hospital Discharges for Primary and Secondary
Diagnoses for Pneumoconioses and Malignancies of the Pleura
(United States, 1991)

Diagnosis (ICD-9 code)	Number of Discharges with Pneumoconiosis or Malignancies of the Pleura as Primary Diagnosis	Number of Discharges with Pneumoconiosis or Malignancies of the Pleura as Secondary Diagnosis
Pneumoconioses		
Asbestosis (501)	479	6,456
Silicosis (502)	–	3,704
Coal workers' pneumoconioses (500)	1,646	10,825
Pneumoconioses due to other inorganic dust (503)	–	46
Pneumopathy due to inhalation of other dust (504) (byssinosis)	235	475
Pneumoconioses, unspecified (505)	–	801
Total	2,360	22,307
Malignancies of the pleura (163.0, 163.1, 163.9)	857	1,843

Source: Data from National Hospital Discharge Survey (Graves 1994).

III.A.2.   Attributable Risk-Based Estimates of Morbidity

III.A.2.1.   Cancer

Among the major causes of morbidity and mortality in the United
States, cancer represents the group of chronic diseases for which occupational etiology is best documented. Nevertheless, cancers are scarcely
recorded in the BLS Annual Survey or in workers' compensation data.
According to the 1992 Annual Survey, among cases with work time lost,
employers reported 103 employees with occupational neoplasms, most
of which were malignant.[12]
   Workers' compensation is another potential source of data for enu-
merating occupational cancers. Like the Annual Survey, many states do
not use a specific category for occupational cancers (e.g., California and

Washington). By contrast, New York and New Jersey do report the number of cancers identified by the workers' compensation systems as being work related. In New York State, eight people had occupational cancer claims accepted for workers' compensation in 1988 (New York Workers' Compensation Board 1993). In New Jersey, an annual average of 131 individuals were recognized as having occupational cancer by the workers' compensation system between 1988 and 1991, whereas the average annual total number of occupational disease awards was 6,340 (New Jersey Workers' Compensation Board 1990). There were 36,896 individuals newly diagnosed as having cancer (excluding basal cell cancer of the skin) and 17,285 deaths from cancer in New Jersey in 1988 (New Jersey Department of Health 1992). While we acknowledge that the cases of cancer awarded workers' compensation in 1988 reflect incident cancer cases from previous years, it is nonetheless clear that a small proportion (i.e., less than 1 percent) of cancers is recognized as being occupational by selected workers' compensation systems.

In order to obtain a more accurate count of the number of cases of occupational illness per year in the United States, we use the proportional attributable risk model to estimate the number of cancers in the United States that are likely to be occupational in origin (sec. II.B). The American Cancer Society (ACS) publishes estimates of the numbers of cases of cancer that occur annually in the United States based on the data collected under the Surveillance, Epidemiology, and End Results (SEER) program of the National Cancer Institute. According to these ACS estimates, there were 1,113,100 malignancies (excluding basal cell cancer of the skin) newly diagnosed among adults 25 years and over in the United States in 1992 (American Cancer Society 1995). Assuming that 6 percent to 10 percent of these cancers are occupational in origin, then 66,790 to 111,310 new cases of cancer were caused by workplace factors in 1992 (table 3.10).

III.A.2.2. Cardiovascular and
Cerebrovascular Disease

As described in section II.B.2, we use an estimate of 5 percent to 10 percent of cases of specific cardiovascular and cerebrovascular disease among people aged 25 to 64, inclusive, as caused by occupational factors.

For accounting of occupational morbidity due to heart disease, the focus is restricted to coronary heart disease, since it is the major cause of heart disease, and current studies support a causal role of occupational factors in the etiology of coronary heart disease. National incidence data for coronary heart disease are less than optimal, since they are extrapolated from the Framingham heart disease sample of approximately 5,000 people. Nonetheless, these data have been used to determine that there are approximately 1.25 million new or recurrent myocardial infarctions each year in the United States, including 530,000 myocardial infarctions among individuals between the ages of 25 and 64, inclusive (Kannel and Thom 1994; American Heart Association 1995; National Heart, Lung, and Blood Institute 1995). Approximately 78,000 of these one-half million heart attacks are fatal. The Framingham database has also allowed an estimation of approximately 200,000 new cases of uncomplicated angina pectoris each year in the United States among people less than 65 years old (American Heart Association 1992, 1993; National Heart, Lung, and Blood Institute 1995).

Applying the proportional range cited previously, there are 36,500 to 73,000 new or recurrent cases of coronary heart diseases (including new or recurrent myocardial infarctions and new cases of uncomplicated angina) each year in the United States due to occupational risk factors (table 3.10).

Data from the Framingham study also allow estimation that 101,000 to 144,000 strokes and transient ischemic attacks occur annually in the United States among people less than 65 years of age (Kannel and Thom 1994; American Heart Association 1992). Since most coronary heart disease and cerebrovascular disease result from the same underlying disease process, atherosclerosis, we use the same range of percentages

TABLE 3.10.   Estimated Incidence of Occupational Illness for Major Causes of Death (United States)

Condition[a]	Estimated Annual Number of New Cases in United States	Percentage Attributed to Occupation	Estimated Number of Cases Due to Occupation
Cancer	1,113,100	6–10	66,790–111,310
Coronary heart disease[b]	730,000	5–10	36,500–73,000
Cerebrovascular disease[b]	101,000–144,000	5–10	5,050–14,400
Chronic obstructive pulmonary disease	1,500,000	10	150,000
Total			258,340–348,710

Source: American Cancer Society 1995.
[a]See table 3.12, note 9, for listing of ICD codes included in these conditions.
[b]Only includes new and recurrent cases of coronary heart disease and cerebrovascular disease among people between ages 25 and 64, inclusive.

(5 percent to 10 percent) as caused by occupational factors. Hence, it is estimated that 5,050 to 14,400 strokes and transient ischemic attacks among people over 25 but under 65 years of age are associated with occupational exposures, for example, job stress, shift work, and noise (table 3.10).

By contrast, the revised Annual Survey recorded 591 work-related cases of ischemic heart disease and 76 people with cerebrovascular disease in 1992.

III.A.2.3. Chronic Obstructive Pulmonary Disease

Despite the fact that chronic obstructive pulmonary disease (COPD) is the fourth leading overall cause of mortality in the United States and increased during the 1980s (American Lung Association 1995), national data on the incidence of COPD are virtually nonexistent. Given the chronic nature of COPD, the impact of this set of diseases has traditionally been measured by its prevalence and mortality rate. The American Lung Association estimates that 15.4 million Americans suffered from COPD in 1992 (American Lung Association 1995). One estimate of the number of new cases of COPD in the United States was 1.5 million in 1984 (Farer and Schieffelbein 1987). Recognizing the dearth of well-founded data in this area, we use this estimate of 1.5 million new cases. Given the rise in COPD mortality from 27.7 per 100,000 in the United States in 1984 to 34.1 per 100,000 in 1992, the estimate of 1.5 million, if accurate, would be an underestimate of the annual number of new cases of COPD in the 1990s. Applying the estimated percentage of COPD attributable to occupational exposures, 10 percent (sec. II.B.3), yields an estimate of 150,000 new cases of COPD each year occurring as a result of exposure to airborne contaminants in the workplace (table 3.10).

In the 1992 BLS survey, 717 cases of work-related COPD were recorded among the illness cases where one or more days of work were missed.

III.B. Occupational Mortality

III.B.1. Specific Occupational Diseases

As discussed previously, though the spectrum of diseases associated with occupations is broad, the diseases uniquely caused by occupational exposures are limited. Included in this group are the pneumoconioses and one type of cancer, malignant mesothelioma of the pleura and peritoneum. Table 3.11 shows the numbers of deaths attributed to these diagnoses as the underlying cause of death and as one of multiple causes of death listed on the death certificate (National Center for Health Statistics 1993a). In 1992, there were 1,136 deaths due to the dust diseases of the lung as the underlying cause, including 631 deaths due to coal workers' pneumoconiosis and 285 deaths due to asbestosis. For malignancies of the pleura, most of which are malignant mesothelioma, there was a total of 477 deaths (National Center for Health Statistics 1993a). Because there is no ICD code specific for malignant mesothelioma of the peritoneum, it is not possible to identify the number of peritoneal mesotheliomas that occurred in 1992.

Table 3.11 also shows the numbers of deaths due to pneumoconioses and malignancies of the pleura when they appear as one of multiple causes of death on the death certificate for the most recent year available, 1990. As expected, the numbers of such deaths are higher than the numbers of death where underlying cause is specified. Citation of a disease among multiple causes can be reasonably interpreted as signifying that it was a contributing factor in death. In 1990, there were 3,659 deaths in which one of the pneumoconioses was a contributing factor and 553 deaths in which malignancy of the pleura was a factor contributing to death (NIOSH 1994; National Center for Health Statistics 1993a).

TABLE 3.11.   Deaths Due to Pneumoconioses and Malignancy of the Pleura Underlying Cause and Multiple Causes (United States, 1990 and 1992)

Cause of Death (ICD-9 Code)	Number of Deaths		
	Underlying Cause (1992)	Underlying Cause (1991)	Multiple Causes (1990)
Coal workers' pneumoconiosis (500)	631	693	1,990
Asbestosis (501)	285	269	948
Silicosis (502)	117	153	308
Other pneumoconioses (503–505)	103	122	413
Total	1,136	1,237	3,659
Malignancy of the pleura (163.0, 163.1, 163.9)	477	452	553

Source: Data from National Center for Health Statistics 1993a.

III.B.2. Attributable Risk-Based Estimates
of Mortality

Table 3.12 provides the results of applying the proportional attributable
risk model as described in Section II.B to the major causes of death in
the United States in 1992. With the exception of pneumoconioses, all

TABLE 3.12.   Estimated Occupational Disease Mortality Due to Selected Causes
(United States, 1992)

Selected Causes of Death[a]	Number of Deaths United States, ages 25 and over	Estimated Percentage due to Occupation	Range Number of Deaths Due to Occupation United States, 1992	Point Estimate
Cancer	517,090	6–10	31,025–51,709	41,367
Cardiovascular and cerebrovascular disease (only ages 25–64, inclusive)	101,846	5–10	5,092–10,185	7,638
Chronic respiratory disease	91,541	10	9,154	9,154
Pneumoconioses	1,136	100	1,136	1,136
Nervous system disorders	26,936	1–3	269–808	538
Renal disorders	22,957	1–3	230–689	460
Total	761,506		46,906–73,681	60,293

Source: Data from National Center for Health Statistics 1994.
[a]Codes of ICD, 9th revision, used for selected causes of death
Cancer: 140–209 (malignant neoplasms)
Cardiovascular and cerebrovascular disease
    401–404 (hypertension, hypertensive heart and renal disease)
    410–414 (ischemic heart disease)
    430–438 (cerebrovascular disease)
    440 (atherosclerosis)
Chronic respiratory disease
    490–496 (chronic obstructive pulmonary disease and allied conditions)
    500–505 (pneumoconioses)
Nervous system disorders
    323.7 (toxic encephalitis)
    331 (other cerebral degenerations)
    332 (Parkinson's disease)
    349.82 (toxic encephalopathy)
    356 (hereditary and idiopathic peripheral neuropathy)
    357.7 (polyneuropathy due to other toxic agents)
    359.4 (toxic myopathy)
Renal disorders: 580–589 (nephrotis, nephrotic syndrome, and nephrosis)

causes of death are associated with an occupational etiology in no more than an estimated 10 percent of cases. Nonetheless, this analysis yields an estimate of 46,909 to 73,681 deaths as a result of occupational risk factors in the United States in 1992. Cancer dominates these estimates due to its high overall incidence and to the restriction of occupationally associated cardiovascular and cerebrovascular deaths to persons under 65 years of age. For each of the three major causes of death, however, the number of deaths, ranging between 5,000 and 52,000, is significant.

To provide a population perspective on this overall estimate of occupational mortality, comparisons to other causes of death may be instructive. In 1992, there were 25,488 deaths from homicides and 33,566 deaths from AIDS. Our lower bound estimate exceeds both of these.

IV. Conclusion

Identifying the true burden of occupational disease in the United States has been an elusive goal for at least 25 years. This goal remains unattained, but recent progress in occupational health surveillance and research allows enhanced estimates of this burden. Specifically, improvements in national data systems for occupational diseases and an accumulating body of epidemiologic and toxicological research provide increasing confidence that the overall magnitude of the problem of occupational disease can be approximated. Proper interpretation of national surveys and prudent application of a proportional attributable risk model to major causes of death and disease in the United States provide the foundation that allows the following conclusions.

Roughly 1,138,512 to 1,228,882 new cases of occupational illness occurred in the United States in 1992. Our point estimate is 1,183,697. This estimate represents a compilation of cases from the Annual Survey (457,400), national surveillance of heavy metal poisoning (14,250), public employees data (92,010), and adjustment for the economic incentive to underreport and proportions of major chronic diseases associated with occupational factors (range from 258,300 to 348,700), as well as accounting for the limited overlap among the sources of data. Much of this disease burden is serious in nature and involves significant lost time from work.

Approximately 47,000 to 74,000 deaths resulted from occupational diseases in 1992. Our best point estimate is 60,293. This estimate includes two types of disease categories: (a) deaths that are

uniquely caused by occupational agents, such as the pneumoconioses and malignant mesothelioma, and (b) a much larger
number of deaths that fall into six major categories of death:
cancer, coronary heart disease, cerebrovascular disease, chronic
obstructive pulmonary disease, nervous system disorders, and
renal diseases.

These estimates should be considered conservative for a variety of
reasons. First, they underestimate important causes of occupational morbidity, including hearing loss, reproductive toxicity, and others. They
were underestimated because they do not cause death or data on their
incidence are not available. Second, limited proportions were used in
the attributable risk model employed in our approach. Third, occupational cardiovascular morbidity and mortality were limited to events
among people less than 65 years old, because the extension of the occupational impact on cardiovascular disease after retirement is uncertain.

CHAPTER 4

Two Methods for Measuring Costs

I. Introduction

Economists have developed two methods for estimating the costs of injuries and illnesses: the Human Capital method and the Willingness-to-Pay (WTP) method.

The outline of the chapter is as follows. Section II explains the Human Capital method. It contains three subsections: introduction, explanation of the method, and critique of the method. Section III explains the Willingness-to-Pay (WTP) method. Several subsections are included in the WTP section. In sections III.A and III.B we explain WTP and comment on its advantages. In section III.C we critique WTP. The critique includes general theoretical criticisms and specific criticisms of individual studies in labor and automotive markets.

II. Human Capital Cost Method

II.A. Introduction

The Human Capital method was popularized by Dorothy P. Rice (1966). It has been applied to a wide variety of injuries and illnesses and continues to be heavily relied on in the medical, public health, and legal literature (American Heart Association 1992; Brown et al. 1993; Hensler et al. 1991; Ireland, Johnson, and Taylor 1997; Miller and Blincoe 1994; National Safety Council 1993; Max and Rice 1993, 1995; Max, Webber, and Fox 1995; Staller, Sullivan, and Friedman 1994; Neumark et al. 1991; Rice, Hodgson, and Kopstein 1985). In what follows, we will first explain the method and, second, critique it.

II.B. Explanation of the Human Capital Method

The Human Capital method posits two broad categories of costs: direct and indirect. Direct costs represent actual dollars spent or anticipated to be spent on providing medical care to an injured or ill person and administrative costs for delivering medical care and for delivering indemnity benefits. Medical costs include doctors' and nurses' services, hospital charges, drug costs, rehabilitation services, ambulance fees, and payments for medical equipment and supplies. Administration costs for delivering medical care include the costs of providing insurance, Medicare, Medicaid, Veteran's Administration, and so on. Administration of indemnity benefits includes the costs associated with providing workers' compensation indemnity, Social Security disability payments, welfare benefits, and private insurance disability payments to injured or sick workers and their families. These are administrative costs, not the dollar amount of the indemnity or welfare benefits. Direct costs are frequently referred to as "accounting" or "out-of-pocket" costs.

Indirect costs are not "accounting" or "out-of-pocket" costs. They represent forgone opportunities for the injured or ill person, his or her family or unpaid caregivers, employer, co-workers, and society at large. Included in this category are the injured or sick workers' lost earnings (Leigh et al. 1995), fringe benefits, and home production, as well as costs of lost productivity among co-workers (Haines 1993), time delays of commuters, and family caregivers' time (Max, Webber, and Fox 1995).[1]

The largest category of indirect costs is the injured or ill workers' lost earnings. Earnings are a measure of output. If the person is no longer earning pay from a job, then he or she is no longer adding to national economic output. This loss is, therefore, not only experienced by the injured worker but also by the economy as a whole. These lost earnings are, in turn, split into morbidity and mortality costs. *Morbidity costs* refers to earnings of the worker with a nonfatal injury or illness and *mortality costs* to the earnings of a deceased worker. Morbidity costs reflect the value of days lost from work. Mortality costs represent the future output that would have been forthcoming if the person had not died young.

II.C. Critique of the Human Capital Method

There are many criticisms of the Human Capital method. Thorough discussions are available (Robinson 1986; Rice et al. 1989a; Hartunian, Smart, and Thompson 1981). Here we mention only the most serious. First, the method is frequently criticized for ignoring costs for non-wage-earning persons, that is, retirees, homemakers, and students. This criticism does not apply to our injury studies, however, since all persons we analyze must have been working for pay prior to the time of the injury. It is relevant for our illness study, but as we will see, injuries generate far more costs than illnesses. Moreover, we also count the value of home production by part-time workers and by workers after they retire. Second, the Human Capital method likely underestimates the cost to women and minorities because the wages for these groups are artificially low due to discrimination in the labor market. The minorities issue is not a strong criticism of our study since our study does not distinguish among races and ethnicities. We simply use average wages for all races and ethnicities. The gender discrimination criticism does apply to our study, but not as significantly as is frequently assumed since we will place a higher value on home production for women than men.

Third, the Human Capital method does not allow for substitution effects. For example, suppose a cashier at a fast-food restaurant is shot during a robbery. A previously unemployed person might now be hired and trained to replace the newly deceased cashier. The economic cost of the murder to society might be merely the costs of locating, training, and hiring the previously unemployed person. There are four responses to this criticism. First, not all workers, for example, police officers, firefighters, pilots, and doctors, are so easily replaced. Second, home production is not so easily replaced, especially for a valued family member. Indeed, lifetime psychological damage can result when a young child loses a parent. Third, virtually all health researchers recognize the need to somehow account for loss of life or functional ability, that is, to account for a net reduction in "aggregate health" even if these are not explicit business expenses. Loss of wages is one way to measure "aggregate health." Another way is to measure years of potential life lost (Cutler and Richardson 1997). Because wages accrue up until age 65 for most people, years of potential life lost and lifetime lost wages are strongly correlated. Fourth, this criticism does not apply to expenditures on medical care, only to the indirect costs component of the Human Capital method.

Despite these criticisms, there is an overarching reason for using the Human Capital method. We seek to compare our costs to costs for other diseases. In virtually all cases, cost estimates for other diseases have used the Human Capital method.

III. Willingness to Pay

III.A. Introduction

The Willingness-to-Pay (WTP) approach is an alternative method for determining the cost of injuries and illnesses. The WTP method is designed to be comprehensive. It does not split costs into direct and indirect components. It attempts to apply prices that are generated in market transactions unfettered by Medicaid, workers' compensation, and other government subsidies. On theoretical grounds, the WTP method is preferred over the more traditional Human Capital cost method by the majority of U.S. academic economists. Outside of U.S. academic economics departments, it has not gained acceptance and has been labeled "a particularly egregious example of junk science" by some judges (Ireland, Johnson, and Taylor 1997).

There are several advantages associated with the WTP approach over the Human Capital approach. First, under the Human Capital approach, retirees, children, and homemakers are greatly undervalued. Their forgone earnings may be minimal. Second, pain and suffering do not enter the Human Capital method. Third, the Human Capital method does not account for the sentiments of the community. Do people, in general, greatly dislike injuries or only mildly dislike them? Some people may actually enjoy taking risks. The WTP method accounts for the value people place on the health of retirees, children, and homemakers; on pain and suffering; and on variation across communities and individuals.

III.B. Explanation of WTP

The idea behind the WTP method is simple (French 1990). Individuals themselves are more likely than a researcher to know the true cost to themselves of any particular injury or illness. Individuals, presumably, are in a better position to evaluate the medical costs, lost earnings, family hardship, pain and suffering, and so on, than any researchers analyzing statistical data. Some people might want to hold onto life no matter what pain must be endured or the costs of drugs or drain on the estate ("Every day above ground is a good day." — Wyatt Earp). Others might prefer suicide if the pain is too great and there are no prospects for recovery ("Some fates are worse than death." — Count Dracula). Some of us with young children might purchase childproof swimming pool covers. Others among us might not. Some buy smoke detectors; others will not. Before laws existed pertaining to air bags, some people ordered air bags for their cars while others did not. In each case, individuals make choices involving risk. In some cases, such as for swimming pool covers, smoke detectors, and air bags, the choices will influence market prices. A risk-for-dollar price trade-off will be observed in the market. Consumers can lower their risks with pool covers, smoke detectors, and air bags if they are willing to pay for these safety items. This is the derivation of the term *Willingness-to-Pay*. There are many influences on market prices for swimming pool covers, smoke detectors, and air bags, such as the costs of producing the covers, detectors, and air bags; the income of consumers; and so on. Nevertheless, with careful econometric analysis, economists have attempted to measure that portion of some market prices that reflect the risk-for-dollar trade-off. The risk premium portion of these prices presumably provides an aggregate estimate of how a typical individual would value an increase or a decrease in risk.

Imagine we have a town of 100,000 residents. Over the next year, suppose 10 will die, but no one knows which 10. The WTP method would, for example, attempt to answer this question: how much would these 100,000 people collectively be willing to pay to reduce the number of deaths to nine, again, not knowing who the nine are? To phrase this a different way, the WTP approach would attempt to answer this question: how much would a typical individual be willing to pay to decrease his or her chances of death in the coming year by 1/100,000?

The most popular WTP technique uses data from the labor market. For example, suppose that in an Oregon and Washington labor market 200,000 high school graduates compete for 100,000 jobs for lumberjacks and 100,000 jobs for plumbers. Imagine that all of the risks of injuries and illnesses for lumberjacks were identical to those of plumbers, except that for death. Suppose that the annual death rate is 11/100,000 for lumberjacks and is 10/100,000 for plumbers. Further assume that all of the prospective employees prefer safety to risk and that all employees and employers are fully aware of the risks. Assume further that all employment transactions are made in competitive markets, without institutions, that is, no labor unions. Finally, assume that workers are consequentialists in utility; that is, they calmly and rationally evaluate the risks of dying. According to an important economic theory — the compensating wages hypothesis — in a competitive labor market, the employers of plumbers would not have to pay as high a wage as employers of lumberjacks. To understand this hypothesis, suppose that the wage of the lumberjacks is $0.05 per hour more than the wage for plumbers. "The market," then, would be putting a price on the risk of death. For $0.05 more per hour, the marginal plumber presumably would be willing to take a job as a lumberjack. This higher wage compensates the worker for taking the job with the higher risk; it is similar to hazard duty pay in the military. The implicit value of life would be $0.05/hour $\times$ 2,000 hours/year $\times$ 1 more death $\times$ 100,000 lumberjacks, or $10,000,000. The 200,000 high school graduates would then be implicitly valuing a life at $10 million.

Assuming workers are well informed, mobile, rational consequentialists, and that markets are free of institutions, the theory that predicts a market trade-off exists between risks of dying on the job and wages cannot be faulted. The theory does not indicate how big the compensating wage or value per statistical life will be, however.

The trade-off will generate a line or curve with a positive slope in a wage and risk diagram. Jobs with high (low) risks should command high (low) wages. In the jargon of economics, the trade-off will generate a collection of equilibrium points that will form the compensating wages curve. The slope of the curve will indicate how much higher wages will have to increase before a marginal worker will take a job with a little higher risk. Econometric techniques that attempt to estimate the compensating wages curve have been applied to labor market data.

III.C. General Critiques of WTP

There are several general criticisms of the WTP approach. First, WTP estimates represent marginal costs; that is, how much more would it cost to save one more life? These marginal costs are more appropriate than average or total costs when attempting to evaluate the benefits and costs of, for example, a new OSHA standard on diesel fuel. They are not appropriate if the goal is to obtain an impression of the overall size of a problem. To estimate the overall national costs of occupational injuries and illnesses is precisely our major goal.

Second, WTP studies of actual markets assume that buyers and sellers in those markets have a reasonable knowledge of the risk involved. As we will see in the specific studies cited subsequently, this is not likely to be true for many persons choosing among safe or dangerous jobs or choosing cars. Nor is it likely to be the case for buyers of air bags, smoke detectors, and pool covers.

Information is likely to be skewed to one side of the market. Employers likely have more information than employees; car, smoke detector, and pool cover manufacturers likely have more information than buyers of those same products. This asymmetrical distribution of information is widely acknowledged by federal and state policymakers, who have passed legislation mandating that manufacturers and sellers must now provide more safety and health information to the public pertaining to, for example, canned, packaged, and bottled foods and beverages and toys, drugs, homes, and day care centers (Leigh 1998). It is also recognized by most advocates of the WTP approach. Viscusi (1992), for example, acknowledges that health risks to workers are "notoriously underreported" (102) by the chemical industry.

A third problem involves rational decision making regarding risk. Few economists have attempted to apply this assumption to behavior involving death. We recognize, for example, that few "agents" would trade off any potential gain, no matter how large, for a 95 percent chance of dying. It is difficult to be rational when contemplating one's own death. Many philosophers argue that the prospect of death has given rise to religious beliefs. People living in flood zones generally do not purchase heavily subsidized insurance even though most benefit-cost studies indicate that they should (Viscusi 1992, 110). Prior to the passage of seat belt legislation in most states, benefit-cost studies showed that most people would have benefited from wearing seat belts but most people did not voluntarily choose to wear them (Viscusi 1992, 10).

The assumptions of rationality when contemplating risk have been an extensive area of study among psychologists and others. One popular view is that for a wide variety of risks people use rules of thumb that frequently violate strict assumptions of rationality. A National Research Council panel of scientists recently summarized these rules of thumb and pointed out the problems they create for advising the public on risk (National Research Council 1976, 111–13; Slovic, Fischhoff, and Lichtenstein 1979).

A fourth problem involves "the market's" ability to generate accurate estimates of a dollar-risk trade-off. Dorman (1996) argues that moral concerns will thwart the market's abilities. Many people have a moral objection to such trade-offs. They believe that risk should be addressed by laws and morals, not markets. Dorman (1996) reported on one study that involved asking respondents whether they would allow a radioactive waste repository in their city in return for a large sum of money. Nearly three-quarters of respondents refused to state the trade-off. These three-quarters did not change their minds even as the sum of money was tripled or quadrupled.

In general, these "refuseniks," as Dorman (1996) labels them, may act in ways that economists view as naive or irrational. They may, for example, assume that the job they are about to take is safe since the employers have a moral and legal obligation to provide safe employment. Some workers themselves would not knowingly violate that moral or law, and they expect others not to violate it either. In any case, any estimated market trade-off of dollar for risk would not reflect the "refuseniks" attitude toward risk.

Another criticism involves the price of medical care. The WTP approach requires that people know the full implications of the risk, in particular that they know the medical care expense associated with improving their health and that they would be required to pay that expense. Neither of these conditions is likely to be true. Outside of financial administrators in hospitals, few persons are knowledgeable about the medical costs of varying therapies and interventions. Moreover, in the United States, some persons face the possibility of paying out of pocket for their entire medical bill while other persons need not pay anything out of pocket.

Many economists have noted that some private WTP valuations will differ with public valuations (Robinson 1986). One example involves wealth and tastes for risk. An 85 year old may be willing to pay more to extend life than a 20 year old. But, society, in general, may not accept a young person's taste for risk as legitimate; that is, young men, in particular, display inordinately high tastes for risk (Leigh 1986c).

Finally, the WTP ignores explicit measurement of medical costs. For better or worse, however, medical costs receive the most attention in the public debate about the economics of health.

III.D. Review of Studies in Labor Markets and Automobile Markets

The most widely cited WTP studies were derived from labor and automobile market studies. In the first part of this section, we review the labor market studies. In the second, we consider an influential automobile market study.

The labor market studies reviewed here used occupational fatalities as measures of hazards to find evidence for compensating wages. The studies fall into seven categories: BLS Annual Survey industry, NIOSH industry/state (NTOF), high-risk occupations, police only, industry and occupation data from New York State, and industries from Texas.

A number of studies used unpublished Annual Survey data from the Bureau of Labor Statistics (BLS) on occupational fatalities within two- and three-digit industries for the 1970s and 1980s. These are the same fatality data that the BLS now regards as unreliable. The BLS no longer releases them to researchers (Kniesner and Leeth 1991). Their unreliability was the primary reason the BLS started the Census of Fatal Occupational Injuries (CFOI). Nevertheless, all studies found some evidence for what appeared to be compensating wages. These studies include Berger and Gabriel 1991; Dickens 1984; Dillingham 1985; Dorsey 1983; Garen 1988; Leigh 1987b; Moore and Viscusi 1988; and Viscusi 1979.

The BLS industry fatality data are limited, however, as each of the authors points out. The industry numbers cannot be reasonably applied to white-collar workers. Root and Sebastian (1981) indicate that approximately four-fifths of all job-related injuries occur among blue-collar and service workers. White-collar work is not nearly as hazardous as blue-collar work; consequently, only blue-collar workers are considered by most authors using BLS Annual Survey industry data. But, wholesale exclusion of white-collar workers creates problems. For industry data, if white-collar workers were exposed to the same amount of risk regardless of industry, their exclusion would not be troublesome. This is unlikely, however. Airplane pilots hold extremely hazardous white-collar jobs. The elevated risk of fatality within the air transportation industry is the result of more pilot (white-collar) fatalities than ground-crew technician and mechanic (blue-collar) fatalities.

Second, the BLS industry fatality numbers from the Annual Survey may be ignoring more than 60 percent of all job-related deaths, as we indicated in chapter 2. The BLS Annual Survey death data are derived only from firms with 11 or more employees. The average number of annual fatalities for all firms of this size combined was estimated to be roughly 4,090 (Macon 1984) in the early 1980s (the time most relevant to the samples in the BLS Annual Survey industry WTP studies). Alternative estimates of annual industries fatalities in all firms during 1984 were roughly 11,000 to 12,000 (Baker et al. 1982; National Safety Council 1983) and 7,000 (National Institute for Occupational Safety and Health 1987). The fact that small firms did not contribute any fatal data poses an even more serious undercount problem than those problems mentioned for nonfatal injuries in the BLS in chapter 2.

Another popular data set has been NIOSH's NTOF discussed in chapter 2. The NIOSH NTOF study provided fatality data by state for nine broad industry categories. Moore and Viscusi (1988) and Viscusi and Moore (1988) found evidence for compensating wages in samples combining blue- with white-collar employees and women with men. Fisher, Chestnut, and Violette (1989) criticized the NTOF study for including information on only nine broad industry categories. Variation in measurements across industries was considerably less in the NIOSH than in the BLS Annual Survey data of three-digit industries.

In the third data set, Thaler and Rosen (1975) and Arnould and Nichols (1983) used fatality numbers in high-risk occupations based on insurance companies' statistics. The insurance data suffered a number of well-recognized weaknesses, however. First, the data confused occupational hazards with lifestyle choices. They represented deaths from all causes, not just job-related deaths. Second, the data applied to only a select group of 37 "extra-risk" occupations. Third, a few of the statistics defied explanation. Cooks, for example, faced three times the risks of firefighters. In an independent test, Leigh (1981) could not replicate Thaler and Rosen's statistically significant results.

Low and McPheters (1983) uncovered a fourth set of data on police fatalities in roughly 70 municipalities. They regressed average police earnings on the number of fatalities and a variety of control variables. They found a positive and significant coefficient on the fatality measure, thus presumably providing evidence for compensating wages. In a comment on their paper, Leigh (1986e) pointed out that they used the wrong explanatory variable. It should have been the death rate, not the *number* of deaths. The raw count alone could be acting as a proxy for city size, and the size of the city police force is known to be strongly correlated with police wages. When equations were reestimated with the death rate on the right-hand side, the estimated coefficient was not significant at conventional levels.

Drawing from workers' compensation files for the state of New York in 1970, Dillingham produced job-related mortality rates for 83 occupations and 157 industries in a fifth data set. But job-related deaths are rare events, as he indicated. Only roughly 600 job-related deaths were reported in New York in 1970. With so few deaths and so many occupations and industries, his mortality estimates "may not reflect the true long-run frequency of fatal injury" (Dillingham 1985, 289). He nevertheless found evidence for compensating wages in a sample of wage earners (not salary earners) who, for the most part, were blue-collar and service workers.

Leigh and Gill (1991) used a seventh data set on female fatalities in Texas. They pointed out that almost all tests for compensating wages were conducted on men, perhaps with good reason. There are a disproportionate number of men in risky jobs (chapter 2, app. B). Leigh and Gill further pointed out that attempts to account for gender differences with a dummy variable are not desirable. Any job risk measure will, therefore, reflect a gender wage differential if women are included in the sample. That is, part of the significance of a coefficient for a variable measuring job hazards could be the result of gender differences in employment in hazardous versus safe jobs. Barry (1985) did not find evidence for compensating wages for various measures of hazards (not deaths) in women-only samples. Leigh and Gill (1991) found evidence for compensating wages among women in union jobs but not among women in nonunion jobs.

In summary, most existing evidence suggests wages are higher for male, blue-collar, and service hourly workers in jobs with high death rates, compared to similar male, blue-collar, and service hourly workers in jobs with low death rates. The most convincing data that provide these results are BLS Annual Survey unpublished two- and three-digit industry data and the NIOSH industry/state data.

Leigh's (1991a, 1995b) studies challenge the most widely cited labor market studies. Both the Annual Survey and the NIOSH NTOF death rates were combined with three national probability samples. Compensating wages were expected in blue-collar, male-only samples but not in male and female clerk samples. An interindustry differentials hypothesis was investigated by alternately including and excluding dummy variables for broad industry divisions. When the seven broad industry dummy variables were excluded in the regressions, a strong partial correlation was observed between death rates and wages. When the dummies were included, the correlations evaporated. These patterns were also observed in samples of clerks — a group of workers not generally believed to receive compensating wages across industries since clerical jobs carry little risk regardless of industry. Evidence thus supported the interindustry differentials hypothesis, not the compensating wage differentials hypothesis. Dorman (1996) found similar results in data from the University of Michigan's Panel Study of Income Dynamics.

The compensating wage hypothesis itself, therefore, cannot be entirely free of scrutiny. Widespread information about job hazards, mobility, and rationality and all employment transactions taking place in markets might be questionable assumptions.

Police officers, firefighters, ironworkers, airplane pilots, and others in obviously dangerous jobs no doubt receive compensating wages. But the U.S. Census lists over 500 occupations and close to 200 two- and three-digit industries. Moreover, as the NIOSH NTOF data demonstrate, substantial variation is apparent across states. Lists of fatality rates by occupation (alone), industry (alone), and state (by industry) are available (Leigh 1995a). As these lists demonstrate, aside from the obvious dangerous jobs, the majority of the others are difficult to rank. Workers may only have to rank two jobs, however. But even paired comparisons are difficult, as a perusal of the lists would illustrate. For example, laborers, apprentices in construction trades, garbage collectors, warehouse workers, truck drivers, delivery workers, and gas station and parking lot attendants have very high rates (Leigh 1995a). Moreover, common misconceptions concerning job-related deaths are pervasive. Firefighters are more likely to die from heart attacks than smoke inhalation, falls, or burns combined (Leigh 1995a). Police officers are as likely to die in a car crash as in a gun battle.

Many economists readily accept that information pertaining to health and preventive medicine varies directly with education (Ippolito and Mathios 1990; Kenkel 1991). It is not surprising, therefore, that a high and disproportionate number of persons with low levels of education occupy dangerous jobs (Leigh 1986b, 1988b).

Poor information on occupational traumatic deaths is widely acknowledged among epidemiologists (Shilling and Brackbill 1987; Behrens and Brackbill 1993). The experts, in fact, could not agree on a definition of a job-related death prior to the 1990s (Windau and Goodrich 1990).

To the extent that occupational disease death rates are correlated with traumatic death rates across jobs, the problem of poor information is even greater. The BLS Annual Survey estimates that disease deaths account for about 10 percent of the total of all occupational deaths (U.S. Bureau of Labor Statistics 1993). In contrast, a New York study suggests that disease deaths are eight to 10 times as many as all traumatic deaths (Markowitz et al. 1989). A study from Pennsylvania suggests that there are 18 disease deaths for each injury death (Neumark et al. 1991). Since the prospects of disease deaths are generally viewed as more menacing than traumatic deaths by the public due to the involuntary nature of exposure to carcinogens (Slovic 1978), poor information combined with public perceptions of threat further complicates the search for compensating wages.

Viscusi (1992) attempts to rebut some of these criticisms. He suggests that workers learn about risks on the job and quit if risks are too great. But a high and disproportionate number of youths and new employees die of on-the job accidents (Division of Labor Research and Statistics 1985; Leigh 1995a). Accidents are sudden, but decisions to leave a job or find a new job may require months or even years.

We are not alone in voicing a concern over the lack of information on hazards available in the labor market. Neumark et al. (1991) are also skeptical. They explicitly ignored WTP estimates because of the information problem. According to Neumark et al. (1991, 976):

[T]he compensating wage differentials approach to estimating costs of occupational hazards (WTP) seem[s] likely to remain seriously flawed until there is an extensive and well-publicized body of literature on the extent and costs of workplace hazards. Only then could workers be assumed to make informed decisions about the amount of risk they are willing to accept on the job.

The assumption of widespread information is also questioned by business professors. Rejda (1984) is the author of the influential reference book *Social Insurance and Economic Security.* He shares, with trade unionists, a widely held belief that, in general, workers, especially nonunionized workers, do not have the bargaining power or information necessary to negotiate with employers over how safe or risky their workplaces should be. He states: "few workers are in a position to determine accurately the probability of an occupational injury and the resulting economic loss" (299–300).

Mobility is another concern. It could be that workers do not receive compensating wages for job risks in secondary (low wage, high turnover) labor markets due to lack of mobility from secondary to primary (high wage, low turnover) labor markets (Robinson 1988b). Moreover, economically disadvantaged people and immigrants may have few options in selecting jobs. It could also be that time is required for persons to make a job change, and during that time, an accident could occur. This would be especially true of persons in their prime earning years who have family obligations and might require substantial training to qualify for a different job.

There is also a problem, alluded to earlier, about rationality when contemplating one's own death. Dickens (1985) and Bryant (1990) make the case that it can be difficult to be completely rational when contemplating one's own death due to job-related events.

Finally, the compensating wage hypothesis assumes that employment transactions occur only in markets. But unions still occupy a significant part of employment relations, and many individual firms have their own internal promotion strategies that are somewhat removed from market transactions. Most of these nonmarket arrangements reject the idea that dangerous conditions can be "paid for" with high wages (Dorman 1996).

In summary, most labor market studies find evidence consistent with the compensating wage differentials. These differentials have been used to calculate a WTP estimate for life. But serious data and assumption problems plague all of these studies.

There have been WTP studies outside of the labor market, including, for example, purchases of smoke detectors and the decision to use a seat belt (Viscusi 1993). One of the most highly regarded studies outside the labor market was conducted by Atkinson and Halvorsen (1990).

Atkinson and Halvorsen (1990) attempted to estimate the value of life based upon consumer purchases of automobiles. Using a variation on the compensating wage approach, they regressed the price of 112 car models from 1978 on characteristics of the cars, characteristics of deceased drivers, and the fatality rates for the cars. The characteristics of deceased drivers and fatality rates for the cars were drawn from the Fatal Accident Report System (FARS) data file at the National Highway Traffic Safety Administration (NHTSA). They found a statistically significant and negative estimated coefficient on their fatality rate variable. With appropriate manipulations, they generated estimates of the value of life that compared favorably with the existing labor market estimates they cited (Leigh and Folsom 1984; Olson 1981; Viscusi 1979).

Their study suffered three data problems, however. The first problem pertained to their fatality rates for the 112 cars, that is, whether the rates applied to the cars or to the drivers of the cars. One view of accidents is that the car is responsible. It is too light, poorly manufactured, not equipped with automatic seat belts or air bags or antilock brakes, or otherwise not crashworthy. Another view would paraphrase the National Rifle Association: it is not cars that kill people, it is drivers that kill people. Teenagers, men, unmarried people, and people with bad driving records are greater accident risks than people with the opposite characteristics.[2] Both views have merit. In any case, it seems appropriate that some characteristics of drivers must be taken into account if a proper estimate of the risk-for-price trade-off is to be discovered.

Atkinson and Halvorsen (1990) followed the approach pioneered by labor economists in which wages were regressed on job fatality rates. Labor economists also invariably include personal characteristics such as years of schooling and work experience as covariates.[3] Atkinson and Halvorsen recognized that they needed driver characteristics in their regressions. They believed driver characteristics could be accounted for by including the average characteristics of deceased drivers. They included the following covariates in their regressions: percentage of decedents age 18 to 24, percentage of male decedents, percentage of decedents with alcohol in the blood, percentage of decedents wearing seat belts, and percentage with no previous offenses. These appear to be reasonable covariates, designed to measure some personal characteristics. Yet, when they were entered into the regressions, they did not generate statistically significant coefficients (134, note 6). In their results on "Age of Drivers" in their table 2, they did not find age to be statistically significant in their regressions. None of the personal characteristics, in fact, were statistically significant either separately or jointly. We are left with the conclusion that personal characteristics of drivers did not influence the price of the car or in any way interfere with the correlation between the car's fatality rate and its price. The personal characteristics they had were apparently not important, and their estimated coefficient on the fatality rate would presumably not be affected by excluding them. These results are alarming.

If drivers were at least partially responsible for a car's fatality rate, and if personal characteristics were correlated with variables influencing the demand for cars, price of cars, and fatality rates, then estimated coefficients and t-statistics on the fatality rate should change as personal characteristics were added or deleted from the regressions. But Atkinson and Halvorsen (1990) did not find that coefficients or t-statistics changed, and they did not find that any personal characteristics were statistically significant. The lack of statistical significance is difficult to explain and raises questions about the reliability of their data.

Second, Atkinson and Halvorsen never explained why 112 cars from only 1978 models were selected for analysis. A personal communication with the person in charge of the FARS file at NHTSA, Louann Hall (telephone call, April 12, 1991), indicated that in 1978, the NHTSA collected data on over 200 car models. Moreover, as Hall indicated, over 200 car models were also available in many other years.

Third, the assumption of good consumer knowledge concerning a car's safety characteristics is not universally accepted. McCarthy (1990) suggests that most new car buyers are not informed about cars' crashworthiness and that market efficiency would be improved by requiring car dealers to post crashworthiness statistics next to the price.

In summary, Atkinson and Halvorsen's (1990) simple idea that we ought to be able to use car prices and car and driver characteristics to estimate the value of life is innovative. But proper estimates would require the careful collection of data on personal characteristics of drivers, such as income, education, marital status, and number of dependents. Believable results would include evidence that the personal characteristics of drivers do make a difference when attempting to estimate a price-fatality trade-off. The fact that Atkinson and Halvorsen's personal characteristics do not make a difference is troubling.

IV. A Willingness-to-Pay Estimate

In this section we generate WTP estimates for injuries and diseases. Because we prefer the Human Capital estimates that appear in chapters 5 and 6, we do not provide detailed analyses or justifications for these WTP estimates. We offer these estimates to demonstrate (a) the general methodology; (b) the large size of the estimates; (c) the corresponding large burden of pain and suffering that is ignored by the Human Capital method.

Several reviews are available that discuss nearly 50 WTP studies (Fischer et al. 1998; Miller 1990; Viscusi 1993). Using data from vehicle crashes, smoke detectors, air pollution, cigarette smoking, automobile prices, and especially the labor market, value of life estimates range between $70,000 and $16 million. Viscusi (1993), the leading researcher in the field, prefers the estimates from the labor market that generally fall in the $3 to $5 million range.

What is noticeable about almost all of these is that they are much larger than would be obtained from the medical cost approach. For example, our average direct cost of injury per death is around $20,000 (chap. 5). Our average of forgone earnings, fringe benefits, and home production is nearly $600,000 per injury death (chap. 5). These sum to roughly $620,000, some $2.4 million below the lowest WTP estimate from the labor market that Viscusi prefers. If WTP death estimates are to be used in lieu of Human Capital death estimates, our estimated costs would increase by factors of three to five for injury deaths alone.

But death is not the only job injury risk. A number of labor market studies have addressed nonfatal injuries. The implicit value of the injury has ranged between $13,810 and $89,408, with the mean value being around $40,000, again, in 1990 (Viscusi 1993).

We will use a $4 million estimate for injury deaths and $40,000 for nonfatal injuries.

Assuming 6,371 deaths at $4 million per death (in 1990), our cost estimate would be $25.484 billion for injury deaths. The calculation for nonfatal injuries is a little more involved, depending on the estimates used for nondisabling injuries. Assuming 13.337 million injuries at $40,000 apiece yields $533.5 billion. But most labor market studies used disabling injuries only when analyzing the WTP for nonfatal injuries. Assuming there were 5.326 million disabling injuries at $40,000 apiece, and $7.1534 million nondisabling injuries at $0 apiece, then our nonfatal injury estimate would be $213.0 billion.

In the first case, including nondisabling injuries, our sum is $559.0. In the second case, excluding nondisabling injuries, our sum is $238.5 billion. There was some 6.8 percent inflation between 1990 and 1992. Our 1992 WTP estimates for injuries would, therefore, be $254.7 billion to $597.0 billion in 1992.

Assuming 60,293 disease deaths at $4 million each generates a total cost of $241 billion for all disease deaths. Assuming 1,183,697 nonfatal diseases at $40,000 per case yields an estimate of $47.5 billion for all nonfatal diseases. But again, not all of these diseases need be disabling. Assuming 39.9 percent are disabling (the same percentage we used for injuries), and assuming the cost for disabling disease is $40,000 each and $0 for a nondisabling disease, our estimate for all nonfatal diseases would be $18.9 billion.

We again generate two estimates for the combined cost of fatalities and nonfatalities for diseases: $260 and $286.5 billion. Applying the 6.8 percent inflation factor yields $278 and $308 billion.[4]

For both injuries and diseases, our estimates would be $533 billion to $902 billion. The disparities between our Human Capital method estimates ($155.5 billion) and these WTP estimates suggest that the value people put on pain and suffering is considerable.[5]

V. Conclusion

This chapter presented methods for the Human Capital and the Willingness-to-Pay approaches. We prefer the estimates based upon the Human Capital method on pragmatic and theoretical grounds. On pragmatic grounds, we know that few WTP estimates are available. Most apply to injury deaths, not nonfatal injuries and not deaths or conditions due to diseases. In particular, we are not aware of any WTP estimates on nonfatal injuries that apply to the convenient WC disability categories from chapter 2. The WTP death estimates, moreover, are hotly debated. The WTP estimates tend to be three to eight times the size of the Human Capital estimates, and thus an occupational injury and illness WTP cost study could not be reasonably compared to existing Human Capital studies of cancer, heart disease, and AIDS. On theoretical grounds, we seek averages and total costs, not marginal ones. In addition, one of the strongest critiques of the Human Capital method — that the costs to children, homemakers, and retirees are underestimated — does not apply to our estimates of people who work for pay.

Finally, the Human Capital method explicitly accounts for medical spending on hospitals, physicians, drugs, and so on. The WTP method does not explicitly count these. But medical costs are easily understood by noneconomists and command the greatest public attention in the debate on costs of health.

The next two chapters estimate the costs of occupational injuries and illnesses using the Human Capital method.

CHAPTER 5

Costs of Injuries

I. Introduction

This chapter presents injury cost estimates using the Human Capital method. The outline of the chapter is as follows. Section II presents our estimates of direct (II.A) and indirect (II.B) costs. Direct costs estimates draw heavily from data from the National Council on Compensation Insurance (NCCI) and from Nelson's (1992, 1993) studies on workers' compensation. Within the indirect cost discussion, we consider NCCI indemnity costs, the present value of lost earnings, and all other indirect costs. A summary table appears in section II.C. Section III reviews existing studies by the National Safety Council (1993); Hensler et al. (1991); Marquis (1992); Miller and Galbraith (1994); Neumark et al. (1991); Nelson (1992, 1993); Burton, Yates, and Blum (1997); Boden and Fleishman (1989); Rice et al. (1989a); Max and Rice (1993); and Blincoe and Faigin (1992). Our conclusion is in section IV.

II. Direct and Indirect Costs Estimates

II.A. Direct Costs

Direct costs are composed of two components: medical and insurance administration. Medical costs cover payments to medical and nursing home care providers such as doctors, hospitals, drug companies, nursing homes, and so on. Insurance administration costs cover the overhead for running an insurance company or an equivalent government agency.

To calculate medical costs we simply multiply our estimates of numbers of injuries in table 2.4 (chap. 2) by our estimates of average costs developed subsequently. The disabling injuries are split into the workers' compensation (WC) categories so that we can match them with average WC cost figures from the National Council on Compensation Insurance (NCCI) Ultimate Reports.[1] The NCCI Ultimate Reports provide information on the average cost for each of the WC categories, including deaths. The amount and detail on WC data the NCCI has are unsurpassed.[2]

The NCCI provides estimates of medical dollars spent and forecasted spending from 38 to 41 states for all WC categories: death, Permanent Total (PT), Permanent Partial (PP), Temporary Total and Partial combined (TTP), and the Medical Only category. All dollars are for cases originating in a given insurance policy year. The estimates are, therefore, incidence based, not prevalence based. The data we used were published in May 1993 and covered policy years 1988, 1989, and a few months into 1990. As mentioned in chapter 2, policy years covered exactly 12 months. Our selected year for research purposes is 1992. We inflated the NCCI cost figures to express them in 1992 dollars and adjusted them slightly upward to reflect the omission of the high medical costs in California and New York.[3]

Table 5.1 presents some medical cost calculations. The first column presents categories of injuries including deaths, PTs, PPs, TTPs, Medical Only, one to seven days lost, and nondisabling. These are WC categories and correspond to our categories from chapter 2. The second column pertains to the dollars per category. They were drawn from the NCCI Ultimate Report (May 1993). They represent what WC would pay for the injuries. Column 3 presents what non-WC charges would be, that is, 89.98 percent of WC charges.[4] Columns 4 and 5 represent our estimates of injuries from chapter 2, table 2.4. The product of the number of injuries in the categories times the average cost per category appears in columns 6 and 7. The sum appears in column 8.

Our total, $20.2246 billion, appears at the bottom. After adjusting for medical inflation and the omission of New York and California, our estimate is $25.9825 billion.

But this $25.9825 billion represents only what is paid to hospitals, doctors, drug companies, and so on. Someone must pay these bills, collect premiums, and service the financial reserves. Insurance companies or their government agency equivalents have costs of administration, maintaining a reserve of funds, interest payments, and, in the case of companies, providing a reasonable profit to owners or shareholders via dividends or value of stock.[5]

We believe insurance administration costs should be included in direct costs. They have not always been so included (Rice et al. 1989a). For injuries qualifying for WC, these costs are reflected in the premiums businesses pay and, therefore, constitute an out-of-pocket cost to business firms. Even when injuries are not covered by WC, there will be some insurance administration, reserve,[6] profit, dividends, and interest

TABLE 5.1. Calculations of NCCI Medical Expenses within Injury Categories

Row	(1) Injury Category	(2) Workers' Compensation Dollars per Injury	(3) Non–Workers' Compensation Dollars per Injury (89.98% of col. 2)	(4) Number of Injuries from table 2.4 Paid by WC (45%)	(5) Number of Injuries Not Paid by WC (55%)	(6) Product Col. 2 × Col. 5 (in $ billions)	(7) Product Col. 3 × Col. 5 (in $ billions)	(8) Sum (in $ billions)
1	Deaths	17,226	15,500	2,867	3,504	0.04939	0.0543	0.10369
2	Permanent Total (PT)	113,372.4	102,012	5,459	665	0.6190	0.0680	
3	Permanent Partial (PP)	15,342.5	13,805	0.33345 million	0.40755 million	5.1160	5.6262	
4	Temporary Total (TT) and Temporary Total and Partial (TTP)	2,782.5	2,504	0.87615 million	1.07085 million	2.4379	2.6814	
5	Medical Only (MO)	294.5	265	See rows 6, 7	See rows 6, 7			
6	One to seven days of disability[a] (work loss)	294.5	265	1.1817 million	1.4443 million	0.3480	0.3827	
7	Nondisabling[a] (no work loss)	294.5	265	3.605 million	4.406 million	1.0617	1.1680	
8	Total					9.6320[b]	10.5926[c]	20.2246
9	Total adjusted for NY, CA, and national medical inflation (× 1.2847)							25.9825

Source: Current study.

[a] We assume that the average Medical Only costs applied equally to the one to seven days of disability and to the nondisability injuries.

[b] Total dollars paid by WC: $9.632 or 47.625%.

[c] Total dollars paid by non-WC: $10.5926 or 52.375%.

expenses, since some other private health insurance company or Medicare or Medicaid would likely cover the injuries not covered by WC.

To estimate these administrative or overhead costs, we begin with WC data in Nelson (1992, 1993). Every three to four years, the Social Security Administration generates national estimates on the annual costs of WC within the states and Washington, DC, as well as the special WC funds for federal government employees, the Black Lung Trust, and the WC program for longshoremen. Nelson's numbers are prevalence based. They cover actual expenses in a given year, not forecasted expenses.[7]

Nelson does not have a separate category for all administrative expenses. We use the difference between the premiums and benefits paid to measure the administrative or overhead costs (Danzon 1992). Using 1991 data (Nelson did not generate a 1992 or 1993 estimate), Nelson calculated that all WC premiums summed to $55.2 billion while all WC benefit payments (medical plus indemnity) summed to $42.1 billion. The difference between these two is 13.1. Now 13.1 divided by 42.1 yields 31 percent. This 31 percent of benefits would represent administrative expenses.

But not all injuries are covered by WC. The estimates from table 2.4, chapter 2, are more than twice the number of actual WC cases. The 31 percent for administrative expense would not necessarily apply to non-WC payments. It is likely that administrative expense would be less for other insurers, especially government insurers. We assume a 15 percent rate, which is drawn from Cutler 1994.[8] But neither the 31 percent WC rate nor the 15 percent non-WC rate would apply to medical costs paid directly by patients. These costs are referred to as out-of-pocket expenses. In 1992, 18.4 percent of medical expenses were out of pocket. Before we apply the 15 percent administrative rate, we must therefore subtract 18.4 percent.

Our administrative costs for WC medical payments are $12.37423 billion × 0.31, or $3.8360 billion. Our administrative costs for non-WC medical payments are [$13.6083 × (1 − 0.184)] × 0.15, or $1.6657 billion. The sum is $5.5017 billion.

Administrative Costs for Indemnity Payments. Calculation of administrative costs for lost earnings is more complicated than for medical expense. Administrative costs would not accrue for earnings or wages but for indemnity benefits. The final number in table 5.3 ($64.5214) is for lost earnings. We first must convert $64.5214 to indemnity benefits. WC undoubtedly contributes the most for total indemnity, but Social Security disability payments, private disability insurance, and welfare payments for the disabled would also contribute some indemnity payments. As will be explained later in our discussion on indemnity benefits, we assume that indemnity benefits cover 50 percent of wage losses. Applying 50 percent to $64.5214 yields $32.2607.[9]

Using the same percentage assumptions as in the preceding for WC and non-WC administrative expense (31 percent for WC; 15 percent for non-WC); assuming the same percentages for WC and non-WC medical care apply to indemnity benefits (47.625 percent for WC; 52.375 percent for non-WC); and assuming 18.3 percent of non-WC expenses are absorbed by patients and families, our administrative cost estimate for indemnity benefits is $6.8296 billion.[10] These $6.8296 can be split into fatality and nonfatality expenses assuming the same percentages as apply for medical care expenditures (0.513 percent for fatalities; 99.497 percent for nonfatalities). We estimate $0.0350 billion for fatalities and $6.7946 for nonfatalities.

Table 5.2 summarizes our data from this section.

II.B. Indirect Costs: NCCI Indemnity, Present Value, and Other Calculations

This section will present a calculation of the indirect costs based upon indemnity data in the NCCI; national government data on employment,

TABLE 5.2.   Estimate of Total Direct Costs

Direct Costs	Billions of Dollars
Total	38.3802
Medical Only	25.9825
Fatalities	0.1332
Nonfatalities	25.8493
Medical administration costs on WC (31%); private insurance, Medicaid, welfare, and Medicare (15%, combined)	5.5017
Fatalities[a]	0.02821
Nonfatalities	5.4335
Indemnity administration costs on WC (31%); private insurance, Social Security, and welfare, (15%, combined)	6.8296
Fatalities[a]	0.0350
Nonfatalities	6.7946

Source: Current study.

[a]Assuming 0.51269% arise from fatalities and 99.4873% from nonfatalities—the same percentages we calculated for medical costs.

earnings, and mortality probabilities; and cost estimates from related studies on indirect costs. As we will see, there are a number of categories for indirect costs, and several sources of data will have to be analyzed to provide a reliable estimate.

The largest category of indirect costs is lost wages. There are two components of lost wages: morbidity costs (nonfatal injuries) and mortality costs (fatal injuries). The NCCI data are useful in estimating morbidity but not mortality costs. We will first analyze morbidity and, second, mortality costs.

II.B.1. NCCI Indemnity

The NCCI reports contain data on the total amount of indemnity dollars paid by WC in the various WC categories: deceased, Permanent Total (PT), Permanent Partial (PP), Temporary Total and Partial (TTP), and Medical Only. Within the deceased category, WC payments are not for lost wages. They are paid to spouses, sometimes as a lump sum death benefit and sometimes as indemnity. They are also paid as indemnity to children up to the age of adulthood. The indemnity payments under the deceased category would not be reliable measures of the present value of lost compensation for the deceased. We therefore will rely on our own present value calculations for the deceased as described subsequently.

The NCCI indemnity payments for PTs and PPs involve some forecasted dollars. The forecasts for PPs and PTs are not necessarily for the lifetime of the injured workers. Many WC boards reason that over time, most workers become accommodated to the permanent injury (especially partial) and find new jobs. The idea of the PP indemnity and, to a much lesser extent, PT indemnity is to allow them time to adapt. Many states and Washington, DC, will pay PP indemnity for only three to 15 years (Berkowitz and Burton 1987; U.S. Chamber of Commerce 1992). On the other hand, all states will allow PT benefits to proceed into retirement age if no alternative work can be found.[11]

The indemnity data for PT, PP, and TTP can be used to construct lost earnings. The NCCI indemnity numbers per case cannot simply be used "as is," however. They underestimate wage loss. The indemnity payments for persons with Permanent Total and Partial conditions have been criticized by a number of researchers as being especially inadequate (Rejda 1994; Berkowitz and Burton 1987; DeVol 1986; and Stern et al. 1997). The percentage of the wage covered by WC indemnity is referred to as the "replacement rate." Most frequently, replacement rates are expressed for *after*-tax wages. We, on the other hand, need *before*-tax replacement rates since it is the before-tax wage that measures output. Indirect costs are not meant to measure the loss of a worker's take-home pay but to measure lost output for the nation.

Berkowitz and Burton (1987) found *after*-tax replacement rates ranged from 75 percent for some TTPs to 25 percent for some PPs.[12] But these 75 percent to 25 percent rates in Berkowitz and Burton were extreme (not average) rates and were also calculated for *after*-tax earnings. Since *before*-tax earnings are greater than *after*-tax, the *before*-tax rate will be less than the *after*-tax rate. In addition, no states awarded an indemnity greater than 66 percent of the *before*-tax wage at the time our NCCI data were collected (1988–92). Stern et al. (1997), in an extensive study of PPs in California, found *before*-tax replacement rates at just under 40 percent. But California is among the least generous of the states (Nelson 1992). Finally, it is generally accepted that replacement rates for most government indemnity plans — including WC — are roughly 50 percent of *before*-tax wages (Ehrenberg and Smith 1991). We will assume that *before*-tax replacement rates were 0.4 for PTs, 0.5 for PPs, and 0.6 for TTPs. We do not use a wage-replacement calculation in the one to seven days lost category. Our 0.4, 0.5, and 0.6 assumptions average to 0.5. But more importantly, as we will see subsequently, the amount of costs for PTs under the 0.4 assumption roughly equals the amount of costs for TTPs. Thus, our weighted average replacement rate for all indemnity categories will be 0.5 — the percentage most frequently assumed by labor economists (Ehrenberg and Smith 1991).[13]

Table 5.3 presents the calculations necessary to estimate the wage losses for Permanent Total (PT), Permanent Partial (PP), Temporary Total and Partial (TTP), and other injuries. Persons who do not report work loss (nondisabling) would have zero wage losses. The WC categories appear in column 1. Column 2 presents the indemnity cost per case. These data are drawn from the May 1993 NCCI Ultimate Report.[14] Column 3 presents the per case cost divided by our assumed replacement rate.

The $288 in row 5 was calculated assuming that, on average, three days of work loss occurred in the category and the average before-tax wage was $12 per hour and the average workday was eight hours. Twelve dollars per hour represents $24,000 per year as an average wage or salary for all employees in 1992 (U.S. Bureau of the Census 1993b).

Column 4 reproduces the estimates from chapter 2, table 2.4. In column 5, the estimated cases in column 4 were multiplied by the per case cost in column 3. Estimates in column 6 adjust for inflation.[15] The total for 1992 — $64.5214 billion — appears at the bottom right corner of table 5.3. This $64.5214 billion does not include administrative costs, fringe benefits, present value of wages for fatalities, and additional indirect costs such

TABLE 5.3. Estimated Before-Tax Wage Loss Based on NCCI Average Indemnity Costs

Row	(1) Category	(2) Per Case ($)	(3) Per Case Divided by Either 0.4 (PT) or 0.5 (PP) or 0.6 (TTP) (one to seven not affected) ($)	(4) 1992 Estimated Cases (chap. 2)	(5) Product (in $ billions)	(6) 1990–92 Wage Inflation Col. 5 × 1.07345[a] (in $ billions)
1.	Deaths[b]			6,371		
2.	Permanent Total	243,187	607,968	12,124	7.3710	7.9124
3.	Permanent Partial	30,239	60,478	741,000	44.8142	48.1058
4.	Temporary Total and Temporary Partial	2,208	3,680	1,947,000	7.1650	7.6913
5.	One to seven days lost	Does not apply	288[c]	2,626,000	0.7563	0.8119
6.	Nondisabling	0		8,011,000	0	0
	Total					$64.5214

Source: Current study.

[a]Wage inflation was estimated with the CPI-U-X1.

[b]Does not apply since death benefits paid to spouse until remarried and children until adulthood.

[c]Assuming 3 days of loss, 8 hours per day, and $12 per hour.

as employer training costs. In the following, we address each of these omitted indirect costs.

II.B.2. Fringe Benefits

For our purposes, employer-financed fringe benefit[16] losses include employer-provided health, dental, life, unemployment, and WC insurance; child care; Social Security contributions; and pensions. Our calculations of fringe benefits will not include employee contributions, supplemental pay (bonuses), or paid vacations or holiday pay. We do not include employee contributions, benefits, vacations, or holiday pay since these are already reflected in our estimate of before-tax earnings.

The U.S. Chamber of Commerce estimated the percentage to be 35 percent of total compensation, or over 54 percent of earnings (35/65 = 0.54) in recent years (U.S. Chamber of Commerce 1993). But some researchers have questioned the methodology of the Chamber of Commerce study. The Chamber of Commerce, for example, looked only at large firms and included paid vacations and holiday pay as part of fringe benefits. Large firms are known to be more generous than small ones (Brown, Hamilton, and Medoff 1990). These 35 percent or 54 percent figures are probably too high.

A BLS study (Brinkley 1994) estimated a 29.6 percent rate for full-time workers and a 20.9 percent rate for part-time workers out of total compensation and (30/70 =) 42 percent and (21/79 =) 26 percent out of wages. But these 29.6 percent and 20.9 percent figures also included vacations and supplemental pay. Subtracting vacations and supplemental pay and attempting to cover all firms, large and small, the BLS estimated employer-financed fringe benefits at 24.7 percent of wages and salaries in 1988 (Piacentini 1990). But wages and salaries do not include bonuses, and our earnings measure does.

Our assumed rate is drawn from the Jacobs 1997 (189) study of 1996 BLS data. Jacobs found that wages and salaries, paid vacations, and bonuses amounted to 81.1 percent of total compensation. Employer-financed fringes made up 18.9 percent. The ratio is 18.9/81.1 = 23.3 percent. This rate is applied to our total earnings figures. Multiplying 0.233 by $64.5214 yields $15.0335 billion, our estimate for fringe benefits for nonfatal earnings losses.

II.B.3. Fatalities

Fatalities require a present value calculation. We assume that persons who died would have earned what others of the same age and gender

TABLE 5.4.   Estimated Number and Percentage Distribution of Fatal Injuries by Gender and Age

	Fatalities	
	Our Estimated Number	Toscano and Windau 1993 Percentage
Total	6,371	100
Sex		
Men	5,925	93
Women	446	7
Both sexes		
Under 20 years	191	3
20 to 24 years	573	9
25 to 34 years	1,529	24
35 to 44 years	1,593	25
45 to 54 years	1,210	19
55 to 64 years	765	12
65 years and older	510	8

Source: Current study and the Census of Fatal Occupational Injuries.

earned. This is the same assumption used by Rice et al. (1989a), Max et al. (1995), Miller and Galbraith (1995), and all other mortality cost estimates using the Human Capital method with which we are familiar.

First, we consider the age and gender composition of our deceased workers. Table 5.4 indicates our estimates of the number of job-related injury deaths in 1992 by gender and age. The percentages were drawn from Toscano and Windau 1993. The estimated numbers of deaths within each category were derived simply by multiplying the percentage with our estimated deaths (6,371). For example, the estimated number of male deaths equals 6,371 × 0.93, or 5,925.

The age and gender data on the deaths were combined with information on wages (U.S. Department of Commerce 1993) and probabilities that persons will survive to age 75 (U.S. Bureau of the Census 1993b), as well as the employment within those categories (U.S. Bureau of the Census 1993). The 65 year was chosen as the average year for retirement.

The present value formula we use is similar to the one in Rice et al. 1989a.

$$PV_{\text{death}} = \sum_{n=y}^{75} P_{y,s,n} \times [M_{s,n} \times (1 + F_{s,n}) \times LFPR_{s,n} + H_{s,n}] \times \frac{(1 + g)^{n-y}}{(1 + r)^{n-y}},$$

where

PV_{death} = present discounted value of loss due to injury death per person;

$P_{y,s,n}$ = probability that a person of sex s and age y will survive to age n;

y = age at which person was injured;

s = sex of person;

n = age of person;

$M_{s,n}$ = mean annual earnings of employed persons of sex s and age n;

$H_{s,n}$ = annual value of household production for person of sex s and age n;

$LFPR_{s,n}$ = proportion of the population of sex s and age n that is employed in the labor market, that is, the labor force participation rate (we assume the $LFPR = 1$ for persons over age 64 at time of death);

$F_{s,n}$ = fringe benefits rate for sex s and age n;

g = rate of increase of labor productivity, assumed to be 1 percent;

r = real discount rate, assumed to be 4 percent.

The *LFPR* in the preceding equation deserves comment. Most people retire at or before age 65. We assumed that persons who died prior to 65 would have a *LFPR* of typical persons now over age 65 (e.g., 0.161 for men and 0.083 for women). However, some of our decedents, prior to death, were over 65 and still working. For these people, we assumed a *LFPR* of 1.0 (i.e., we assumed that they would have continued working until age 75). We assumed no one would work beyond age 75.

Tables are available from the authors that present the present value calculations for women and men. We were able to find data only within age categories, not within each age. The present value tables have information on the following: probabilities of survival from one age category to the next (U.S. Bureau of the Census 1993b; U.S. Department of Health and Human Services 1994); ratios of the productivity to the discount rate factors; average annual earnings for full-time and part-time employees (U.S. Department of Commerce 1993); the annual value of household production (Douglas, Kenny, and Miller 1990); the fringe benefits (0.233); and the labor force participation rate (U.S. Bureau of the Census 1993a).

The contribution of the individual worker to economic and social output should include home production. Home production included changing diapers, reading to children, home repairs, building cabinets, plumbing repairs, and so on (and on!). Home production can take place any time of the day. Estimates on home production were drawn from Douglas, Kenney, and Miller 1990 and updated to 1992 using the Consumer Price Index for Urban Dwellers (CPI-U-X1). These Douglas, Kenny, and Miller estimates assume the following: (1) higher productivity in the labor market implies higher productivity at home; (2) women, because of socialization and job market discrimination, have more home production than men; (3) women of child-rearing age provide the greatest amount of home production; and (4) women are more likely than men to work part-time and work more hours than men at home.

Our results appear in table 5.5. Columns indicate gender and total; rows indicate earnings, fringe benefits paid by employers, home production, and total. The grand total for indirect costs for all deaths is $3.6865 billion. This represents a per person cost of $578,638 for all lost production and a per person cost of $422,069 for earnings only.

These $578,638 and $422,069 per person estimates are a little smaller than the amount we found on a per case basis for Permanent Total injuries ($607,968). This can be explained by the age differences for fatalities and nonfatalities. Nonfatal injury rates are more frequent among the young than the old, whereas the opposite is true for fatal injury rates (chap. 2, app. B, table B2.1). This $578,638 is also less than the $744,000 for CFOI deaths in New Jersey (Roche 1995). But Roche's study did not adjust for the probability of survival from one age to the next. Moreover, New Jersey wages are higher than the national average. The $578,638 is more than the $317,181 in Rice et al. 1989a in part because the Rice estimate applied to 1985 and in part because the Rice estimate applied to all people, whether working or not.

TABLE 5.5.   Present Value of Lost Earnings, Fringe Benefits, and Home Production

	Women	Men	Total (or average, per person)
Earnings	$0.0940 billion	$2.5950 bllion	$2.6890 billion
per person	$210,762	$437,900	$422,069
Fringe benefits	$0.0219 billion	$0.6046 billion	$0.6265 billion
per person	$49.103	$102,042	$98,336
Home production	$0.0546 billion	$0.3164 billion	$0.3710 billion
per person	$122,498	$53,408	$58,233
Total	$0.1705 billion	$3.5160 billion	$3.6865 billion
per person	$382,363	$593,418	$578,638

Source: Current study.

II.B.4. Home Production

We assume that home production losses for nonfatal injuries would be proportional to those for fatal injuries. The ratio of home production losses to lost earnings for the fatalities for men and women combined is 0.138. Assuming the same percentage applies to nonfatal injuries, our estimate of home production losses would be 0.138 × $64.5214 = $8.9040 billion.

II.B.5. Training, Disruption Costs

Any injury resulting in work loss will create some disruption at the workplace. For fatalities, Permanent Total, and Permanent Partial injuries, these will be serious disruptions. In the short run, other workers will have to fill in for the deceased or injured worker. In the long run, new persons will have to be hired and trained.

The costs for hiring and training are difficult to estimate. Few studies have addressed the issue. Here we will review those by Barron, Black, and Lowenstein (1989), Flynn (1995), Mincer (1962), and Smart (1987).

Barron, Black, and Lowenstein (1989) estimated that 161 hours of managers' and co-workers' time are required to hire and train new workers during the first three months of the new hire's tenure. Assuming $15.24 (1992) for average total compensation (wages and fringes) per hour for managers' and co-workers' time, hiring and training costs would be $2,454 (161 × 15.24).[17]

But the Barron, Black, and Lowenstein 1989 study was drawn from a sample with a high percentage of firms paying low wages and from employees with few skills. It is likely that Barron, Black, and Lowenstein underestimated the hours required for average to above average skilled workers, that is, for persons with greater skills who have worked at the same firm for a number of years and acquired considerable amounts of "specific" human capital (Mincer 1962).[18] Moreover, Barron, Black, and Lowenstein only considered the costs for the first three months. Training for many jobs requires more than three months. An Employment Management Association study estimated that hiring costs alone averaged $3,310 in 1994 (Flynn 1995). Finally, any costs associated with grief or shock of co-workers were also ignored (Haines 1993).

We assumed that these hiring, training, and disruption costs will add $2,453.64 to costs for the company for every death, Permanent Total injury, and Permanent Partial injury. We assumed that Temporary injuries will add $149 apiece and all other disabling injuries will cost $12 apiece.[19] Our estimate of workplace hiring, training, and disruption costs is then $(6,371 \times \$2,454) + (12,124 \times \$2,454) + (741,000 \times \$2,454) + (1,947,000 \times \$149) + (2,626,000 \times \$12) = \$2.1853$ billion.

II.B.6. Other Indirect Costs

We omit costs for travel delays, home health care, family disruptions, and innocent third parties. These are discussed briefly at the end of the cost section and in our chapter on limitations (chap. 10).

II.C. Summary Table

Table 5.6 summarizes the direct and indirect costs using the NCCI data combined with present value calculations and other sources. Our preferred estimates include direct costs, estimated to be $38.3802; indirect costs, $94.3307; and total costs, $132.7109. We also calculated $3.76531 for mortality costs and $128.9456 for morbidity costs (table 1.1).

II.D. Advantages and Disadvantages

There are many advantages and disadvantages to this approach of multiplying NCCI average cost estimates times the number of injuries. We first consider the advantages.

First, the NCCI data are the only national data that are available on costs for the categories of WC.

Second, the medical costs include all customary costs for ambulances, emergency rooms, physicians, therapists, nurses, hospitals, rehabilitation, and so on. By relying on the NCCI data, we avoid problems associated with creating our own estimates of costs for ambulances, therapists, and so on. We do not become entangled with ferreting out differences between, for example, hospitals and insurers in what was supposed to be paid versus what was actually paid.

Third, in the years we rely on (1988 to 1990), WC almost always paid for 100 percent of medical expenses. Few, if any, co-payments or deductibles occurred. We therefore avoid questionable assumptions about deductibles and co-payments that would have to be made using private health insurance data.

Fourth, the NCCI data are incidence based and follow each case for at least three years. We do not have to make our own forecast for how the expense of the case would vary over the first three years.

Fifth, these are simple calculations. They do not require that we match cost data to hospitalizations to injuries based on the part of the body affected. There is a serious difficulty associated with cost measurements based on body parts. Perhaps as many as 40 percent of all injuries affect more than one body part (Hensler et al. 1991; Hall and Owings 1994).

Sixth, the NCCI cost data are widely cited (Nelson 1992, 1993; Boden and Fleishman 1989; Rice et al. 1989a; National Safety Council 1993, 1994).

The first disadvantage is that there are nonparticipating states — California, Minnesota, Nevada, New York, North Dakota, Ohio, Washington, West Virginia, and Wyoming (and Delaware and Pennsylvania

TABLE 5.6. Summary of Costs

Total direct costs	38.3802
Medical Only	25.9825
Fatalities (0.51269%)	0.1332
Nonfatalities (99.4873%)	25.8493
Medical administration costs on WC (31%); private insurance, Medicaid, welfare, and Medicare (15%, combined, excluding out of pocket)	5.5017
Fatalities[a]	0.02821
Nonfatalities	5.4735
Indemnity administration costs on WC (31%); private insurance, Social Security, and welfare (15%, combined, excluding out of pocket)	6.8296
Fatalities[a]	0.0350
Nonfatalities	6.7946
Indirect costs	94.3307
Lost earnings	67.2604
Fatalities	2.6890
Nonfatalities	64.5214
Fringe benefits (23.3% of earnings)	15.6600
Fatalities	0.6265
Nonfatalities	15.0335
Home production	9.2750
Fatalities	0.3710
Nonfatalities (same as average percentage for fatalities: 13.8% of earnings)	8.9040
Workplace training, restaffing, disruption	2.1853
Fatalities	0.0156
Nonfatalities	2.1697
Grand total	132.7109

Source: Current study.

[a]Assuming 0.51269% arise from fatalities and 99.4873% from nonfataliites. These are the percentages we calculated for medical costs.

on Medical Only costs). California and New York account for over 70 percent of the population of these omitted states (U.S. Bureau of the Census 1993), however, and we did explicitly account for these two.

Second, we must assume that the large self-insured firms (excluded from NCCI) have similar average costs as the firms included in the NCCI numbers. This second assumption does not appear to create any obvious bias, however.

Third, the administrative charges for WC were based on total benefits to premium differences. Total WC benefits include indemnity. It could be that indemnity administration is more expensive than medical administration due to litigation. Medical expenses are less often subject to litigation than indemnity expenses. Hence, we may be overestimating insurance administration for medical expenses. But we used this assumption for our analysis of indemnity; hence, we may have underestimated administrative costs for indemnity. Moreover, total indemnity expenses are greater than total medical expenses. Thus, by applying the same percentage for both medical and indemnity expenses, we may underestimate combined total administrative costs for medical and indemnity benefits.[20]

The fourth limitation is that we must assume the average costs for the illnesses are the same as those for the injuries. This fourth assumption is not terribly problematic given that illnesses probably comprise less than 3 percent of total WC costs (Boden and Fleishman 1989; Rossman, Miller, and Douglas 1991).

III. Literature Review

This section will address how our estimates compare with those in the literature. Unfortunately, few studies have been conducted. A literature search uncovered several occupational injury studies and a handful of related studies. We will begin with the two most widely cited studies, National Safety Council 1993 and Marquis 1993. The remaining occupational injury studies are considered next: Miller and Galbraith 1994; Neumark et al. 1991; Nelson 1992, 1993; Burton, Yates, and Blum 1997; and Boden and Fleishman 1989. We then move on to related literature on the costs of all injuries (Rice et al. 1989a), costs of firearms (Max and Rice 1993), and costs of motor vehicle crashes (Blincoe and Faigin 1992).

III.A. Job Injury Studies

Our review of job injury studies will lodge a number of constructive criticisms of these studies. We have great respect for the authors of these studies, and we have used many of their analyses and estimates in developing our own.

III.A.1. National Safety Council (NSC)

The NSC injury and cost estimates are widely cited by researchers and the news media. We cited estimates from the NSC book *Accident Facts* in chapter 2. The NSC collects and presents more data on accidents, injuries, and their costs than any other private firm or federal agency. However, despite their expertise in the area, the authors of *Accident Facts* are cautious in presenting their data. For example, this footnote appears on page 1 of *Accident Facts* 1993.

Injuries are not reported on a national basis [by researchers other than those at the NSC], so the totals [the NSC publishes] are approximations based on ratios of disability injuries to deaths developed from a 1990 NSC study. The totals are the best estimates for the current year; however, they should not be compared with totals shown in previous editions of *Accident Facts* to indicate year-to-year changes or trends.

On page 35 of *Accident Facts* 1993, we encounter these sentences pertaining to the costs of work accidents.

Cost estimating procedures were revised for the 1993 edition of *Accident Facts*. In general, cost estimates are not comparable from year-to-year. As additional or more precise data become available, they are used from that year forward. Previously estimated figures are not revised.

In other words, counting the numbers of accidents and injuries nationwide and calculating their costs are difficult tasks. These counting and costing attempts are constantly being improved.

With these caveats in mind, we turn to the NSC estimates. The total cost for job-related nonintentional injuries was $115.9 billion in 1992. This $115.9 billion estimate, like our $132.7 billion estimate, is an incidence, not a prevalence, estimate. The largest portion of NSC job-related costs came from wage and productivity losses ($62.5 billion) and medical expenses ($22.0 billion). The other categories of expenses are itemized as administrative expenses ($14.5 billion), employer costs ($10.2 billion), motor vehicle damage ($3.4 billion), and fire losses ($3.3

billion). The NSC also includes fringe benefits, household production, and travel delays within their wage and productivity losses category and includes expected future medical costs within their medical expenses category.

The NSC, like us, use the difference between premiums paid to insurance companies and claims paid out by those companies to estimate administrative costs. We also concur with the NSC inclusion of costs to uninjured workers' and firms' production slowdowns, training of replacement workers, and extra cost of overtime for noninjured workers. We differ in that we do not include fire losses or motor vehicle damage, reasoning that these are not *injury* costs per se.

The NSC also presented cost estimates for the cost per death ($780,000) and per disabling injury ($27,000) — defined as any injury resulting in one or more days of lost work.

Our $132.7 billion estimate is larger than the NSC's $115.9 billion estimate. The disparity is largely the result of two factors: (1) the NSC explicitly ignored violent incidents (assault, murder, suicide), and more importantly, (2) the NSC relied on the NHIS estimate of nonfatal work injuries. As we argued in chapter 2, appendix A, the NHIS only captures roughly 50 percent to 60 percent of all nonfatal injuries.

Additional NSC estimates pertained to back injuries. A section in *Accident Facts* indicates that an NCCI report on 600,000 WC claims found nearly one-third (31 percent) of lost-time WC claims were due to back injuries. Because the average costs of back injury claims were roughly one-third more than the average costs of all other lost-time claims, the total WC lost-time costs associated with back injuries were more than 40 percent of all lost-time (disability) claim costs. Most back injuries were the result of lifting.[21]

III.A.2. Marquis 1992 and Rand, Hensler et al. 1991

The Rand corporation study of *all* injuries by Hensler et al. (1991) together with the companion study on *only* job-related injuries by Marquis (192) was introduced in chapter 2. They were drawn from a large household survey independently conducted by researchers at Rand. In this section, we will first present an overview of their cost findings and, second, discuss their methodology.

Marquis's estimates applied to nonfatal traumatic injuries. Fatalities and all occupational diseases including carpal tunnel syndrome were excluded. She estimated that seven million Americans experienced on-the-job injuries in 1989. Another four million suffered in 1989 as a result of an injury that occurred prior to 1989. Roughly 11 million persons were suffering from an on-the-job injury in 1989 that either occurred in that year or a previous year.

She estimated a total cost of $83 billion in 1989 — almost 2 percent of GDP. Roughly 40 percent of that amount was spent on direct (medical) cost, and 60 percent resulted from work loss costs. Marquis pointed out that workplace injuries were more costly than non-workplace injuries. Only roughly 20 percent of all injuries in the Hensler et al. 1991 study were job related, but workplace injury costs claimed nearly 50 percent of all costs. Workplace injuries generate more indirect costs than non-workplace injuries since many people experiencing non-workplace injuries did not hold jobs.

Marquis (1992) did not place a dollar value on the loss in home production. She did, however, estimate that for every day missed from work, roughly two-thirds of one day was missed from home production.

Finally, Marquis (1992) looked at who paid the costs. She estimated that 45 percent of medical and wage losses were born by the individuals and their families. The remaining 55 percent was split among a variety of payers: WC (27.5 percent), private insurance (11 percent), employer-provided benefits (5.5 percent), Medicare, Supplemental Security Income and Social Security Disability Insurance (5.5 percent), and, finally, tort liability (5.5 percent).

The Hensler et al. 1991 and especially the Marquis 1992 studies are limited. First, fatalities were excluded. Second, given the nature of the questions on their questionnaires about accidents and injuries, a considerable number of assaults, attempted murders, and suicides were excluded. Third, a great number of minor injuries, involving one to four days of work loss, were excluded.[22]

A fourth limitation is that they underrepresented minorities and the poor — groups that are more likely than other groups to experience injuries on and off the job (Wildarsky 1980).[23]

Fifth, their cost estimates were prevalence based, not incidence based. The incidence cost approach is used by almost all other authors of injury studies we found in the literature.

III.A.3. Miller and Galbraith 1994

Miller and Galbraith's study (1994) used injury statistics from 1989 and produced cost estimates for December 1990.[24] They estimated 10,958,000 injuries (disabling and nondisabling) in 1990. The total amount of their estimated direct and indirect expenses was $96.6 billion. They also estimated an additional $61.8 billion based on Willingness-to-Pay methods.[25] This $96.6 billion applied to 1990. Assuming a 7.345 inflation rate between 1990 and 1992, Miller and Galbraith's estimate would be $103.7 billion in 1992. This estimate is only roughly 11 percent less than the NSC estimate for 1992.

The largest expense was again associated with work loss ($41.6 billion), followed by medical and emergency services ($17.5 billion). Somewhat surprising categories entered third and fourth: motor vehicle liability insurance ($11.2) and workplace disruption ($10.0 billion).[26] The liability insurance dollars were for claims paid to nonemployees resulting from crashes caused by employees. Workplace disruption included overtime pay, lost production for co-workers, and recruitment and training costs.[27]

Household production has been ignored by some researchers, but Miller and Galbraith devoted considerable effort to estimating its value. It is useful to compare ratios of home production to wage loss. Miller and Galbraith's ratio was 18 percent. Ours is 13.8 percent. It is reassuring that our percentage is relatively close to theirs.

Miller and Galbraith's medical costs were drawn from an NCCI Ultimate Report not covering all states or all firms. They, like us, nevertheless argue that the per case estimates should be representative.

Miller and Galbraith also used Nelson's medical cost (not indemnity cost) estimates from the *Social Security Bulletin* (Nelson 1993). Nelson's estimates were prevalence based, however. We prefer incidence-based cost estimates for injuries.[28] Miller and Galbraith also estimated wage losses for nonfatal injuries using techniques similar to ours. They relied on NCCI indemnity data and assumed that WC compensated 60.3 percent of the *before*-tax wage loss and none of the fringe benefit loss.

III.A.4. Neumark et al. 1991

Neumark et al. (1991) estimated the incidence cost of occupational injuries and diseases in Pennsylvania in 1987, 1988, and 1989. The epidemiological part of the study was conducted by researchers at the Pennsylvania Department of Health. The document they produced — *Occupational Disease and Injury in Pennsylvania* — was apparently not intended for public use. The Pennsylvania Department of Health will not release the document or even an abstract. Moreover, the document has not been published in the scientific literature.

Neumark et al. (1991) nevertheless presented some of the Pennsylvania Department of Health epidemiological estimates. We will review these epidemiological estimates before examining their cost estimates.

Pennsylvania's contributions to nonfatal injuries and illnesses were drawn from the BLS's Annual Survey for 1987. The nonfatal injuries were estimated to be 140,908, whereas the nonfatal illnesses were estimated to be 19,982. The total was 160,890. The injury deaths were counted using Pennsylvania's WC records. Among fatalities, 267 were identified as due to injuries, 139 as due to poisoning, and 4,715 as due to diseases. The total number of disease and poisoning deaths was 4,854. Dividing this number by 267 yields 18.2. In other words, 18.2 disease and poisoning deaths were found for every injury death in the Pennsylvania Department of Health study. We found roughly 9.5 disease and poisoning deaths for every injury death (chaps. 2 and 3).

We turn now to the cost estimates. Neumark et al. (1991) provided separate direct cost estimates for injuries and illnesses. Although separate indirect cost estimates were not provided in the text, their tables are well organized, so that they can estimate separately the cost of injuries and illnesses.

Neumark et al. (1991) used NCCI data to calculate medical costs, as well as state of Pennsylvania data. Neumark et al. calculated the medical costs of injuries to be $568.3 million. Their direct and indirect cost estimates for injuries summed to $741.3 million. This represented roughly 31 percent of all injury and illness costs. Our estimate is roughly 85 percent.

They extrapolated to the United States and found a mean estimate of $54.5 billion for injuries *and* illnesses. Multiplying this $54.5 billion by 31 percent yielded $17 billion in 1989. This $17 billion would then be the Neumark et al. 1991 estimate of direct and indirect costs for all occupational injuries in the United States in 1989.

We can further split this $17 billion into direct and indirect components. Assuming the same percentages of direct and indirect costs apply to Pennsylvania as to the nation, direct costs would be $13 billion, and indirect costs would then be $4 billion.

There are several limitations to the Neumark et al. 1991 study. (1) The deficiencies of the BLS's Annual Survey were never mentioned or accounted for. (2) The deficiencies of WC were mentioned but never corrected. (3) The results for indirect and direct costs are difficult to accept. Generally, indirect injury costs exceed direct costs by factors of 3, 4, or more. In the Neumark et al. estimates, direct costs exceed indirect costs by threefold. (4) It is difficult to extrapolate the experience of one state to the entire United States. (5) They ignore recruitment and retraining expenses and disruption of work. (6) The forgone earnings estimate ignores fringe benefits. (7) The final injury estimate, $17 billion, is far less than WC expenses for the same year (Nelson 1992). (8) But the most serious criticism is the most obvious: the initial epidemiological study by the Pennsylvania Department of Health is not available for public scrutiny nor has it ever been published.

The Neumark et al. 1991 study nevertheless was the first to publish estimates for direct and indirect costs of occupational injuries *and* illnesses. In fact, they cited our papers as the only previous studies on the subject: Markowitz et al. 1989b (New Jersey) and Fahs et al. 1989 (New York). The Neumark et al. study was a pioneering study that proved useful. For example, we followed their approach to the NCCI medical data by multiplying numbers of injuries by NCCI average costs. Second, they, like us, explicitly ignored Willingness-to-Pay methods. Neumark et al. were skeptical of the reliability of WTP estimates (see chap. 4).

III.A.5. WC Data in Nelson 1992 and 1993; Burton,
Yates, and Blum 1997; and Boden and Fleishman 1989

Nelson. Every three to four years, the staff of the Social Security Administration used to generate national estimates on the annual prevalence costs of WC (Nelson 1992, 1993). Nelson culled data from a variety of sources, including A. M. Best Company (a national data-collecting agency for private insurance), the National Council on Compensation Insurance (NCCI), the federal Black Lung program, the federal Employees Compensation program, and the federal Longshoremen and Harbor Workers' Compensation program. The A. M. Best and NCCI data cover the traditional WC programs within the states. All other programs are federal and, technically, not part of the traditional state-based network of WC.

Rossman, Miller, and Douglas (1991, 32), Boden and Fleishman (1989), and Nelson (1993) estimate that roughly only 2 percent of WC costs cover illnesses. As a result, statements about the size of WC costs generally apply to injuries.

In 1991, Nelson estimated total WC premium costs of $55.2 billion (1992 estimates were never made). Roughly $42.1 billion of this was spent on benefits, and $13.1 billion was retained for administration expense. Of the $42.1 billion, roughly $16.8 went for medical costs and $25.3 went for indemnity costs.

Burton. John F. Burton Jr. is perhaps the most widely cited economist writing about the overall costs of WC. He produces national estimates of overall costs annually as well as providing extensive analyses of many WC economic issues every two months in his *Workers' Compensation Monitors* and his *WC Year Books* (Burton 1993; Burton and Schmidle 1994; Burton, Yates, and Blum 1997).

Burton makes extensive use of the data in Nelson 1992 and 1993 but also considers data from A. M. Best. He relies on econometric models to update Nelson's and Best's estimates.

He revised his methods in 1997 and adjusted upward all his previous estimates for the 1990s. Prior to the revisions, his estimates were $57 billion (1991) and $60 billion (1992). After his revisions, his estimates were $66.7 billion (1991) and $73.5 billion (1992). His estimate for 1996 was $92.7 billion.

Burton also finds that WC costs as a percentage of total payroll average 2.57 percent. From 1979 to 1990, Burton finds *total* benefits have shown an *annual* rate of increase of around 12.2 percent. These increases are due largely to the rising cost of medical care, growing numbers of people in the workforce, and the growing number of people filing successful claims.

Burton does not estimate medical only costs or indemnity only costs in 1992. He simply reproduces Nelson's estimates from 1990. In 1990, medical payments comprised 41 percent of all benefits paid, while indemnity payments comprised 59 percent of all benefits paid.

We know that $55.2 billion (Nelson) or $60 or $73.5 billion (Burton) are too low as estimates of *all* job-related injury costs. First, WC captures only about 45 percent of all injuries. Second, indemnity payments cover only about 50 percent of lost wages. Third, WC does not pay for lost fringe benefits or lost home production.

Boden and Fleishman. Boden and Fleishman (1989) were commissioned by the Workers' Compensation Research Institute to study time trends and state by state variations in WC costs. The analysis was based on information from 42 states and Washington, DC, and included data from 20 years — 1965 to 1985. The data were drawn from the NCCI and independent insurance rating bureaus in California, Massachusetts, Minnesota, New Jersey, New York, and Texas as well as from exclusive state funds. They did not analyze data from self-insured employers.

Boden and Fleishman's (1989) more important findings included these. (1) The rate of growth in WC medical costs was less than that of other non-WC medical costs from 1965 through 1977. The growth rate in WC medical costs began exceeding the rate for non-WC medical spending in the late 1970s and accelerated its pace in the 1980s. (2) The growth rate was high in some states and low in others. Low states or jurisdictions (for 1980 to 1988) included Washington, DC (2.2 percent), Arkansas (5.8 percent), Michigan (3.3 percent), North Carolina (4.6 percent), Ohio (4.2 percent), and Massachusetts (4.1 percent). High growth states included Texas (12.7 percent), Louisiana (13.5 percent), California (10.1 percent), Oregon (11.5 percent), and Oklahoma (11.3

percent). There were many reasons for the variation across states including the following: the high costs for medical services in some states and low costs in others; the industrial and occupational mix; and the financial parameters of WC payments. For example, states with long waiting periods (seven days) tended to have higher average costs than states with short waiting periods (three days). The longer the injured worker is away from the job, the more serious the injury is likely to be. (3) Finally, Boden and Fleishman documented a direct relationship between unemployment and *average* medical costs. After accounting for the secular upward trend in costs, as unemployment increased (decreased), *average* medical costs for workers' compensation increased (decreased). They explained these results this way.

> During recessions, less experienced workers — those with more, but generally less severe, injuries — are laid off first. With the declining incidence of less severe injuries, average severity increases. During periods of high unemployment, the duration of indemnity benefit payments increases because injured workers have more difficulty finding jobs . . . average medical costs per claim go up. Another product of increased duration is more litigation about the timing of return to work, which itself increases medical costs. . . .
>
> . . . Unemployment rates generally were higher in the 1980s than in the 1960s. Because higher unemployment is associated with greater average severity of injuries, claim duration, and medical-legal costs, worsening labor market conditions may account for part of the acceleration in the growth of per-claim medical costs.

III.B. Studies Not Dealing Exclusively with Job-Related Injuries

III.B.1. Rice et al. 1989a and Max, Rice, and MacKenzie 1990

Rice et al. (1989a) and Max, Rice, and MacKenzie (1990) analyzed incidence cost of all injuries for 1985. Rice et al. is the most widely cited study on the costs of injuries for all persons of all ages (infants, as well as the elderly, were included). They had a number of notable findings and methods. (1) In 1985, 56.9 million persons were injured, including 143,000 fatalities, 2.3 million injured persons requiring hospitalizations, and 54.4 million nonhospitalized injuries requiring medical attention or resulting in one or more days of restricted activity. (2) 13,000 of the 143,000 deaths were for people who died after 1985 due to injuries sustained in 1985. (3) In 1985, costs were $157.6 billion, or $2,772 per injured person. Direct costs amounted to 29 percent of total costs. Morbidity costs were 41 percent, and mortality costs were 30 percent. (4) Men generated a little over two dollars of costs for every one dollar generated by women. (5) The researchers accounted for home production and assigned different amounts depending upon age and gender. Men were assumed to contribute the equivalent of roughly 7.7 percent of their wages in home production, and women were assumed to contribute the equivalent of 38 percent of their wages in home production. (6) The Rice et al. estimates do not rely on a single source for their costs. They could not, given that there is no national data set on injuries and costs. Many studies were cited, and myriad assumptions were made in their explanations for their calculations on their pages 72 to 81. (7) They point out that "the data sets employed differ significantly as to how the cost data can be broken down, necessitating many assumptions. For this reason, a breakdown of costs by causes, nature, or intent of injury would be unjustified by the available data."

We have several advantages over Rice et al. 1989a. First, we were able to rely on the CFOI, NTOF, SDS, and Annual Survey, which are large government efforts specifically designed to count job-related injuries. Apart from the NHIS, no government efforts exist to count all injuries. And, as we have seen, the NHIS has some severe limitations, especially when injuries involve violent acts.

Second, we rely on WC data from over 40 states collected and distributed by the NCCI. The cost data in the NCCI reports pertain directly to job-related injuries. Again, there are no firms or agencies collecting such a large amount of primary data for all injuries combined. Moreover, the NCCI provided data on indemnity or wage loss benefits on nonfatal injuries that allowed us to generate estimates of indirect morbidity costs. Unlike Rice et al. (1989a) we did not have to estimate how many days of work loss would have resulted from a given injury and then multiply that by an assumed wage.[29]

III.B.2. Violence: Max and Rice 1993

Murders are a leading cause of job-related deaths for lawyers, taxi drivers, restaurant and bar managers, gas station attendants, sales managers, bank tellers, cashiers, secretaries, parking attendants, guards, bartenders, entertainers, waiters and waitresses, receptionists, janitors, general managers, and convenience store clerks (Leigh 1995a). These murders more often than not involved robberies — not worker, co-worker, or supervisor quarrels. These murders could be reduced by requiring armed guards at all late-night convenience gas and liquor stores, restaurants, taverns, and so on (Friedman 1994). In light of this evidence, we view the Max and Rice 1993 study on the costs of firearm fatal and nonfatal injuries.

The Max and Rice 1993 estimates were incidence based. In 1988, "firearm injuries resulted in nearly 34,000 deaths including 1,801 unintentional deaths, 18,169 suicides, 13,645 homicides, and 442 deaths of unknown intent." Many of these deaths occurred among young people, so that the years of potential life lost were staggering: 1,350,467 in 1985.

They also found that the ratio of fatal to nonfatal injuries was much higher for firearm injuries than all other injuries. For every fatal firearm injury, there were 7.4 nonfatal injuries. But the ratio is closer to 1 to 2,000 for every non-firearm-related occupational injury. Firearm injuries are more likely to result in death than any other category of injury.

The total costs of firearm injuries in 1985 were estimated to be $14.4 billion, of which about 66 percent was for lost productivity and 33 percent was for medical costs.

III.B.3. Vehicle Crashes: Blincoe and Faigin 1992

The Blincoe and Faigin 1992 study appears to be the most comprehensive of all studies on the costs of vehicle crashes. Unlike prior studies on the costs of vehicle crashes, Blincoe and Faigin included property damage, costs of uninjured occupants, legal and court costs, workplace disruption, and delay costs. Theirs was an incidence cost study, and they also used a 4 percent discount rate on future dollars.

Editors of the *Morbidity and Mortality Weekly Report* (a government publication) summarized the Blincoe and Faigin 1992 estimates of costs on motor vehicle crashes this way.

> Motor-vehicle crashes during 1990 accounted for 44,531 fatalities, 5.4 million non-fatal injuries, and 28 million damaged vehicles, and an estimated total cost of $137.5 billion. Major sources for cost were property damage ($45.7 billion; 33 percent), productivity losses in the workplace ($39.8 billion; 29 percent), medical care expenses (13.9 billion; 10 percent), and losses related to household productivity ($10.8 billion; 8 percent).
>
> The greatest unit cost was associated with fatalities — approximately $702,000 per fatality. The economic impact of motor vehicle crashes during 1990 was approximately 2.5 percent of the Gross Domestic Product in the United States. Although most motor-

vehicle crashes involved no injury, crashes resulting in injuries and fatalities accounted for three-fourths of all crash costs. Nearly 30 percent of the first-year medical costs of hospitalized persons injured in a motor-vehicle crash in the United States is paid by federal, state, and local government sources such as Medicaid and Medicare.

In addition, Blincoe and Faigin found that approximately 22 percent of people in crashes involving injuries did not file a police report. This is a significant finding. Apparently the problem of inadequate records is not unique to workers' compensation reports.

III.B.4. Other Studies

A literature search did not uncover any comprehensive study of job-related injury costs in other countries. However, there are a number of related studies. A particularly notable one is by Oxenburgh (1991). Oxenburgh produced a "how to" book for Australian businesses. The "how to" here refers to the methods whereby simple cost-benefit analyses of safety and health measures can be assessed on a firm-by-firm basis. His thesis is that businesses would invest more in safety and health if only they knew the considerable costs, sometimes hidden costs, associated with injuries and illnesses. Oxenburgh focuses on injuries, however, given the easier task of identifying job-related injuries as opposed to job-related illnesses. Oxenburgh points out that practical business people ought to be aware that injuries and illnesses can reduce profit through increasing the need for overtime and adding the costs of extra staffing, training, and lost morale in addition to the traditional lost production time due to an absent employee. Oxenburgh does not produce a total estimate for Australia.

The OSHA is sometimes compared to the EPA. The Environmental Protection Agency (EPA) has produced an in-house study of the costs of pollution. That cost was estimated to be $1.3 trillion in 1990 (Crandall, Rueter, and Steger 1996, 46). However, the EPA methodology relied on WTP methods and, to our knowledge, has yet to be published.

IV. Conclusion

Table 5.6 summarizes our cost findings. Our direct costs ($38.3802) and our indirect costs ($94.3307) sum to $132.7109 billion. We believe our cost analysis is more reliable than any prior study. We include home production losses, fringe benefits losses, insurance administrative costs on medical care and indemnity, and workplace training losses. We believe these are underestimates. Because of data limitations we did not account for property damage, time delays, police and fire services, family home health care, costs to innocent third parties, and pain and suffering.

The major point of our review of the existing literature is to affirm that our methods and assumptions are reasonable. In as many cases as possible, we relied on the literature to support our methods and assumptions. We did not create new methods.

We compare our estimates with a number of other studies, including three explicitly on occupational injuries and illnesses. The National Safety Council (NSC) (1993) estimated $116 billion of costs for injuries only in 1992. But the NSC ignored assault, murder, suicide, and other acts of violence. Moreover, the NSC relied on the National Health Interview Survey (NHIS), which we believe underestimates job-related injuries. Marquis (1992) estimated the direct and indirect costs of injuries to be roughly $83.2 billion in 1989. But the Marquis study greatly underestimated nondisabling injuries; ignored deaths; ignored assaults and acts of violence; and undersurveyed the poor, who are more likely to experience job-related injuries than middle or upper income groups; and the dollars applied to 1989, not 1992. Miller and Galbraith (1994) estimated $96.6 billion in costs. But Miller and Galbraith relied on the NHIS, and their cost applied to 1990. Finally, we do not believe that any of the studies we reviewed, including the three national studies on job-related injuries, properly accounted for insurance administration costs.

The next chapter considers the cost of occupational illnesses.

CHAPTER 6

Costs of Disease

by Marianne Fahs and J. Paul Leigh

1. Introduction

In this chapter we present estimates of the costs of occupational diseases and conditions for 1992. We use similar cost categories and the same general methodology as in chapter 5. We rely on the epidemiological estimates in chapter 3. We consider the six leading causes of death and morbidity: cancer, cardiovascular and cerebrovascular disease (circulatory disease), chronic respiratory disease, pneumoconiosis, nervous system disorders, and renal disorders. These diseases garner our greatest attention because they generate the greatest costs. We also estimate costs for nonfatal occupational illnesses and conditions such as carpal tunnel syndrome.

II. Method

II.A. Introduction to Method

We again rely on the Human Capital method to apportion costs between direct and indirect components. Unlike our methods with injury, however, our methods for estimating direct costs of disease will mix prevalence with incidence approaches. We use the incidence approach for nonfatal diseases and conditions — just as we did for nonfatal injuries. Reasonably good data are available on the numbers of new cases (BLS's Annual Survey) and the price per case (Neumark et al. 1991). The same cannot be said for fatalities and costs involving the six deadly diseases (cancer, circulatory, and so on). We adopt the prevalence approach for counting and measuring direct costs for the six deadly diseases. On the other hand, incidence data for indirect costs were available, and so the incidence method is applied to indirect costs for fatalities and nonfatal illnesses alike. Our mixed incidence and prevalence approach is consistent with the literature on counting and estimating costs for these diseases (Markowitz et al. 1989a; Fahs et al. 1989) as well as most studies on the costs of other illnesses (Rice and Hodgson 1985; Rice 1966; Hodgson 1982; Yelin and Callahan 1995).

The reason the majority of researchers use the prevalence method for measuring the direct costs is that an incidence approach is not feasible unless numerous questionable assumptions are invoked. Consider what an incidence study for cancer must assume. We must first assume a worker is exposed to a carcinogen in 1992 or an accumulation of years through 1992. Second, we must assume when that worker will manifest the cancer after that exposure. This might be one or perhaps 40 years later. Third, we must assume (guess?) some time course for the natural history of a cancer, the severity of the disability that results, and the therapies that will be attempted one to 40 years into the future. Fourth, we must assume (guess?) when and if a cancer will kill a worker. Finally, we must assume costs for treatment and costs surrounding the possible cancer death from 1992 through perhaps 2042.

On the other hand, the prevalence method for estimating direct costs is straightforward since it involves only numbers and costs from 1992. Consequently, virtually all chronic illness cost studies use prevalence, not incidence.

Indirect costs for 1992 and beyond are easily estimated, given the prevalence of disease and direct costs from 1992. The disease death and morbidity are analyzed just as an injury death would be analyzed in 1992: we simply calculate the present value of lost earnings, home production, and so on, from 1992 on. If morbidity results, we estimate the present value in lost earnings, home production, and so on, from 1992.

In short, our mixed incidence/prevalence method is not confusing. We simply treat all of the disease estimates from chapter 3 as if they were new illnesses. However, the direct cost estimate for the six diseases will take a macro, or "top-down," approach. The estimate of direct costs for the nonfatal diseases as well as the estimate for indirect costs for the six deadly diseases and the nonfatal illnesses will take a micro, or "bottom-up," approach.

II.B. Macro or Direct Cost Approach for the Six Diseases

Our "top-down" approach is similar to that of Fahs et al. (1989, 1998), Rice, Hodgson, and Kopstein (1985), and Rice et al. (1989a). Estimates rely on ratios involving hospital days multiplied by national estimates of medical spending.[1] These hospital day ratios act as anchors in the estimation of all direct costs. Hospitalization data are highly regarded, are collected annually, and are summarized within the same definitions, thus permitting comparisons across diseases. Similar data are not available for doctor's visits or drug use. Moreover, hospitalizations are the most expensive (broad) category of medical care, contributing to 44.6 percent of medical costs in 1992. Doctors' services were second at 20.9 percent (Burner and Waldo 1995). We assume that spending on all other direct costs is proportional to hospital spending.

Our "top-down" approach begins with an estimate of national expenditures on medical care — $820.3 billion, or 13.6 percent of the gross domestic product in 1992. This is equivalent to spending of $3,086 per person. Medicare and Medicaid contributed 16.9 and 13.2 percent; other third-party government spending contributed 13.6 percent; direct out-of-pocket expenditures contributed 18.9 percent. The remainder, 37.9 percent, was contributed by private health insurance and HMOs. This $820.3 billion in health care expenditures included payments for hospitalizations, doctor and dentist visits, nursing home care, drugs, and medical supplies. The figure also includes public health care expenditures, such as construction of hospitals and offices, government public health activities, and research, as well as some estimate of "program administration and net cost of public health insurance" (Burner and Waldo 1995). We include public health care expenditures on the grounds that without these occupational diseases, some portion of these public expenditures would not be necessary. We did not include the last category, "program administration," in our calculations, however. We believe it is an underestimate. The NCHS believes this amount to be $39.5 billion. This would be the equivalent of $(39.5/780.8 = 0.0506)$, roughly 5.06 percent of expenditures. Studies have shown that administrative costs can add an additional 3 to 45 percent to the total cost of medical care (Woolhandler and Himmelstein 1991; Thorpe 1992; Danzon 1992; Cutler 1994). Cutler's (1994) estimate of 15 percent appears to be the most reliable, and it is the one we used in chapter 5. As a result, we will exclude the $39.5 billion but ultimately include a 15 percent administrative expense in our calculations. We therefore use $820.3 - 39.5 = 780.8 to begin our calculations.

Using the National Hospital Discharge Survey (Graves 1994), we then calculate the total number of days spent in the hospital by patients with a primary diagnosis for each of the attributable occupational diseases in chapter 3. Total days of hospitalization by one of the six diseases are then divided by total hospital days for all diseases and injuries in the United States in 1992 (190,386,000). This percentage is then multiplied by $780.8, which in turn is multiplied by the ratio of occupational deaths to total deaths from chapter 3. The procedure can be displayed in equation (6.1), which calculates the estimate for cancer.

Med$Cancer = $780.8 × (Cancer Days/Total Days) ×
(OccCancerDeaths/TotCancerDeaths),   (6.1)

where
Med$Cancer = medical dollars spent for occupational cancers;
CancerDays = number of days in the hospital attributed to
            cancer;
TotalDays = number of days in the hospital attributed to *all*
            diseases and injuries in the United States in 1992;
OccCancerDeaths = number of cancer deaths attributed to
            occupations (from chap. 3);
TotCancerDeaths = total number of cancer death due to all
            causes.

Formulas—such as (6.1)—for each disease generate cost estimates for each of the six diseases. These estimates will not include an estimate of the administrative costs, however. To obtain each of these for the six diseases, we assume (1) $630.2 billion of spending was conducted by insurance companies and governments ($150.6 billion by individuals in out-of-pocket expenditures is subtracted from $780.8 to obtain $630.2), and (2) the average of private and public insurance administrative costs is 15 percent (Cutler 1994 and chap. 5). Our effective multiplier is 0.1211 ((0.15 × 630.2)/780.8), which is multiplied by the preceding estimate to derive the overall administrative costs.

These calculations are carried out in row 10 of table 6.1. To account for administrative costs, we add an additional 15 percent as indicated in rows 10 and 11. Insurance administration is assumed to be 15 percent of one-half of lost earnings. In other words, following our discussion in chapter 5, we assume an earnings replacement rate of 50 percent and an administrative charge of 15 percent on indemnity and survivor's payments.[2] Row 12 presents our grand total—$10.5978 billion.

II.C. Indirect Costs for the Six Deadly Diseases

Indirect costs were estimated using the present value equation in chapter 5 on the costs of injuries. Unlike in the injury application, however, no one was assumed to have a labor force participation rate of 1.0 beyond age 65. We simply used the labor force participation rates for all Americans.[3] Information for use in the present value equation applied to age-specific, sex-specific, and disease-specific mortality data from the National Center for Health Statistics, Vital Statistics Division, as well as life table estimates (U.S. National Center for Health Statistics 1993b; U.S. Department of Health and Human Services 1993, 1994; Rogot, Sorlie, and Johnson 1992) and earnings and labor force participation data from the Bureau of Labor Statistics, *Employment and Earnings.* By applying the attributable risk proportions, presented in chapter 3, to the total estimates of individual costs by disease, the present value of the indirect cost of premature mortality is estimated for the base year 1992.

Finally, we calculated national disease-specific ratios for morbidity costs to direct costs and for morbidity costs to mortality costs (Rice, Hodgson, and Kopstein 1985; Rice et al. 1989b) to obtain an estimate of the morbidity costs for the occupational diseases that comprise the major causes of death. Two different recent estimates were obtained. These can be illustrated with equations (6.2) and (6.3) as they apply to cancer.

Our first estimate of morbidity costs for cancer = (Rice's morbidity costs for cancer/Rice's direct costs for cancer) ×
our direct cost for cancer. (6.2)

Our second estimate of morbidity costs for cancer = (Rice's morbidity costs for cancer/Rice's mortality costs) × our mortality costs. (6.3)

The "Rice" in the preceding equations refers to the estimates of Rice, Hodgson, and Kopstein (1985) and Rice et al. (1989b).

II.D. Direct and Indirect Costs for Nonfatal Conditions

To obtain the medical costs for nonfatal conditions, we multiplied the number of new cases times the average cost per case. Numbers of new cases are estimated in chapter 3. Average costs per case are derived from NCCI data and a dermatologist survey in Neumark et al. 1991, as well as from Feurstein et al. 1998 for carpal tunnel syndrome. Following our injury method, again, 31 percent and 15 percent insurance administrative costs were assumed. The 31 percent applies to the BLS estimate, assuming the BLS numbers were reported to WC.[4] The 15 percent applied to all other costs except those that were assumed to be out of pocket. Morbidity costs were calculated by multiplying days lost by wage rates, fringe benefits rates, and home production rates.

TABLE 6.1. Direct Costs Only

Row	Neoplasms; Cancer (codes: 140–239)	Circulatory System (codes: 390–459)	Chronic Respiratory Diseases (COPD) (codes: 490–496)	Pneumoconiosis (codes: 500–505)	Nervous System Disorders (codes: 323.7, 331, 332, 349.82, 356, 357.7, 359.4)	Renal Disorders (codes: 580–589)	Total
1 Disease hospital days[a] (in thousands)	15,379	39,379	5,052	21[b]	487[c]	892[d]	
2 Total hospital days[a] (in thousands)	190,386	190,386	190,386	109,299[b]	190,386	190,386	
3 Ratio of disease/total	0.08603	0.20884	0.02655	0.000192	0.002558	0.004685	
4 National spending[e,f] (in $ billions)	$780.8	$780.8	$780.8	$780.8	$780.8	$780.8	
5 National spending × ratio of disease/total	$67.1722	$163.0623	$20.7302	$0.1499	$1.9973	$3.6580	
6 Total deaths[g]	517,090	913,908	91,541	1,136	26,936	22,957	
7 Occupational deaths	41,367	7,638	9,154	1,136	538	460	

8 Ratio of occupational to total deaths	0.0799	0.0083575	0.1000	100%	0.02	0.02	
9 Row 5 × row 8	$5.3731	$1.3628	$2.0730	$0.1499	$0.03995	$0.07316	$9.07191
10 15% administration costs on all medical costs except out-of-pocket expenses[h]	$0.65068	$0.1650	$0.2511	$0.01815	$0.0048	$0.00886	$1.09859
11 15% administration costs on 1/2 of all lost earnings	$0.2481	$0.0978	$0.0641	$0.0108	$0.0023	$0.0042	$0.4273
12 Total	$6.2725	$1.6256	$2.3882	$0.1789	$0.0471	$0.08626	$10.5978

[a]Graves 1994.
[b]Number of discharges, not days. Hospital days were not available for pneumoconiosis.
[c]Hospital days were only available for 331, 332, 349.8, and 356.
[d]Hospital days were only available for 581, 583, 584, 585, and 586.
[e]Excludes NCHS category for "Program administration and net cost of private health insurance."
[f]Burne and Waldo 1995.
[g]Kochanek and Hudson 1994; and preprints from the NCHS.
[h]$780.8 - 150.6 = 630.25$; $15\% \times 630.2 = 94.53$; $94.53/780.8 = 12.11\%$. Thus this is equivalent to 12.11%.

III. Results

III.A. Fatal Diseases

III.A.1. Direct Costs

Table 6.1 presents the numbers for each of the variables mentioned in equation (6.1). Diseases are listed across the top. Variables that enter equation (6.1) are listed along the left side of table 6.1.

The hospital days and national health care spending are drawn from Graves 1994. These variables occupy the first five rows. In row 1, the hospital days for the specific disease are included. For example, hospital days for cancer were 15,379,000. Row 2 includes hospital days for all diseases and injuries: 190,386,000. This number is the same for each column. Row 3 presents the ratio of row 1 numbers to row 2 numbers, for example, for cancer that is 15,379/190,389 or 0.08603. Row 4 provides the estimate of national spending, excluding what the NCHS terms *program and administrative costs:* $780.8. Row 5 multiplies entries in row 3 with entries in row 4, for example, 0.08603 × $780.8 = $67.1722.

Row 6 presents all U.S. deaths regardless of age in one of the six categories. Row 7 presents our estimate of the numbers of deaths due to occupations. The ratio of occupational to total U.S. deaths is entered into row 8. Row 9 multiplies row 7 by row 8. Rows 10 and 11 adjust for administrative costs, and row 12 presents the totals. The grand total— $10.5978 billion—appears in the lower right-hand side. We did not adjust for age since age was implicitly accounted for in row 8.

III.A.2. Indirect Costs

Table 6.2 describes the indirect mortality and morbidity costs for the six deadly diseases. Diseases are listed across the top, in the columns. Numbers of deaths and categories of indirect costs are listed along the left-hand side in the rows. The numbers of deaths are drawn from chapter 3. The estimates on the gender composition are unique to this chapter. We assume 62 percent of the deaths among males and 38 percent among females. These percentages correspond to the gender contribution to employment in 1970. We use 1970 because these diseases generally require years of exposure to a risk and years of gestation. We did not use the male/female percentages for all deaths in 1992 since they would not reflect job-related gender differences. We did not adjust for any gender differences in the type of employment; that is, men are likely to hold a disproportionately greater number of blue-collar jobs than are women, and blue-collar jobs likely expose workers to more risks than white-collar jobs. Our pneumoconiosis estimates from chapter 3 apply only to men, however.

In calculating lost earnings, fringe benefits, and home production, we assumed the same age structure for occupational deaths as for all deaths in a given disease. These data are drawn from Kochanek and Hudson 1994 and National Center for Health Statistics 1996. Again, we assumed that no disease develops before age 25 and for circulatory disease, after age 64.

Cancer contributed the most: $3.984 billion for mortality and $0.662 for morbidity. Again, the mortality costs are derived from the economic production and home production that were lost because the person died prematurely. The morbidity costs are derived from those persons who contract cancer, experience some disability and lost economic and home production, but do not die from cancer.

The second greatest amount of indirect cost arise from circulatory disease: $1.570 billion for mortality and $0.261 billion for morbidity. Chronic respiratory disease is third with a total amount of $1.201 billion followed by pneumoconioses with $0.192, renal disease with $0.08 billion, and nervous system disorders with $0.044. We were able to estimate morbidity costs for all diseases since our estimating technique relied on ratios from Rice, Hodgson, and Kopstein 1985 and Rice et al. 1989b, not on the incidence of new disease in chapter 3.

Our totals for all diseases are listed in the lower right-hand corner: $6.175 for mortality, $1.819 for morbidity and $7.994 for the sum.

But this $7.994 figure does not include government program and insurance administrative costs for indemnity and survivor's payments. Indemnity is not the same as for injuries, however. WC covers a significant amount of job-related injuries. WC covers very little of disease, and most of these will be in the nonfatal categories reported to the BLS, which we account for in the section on the Annual Survey, which follows. Virtually all of these indemnity payments would be paid by the Social Security Administration for worker's death prior to retirement (survivor benefits) or for Social Security Disability Insurance (SSDI). To calculate these administrative costs we assume a 50 percent earnings-replacement rate and a 15 percent administrative cost out of indemnity (these are the same percentages we assumed in chap. 5 for non-WC payments). This $0.4273 of indemnity administration costs is accounted for in row 11 of table 6.1 since it is technically a direct cost.

TABLE 6.2. Indirect Mortality and Morbidity Costs

	Cancer	Circulatory Diseases	Chronic Respiratory Diseases	Pneumo-conioses	Nervous System Disorders	Renal Disease	Total
Number of deaths							
Female[a]	15,719	4,736	3,479	0	204	175	24,313
Male	25,648	2,902	5,675	1,136	334	285	35,980
Total	41,367	7,638	9,154	1,136	538	460	60,293
Lost earnings (in $ millions)							
Mortality	2,917	1,141	353	59	18	25	4,513
Morbidity[b]	485	190	525	88	14	30	1,332
Total	3,402	1,331	878	147	32	55	5,845
Lost fringe benefits (in $ millions)							
Mortality	680	266	82	14	4	6	1,052
Morbidity[b]	113	44	122	21	3	7	197
Total	793	310	204	35	7	13	1,362

Lost home production (in $ millions)							
Mortality	387	163	48	4	3	5	610
Morbidity[b]	64	27	71	6	2	6	176
Total	451	190	119	10	5	11	786
Total lost earnings, benefits, productions (in $ millions)							
Mortality	3,984	1,570	483	77	25	36	6,175
Morbidity[b]	662	261	718	115	19	44	1,819
Total	4,646	1,831	1,201	192	44	80	7,994

Source: Current study.

[a] We assume 62% deaths among males and 38% among females. This 62/38 split corresponds to the percentage contributed to employment in 1970.

[b] We assume the same morbidity to mortality cost ratios as Rice, Hodgson, and Kopstein (1985) and Rice, Hodgson, and Capell (1989b).

III.A.3. Total Costs

Table 6.3 describes the total costs for the six deadly diseases. Cost categories appear along the left-hand side. Direct costs were split into medical costs and administrative costs. Administrative costs in turn apply in part to spending for medical care and in part to spending for indemnity benefits from, for example, the Social Security Administration. Indirect costs are also split into the categories of mortality costs and morbidity costs. These morbidity costs in table 6.3 relied on the calculations in equation (6.2); that is, they were anchored to mortality costs in Rice, Hodgson, and Kopstein 1985.

The direct costs include persons who die in 1992 as well as those who survive but are treated, for example, for cancer in 1992. The indirect costs explicitly account for those dying and those surviving with mortality and morbidity costs.

Cancer generates the greatest costs with $10.9185 billion, followed by chronic respiratory disease ($3.579 billion) and cerebrovascular and cardiovascular disease ($3.4566 billion). The first three — cancer, circulatory, and chronic respiratory — accounted for roughly 96 percent of the cost of the six deadly diseases combined. The rank order of the remaining diseases is pneumoconioses ($0.3809 billion), renal disorders ($0.167 billion), and nervous system disorders ($0.091 billion). Overall, roughly 57 percent of these costs arise in the direct category and 43 percent in the indirect. This is in contrast to the injuries, for which roughly 32 percent was estimated to direct cost and 68 percent to indirect cost. The explanation is simple: injury deaths occur more frequently than disease deaths among young workers. Finally, total mortality costs are roughly 3 1/3 times total morbidity costs. Again, there is a simple explanation: the highest morbidity to mortality cost ratios were for cancer and circulatory diseases. Lost work and home production are generally far larger for a premature death than a flare-up of cancer or circulatory disease from which the patient might fully or even partially recover. Pneumoconioses and, to a lesser extent, chronic respiratory disease do not fit this pattern. Both of these conditions frequently result in slow deterioration, disability, and eventually death. Considerable morbidity costs therefore result.

In order to assess the reliability of our morbidity estimates, we performed a sensitivity analysis. We analyzed the effect on our results of the assumptions used to estimate morbidity costs. To perform the sensitivity analysis, we calculated morbidity costs two ways. In tables 6.2 and 6.3, we presented estimates based on the calculations of morbidity cost as a ratio to mortality costs. In Leigh et al. 1996 we present estimates based on the calculation of mortality costs as a ratio to direct costs (Rice,

TABLE 6.3. Total Costs of Fatal Occupational Diseases by Direct and Indirect Costs by Disease (midpoint estimates) (costs in $ billions)

	Cancer	Cerebrovascular and Cardiovascular Disease	Chronic Respiratory Disease	Pneumoconioses	Nervous System Disorders	Renal Disorders	Total
Direct cost	6.2725	1.6256	2.3882	0.1789	0.0471	0.08626	10.5978
Medical cost	5.3731	1.3628	2.0730	0.1499	0.03995	0.07316	9.0719
Administration							
Medical administration	0.65068	0.1650	0.2511	0.01815	0.0048	0.0089	1.0986
Indemnity administration	0.2481	0.0978	0.0641	0.0108	0.0023	0.0042	0.4273
Indirect cost	4.646	1.831	1.201	0.202	0.044	0.0800	7.994
Mortality	3.984	1.570	0.483	0.077	0.025	0.036	6.175
Morbidity	0.662	0.261	0.718	0.115	0.019	0.044	1.819
Total	10.9185	3.4566	3.5792	0.3809	0.0911	0.16626	18.5918[a]

Source: U.S. Health Care Financing Administration, *Health Care Financing Review* fall 1994; Graves 1994; National Nursing Home Survey, National Center for Health Statistics 1985; Medical Care Component, Consumer Price Index, U.S. Bureau of Labor Statistics, Department of Labor 1995; Money Income of Households, Families and Persons in the United States 1992; U.S. Bureau of the Census 1993.

[a]Rows and columns may not exactly sum due to rounding.

Hodgson, and Kopstein 1985; Rice et al. 1989b). We find the method used did not affect the final estimate of total cost of occupational disease. The total economic cost estimates varied by less than 3 percent at midpoint.[5]

Indemnity administrative costs are the smallest category in table 6.3. Indemnity administrative costs arise from WC and Social Security Administration of indemnity payments to survivors of the illness. That is, these costs only apply to morbidity costs.

Table 6.4 presents the range for the total cost using the percentages identified in chapter 3. Diseases are listed down the left-hand side of table 6.4. The widest ranges are for cancer and circulatory diseases, whereas the narrowest ranges are for pneumoconioses and chronic respiratory disease. Overall, our estimate of the lower bound for all costs of these six diseases is $14.6 billion; the upper bound is $22.6 billion.

III.B. Nonfatal Diseases and Conditions

III.B.1. Direct Costs

Table 6.5 presents the number and estimated total medical costs of new cases of nonfatal occupational illness. These costs amount to over $2.0

TABLE 6.4.   Range of Total Costs of Fatal Occupational Diseases
(costs in $ billions)

Disease	Percentage Range[b]	Low Estimate	High Estimate	Midpoint Estimate
	Total Costs[a]			
Cancer	6–10	8.1889	13.6481	10.9185
Cardiovascular and cerebrovascular disease	5–10	2.3044	4.6088	3.4566
Chronic respiratory disease	10	3.5792	3.5792	3.5792
Pneumoconiosis	100	0.3809	0.3809	0.0911
Nervous system disorders	1–3	0.055	0.1367	0.1078
Renal disorders	1–3	0.08315	0.2495	0.1663
Total		14.6016	22.6031	18.5918

Source: U.S. Health Care Financing Administration, *Health Care Financing Review* fall 1994; Graves 1994; National Nursing Home Survey, National Center for Health Statistics 1985; Medical Care Component, Consumer Price Index, U.S. Bureau of Labor Statistics, Department of Labor 1995; Money Income of Households, Families and Persons in the United States 1992; U.S. Bureau of the Census 1993.
[a]All cost estimates are in 1992 dollars.
[b]Estimated proportions are from chapter 3.

TABLE 6.5. Direct Medical Costs for Nonfatal Diseases and Conditions

Disease/Condition	Number of New Cases	Average Cost ($)	Total[a] Cost ($)
Skin diseases (e.g., dermatitis, eczema, rash, chemical burns)	62,900 132,276[b]	404[c]	53,440,594
Dust diseases (e.g., pneumoconioses)	2,800 5,888[b]	See table 6.1[d]	
Respiratory conditions due to toxic agents	23,500 49,420[b]	3,280[e]	162,097,600
Poisonings	3,500[f]		
BLS	7,360	3,208[e]	23,610,880
Lead surveillance (chap. 3)	14,500[b]		45,714,000
Disorders due to physical agents (e.g., sunstroke)	22,200 46,687[b]	3,280[e]	153,132,040
Disorders associated with repeated trauma (e.g., carpal tunnel syndrome)	281,800 592,625[b]	2,674[g]	1,584,680,300
All other illnesses	55,815[h] 117,379[b]	3,280[e]	385,003,120
Total			2,022,675,200

[a]Administrative costs are not included in this table. They are calculated as follows: 31% on $1.063 billion plus 15% on $1.172 billion. We assume that WC covers the same illnesses reported to the BLS ($1.063 billion) but not those illnesses not reported ($1.172 billion). We assume 19.3% of 1.172 paid with out-of-pocket funds (1.172 − out-of-pocket percentage) × 0.15 = $0.1419 billion, 1.063 × 0.31 = 0.3295.

[b]We assume the same undercount that applies to BLS injuries applies to BLS illnesses: (13.337/6.342 = 2.103). Our adjustment accounts for the fact that the Annual Survey does not count illnesses among federal, state, and local government workers, and the self-employed, and the economic incentives to underreport.

[c]Drawn from Neumark et al. 1991: $315 × inflation adjustment where $315 is average cost to treat dermatitis in 1988.

[d]Dust diseases are accounted for with morbidity costs for pneumoconioses in table 6.1.

[e]Estimated with our average injury cost data and average injury cost and average illness cost from Neumark et al. (1991): $1,938 × ($6,825/$4,033) where $1,938 is our average medical cost per injury; $6,825 and $4,033 are average medical costs for illnesses and injuries from Neumark et al. 1991.

[f]Excludes 3,500 BLS cases that are assumed to be accounted for in lead surveillance.

[g]Average cost for carpal tunnel syndrome from Feurstein et al. 1998 minus inflation adjustment since the Feurstein et al. 1998 data were for 1994.

billion. Administrative costs can be calculated by assuming 31 percent of the illnesses likely covered by WC ($1.063 billion) and 15 percent on the remainder excluding out-of-pocket expense. These calculations yield $0.3294 + $0.1419 + $0.4713. Total direct cost of nonfatal disease would then be $2.023 for medical and $0.4713 for administration costs, or $2.4943 total.

We assume that all cases in table 6.5 are acute conditions. We assume these cases are resolved during the year and that full recovery ensues. That is, the costs end December 31, 1992. This is a conservative assumption. Hearing loss is permanent, and perhaps later in life a person will purchase a hearing aid. Several severe acute respiratory conditions can permanently compromise lung capacity. Acute skin diseases can leave the skin especially sensitive to any harmful exposures in the future. In the interest of simplicity and being conservative, we ignore all these possible future complications associated with the diseases and conditions mentioned in table 6.5.

III.B.2. Indirect Costs

Table 6.6 presents our calculations for indirect costs. Diseases and conditions appear across the top of the table. Statistics and calculations are described on the left-hand side corresponding to the rows.

Numbers of new cases are in row 1. The percentage involving days lost are in row 2. This percentage information is only available at the aggregated "all illnesses" level; hence it is the same for every disease or condition — 48.73 percent. Row 3 multiplies the number of new cases by the percentage involving days lost. We conservatively assume that illnesses that do not generate at least one day of work loss do not count. This is conservative because many cases may involve one to seven hours of work loss yet still not be counted as a full day of work loss.

The median days lost data were drawn from a table in the Annual Survey that does not exactly follow the same classifications as appear across the top of table 6.5. Skin diseases, respiratory conditions, physical agents, heatstroke, and so on, had corresponding categories on all Annual Survey tables. Repeated trauma and "all other" did not. We substituted carpal tunnel syndrome for repeated trauma and the average for all illnesses for "all other."

Wages are drawn from U.S. Bureau of the Census 1993a. Fringe benefits were estimated to be 23.3 percent (chap. 5). Home production averages 13.79 percent of earnings.

The entries in row 10 sum to $1.410 billion (see row 11), our estimate of indirect cost. Many of these illnesses will generate indemnity

TABLE 6.6. Indirect Costs for BLS Nonfatal Diseases and Conditions

Row	Statistics and Calculations	Skin Disorders	Respiratory Conditions	Poisonings	Disorders Due to Physical Agents	Repeated Trauma	Others	Total
1	Number of new cases	132,276	49,420	21,610	46,687	592,625	117,379	
2	Percentage involving days lost[a]	48.73%	48.73%	48.73%	48.73%	48.73%	48.73%	
3	Row 1 × row 2	64,458	24,082	10,531	22,751	288,786	57,199	
4	Median days lost	3[b]	5[b]	2[b]	3[b]	32[b]	5[b]	
5	Row 3 × row 4 (total days lost)	193,374	120,410	21,062	68,253	9,241,152	285,995	
6	Wages per day[c]	$103.59	$103.59	$103.59	$103.59	$103.59	$103.59	
7	Fringe benefits (per day, % of wages)	23.3%	23.3%	23.3%	23.3%	23.3%	23.3%	
8	Home production (per day, % of wages)	13.79%	13.79%	13.79%	13.79%	13.79%	13.79%	
9	Row 6 + row 7 + row 8	$142.01	$142.01	$142.01	$142.01	$142.01	$142.01	
10	Row 5 × row 9	$27,461,041	$17,099,424	$2,991,015	$9,692,609	$1,312,335,900	$40,614,149	
11	Total							$1,410,194,000
12	Administrative cost							
	31% on BLS estimates							$207,897,300[d]
	15% on all else except out of pocket							$89,575,853[d]

[a]This percentage was calculated as follows: 222,900/457,400 = 48.73%; 222,900 = number of illness cases involving time lost; 457,400 = total number of cases.

[b]U.S. Bureau of Labor Statistics 1995a, table 21, 174–99. (Repeated trauma = carpal tunnel syndrome, Others = average for all).

[c]U.S. Bureau of the Census 1995.

[d]These administration costs are direct costs.

benefits from WC, Medicaid, Medicare, and private disability insurance. We assume this will add an additional 31 percent and 15 percent to the costs. Our administrative costs estimate for indirect cost estimate is then $0.397 billion.

III.C. Grand Total

Table 6.7 presents our estimates for the total cost. The grand total for all costs is $22.7925 billion. These costs include $13.3885 billion (59 percent) in direct costs and $9.404 billion (41 percent) in indirect costs. Within the direct costs category, medical expenses are the largest, contributing 83 percent. The contributions to the indirect category include

TABLE 6.7.   Summary of Costs of Illness

	Total (in $ billions)[a]
Direct	13.3885
Medical	11.0949
Fatals	7.2853
Nonfatals[b]	3.8096
Administrative on medical	1.5703
Fatals	1.0311
Nonfatals[b]	0.5392
Administrative on indemnity	0.7233
Fatals	0.4749
Nonfatals[b]	0.2436
Indirect costs	9.404
Lost earnings	6.8740
Fatalities or mortality	4.513
Nonfatalities or morbidity	2.3608
Fringe benefits	1.602
Fatalities or mortality	1.052
Nonfatalities or mortality	0.4370
Home production	0.928
Fatalities or mortality	0.610
Nonfatalities or mortality	0.318
Workplace training, restaffing	0
Grand total	22.7925

Source: Current study.
[a]Because of rounding, not all subcategories will sum exactly.
[b]Assuming 65.663% are due to fatalities and 34.337% are due to nonfatalities. These percentages are based on ratios of fatal to nonfatal dollars to indirect costs.

lost earnings (74 percent), lost fringes (16 percent), and lost home production (10 percent).

IV. Discussion

IV.A. Limitations

A full accounting of the limitations of our analysis of the cost of illness is presented in chapter 10, "Limitations and Assumptions." Nevertheless, we will mention three of the most significant here.

First, and most important, there is no single data set that contains the information required to estimate illness costs. Occupational health costs analysis is severely hampered by the fragmented information systems that are associated with the over 1,500 employer-based health insurance plans for working populations. In addition, the loss of continuous medical history and follow-up data due to the separation of Medicare from private employer-based insurance information systems further limits the data accessibility that is necessary to understand the full spectrum of the costs over the life span.

Second, there are assumptions that should be tested in future research. For example, the assumption that occupational death rates are identical to national average and age-specific data rates should be examined. If, for instance, workers with occupationally acquired cancer die at an earlier age than patients whose cancers are caused by nonoccupational factors, our economic cost estimates are likely to be biased downward. A faster transition time between stages of severity would be consistent with higher concentrations of toxins at the workplace as opposed to the nonwork environment. In general, future researchers should examine whether an occupationally acquired disease differs in any systematic way from the same disease that was not caused by the occupation.

Data gathered to document both the social severity and the clinical severity of occupationally related disease would be extremely useful and would enhance the validity of economic estimates. Varying transition times and progression probabilities between stages of disease severity can substantially affect the economic estimates. For example, for heart disease, a stochastic model that incorporated mathematical decay functions for declining rate of mortality from heart disease after age 65 due to occupational hypertension acquired before age 65 would substantially improve the economic cost estimates. Lacking these data, we simply assumed no economic costs were attributed to death due to heart disease after age 65.

The analysis of nonfatal illnesses is likely to underestimate indirect costs by a significant amount. The BLS Annual Survey is widely known to underreport the number of work loss days resulting from the illness (in addition to the underreporting of numbers of illnesses). Estimates from the literature indicate the underreporting of work loss days may be as much as threefold (Oleinick et al. 1993). Whereas we made an adjustment for the undercount of numbers of illnesses, we did not do so for the number of days lost.

Finally, the prevalence estimate of costs essentially reflects workplace exposures and number of workers from 10 to 40 years prior to 1992. This has two implications. First, workplaces may be cleaner in 1992 than in prior years. Second, every year, the workforce grows. These two implications result in conflicting biases on our estimates. It remains unknown whether an accounting of illnesses due to exposure in the 1990s would be more or less than the costs we estimate here.

IV.B. Comparisons to Other Studies of Occupational Disease

We are aware of only four prior studies of the costs of occupational illness in the United States: Two by ourselves (Fahs et al. 1989; Markowitz et al. 1989a, 1989b) for New York State and New Jersey, another by Neumark et al. (1991) for Pennsylvania, and a fourth by Farquhar et al. (1998).

Our methods in the New York and New Jersey studies are consistent with the methods we rely on for this national study. The Farquhar et al. 1998 study heavily relied on our unpublished NIOSH report that serves as a supporting document for this book (Leigh et al. 1996). In particular, all three focus attention on a few fatal diseases — cancer, circulatory, chronic respiratory, pneumoconioses, and renal disease. Our current national study, however, adds nervous system disorders as well as the nonfatal illnesses reported to the BLS Annual Survey. In addition, we add our own estimates of administrative costs, lost home production, and the cost of nonfatal conditions that were not included in our prior studies using New York and New Jersey data.

Neumark et al. (1991) speculate that if Pennsylvania is representative of the nation, occupational illness and injuries would cost roughly $54.5 billion in 1989. They (implicitly) attribute roughly $17 billion to injuries and $37.5 to diseases (see chap. 5 for more complete discussion of Neumark et al. 1991). This $37.5 billion exceeds our estimate of $25 billion. This disparity, in part, may be due to the nonrepresentativeness of Pennsylvania — a state that is heavily industrialized. For example,

20.5 percent of Pennsylvania's workforce is employed in manufacturing and 3.6 percent in metal industries, although only 18.5 and 1.8 percent of the national workforce are so employed in these industries at the time of the Neumark study. Manufacturing contributes the highest number of illness cases (Fahs et al. 1989). Moreover, metal industries in particular contribute a high percentage of illnesses relative to their employment (U.S. Bureau of Labor Statistics 1994a, 1994b).

Another reason for their relatively high estimate is their assumption about the average age at death (Oleinick and Gluck 1992). They use the same age (44.1 years) for both injuries and diseases. The 44.1 years was a WC and BLS estimate of average age of job-related death in Pennsylvania and was heavily weighted by injury deaths. This 44.1 years would result in an overestimate for illness and an underestimate for injuries, since the average age of an injury death is much younger than a disease death. We did not use one average estimate for both illnesses and injuries. Ours differed by age bracket and gender and especially for injuries and diseases.

In short, we believe our $22.8 billion estimate is more reliable than the $37.5 billion estimate of Neumark et al. (1991).

IV.C. Comparison to Other All Disease Studies

In chapter 11 we compare our costs of illness and injuries with 1992 estimates of the cost of AIDS, Alzheimer's disease, circulatory disease, cancer, and arthritis. In this short section in chapter 6 we simply note some important findings and compare data with one of the most widely cited costs of illness studies. Rice, Hodgson, and Kopstein (1985) provided estimates for 14 diseases and disorders as well as one estimate for all injuries and poisons. In 1980 dollars, the total bill for all of these diseases, disorders, and injuries was $455 billion, of which about $211 billion was for direct costs and $244 was for indirect costs (assuming a 4 percent discount rate). Diseases of the circulatory system as well as injuries and poisonings were the most costly. The disease or conditions are ranked as follows: circulatory disease cost $85 billion ($32.5 direct, $52.5 indirect); injuries and poisonings cost $83 billion ($18.7 direct, $64.3 indirect); cancers cost $50.5 billion ($13 direct, $37.5 indirect); and diseases of the respiratory system cost $33 billion ($16.7 direct, $16.3 indirect). Since 1980, there have been considerable inflation, especially in medical prices; changes in treatments; and changes in the numbers of people dying from any given disease or injury. In addition, Rice, Hodgson, and Kopstein did not account for some of the factors we did, such as for insurance administration for indemnity benefits. Nevertheless, it is useful to note that the diseases that have a significant job-related component also generated considerable costs overall.

V. Conclusion

Standard techniques developed by Rice, Hodgson, and Kopstein (1985) and others were applied to estimate costs. Estimated costs for job-related diseases and conditions summed to roughly $23 billion in 1992. Approximately 59 percent came from direct costs and 41 percent from indirect costs. The bulk of these costs—nearly 82 percent—arose from six fatal diseases such as cancer (roughly 18 percent), and the remainder came from nonfatal ones such as carpal tunnel syndrome.

CHAPTER 7

Workers' Compensation Costs across Occupations

I. Introduction

This chapter uses the BLS's Supplementary Data System (SDS) to determine which occupations generate the greatest and least costs. These cost rankings of occupations may be useful for policymakers interested in targeting specific jobs for interventions. They may also be useful for individual employees interested in rankings of the overall risk associated with any particular job. Relative rankings measured with costs can indirectly serve as risk rankings since costs combine fatalities, injuries, and diseases into one metric. A similar study of industries has also been conducted (Leigh and Miller 1998a).

The SDS data have a number of limitations as indicated in chapter 2 and in Leigh and Miller 1997. For the purposes of this chapter, they appear to be unsurpassed by any other data set. They contain information on workers' compensation categories of disabilities (i.e., death, Permanent Total, Permanent Partial, Temporary Total and Partial, and Medical Only). Information from these categories can be matched to our cost data from chapter 5 to produce cost estimates within one- and three-digit occupations. Also, unlike the CFOI and the NTOF, the SDS includes diseases. The CFOI excluded some 18 percent of deaths judged to be due to diseases. Moreover, the CFOI and NTOF do not include nonfatal injuries. Finally, the SDS data are superior to the BLS Annual Survey data, which contain neither WC disability categories nor fatality data.

Two drawbacks should be mentioned at the outset, however. These data are drawn exclusively from workers' compensation (WC) records. Our rankings and estimates will suffer to the extent that WC records do not reflect all job injuries and illnesses within all occupations. As we saw in chapters 2 and 3, WC likely (1) underestimates deaths from motor vehicles and violent acts and greatly undercounts diseases; (2) ignores many nondisabling injuries; and (3) does not comprehensively cover occupations such as miner, farm laborer, domestic, or the self-employed. Another drawback is that our analysis within this chapter relies on data from 1985 and 1986. Due to the reliance on 1986 WC data, these relative costs cannot be compared to our national costs estimates in chapters 5 and 6.

We generate four tables. Table 7.1 ranks six broad occupation categories by total costs. Table 7.2 ranks six broad occupations by cost per worker. Table 7.3 ranks 40 of 419 specific three-digit occupations by total costs. Table 7.4 ranks 40 of 223 specific occupations by cost per worker.

II. Data and Method

II.A. Supplementary Data System (SDS)

The Supplementary Data System was described in chapter 2. In this chapter we only considered data from eight states and only from 1985 and 1986: Arkansas, 1985, 1986; Colorado, 1985; Delaware, 1985, 1986; Iowa, 1985, 1986; New York, 1985, 1986; North Carolina, 1985, 1986; Oregon, 1985, 1986; and Wisconsin, 1985, 1986. On average, these states contributed to 16.51 percent of U.S. employment for the two years combined. Although the SDS contains information from 1976 through 1988, the most recent years available with WC disability categories are 1985 and 1986. The BLS has ended the SDS effort; hence, 1986 is the most recent year available.

The BLS continues to have confidence in the SDS in its ability to provide *relative* comparisons, not total counts of deaths, injuries, and illnesses (chap. 2, app. A). In using these SDS data, we only seek relative rankings of occupations, not total national estimates. The SDS data are limited. Nevertheless, given that so little is known about costs across occupations, an analysis of these limited data seems warranted. Future analysts will undoubtedly improve on our rankings but will likely be informed by the procedures and rankings in our study.

Our methods involved aggregation of the data within various combined categories, that is, number of deaths, Permanent Totals (PTs), Permanent Partials (PPs), and Temporary Totals and Partials (TTPs) within over 300 occupations coded according to 1980 U.S. Census categories. Since we merely seek to describe numbers contained in the SDS we did not conduct any statistical tests.

II.B. Costs

Data on costs were derived from chapter 5 and deflated to reflect 1986 dollars. Costs were assigned to each of the following categories: fatalities, Permanent Total disabilities, Permanent Partial disabilities, Temporary Total and Partial disabilities. These cost figures are comprised of direct and indirect components. Total costs within occupations were calculated by multiplying average costs for the WC category by the number of episodes within that category.

The calculation of total costs within an occupation does not require knowledge of the number of incumbents in the occupation. The calculation for a per worker cost, or cost rate, within an occupation involves a ratio. The costs are in the numerator, and the estimated number of persons employed is in the denominator. The cost calculations were described previously. The estimated number employed was drawn from BLS published tables on employment within occupations (U.S. Bureau of Labor Statistics 1985, 1986).

The cost rate is easily understood if attention is restricted to a single occupation, say, lumberjacks. The calculation is represented in equation (7.1).

$$\text{Cost rate for lumberjacks} = \frac{\sum_{i=1985}^{1986} \sum_{i=1}^{I} \text{Costs}_{it}}{\sum_{t=1985}^{1986} \text{USEmp}_t \times \text{StatesPercent}_t}, \qquad (7.1)$$

where $t = 1985$ and 1986; $I =$ the number of states and varies by year: eight in 1985, seven in 1986; and $\text{Costs}_{it} =$ the total costs for lumberjacks in the ith state in the tth year. The double summation symbols indicate that costs are summed across states and over time. $\text{USEmp}_t =$ the number of employed lumberjacks in the year t for the United States; $\text{StatesPercent} =$ the percentage of national employment contributed by the seven or eight states in year t.

The ratio in equation (7.1) was calculated for 223 specific occupations and six broad occupation groups.

We also calculated total costs within occupations. These calculations did not require denominator data. We ranked 419 specific occupations and six broad occupation groups based on total costs.

III. Results

Four tables are presented for ranking occupations by total direct and indirect costs. These costs are the total *annual* costs. Costs from both years are expressed in 1986 dollars. In table 7.1, broad occupation groups are ranked according to their overall contribution (total costs), without adjusting for employment within occupations. In table 7.2, the broad occupation groups are ranked on a per worker basis (average costs). Table 7.3 presents the rankings for 40 (of 419) specific occupations by total costs; table 7.4 ranks 40 of 223 specific occupations by average costs. Results for all 419 and 223 occupations are available from the authors.

Table 7.1 follows a simple format. The rank of the occupation group appears in the first column. Column 2 presents the three-digit 1980 Census occupation codes. The description of the occupation group is in column 3. Total costs generated by the occupation group appear in column 4.

As table 7.1 illustrates, traditional blue-collar jobs (operatives, laborers, precision production, craft, and repair occupations) generate the greatest total costs. Service, sales, and administrative support (clerical) occupations are next in line. Management and professional occupations rank fifth, while occupations in farming, forestry, and fishing are at the bottom of the total cost list.

Table 7.2 depicts the average annual cost, again expressed in 1986 dollars. At the top of the list are operators and laborers with $898 per worker, and at the bottom are managers and professionals with $85 per worker. The larger costs, $898 and $556, may appear high to some

TABLE 7.1.   Broad Occupation Groups by Total Costs

(1) Rank	(2) 1980 Census Codes	(3) Description of Occupation Group	(4) Total Costs (1986 $)
1	700–899	Operators and laborers	2,544,000,000
2	500–699	Precision production, craft, and repair occupations	1,231,000,000
3	400–469	Service occupations	1,051,000,000
4	201–399	Technical, sales, administration support occupations	659,000,000
5	001–199	Managerial and professional occupations	371,000,000
6	470–499	Farming, forestry, fishing occupations[a]	209,000,000

Source: Current study.

[a]Workers' compensation data underrepresent farming, forestry, and fishing occupations.

readers. It should be recalled, however, that these costs reflect indirect costs, that is, lost wages, benefits, and home production, in addition to medical expenses.

The only difference in the rankings between tables 7.1 and 7.2 pertains to farming, forestry, and fishing occupations. In all likelihood, our rankings do not adequately reflect the true costs of injuries and illnesses associated with these occupations. Many studies suggest farming generates more deaths, injuries, and illnesses on a per capita basis than any other broad group of occupations (Toscano and Windau 1993; Berkowitz and Burton 1987; Jenkins et al. 1993; Stout and Bell 1991; Baker et al. 1982; Bell et al. 1990; Meng 1991). The reason tables 7.1 and 7.2 do not reflect this results from our exclusive reliance on WC records that systematically exclude large numbers of farmers and farmworkers (U.S. Chamber of Commerce 1992).

Table 7.3 ranks 40 of 419 specific occupations by total costs.

Truck drivers occupy position one with a total cost of $365 million. Laborers outside construction are in position two with $330 million.

Machine operators, not specified, rank third in table 7.1; their total costs are $260 million. Ranked fourth is occupation not classified. It is tempting to discard these categories (e.g., "not specified," "not classified") from our tables altogether. But that would be a mistake. The fact that these categories, together with those in the "miscellaneous" and "not elsewhere classified" (n.e.c.) categories, are so high on the list

TABLE 7.2.   Broad Occupation Groups by Average Annual Cost

Rank	1980 Census Codes	Description of Occupation Group	Average Cost (1986 $)
1	700–899	Operators and laborers	898
2	500–699	Precision production, craft, and repair occupations	556
3	400–469	Service occupations	434
4	470–499	Farming, forestry, fishing occupations[a]	368
5	201–399	Technical, sales, administration support occupations	116
6	001–199	Managerial and professional occupations	85

Source: Current study.

[a]Workers' compensation data underrepresent farming, forestry, and fishing occupations.

TABLE 7.3. Costs by Specific Occupation, Averaged over 1985 and 1986

Rank	1980 Census Code	Description	Total Annual Costs (1986 $)
1	804	Truck drivers, heavy	365,167,487
2	889	Laborers, except construction	330,677,638
3	779	Machine operators, not specified	260,453,369
4	999	Occupations not classified	238,922,707
5	453	Janitors and cleaners	226,284,072
6	447	Nursing aides, orderlies, and attendants	205,145,880
7	869	Construction laborers	146,916,938
8	785	Assemblers	138,739,788
9	260	Sales workers, retail, n.e.c.	130,264,003
10	777	Miscellaneous machine operators, n.e.c.	129,851,659
11	567	Carpenters	125,085,238
12	883	Freight, stock, and material handlers, n.e.c.	113,922,192
13	19	Managers and administrators, n.e.c.	103,023,173
14	549	Not specified mechanics and repairers	97,303,525
15	444	Misc. food preparation occupations, n.e.c.	78,658,802
16	496	Timber cutting and logging occupations	73,790,081
17	633	Supervisors, production occupations	73,280,259
18	575	Electricians	70,464,255
19	436	Cooks, except short order	66,711,100
20	243	Supervisor and proprietors, sales	66,308,382
21	505	Automobile mechanics	64,710,729
22	783	Welders and cutters	64,416,276
23	418	Police and detectives, public service	63,591,968
24	877	Stock handlers and baggers	63,227,739
25	479	Farmworkers	61,379,120
26	686	Butchers and meatcutters	60,995,610
27	585	Plumbers, pipe fitters, and steamfitters	51,212,922
28	449	Maids and housemen	50,030,491
29	95	Registered nurses	49,787,372
30	806	Driver-sales workers	45,818,119
31	873	Production helpers	44,931,296
32	364	Traffic, shipping, and receiving clerk	44,245,507
33	417	Firefighting occupations	43,549,377
34	486	Groundskeepers and gardeners	43,447,140

TABLE 7.3. (*Continued*)

Rank	1980 Census Code	Description	Total Annual Costs (1986 $)
35	808	Bus drivers	43,355,950
36	550	Construction occupations, n.e.c.	43,347,324
37	518	Industrial machinery repairers	43,082,013
38	637	Machinists	41,283,280
39	424	Correctional institutional officers	39,889,505
40	379	General office clerks	38,759,801

Source: Current study.

underscores our lack of knowledge about the jobs that are generating high costs and the persons who hold those jobs. It seems reasonable to conclude that persons holding jobs that require well-defined skills would not be included in these amorphous "not classified" or "miscellaneous" categories.

Janitors and cleaners rank fifth with $226 million in costs. Nursing aides are in the sixth position with $205 million. Construction laborers ($146 million), assemblers ($138 million), retail sales workers, n.e.c. ($130 million), and miscellaneous machine operators, n.e.c. ($130 million) round out the top 10.

There is a striking contrast between white-collar occupations and all other occupations. Our definition of "white collar" includes all occupations with a census category of 399 or less. These would include managers and professionals as well as technical, sales, and administrative support occupations. Our definition of all other occupations includes all occupations with a census category of 400 or more. These would include the following: service occupations; farming, forestry, and fishing occupations; as well as the traditional blue-collar jobs of precision production, craft, and repair occupations, operators, fabricators, and laborers. Occupation codes 999 and 910 (occupations not classified) are not included in either the white-collar or the "all other" category.

Out of the top 50 occupations, 42 are in the "all other" group and seven are in the white-collar group. Within the bottom 50 (ranks 369 to 419—available from the authors), 15 are in the "all other" group and 34 are in the white-collar group (occupation not classified, code 910, occupies position 412). These striking contrasts are consistent with the ranking by broad occupation groups in table 7.1.

The bottom 25 occupations (ranks, costs in thousands) are these: physicists and astronomers (395, $104); geologists (396, $98); marine engineers (397, $93); health diagnosing practitioners, n.e.c. (398, $92);

social scientists (399, $79); tool programmers (400, $71); nuclear engineers (401, $66); actuaries (402, $66); classified ad clerks (403, $63); captains of fishing vessels (404, $63); mathematical scientists, n.e.c. (405, $60); authors (406, $60); samplers (407, $46); longshore equipment operators (408, $44); aerospace engineers (409, $43); air traffic controllers (410, $41); petroleum engineers (411, $38); hunters and trappers (412, $11); optometrists (413, $8); podiatrists (414, $5); telegraphers (415, $5); occupations not classified (416, $5); legislators (417, $3); agricultural workers (418, $2); atmospheric and space scientists (419, $2).

The white-collar and clerical workers that generate the most total costs include the following: retail sales workers, n.e.c. (rank = 9, $130 million); managers and administrators, n.e.c. (13, $103 million); sales supervisors and proprietors (20, $66 million); registered nurses (29, $50 million); shipping and receiving clerks (32, $44 million); general office clerks (40, $39 million); secretaries (44, $35 million); teachers, n.e.c. (52, $30 million); management related occupations, n.e.c. (54, $29 million); sales engineers (57, $27 million); licensed practical nurses (62, $24 million); administrative support occupations, n.e.c. (78, $20 million); bookkeeper (46, $16 million); secondary school teachers (90, $17 million); teacher's aides (95, $14 million).

Professionals are a subcategory of white-collar workers. As the preceding list demonstrates, the following professionals (without n.e.c. classifications) generate sizable costs: registered nurses, licensed practical nurses, and secondary school teachers. As we will see, nurses are also high on the per employee list compared to other professionals. This suggests that nurses experience a considerable number of injuries and illnesses on the job both collectively and individually. Secondary school teachers are relatively low on the per employee list. We conclude that the high ranking of secondary school teachers in the per occupation listing is due to the great numbers of people employed as secondary school teachers.

Table 7.4 presents the per worker (average) cost ranking. The rank appears in column 1. The occupation code is in the second column. Description of the occupation is in column 3. The last column presents the average cost rates.

There are several results that emerge from table 7.4. First, many of the occupations with the highest rankings are poorly paid, for example, production helpers, laborers in and out of construction, meatcutters, grinding machine operators, kitchen workers, punching press operators, furnace machine operators, nursing aides, helpers, assemblers, miscellaneous food preparation operators, and janitors and cleaners.

Second, the highest ranking occupations are dominated by non-white-collar, nonclerical categories. This is most quickly seen by perusing

TABLE 7.4. Costs per Employee, or Average Cost by Specific Occupation, Averaged over 1985 and 1986

(1) Rank	(2) 1980 Census Code	(3) Occupation	(4) Cost per Employee (1986 $)
1	496	Timber cutting and logging occupations	5,733
2	873	Production helpers	3,679
3	889	Laborers, except construction	1,777
4	727	Sewing machine operators	1,691
5	544	Millwrights	1,670
6	424	Correctional institution officers	1,389
7	686	Butchers and meatcutters	1,297
8	806	Driver-sales workers	1,291
9	417	Firefighting occupations	1,287
10	709	Grinding, buffing, polishing machine operators	1,250
11	804	Truck drivers, heavy	1,226
12	869	Construction laborers	1,198
13	439	Kitchen workers, food preparation	1,156
14	878	Machine feeders and off-bearers	1,144
15	853	Excavating and loading machine operators	1,085
16	706	Punching, stamping, press machine operators	1,085
17	527	Telephone line installers and repairers	1,059
18	704	Lathe and turning machine operators	1,026
19	423	Sheriffs, bailiffs, and officers	1,006
20	766	Furnace, kiln, and oven operators	989
21	418	Police and detectives, public service	958
22	447	Nursing aides, orderlies, and attendants	957
23	577	Electrical power installers and repairers	945
24	865	Helpers, construction trades	872
25	653	Sheet metal workers	839
26	769	Slicing and cutting machine operators	826
27	593	Insulation workers	819
28	785	Assemblers	772
29	657	Cabinetmakers and bench carpenters	760
30	696	Stationary engineers	759
31	444	Misc. food preparation occupations, n.e.c.	748
32	844	Operating engineers	734
33	199	Athletes	706·
34	783	Welders and cutters	683
35	526	Household appliance, power tool repairers	681
36	768	Crushing and grinding machine operators	678
37	575	Electricians	672
38	453	Janitors and cleaners	660
39	585	Plumbers, pipe fitters, and steamfitters	656
40	563	Brickmasons and stonemasons	650

Source: Current study.

the occupation code numbers. Code numbers over 399 indicate non-white-collar occupations. Numbers under 399 indicate white-collar occupations. Within the highest ranking 100 occupations only 11 are white collar or clerical (professional athletes; shipping and receiving clerks; managers; stenographers; transportation reservation agents; teachers, n.e.c.; recreation workers; pilots; licensed practical nurses; general office clerks; and inventory clerks).

Third, teachers, except for those in the n.e.c. category, appear at the bottom of the list (available from the authors). Since this list in table 7.4 adjusts for the number of incumbents, and given these low rankings for teachers, it is tempting to conclude that teaching is among the safest of jobs. This conclusion would be premature, however. The SDS greatly underreports government workers, whereas the denominator data do not. A high percentage of teachers are government workers; hence average cost estimates would be artificially low.

IV. Discussion

Extensive discussions of the limitations of these data from the Supplementary Data System (SDS) are available in chapter 2 and in Leigh and Miller 1997. We therefore turn to comments on important findings and comparisons to other studies.

One important finding pertains to the occupations that most frequently appear high on our lists: laborers (both in and out of construction), janitors and cleaners, and general machine operatives ("not elsewhere classified" or "not specified"). These occupations are highly ranked for total and average costs. These results are consistent with those on predominantly injury death rates, indicating high rates for janitors and cleaners; machine operatives, not elsewhere classified; and especially laborers in and out of construction (Dieterly 1995; Toscano and Windau 1994; Meng 1991; Leigh 1995a). They are also consistent with an influential early study using the SDS by Root and Sebastian (1981), who calculated a hazard index. The job hazard index applied to roughly 60 occupations and 180 occupation and industry combinations. The index was created by calculating a ratio. In the numerator was the percentage of total injuries contributed by a particular occupation or occupation-industry cell, and in the denominator was the expected percentage for that occupation or cell. They found that more than 99 percent of the cases were not fatal. Occupations with the highest indexes were, in order, warehouse laborers, all other laborers, structural metal crafts workers (ironworkers), roofers, sheet metal workers and apprentices, construction laborers, freight handlers, millwrights, and truck drivers. Root and Sebastian also found that, overall, blue-collar work was twice to eight times as hazardous as white-collar work, depending on the industry examined.

A related finding is that operators and laborers with the "miscellaneous," "not specified," "not elsewhere classified (n.e.c.)" categories rank high in both table 7.3, for total cost contribution, and table 7.4, for average cost or per worker contribution. These jobs and apparently these workers were not easy for the U.S. Census or the Bureau of Labor Statistics to classify. It is likely that many of these jobs do not require a great deal of skill. Skilled jobs are more likely than nonskilled jobs to have specific titles. Unskilled and semiskilled jobs employ many workers who are new to the tasks: youths, persons lacking high school diplomas, immigrants, and so on. This interpretation is consistent with the finding discussed earlier pertaining to the high risk for laborers, janitors and cleaners, and general machine operatives. All of these unskilled and semiskilled jobs pay low wages. If costs can be viewed as an index of hazardous conditions then these results are consistent with the hypothesis that the most dangerous jobs command low pay.

It could be argued that incumbents in these occupations are especially prone to filing WC claims since the WC benefits might be especially generous in comparison to the low wage that laborers, operatives, and janitors and cleaners receive. That is, it could be that many of these claims are fabricated. But this argument is difficult to accept for deaths.

On the other hand, there are many factors that would contribute to high injury and illness rates among these occupations. Laborers, operatives, and janitors do not require much training and are frequently new employees. New employees, like green troops, are prone to engage in risky behavior. They may be unaware of the hazards or they may want to impress their bosses. Alternatively, youths frequently populate these unskilled and semiskilled positions, and many youths feel impervious to hazards. New employees may also be less likely to receive proper safety and health training. Business calculations might reveal that the costs of providing the training exceed the benefits.

The occupations at the bottom of the list of costs per occupation tend to have a few members (nuclear engineers, authors, podiatrists). Telegraphers are virtually extinct today. However, this is not true for all the occupations at the bottom. Agricultural workers and fishers are numerous. Their low ranking is likely due to the fact that these occupations frequently lie outside WC coverage (U.S. Chamber of Commerce 1992). Finally, as indicated previously, it is likely that teachers' low average cost ranking is largely due to the fact that they lie outside many traditional WC systems.

Recent BLS reports have attempted to rank three-digit occupations according to the total number of days lost due to nonfatal injuries and illnesses using data from the Annual Survey of Occupational Injuries and Illnesses. This Annual Survey ranking would be most similar to our table 7.3 since it attempts to rank by total volume or burden of the problem, not average or per worker volume. In a May 8, 1996, BLS news bulletin (U.S. Bureau of Labor Statistics 1996), the following occupations were identified as contributing the greatest volume of cases involving days away from work in 1994: truck drivers, nonconstruction laborers, nursing aides, janitors and cleaners, construction laborers, assemblers, carpenters, stock handlers and baggers, cooks, and cashiers. This ranking bears a strong resemblance to our table 7.3. This is striking since the BLS list corresponds to the 1990 Census code while ours corresponds to the 1980 code and, more importantly, since there are so many differences in the data sources. The 1980 code, for example, does not have an entry for cashiers. It is likely that the 1980 code for "retail sales workers, n.e.c.," contains cashiers. If so, the top 10 BLS occupations are all included in our top 24. Moreover, the top two occupations on both lists are the same.

The BLS also recently began publishing rankings on relative per capita risks for the top 10 occupations, again using days of absence data in the Annual Survey. This relative risk ranking corresponds to our average cost ranking in table 7.4. Days of absence are divided by employment within the occupation (Toscano and Windau 1994). For men, the following occupations received the highest ranking: nonconstruction laborers, kitchen workers, nursing aides, construction laborers, driver-sales workers, construction trades helpers, miscellaneous food preparation occupations, transportation and reservation ticket agents, sheet metal workers, and freight handlers. For women, the list included miscellaneous food preparation workers, nonconstruction laborers, kitchen workers, public transportation attendants, nursing aides, freight handlers, bus drivers, truck drivers, janitors and cleaners, and waitresses' assistants.

Again, despite the differences in the Annual Survey data and the SDS data, this BLS relative risk ranking also bears a strong resemblance to our table 7.4. With the exception of waitresses' assistants, which was not a category in the 1980 census and hence does not appear anywhere on our lists, the other occupations mentioned for both men and women rank in our top 40 slots.

A handful of occupations has also been ranked by relative risks of injury fatality using the Census of Fatal Occupational Injuries (U.S. Bureau of Labor Statistics 1995b). The following ranking was obtained (with our ranking from table 7.4 in parentheses): lumberjacks (1), airline pilots (87), fishers (N.A.), supervisors to farmworkers (N.A.), taxi drivers (43), farm managers (N.A.), construction laborers (12), electric power install-ers and repairers (23), roofers (48), sheriffs (19), truck drivers (11), driver-sales workers (8), and farmworkers (N.A.). The N.A. indicates "not applicable"; that is, we know that the SDS undercounts fishing and farming work. Apart from airplane pilots and the farming and fishing occupations, this Census of Fatal Occupational Injuries relative risk list is similar to our table 7.4. The exception for airplane pilots is easily ex-plained. Pilots are likely to have a high death rate but not necessarily a high nonfatal injury rate. Airplane crashes tend to generate a higher death to nonfatal injury ratio than any other accident-causing event.

The Census of Fatal Occupational Injuries can also be used to rank occupations according to the number of deaths, not accounting for em-ployment. This would be analogous to our table 7.3. The following list (and numbers of deaths) was obtained: truck drivers (731), farmers (328), construction laborers (218), managers and administrators (213), noncon-struction laborers (202), farmworkers (184), lumberjacks (124), military occupations (121), taxi drivers (113), airplane pilots (104), street and door-to-door salespersons (101), police and detectives (101), guards and police except public service (86), janitors and cleaners (83), fishers (79). Again, there are similarities to our table 7.3, which includes 11 of these 15 within the top 30 occupations.

The fact that rankings from these four BLS studies using data from the Annual Survey and the Census so strongly resemble our rankings lends credibility to our rankings, despite the limitations mentioned in Leigh and Miller 1997.

V. Conclusion

Tables 7.1 through 7.4 present rankings of occupations based on their annual costs. The SDS data were drawn from eight states, each repre-senting a different region in the United States. These rankings are lim-ited. Only information from the SDS/WC data set was used. These rankings do *not* reflect a compilation of the many injury and disease data sources we identified in chapters 2 and 3. As a result, for example, we underestimate the costs of coal mining, fishing, and agriculture. Never-theless, these rankings appear to be the only such lists available in the literature. Moreover, the rankings appear reasonable. We have seen that our rankings are similar to those provided by the BLS in their Census of Fatal Occupational Injuries studies and their Annual Survey studies. We conclude that, after noting the caveats and limitations listed in Leigh and Miller 1997, our rankings provide a reasonable basis to begin a more thorough investigation of costs within occupations.

CHAPTER 8

Who Pays?

I. Introduction

Our analysis of who pays for occupational injuries and illnesses is split into two parts: nominal aspects of who pays, and incidence aspects of who pays are considered.[1] In the nominal view, the origin of funds is presumed to be with the firm, agency, or person that actually writes the check or signs the credit form or pays the cash.[2] In the incidence view, the origin of funds is not readily apparent. Economic analysis is required to assess incidence. For example, workers' compensation (WC) insurance companies write the checks to pay for many injured workers. The insurer derives funds from employers' premiums, and employers in turn might pass on the high WC premium to consumers in the form of high prices for the goods the employer sells. In the incidence view, it may be consumers who ultimately pay for occupational injuries and illnesses.

Unfortunately, there have not been any definitive studies of the incidence of WC premiums. Moreover, there have not been any studies whatsoever of the incidence of occupational injuries and illnesses not covered by WC. Our analysis is therefore merely a sketch of what a thorough incidence study would have to address, and our estimates should be viewed in that light. Accordingly, we place greater emphasis on the well-documented and commonsense analysis of nominal payment.

The outline of the chapter is as follows. Section II discusses nominal payment. Section III considers incidence payment. Two main subsections appear in section III: "Who Pays for WC?" and "Incidence for WC and Non-WC Costs." Within the "Who Pays for WC?" subsection, we provide an introduction (III.A.1), theory (III.A.2), and evidence (III.A.3). The chapter closes with a conclusion (sec. IV).

II. Nominal Payment

Our analysis of nominal payment is constructed around tables 8.1 and 8.2, which were drawn from the Health Care Financing Administration

(Levit et al. 1994). Table 8.1 presents 1992 national health spending by who receives the payment. A familiar pattern emerges. Hospitals receive the most (37.3 percent), followed by physician services (19.7 percent), drugs (8.6 percent), and nursing home care (8.0 percent).

Table 8.2 apportions spending according to who pays the nominal cost. Private funds contribute the most (56.4 percent). Within the private funds rows, private health insurance contributes 33.2 percent, and out-of-pocket expenses by consumers amount to 18.4 percent. Within the public fund rows, the federal government pays for 31 percent, while state and local governments pay for 12.6 percent.

Table 8.3 is constructed assuming workers' compensation (WC) covers 45 percent of all medical expenses and the other 55 percent is paid for with the same percentage identified in table 8.2.[3] These percentages are not based upon a 100 percent total, however, but a 55 percent total. That is, in table 8.2 all private funds (row I) were assumed to draw 56.4 percent out of a total of 100 percent. In table 8.3, all private funds (row II) were assumed to draw 56.4 percent out of 55 percent (i.e., 31 percent of the total costs of occupational injuries and illnesses). For example, the 18.3 percent in row II.A.1 (table 8.3) was calculated by multiplying

TABLE 8.1. National Health Expenditures (billions of dollars, 1992)

	Total	Percentage
Total	820.3	100.0
Health services and suppliers	729.9	96.7
Personal health care	729.7	89.0
Hospital care	306.0	37.3
Physician services	161.8	19.7
Dental services	34.7	4.2
Other professional services	46.4	5.7
Home health care	16.8	2.0
Drugs	70.8	8.6
Vision products	12.0	1.5
Nursing home care	65.5	8.0
Other personal health care	15.8	1.9
Program administration and net cost of private insurance	39.5	4.8
Government public health activities	23.7	2.9
Research and construction	29.0	3.3
Percentage of GDP		13.6

Source: Data from Burner and Waldo 1995.

TABLE 8.2. National Health Expenditures by Source of Funds (billions of dollars, 1992)

	Billions of Dollars	Percentage
Total	820.3	100.0
I. Private funds	462.3	56.4
A. Consumer payments	423.3	51.6
1. Out of pocket	150.6	18.4
2. Private health insurance	272.7	33.2
B. Other private funds	39.5	4.8
II. Public funds	357.5	43.6
A. Federal funds	254.3	31.0
1. Medicare	138.3	16.9
2. Medicaid[g]	68.3	8.3
3. Other federal	47.8	5.8
B. State and local funds	103.2	12.6
1. Medicaid[a]	39.7	4.8
2. Other state and local	63.5	7.7

Source: Health Care Financing Administration, Office of the Actuary, Data from the Office of National Health Statistics.
[a]Total Medicaid (federal and state) is $108.0, or 13.2%.

TABLE 8.3. Direct Cost for Occupational Injuries and Illnesses by Source

	Billions of Dollars	Percentage
Total	51.7687	100.0
I. Workers' compensation	23.2959	45.0
II. Non–workers' compensation	28.4728	55.0
A. Private funds	16.0483	31.0
1. Private health insurance	9.4736	18.3
2. Out of pocket and other	6.5746	12.7
B. Public funds	12.4244	24.0
1. Federal funds	8.8007	17.0
a. Medicare	2.6480	9.3
b. Medicaid[a]	1.3012	4.57
2. State and local	3.6238	7.0
a. Medicaid[a]	.7517	2.64

Source: Current study.
[a]Federal plus state Medicaid is $2.0529, or 7.21% of total direct costs.

0.332 from table 8.2 (row I.A.2) with 0.55, our assumed percentage of non-WC payments.

As can be seen from table 8.3, the nominal direct cost for occupational injuries and illnesses is spread among many payers. This is an important point. Our nominal cost analysis suggests that many groups in the economy—non-WC private insurers, Medicare, and Medicaid (taxpayers)—not just employers and employees, pay for the cost of occupational injuries and illnesses.

A noteworthy row in table 8.3 is II.A.2: out of pocket and other. These nominal expenses are paid for by the injured or ill worker or by another private party. If we apply the same percentages available in table 8.2 to our 55 percent of non-WC payment, we find that out of pocket spending by workers was 10 percent and spending by other private persons was 2.7 percent.

Another noteworthy row is II.B. Taxpayers are paying roughly 24 percent of the nominal direct costs.

We turn now to the indirect costs. In table 8.4, columns 1 and 2 sum to 100 percent. Columns 1, 3, and 6 also sum to 100 percent. Finally, columns 1, 4, 5, 7, and 8 sum to 100 percent. The structure of these columns is identical to the structure of rows in table 8.3. Consider the first row in table 8.4—lost earnings. We assume that WC would cover 45 percent of all persons and costs but that indemnity would only pay for 50 percent of the before-tax wage. Hence, the first cell is 0.45 × 0.5 = 22.5 percent. The second cell is simply 1 − 0.225, or 77.5 percent. Except for the out of pocket cell, all other cells in row A multiplied percentages in table 8.3 by 0.5. The cells and their corresponding multiplications are provided in row A. The cell that picked up all of the remaining cost was out of pocket and other. This category would be composed primarily of the workers and their families. The remaining costs comprise 56.35 percent of the total. We first assume that, once injured, the worker maintains some fringe benefits but that these are not paid by WC but by private sources. We assume that the same percentages that apply to lost earnings also apply to lost fringe benefits.

We assume that home production losses nominally fall on the worker and his or her family: 100 percent in the out of pocket and other category.

We assume that workplace training and disruption costs are normally borne by the employer. But the employer may be private or public. We assume that 80 percent would be private, 10 percent federal government, and 10 percent state and local government.

After applying the percentages in table 8.4 to indirect cost calculations from chapters 5 and 6, we produce table 8.5, which combines direct

TABLE 8.4. Percentages Assumed in the Construction of Source of Payment for Indirect Costs

Indirect Cost	(1) Workers' Compensation	(2) Non-Workers' Compensation	(3) Private	(4) Private Insurance	(5) Out of Pocket Other	(6) Public	(7) Federal	(8) State and Local
A. Lost earnings	$(0.5 \times 45 =)$ 22.5%	$(1 - 22.5\%)$ 77.5%	65.5%[a]	$(0.5 \times 183 =)$ 0.15%[a]	(remainder) 56.35%[a]	$(0.5 \times 0.24 =)$ 12%[a]	$(0.5 \times 17 =)$ 8.5%	$(0.5 \times 0.07 =)$ 3.5%
B. Fringe benefits	0	77.5%	84.5%[b]	11.8%[b]	72.7%[b]	15.5%[b]	11.0%[b]	4.5%[b]
C. Home production	0	100%	100%	0	100%	0	0	0
D. Workplace training	0	100%	80%	0	80%	20%	10%	10%

Source: Current study.

[a]Health insurance + out of pocket + public = non–workers' compensation. Only insurance and public are assumed to provide indemnity; hence 0.183 must be multiplied by 0.5, and 0.24 must be multiplied by 0.5. The remainder, 56.35%, must be absorbed by workers and their families.

[b]Ratios of percentages from lost earnings are used to calculate fringe benefits. For example, under the private column, 8.45% = 655/77.5. Under the out of pocket column, 72.7% = 84.5% × (56.35/65.6).

TABLE 8.5.   Direct and Indirect Costs by Source, Nominal Payment

	Billions of Dollars			Percentage of Total
	Direct	Indirect	Total	
Total	51.7687	103.7347	155.503	100.0
Workers' compensation	23.2959	18.92	42.216	27.1
Non–workers' compensation	28.4728	84.81	113.283	72.9
Private funds	16.0483	68.72	84.768	54.7
Private health insurance	9.4736	6.61	16.084	10.3
Out of pocket, other	6.5746	62.11	68.685	44.2
Public funds	12.4244	16.09	28.510	18.3
Federal	8.8007	9.74	18.541	12.1
State and local	3.6238	6.297	9.9138	6.1

Source: Current study.

with indirect costs. Table 8.5 therefore summarizes our estimates of who nominally pays for occupational injuries and illnesses.

One notable result from table 8.5 pertains to workers' compensation, which we estimate to cover roughly only 27 percent of all costs. Using a similar approach, Marquis (1992) also found WC contributed roughly 27 percent to overall costs. Another important result pertains to the large contribution of the out of pocket category — 44.2 percent — the lion's share of which is borne by injured workers and their families. In fact, the out of pocket category is the largest of all the subcategories and larger than the contribution of WC. Marquis found 45 percent of the costs to be borne by workers and their families. Finally, governments, that is, taxpayers, bear a significant burden — $28.5 billion.

III. Incidence of Costs

III.A. Who Pays for WC?

III.A.1. Introduction

Chelius and Burton (1992, 1994) present an exceptionally well-written, nontechnical explanation of the theory and evidence on the incidence of who bears the burden of WC premiums. Much of our discussion on WC is drawn from their articles, although our conclusions will differ slightly. We are deliberately brief. Readers are referred to the Chelius and Burton 1992, 1994 articles for more detail.

III.A.2. Theory

Three groups in the economy are most frequently assumed to bear the incidence burden of WC premiums: employers, consumers, and employees. As a matter of law, payment falls entirely on the employer. That is, the insurance premium invoice is mailed to the employer, and the employer writes the check to the WC insurance carrier. The employer bears 100 percent of the *nominal* burden.

Incidence analysis suggests that the employer may try to pass on the cost of the WC premium up to the consumer or down to the worker. If WC costs are passed up, the firm will increase the price of its product or service to the consumer. If WC costs are passed down, all workers will receive lower wages, whether or not they are injured. Last, firms may have to absorb some of the cost themselves and thus experience lower profits than they otherwise would.

The pass-through mechanisms do not occur quickly. The firm does not immediately increase price or ask workers to take a pay cut the day after the WC premium increases. The pass-through effects require months or even years. Moreover, when the premium is passed down, firms will seldom ask workers to take a pay cut. They will simply not allow the wage to increase over time as fast as it otherwise would.

The ability of the firm to pass on the cost depends on consumers' sensitivities to price increases and workers' sensitivities to wage decreases. If the WC premium increase applied only to one firm, that firm might not have much success passing the cost on to either consumers or workers. Imagine that the premium hike applied to video rental store A but not to any other video store in your neighborhood. If firm A tried to pass on the cost to consumers, many or most consumers might begin to rent videos from an alternative store. On the other hand, if store A tried to hold the line on wage increases while all other stores were granting raises, store A might lose employees. In this case, firm A would likely have to absorb the premium increase internally; that is, its profits would fall.

On the other hand, suppose all video stores everywhere experienced the same WC premium hike. Further suppose that no other firms outside the video rental industry experienced premium increases. Under these circumstances, video rental stores might try to pass on the cost to consumers. Consumers who wish to rent videos would have no other alternative. Sales workers, on the other hand, would have many alternatives. They could work in a clothing store or a fast-food restaurant.

Ultimately what matters is who has the greater alternatives: consumers or workers. Unfortunately, there is no consensus among economists in answering this question.

It would appear that workers may not have many choices if the great majority of U.S. workers work in firms or government agencies that are covered by private or government WC. If a person has made the decision to work, it is likely that he or she will work for employers covered by WC. But WC premiums do vary across firms. Some firms are experienced rated, meaning that their premiums are proportional to their own injury and illness rates. Other firms are charged premiums according to their industry and size. Finally, some small firms are exempt from WC altogether. In other words, there is likely to be a variety of firms and governments with varying WC premiums from which a worker may choose a job.

Consumers also would appear to have few choices since WC coverage is so widespread. Consumers, however, can buy imports, save rather than spend, or buy goods and services from firms exempt from WC coverage. Moreover, consumers can buy goods and services from states with low WC costs.

Consumers' demand for *all* products and services produced by firms covered by WC may be fairly unresponsive to increases in price, and workers may be unresponsive to wage drops. What is critical for the economic theory of incidence is which group is least responsive. That is, if workers are less likely to respond to a wage drop than consumers are likely to respond to a price increase, workers will ultimately bear more of the cost than consumers. On the other hand, if both are responsive, profits may be significantly less. Economists have turned to empirical tests to resolve the issues of the incidence of WC premiums.

III.A.3. Evidence

Chelius and Burton (1994) review three categories of empirical studies. First, they consider studies that examine employer and employee responses to changes in all labor costs. These studies show that, for example, middle-aged male workers will continue working virtually regardless of the wage. Second, they consider studies of payroll taxes, such as Social Security taxes. One study, in particular, presented some convincing evidence. In Sweden, payroll taxes grew from 6 percent in 1950 to 40 percent in 1979. The study found that within one year of each payroll tax hike, roughly 50 percent had been shifted to workers in the form of lower wages (or lower wage raises).

Redja (1984) concurs with this view. Redja suggests that since the

WC insurance premium is based on the firm's payroll, "its economic effects may be similar to those of a payroll tax and current research suggests that in the long run, most payroll taxes are borne by labor" (303).

These studies on tax shifting for the payroll tax are important for us since a considerable portion of the costs of job-related injuries and illnesses is nominally paid by Social Security Disability Insurance and by Medicare, both of which are financed with a payroll tax.

The third set of studies is drawn from the literature on compensating wages for job risks (see chap. 4). These studies tend to show that the more generous the WC benefits are, the lower the compensating wages generated in the labor market. The trade-off between WC costs and wages was almost one to one in some of these studies. That is, one more dollar of annual WC costs was almost equally matched by one less dollar in an annual earned wage. Other studies find no trade-off of WC benefits for wages (Dorman and Hagstrom 1998).

Chelius and Burton (1994) conclude that all premiums are passed down to workers in the form of lower wages. They acknowledge that their conclusion is "radical" (25). In fact, it is not a view that mainstream conservative economists would accept, many of whom see a role for WC premiums and other "injury taxes" in reducing the toll of occupational injuries and illnesses (Smith 1974; Viscusi 1998). First, employers seem to be especially resistant to increases in WC premiums. If all of the WC costs were passed on to workers, employers would not be annoyed by WC premium increases. Yet complaints and well-orchestrated advertising by businesses executives about the high cost of WC premiums were what drove the California legislature to severely tighten eligibility standards in the now-historic changes in WC law. Moreover, unions, in general, tend to support more generous WC benefits and, by implication, higher premiums. We should not presume to know unions interests better than they do. In addition, as indicated in our literature review of the WTP studies (chap. 4), most compensating wage studies have a number of serious limitations.

The comparison between WC and payroll taxes may not be accurate. First, WC has far more variation than the payroll tax. WC rates vary by injury and illness and across states.[4] The payroll tax is a flat rate for most workers. WC may more closely resemble a fringe benefit, and the evidence suggests that, in general, fringe benefits augment wages, rather than replace them. Finally, it should be understood that there have not been any "before and after" tests of the incidence of WC premium hikes.[5]

Given the lack of consensus among economists, we offer the following examples and that in III.B as merely a suggestion.

We assume the following incidences for WC costs.

Employers: 40 percent
Consumers: 20 percent
Workers: 40 percent

It is important to note that "workers" in this analysis applies to all employees covered by WC. This does not only include injured or ill workers. That is, even if an employee were never to have a job-related injury or illness, he or she would nevertheless pay for WC through lower wages.

In table 8.5, we calculated that $42.2 billion would be nominally paid by WC. This $42.2 billion can be split among our three "actual" payment groups as follows.

Employers: $0.4 \times 42.2 = \$16.88$ billion
Consumers: $0.2 \times 42.2 = \$8.44$ billion
Workers: $0.4 \times 42.2 = \$16.88$ billion

III.B. Incidence for WC and Non-WC Costs

In table 8.5, we identified four non-WC payers who share the cost: private health insurance; out of pocket and other; federal government; and state and local government. There are a number of reasons for this lack of complete coverage, including the fact that many small firms with one to five employees are frequently exempt from WC laws. Workers in these firms can be injured or become ill and when they do, they frequently receive benefits from Social Security or welfare. These small firms essentially pass on the cost of workplace safety and health to society at large (Rejda 1984).

Private health insurance, if it is derived as a fringe benefit from the job, would have essentially the same effects as WC. It is another labor cost to the employer, just like WC. Not all private health insurance is derived from employment, however. Health insurance paid by an individual worker would be nominally and actually paid by him or her. We therefore assume the following split among employers, consumers, and workers for private health insurance: 35 percent, 15 percent, 50 percent.

We assume that the lion's share of out of pocket and other contributions would fall on workers (80 percent). Most of the nominal costs of out of pocket and other also fall on workers. We assume firms would be successful in shifting some of their nominal costs onto consumers (5 percent) and some to workers (5 percent) but retain half (10 percent). Our percentages for out of pocket and other would then be 10 percent, 5 percent, 85 percent. These are summarized in table 8.6.

The great majority of federal contributions would be derived from Social Security and Medicare payroll taxes. We assume 100 percent of the payroll tax is borne by workers.

State and local contributions would likely come from general, not payroll tax, revenues. We assume consumers (taxpayers) would pay 100 percent of general tax revenue.

If the percentages in table 8.6 are applied to the nominal payer amounts in table 8.5, we can generate the incidence of costs in table 8.7. Workers shoulder most of these costs through lower wages, but a significant amount is passed on to consumers through higher prices and to employers through lower profits.

TABLE 8.6.   Assumed Percentages of Incidence Allocation

Nominal Payment Category	Incidence Payment Category			
	Employer (%)	Consumer (%)	Worker (%)	Sum (%)
Workers' compensation	40	20	40	100
Non–workers' compensation				
Private funds				
Private health insurance	35	15	50	100
Out of pocket, other	10	5	85	100
Public funds				
Federal	0	0	100	100
State and local	0	100	0	100

Source: Current study.

TABLE 8.7.   Incidence of Costs

Category	Billions of Dollars	Percentage
Employer	29.38	19
Consumer	24.26	16
Worker	101.85	65
Total	155.50	100

Source: Current study.

IV. Conclusion

As tables 8.5 and 8.7 indicate, the costs of occupational injuries and illnesses are spread throughout the economy. We regard this conclusion as one of the most important in our study. The incidence analysis, which we regard as preliminary, indicates that these costs are borne by consumers, firms, and workers, most of whom never experience an injury or illness. The nominal analysis indicates that whereas a large share of costs are borne by the injured or ill workers and their families, a sizable percentage is paid by private non–workers' compensation insurers, Medicare, and Medicaid. In the nominal analysis, WC covers 27 percent of the costs, whereas taxpayers cover 18 percent.

CHAPTER 9

Policy and Cost Comparisons

I. Introduction

This chapter will briefly suggest some policy proposals as well as make cost comparisons between occupational injuries and illnesses on the one hand and AIDS, Alzheimer's disease, arthritis, circulatory disease, and cancer on the other.

II. Policy

II.A. Introduction

Suggested policy proposals involving OSHA, workers' compensation, injury taxes, and so on, are too numerous to list, let alone discuss.[1] They range from radically increasing the number of OSHA inspectors to abolishing OSHA altogether.[2] Our purpose in this chapter is briefly to mention six policy changes. The first of these ("A Report Card") is a new idea. The others are old but now carry more significance, given our results on costs. Accordingly, most of our attention will be on the Report Card proposal.

II.B. A Report Card for Occupational Injuries and Illnesses

II.B.1. Introduction

In recent years, government policies have proliferated that require sellers, hospitals, firms, and employers to reveal information pertaining to the health consequences of products and services (Leigh 1998). In 1996, national legislation was passed that required that public water utilities to provide information to consumers regarding the chemicals present in tap water. Hospitals now routinely provide mortality data to government authorities, who, in turn, make them available to print and broadcast

182

media (Mennemeyer, Morrisey, and Howard 1997). Canned, packaged, and bottled food and beverages now have labels revealing ingredients and nutritional content. Tobacco and toy firms are required to inform consumers of the health and safety aspects of their products. Drug companies must inform consumers of possible side effects of their drugs. A panel of scientists at the National Research Council has advocated requiring auto companies to provide to consumers information and numerical rankings on the crashworthiness of new cars (Morgan et al. 1996). As a result of the Valujet crash in May 1996, the Federal Aviation Administration (FAA) now provides crash statistics on airlines via the Internet ("FAA will offer"). The state of Massachusetts now prepares report cards on physicians that include information on malpractice awards (Green 1996). Report cards are also being used by many health plans to inform consumers (Hibbard and Jewett 1997). Finally, although not sponsored by government, *Consumer Reports* magazine frequently has stories on the health and safety aspects of a variety of products, services, and firms, including HMOs.

The Information Age is transforming buying and selling transactions throughout our economy. This is especially true for health and safety information. Moreover, the information and government policies enjoy widespread political support. The water utilities legislation alluded to above was overwhelmingly passed by the Republican-controlled House in the summer of 1996. A Harris poll indicated that 66 percent of people surveyed would like to see report cards for hospitals, and 58 percent would like to see consumer ratings of physicians ("FAA will offer" 1997).

II.B.2. A Policy Proposal

The Occupational Safety and Health Administration (OSHA) has also embraced this policy of providing information. The original 1970 OSH Act contains a standard pertaining to access to injury and illness records (Title 29, Code of Federal Regulations, pt. 1904). This Injury and Illness Recording Standard gives employees the right to examine and copy the injury and illness log. A standard from the 1980s pertained to access to medical and exposure records (Title 29, Code of Federal Regulations, pt. 1910.20). This Access-to-Records Standard requires employers to inform employees of the availability of medical records information on an annual basis. The point of our policy proposal is to suggest that these standards ought to be provided to current and prospective employees, and that they ought to be presented so that they are intelligible to the average American. These suggestions could be carried out by simply amending the Recording Standard (29 CFR 1904). One approach would require that some abbreviated version of these data be included in a report card and be attached to every job application form. Another approach would require that this report card be circulated among employees each year.

The report card should contain national death, injury, and illness rates as well as costs for specific occupations corresponding to the industry in which the firm operates. Information on the most frequent causes of these deaths, injuries, and illnesses should also be included. Experts could be consulted on how the rankings, rates, and report card would be presented so that the average employee and employer would find them useful (Morgan et al. 1996). Percentiles rather than rates, for example, might be most useful. Costs might be an alternative method to communicate the risk, given that costs combine deaths, injuries, and illnesses in a metric most people easily understand — dollars.

II.B.3. Data

The report card would not be expensive. The Bureau of Labor Statistics (BLS) annually collects and publishes extensive information on job-related injuries and illnesses in the Census of Fatal Occupational Injuries (Census) (Toscano et al. 1995) and the Annual Survey of Occupational Injuries and Illnesses (Annual Survey). The Annual Survey data are derived from the logs required by the Recording Standard.

Whereas the BLS publications using the Census and the Annual Survey are extensive, they do not yet publish the data that would be most useful for the employee and employer: the death rates, the nonfatal injury and illness rates, and the costs rates, as well as the causes of these deaths, injuries, and illnesses for as many specific occupations and industries as possible (Leigh 1995a).[3]

II.B.4. Limitations of the Proposal

There are a number of problems associated with these data and this recommendation to provide injury and illness information. First, there are data problems as noted in our discussion of the Census and the Annual Survey in chapter 2. Moreover, as noted in chapter 2 (CFOI) and chapter 3 (Annual Survey), neither database adequately addresses illnesses. These problems could be minimized with more resources devoted to BLS data-gathering efforts and with a more aggressive OSHA that imposes fines on firms that underreport. Moreover, existing injury data may not be terribly biased if the goal is to compare injury and illness rates across occupations and industries; that is, if firms underreport by similar percentage amounts, relative rankings will still be useful.

There may be legal issues associated with the release of these BLS data. The persons and firms supplying the raw data to the Census and the Annual Survey are guaranteed confidentiality by the BLS. One way to minimize the risk of breaching confidentiality agreements is to keep the data at a sufficiently aggregated level—for example, at the three-digit occupation and one-digit industry levels. Another way is to present the data as costs rather than numbers of deaths, injuries, or illnesses.

Some readers might envision a limitation involving additional record keeping by individual firms. Our specific proposal, however, involves occupation/industry cells aggregated from nationwide data. The data would be provided by the U.S. Department of Labor to firms and workers. As a result, individual firms would not be burdened with generating their own data for all occupations. A related problem concerns effectiveness. It might be argued that the most effective statistics for policy purposes would be firm specific. Firm-specific data from new or small firms, or firms experiencing wide employment swings, would be especially problematic. Rate data may not be reliable due to small numbers or rapidly changing numbers in the denominator. Numerator data may also be unreliable. Injury deaths are relatively rare and may not have occurred for a new or small firm. That fact alone might lull the manager or owner of the firm into a sense of complacency.[4] Small firms, in general, have especially high injury death rates. Moreover, as mentioned, there might be legal problems associated with releasing these firm-specific data directly to the public. Finally, calculations of rates and rankings by individual firms would impose an additional burden on businesses. For these reasons, the provision of national occupation and injury-specific data would have some effectiveness not available with firm-specific data and might be more practical than firm-specific data.

II.B.5. Benefits of the Proposal

An extension of the Recording Standard would set in motion a number of forces that would improve working conditions, especially for jobs heretofore not widely recognized by the public as hazardous, such as nursing home work. First, news media attention will be directed toward those jobs at the top of the list. Responsible employers will seek to improve their image by offering safer workplaces. This heightened public awareness will be perhaps the most significant effect of the provision of information. Public support for additional OSHA regulations is likely to grow.

For example, the Census data have been used to focus attention on homicides in the workplace. Newspaper articles (Kilborn 1991) and television programs have addressed the hazards of employment in convenience stores. One program presented the response of the Gainesville, Florida, police department to convenience store crimes. The response ultimately resulted in a sharp drop in crimes in convenience stores. This increased media attention may already have had some effect. The latest Census data indicate that for the first time since records have been kept, national work homicides decreased from 1993 to 1994 (Toscano 1996).

Second, employees and employers will be alerted to the most probable injuries and illnesses in their line of work. This will be especially important for new, small companies with little history of occupational safety and health problems; it will also be important for employees in all jobs. A firm with no history of deaths would become aware of how these are likely to occur and could take preventive measures to avoid them.

Finally, provision of information will help "the market" reduce injuries and illnesses (Schroeder and Shapiro 1984). There is a "free market" force, an invisible hand, that works to reduce injuries and illnesses without government intervention. That force is referred to as the compensation wage hypothesis by economists (see chap. 4). It rewards firms with safe working conditions and punishes firms with dangerous conditions. Empirical evidence for the existence of compensating wages is mixed. Some economic studies find evidence for compensating wages (Viscusi 1992), while others do not (Dorman 1996; Leigh 1995b). The most highly regarded advocate of the hypothesis, Kip Viscusi (1992), asserts that the free market force has been more effective than all of OSHA's efforts to reduce injuries and illnesses. All economists will agree, however, that if the free market force is to work, employees must know the risks they face.

We turn now to additional policies.

II.C. Five Additional Policies (Greer 1992)

Fines for Willful Underreporting. As noted in appendix A to chapter 2, when OSHA started issuing fines to large manufacturing companies for "willful" underreporting, the recorded number of cases leaped over 100 percent.[5] A number of firms pleaded guilty (Caterpillar, Chrysler, General Dynamics, and Scott Paper) and received fines (Greer 1992), and considerable undesirable publicity surrounded those fines. But the fines were targeted only at large manufacturing concerns. If OSHA were to announce that all firms were likely to receive fines and if OSHA carried out this threat, we might have a better understanding of the magnitude of occupational safety and health problems.

Increase WC Premiums, Benefits, and Coverage. Due to the moral hazard associated with receiving WC benefits, the benefits must be less than fully compensating for an injury or illness. But our results suggest that WC covers less than 55 percent of the true cost of injuries and perhaps less than 5 percent for illnesses. A case could be made for increasing premiums and benefits and for widening WC coverage to all firms but the self-employed.[6] Benefits ought to be raised so that the effective wage replacement rate is 0.66, not 0.4 for permanent disabilities.

A drawback to this proposal to raise premiums and benefits is that some investigators maintain that generous WC benefits would result in more injuries occurring and greater time away from work (Falaris, Link, and Staten 1995). This theory holds that workers are aware of the WC benefits they qualify for in the event of an injury and that if those benefits are sufficiently generous, some workers may take fewer precautions at work than if the benefits were stingy. Alternatively, workers may discover how generous WC benefits are after qualifying for WC and decide that a few more days or weeks spent recovering from or nursing an injury would be financially rewarding. This is the so-called moral hazard problem identified in the insurance literature. Studies on this moral hazard problem were mentioned in chapter 2 (app. A, Annual Survey section). Ruser (1991, 1993) found that generous WC benefits were associated with increased nonfatal (but not fatal) injury rates and length of time away from work. Cheadle et al. (1994), on the other hand, did not find any statistical significant associations.

Any investigation of WC benefits, injury rates, and duration of time off work will confront a mutual causality statistical problem that few studies have investigated. Positive partial correlations between injury rates or time loss from work and generous benefits do not necessarily imply that generous benefits result in more injuries or longer durations. It could be that state legislators and insurance commissioners who establish the benefits are simply responding to constituencies. Injured workers who vote may let their elected representatives know that they want generous benefits. The more injured or ill workers there are in a state, other things equal, the larger the constituency that would support generous benefits. Leigh (1985b) found that the estimated effect of generous benefits on injury and illness rates is less after accounting for mutual causality bias than before accounting for it.

Another problem not addressed by researchers who allege a strong moral hazard problem concerns the Willingness-to-Pay (WTP) and Human Capital estimates found here as well as the disincentives workers face in filing WC claims (chap. 2). In our research into WTP, we found that virtually all WTP estimates of values of life, injuries, and diseases were three to six times greater than the Human Capital costs of the same lives, injuries, and disease. Moreover, our Human Capital indirect costs estimates were roughly 35 percent more than lost wages, that is, fringe benefits and home production. It would appear that the WTP costs to the individual would far exceed, and Human Capital indirect costs would significantly exceed, the WC benefits, especially given that WC covers only roughly 40 to 60 percent of the before-tax wage. Given the magnitude of the differences between either WTP or Human Capital costs on the one hand and WC benefits on the other, it would appear that not a great number of workers would find it profitable to experience an injury or illness and subsequently collect benefits. In addition, workers might worry that filing a WC claim would reduce their future raises and employment prospects. In summary, we do not regard the moral hazard problem as especially troublesome unless WC benefits were raised an inordinate amount.

Better Illness Data Collection. Given the dearth of data on occupational illness, it seems appropriate that the BLS, NIOSH, and OSHA form a scientific panel to discuss ways whereby data could be collected and published. A Census of Fatal Occupational Diseases might be created.

Small Firms. As we have seen (chap. 2), small firms are especially hazardous. They should not receive special "hands-off" treatment by the OSH Administration or BLS data gatherers. To the contrary, they should receive increased regulatory attention. Small firms should not be exempt from WC coverage.

General Industry Tax or OSHA Trust Fund (Smith 1974). A nationwide tax should be levied on firms based upon the experience of their industry. Contributions to the illness burden could be assessed for each industry using NIOSH industry-specific data on deaths from circulatory diseases, cancer, COPD, and so on. Contributions to the injury burden could be assessed with Annual Survey data for each industry. Part of this general tax should be used to pay back to Medicare and Medicaid the amount that Medicare and Medicaid currently pay for occupational injuries and illnesses. The general tax would be similar to the tax all coal companies pay into the federal Black Lung Trust. Similar arguments have been advanced by attorneys general from a variety of states in connection with the cost of tobacco-related illnesses to state medical funds.

III. Cost Comparisons with Other Diseases

In the first subsection, we will compare our costs with costs of other diseases. In the second, we will indicate how the economic laws of diminishing returns and increasing opportunity costs suggest medical dollars might be reallocated between heart disease and occupational injuries and illnesses.

III.A. Costs of AIDS, Alzheimer's Disease, Arthritis, Circulatory Diseases, and Cancer

Costs of occupational injuries and illnesses are large when compared to other diseases. The direct and indirect costs of AIDS were estimated to be roughly $30.0 billion in 1992 (Hellinger 1992; Farnham 1995), excluding insurance administration costs. Roughly $6.8 billion arose from direct costs and $23.2 from indirect costs. The ratio of indirect to direct costs is high (4 to 1) because so many AIDS patients die before retirement. Our occupational injuries and illness costs, excluding insurance administration, were approximately $140 billion.

Alzheimer's disease was recently estimated to generate $20.6 billion in direct costs and $46.7 billion in indirect costs, including administration (Ernst and Hay 1994). The ratio of indirect to direct costs was a little over 2 to 1. The reason for the relatively low ratio is that most people do not develop Alzheimer's disease until they retire. Again, our direct cost estimate was $52 billion and our indirect estimate was $104 billion for injuries and illnesses.

The costs of all musculoskeletal conditions (mostly arthritis) were roughly $149 billion in 1992 (Yelin and Callahan 1995).

The economic costs of cancer were estimated to be roughly $96 billion in 1990 (Brown, Hodgson, and Rice 1993). The Brown study did not account for insurance administration, and there have been inflation and a rising trend in cancer prevalence. We therefore developed our own estimate based on the Rice, Hodgson, and Kopstein 1985 study. We assumed a 154 percent increase in general medical prices from 1980 to 1992; a 33 percent increase in the number of afflicted people from 1980 to 1992; a 70 percent increase in economy-wide prices for indirect costs; and a 10 percent additional increase in costs for cancer therapy. Our calculations (Leigh et al. 1996) generated a cost of $171 billion for 1992. The ratio of indirect to direct costs was roughly 3 to 1.

Circulatory diseases—heart attack, stroke, and high blood pressure—are responsible for more deaths than any other disease or injury in the United States. Unfortunately, the most reliable estimate of the costs of all circulatory diseases dates to 1980. Rice, Hodgson, and Kopstein (1985) estimated $32.5 billion in direct costs and $47.1 billion in indirect costs in 1980. The American Heart Association (1992) attempted to adjust these estimates to reflect inflation and changes in the numbers of people with heart diseases from 1980 to 1982. The American Heart Association estimate for 1992 was $108.9. The Association did not fully account for the mortality aspect of indirect costs, however. The Heart, Lung, and Blood Institute estimated the cost to be $189 billion (Fox et al. 1996) and did attempt to fully account for indirect costs. The ratio of indirect to direct costs was roughly 1.5 to 1. We prefer the NHLBI estimate of $189 billion.[7]

III.B. Reallocation between Circulatory Disease and Occupational Injuries and Illnesses

In this section we present a suggestion concerning how our estimates might be used to allocate preventive medicine dollars. We emphasize the word *suggestion*. A thorough benefit-cost study of the allocation of preventive medicine dollars would require a book unto itself. We will compare spending for all circulatory diseases with occupational injuries and illnesses (excluding job-related circulatory diseases).[8]

Occupational injuries and illnesses (excluding job-related circulatory diseases)[9] cost roughly 82 percent as much as all circulatory (heart and stroke) diseases. This does not necessarily imply that if, for example, Congress and the president find an additional $100 million dollars of unallocated preventive medicine spending, they should spend it reducing occupational injuries and illnesses. Since this $100 million could be used for either of the two problems, the relevant question is this: where will the dollars of spending generate the greatest cost savings — in circulatory disease or occupational injuries and illnesses? A definitive answer to this question would require information on marginal costs. A suggestive answer can nevertheless be made with information on average and total costs.

Two of the most important lessons of economics involve the laws of diminishing returns and of increasing opportunity costs. These laws are so widely accepted that they are discussed in the opening chapters of every introductory economics text. In our context, suppose that $1 billion is being spent on the prevention of circulatory disease. The law of diminishing returns suggests that the first, say, $100 million spent on reducing circulatory disease (from 0 to $100 million) will probably yield a larger reduction in risk than the last $100 million spent (from $900 million to $1 billion).

An analogy might help explain the idea. Suppose that circulatory disease risk can be reduced through jogging. The law of diminishing returns suggests that the decrease in risk would be greater for the sedentary person (who never jogged) who now decides to jog 15 minutes a day as opposed to the active person (who used to jog one hour a day) who now jogs one hour and 15 minutes. The 15 additional minutes to the sedentary person would likely reduce his or her risk more than the 15 additional minutes would reduce the risk for the active person. If the goal were to increase aggregate health (the sum of the health between the two persons) and if a choice has to be made between the two persons the 15 minutes ought to be applied to the sedentary person.

The law of increasing opportunity costs extends the law of diminishing returns to the production of two goals. Imagine our two goals are winning horse races and basketball games. The law of increasing opportunity costs states that some factors of production (land, labor, or capital) are more suitable in the winning of races than in the winning of games. Short persons can play basketball, but they are not likely to score as many points or win as many games as tall persons. Tall persons can ride horses, but they are less likely than short persons to win horse races. If total wins are to be maximized, we should allow short persons to specialize as jockeys and tall persons to specialize as basketball players.

In our context, the goals would be the production of health, free from circulatory disease and/or free from occupational injuries and illnesses. The law of increasing costs relies on the notion of the substitutability of factors. The word *factor* here means something that helps produce health — such as biochemists who attempt to improve cholesterol-lowering drugs[10] and safety experts for occupational safety and health. The safety experts may have special abilities to spot safety hazards. These abilities may not be possessed by biochemists. Biochemists, on the other hand, may have abilities that safety experts do not possess. To produce more health free from circulatory disease could eventually require that some safety experts be trained as biochemists. These new biochemists may not have the same intrinsic biochemical abilities as the old biochemists. In a similar vein, to produce more health free from occupational injuries and illnesses would eventually require that biochemists be trained as safety experts. These new experts may not have as much ability as the old experts in spotting occupational hazards.

The experts and the biochemists are "factors." They possess different abilities. People who freely choose to become biochemists probably have more ability in those tasks than people who are forced out of a safety expert job into a biochemist's job. Likewise, biochemists forced into a safety expert job may not make good safety experts.

As we require more and more production of health free from circulatory disease, we essentially reach a point where factors more adept in
the production of health free from occupational injuries and illnesses
are forced into circulatory disease risk reduction. The point is that some
factors (land, labor, or capital) are more suitable in producing health free
from circulatory disease than in producing health free from occupational
injuries and illnesses. If we force those factors to produce things for which
they are ill suited, our increase in production will be small.

If our goal is to prevent both circulatory disease and occupational
injuries and illnesses, then some *balance* of factors or resources between
these two preventive activities would be warranted.[11] This plea for balance is especially strong, given that the total costs of the two problems are
of roughly similar magnitudes. There does not appear to be a balance,
however. Far more resources appear to be applied to circulatory disease
than occupational injuries and illnesses. By virtually any measure —
research dollars, numbers of cardiologists versus occupational medicine
physicians, dollars spent on cholesterol-lowering drugs, number of
OSHA inspectors or safety experts, paperback self-help books, news
articles, television shows, and so on — physicians, politicians, nurses, authors, media representatives, drug company CEOs, and U.S. consumers
spend far more attention on circulatory disease than on occupational
injuries and illnesses. If some of these circulatory disease dollars and
attention were redirected at occupational injuries and illnesses, we might
experience a slight increase in circulatory disease costs but a much larger
reduction in occupational injury and illness costs.

This analysis of circulatory disease costs is merely an example of an
application of the laws of diminishing returns and increasing costs. We
do not wish to single out circulatory disease as getting too much public
and scientific attention. Our analysis could equally be applied to AIDS,
cancer, Alzheimer's disease, arthritis, or any other health problem. Our
point is simple: a reallocation of resources from any of a number of
health problems to occupational safety and health might result in a net
gain in lives saved as well as in injuries, illnesses, and costs avoided.[12]

IV. Conclusion

In this chapter we mentioned several policy options and compared costs
of occupational injuries and illnesses with those of other diseases.

Regarding policy, we argue that the Reporting Standard should be
extended to include national summary statistics on injuries and illnesses
that would be useful for the average American. These statistics should
be placed on job application forms. There are several reasons for provid-

ing this information. There is considerable legal precedent. The policy would not be costly since the data are already available. Finally, the provision of information would set in motion strong political and economic forces that would reduce injuries and illnesses.

Also regarding policy, we listed five specific suggestions: (1) fines for willful underreporting; (2) increased WC premiums and benefits; (3) better illness data gathering; (4) greater attention to small firms; (5) a general industry tax, or OSHA Trust Fund.

This chapter also estimated costs for other diseases. Occupational injury and illness costs are roughly five times the costs for AIDS, three times the costs for Alzheimer's disease, more than the cost for musculoskeletal diseases, roughly 91 percent of the costs for all cancers, and 82 percent as big as the costs of all heart diseases and strokes. By virtually any measure, occupational injuries and illnesses do not receive the same scientific, government, medical, media, or public attention commanded by AIDS, Alzheimer's disease, arthritis, cancer, or heart disease. Some reallocation of resources from any one of the former to occupational injuries and illnesses might improve the overall health of the nation.

CHAPTER 10

Limitations and Assumptions

I. Introduction

In this chapter we discuss some of the limitations, assumptions, and advantages of our study. Space prohibits an evaluation of all criticisms, limitations, and advantages as well as a discussion of every assumption we made. We therefore selected the limitations that were the most controversial and the assumptions that had the greatest consequences for our estimates.

Two sections follow this one. In Section II, we consider the limitations and criticisms of our study and our rebuttals to these criticisms. Limitations include the following: no single source of data; fraudulent claims; more injuries occur at home than at work; WC medical costs exaggerate true medical costs; full employment; Human Capital costs and QALYs; generous WC benefits increase injuries; total and average costs versus marginal costs.

The chapter closes with a conclusion (sec. III). In appendix A, we list 31 of the most important assumptions and note whether they result in a high or low estimate for numbers of injuries and illnesses and for costs. Appendix B considers incidence and prevalence costs.

II. Limitations and Criticisms

II.A. No Single Source of Data

Our most serious limitation was that there was no single source of data available to provide all of the information we required. We had to analyze data from a variety of sources. In all, we considered over 20 primary sources and over 300 secondary sources. Each source had limitations, and numerous assumptions had to be made in calculating our final estimates.

In appendix A of this chapter, we mention 31 of the major assumptions of the study. We do not elaborate on these assumptions here. Rather, we refer the reader to the place in the text where the assumption is invoked and discussed. A word precedes each item in our list of

194

assumptions. The word *Low* indicates that this assumption would result in a lower estimate than would be obtained with alternative assumptions. The word *High* indicates the assumption led to a higher estimate than would have been obtained with alternative assumptions. Note that Low assumptions outnumber High assumptions: 25 Lows, two Highs, and four of unknown bias. Moreover, each High assumption receives quite a bit more attention and justification in the text referenced than the Low assumptions. We invoked High estimate assumptions only when we believed there was overwhelming evidence to support them.

II.B. Fraudulent Claims

A popular perception is that many job-related injuries and illnesses are fraudulent. This perception is especially strong for a WC claim. For example, some people fake back pain or exaggerate the pain they feel, hoping to qualify for WC benefits.

There are several responses to this criticism: First, if the dollar amount of the fraud were large, it would behoove WC insurance firms to find and prosecute the perpetrators. After all, fraud reduces these firms' profits. In other words, there are economic forces that automatically work to minimize fraud.

Second, the extent of the fraud, whether big or small, has never been carefully documented. In the study with which we are familiar, the Ohio Bureau of Workers' Compensation employed 80 investigators to ferret out fraud (Smith 1995). In 1994, they found $52 million of fraudulent claims. Fifty-one persons were convicted. If Ohio is representative of the nation and if this $52 million only applied to 1994 (which is unlikely since many large claims involve more than one year) then we estimate roughly $1.2 billion in fraudulent claims. Now $1.2 billion is a lot of money, but it is only roughly 2 percent of all WC dollars spent in 1994 and less than 1 percent of all costs as estimated in this study. In another study the actual number of fraud cases sent by insurance companies to prosecutors was less than 1 percent of all claims (Fricker 1997).

Smith (1992) indirectly tested the fraud hypothesis by looking at frequencies of claims on Mondays as opposed to all other days of the week. Smith hypothesized that some workers may have actually been injured over the weekend, but claimed to their employer that the injury occurred on Monday, thus qualifying them for WC benefits. As we indicated in chapter 2 (app. A, the Annual Survey section), however, Smith ignored the medical literature showing at least part of the increase of incidents on Mondays could be attributed to the body's physiological response to the reintroduction of job hazards. This would be especially true on Mondays following vacations.

Questions of fraud have been addressed in a closely related area — the Social Security Disability Insurance (SSDI) program (Bound 1989). In the early 1980s, the Reagan administration began making it difficult for people to qualify for SSDI. From 1980 to 1982, the number of new successful claims dropped 25 percent. At the same time, more than 20 percent of cases of persons receiving benefits were reviewed and denied. Most of those among the 20 percent who appealed won their appeal. The aggressive Reagan policies ended in 1984, when Congress enacted new legislation governing SSDI.

John Bound (1989) tested the hypothesis that a high percentage of SSDI recipients was able to work. He analyzed persons who were denied benefits. Presumably, an even higher percentage of those who were *denied* benefits as opposed to those who were awarded benefits would have the ability to work. Social Security data on prime-age men rejected from SSDI showed, however, that fewer than 50 percent went back to work. Moreover, among those who did find work, their earnings were 30 percent less than their predisability earnings.

Boaz and Muller (1990) considered the fraud issue from a different perspective. They analyzed roughly 11,000 people in the Social Security Administration's Retirement History Survey (RHS). They found that self-reported health status was not only a strong predictor of early retirement but of premature death as well. The probability of dying "within two years after retiring and the probability of seeking medical care at the time of retiring are much higher for those who report work-limiting health problems before age 65." Similar results were found for those who applied for SSDI, regardless of whether they were eventually awarded benefits (Boaz and Muller 1990).

Both the Bound (1989) and Boaz and Muller (1990) studies suggest that reports of extensive fraud in the SSDI program were exaggerated. They also suggest that future WC research ought to investigate the health outcomes of persons who had their WC claims rejected.

It is often alleged that "job-stress" claims dominate WC caseloads. Stress claims were increasing significantly during the 1980s, especially in California. Nationwide, stress claims are not significant. Burton estimated them to be one-half of 1 percent of all WC claims in the late 1980s (Burton 1988).

Elisburg (1994) points out that the majority of stress cases are not terribly controversial. Elisburg identifies three categories of stress claims. The first type of stress claim involves a mental problem that resulted from a traumatic injury in the workplace. Many suicides fall into this category. A formerly active person becomes a quadriplegic as the result of a job-related injury and commits suicide a year or two later. The second category involves a mental condition that leads to a job-related injury. For example, a sudden noise could result in paralysis that, in turn, could result in physical injury.

The third and the most controversial is that a mental condition in the worker could result from an incident at the job that may not have resulted in any physical injury to the worker filing the claim. Even within this category, however, many of the cases appear unimpeachable. For example, Elisburg (1994) cites one case in which a worker suffered a severe anxiety reaction after accidentally running over and killing a fellow employee.

A related criticism involves the alleged waste and inefficiencies in medical care for injured or ill workers. Waste and ineffective treatments undoubtedly exist. There is always room for improvement in providing care. Waste and ineffective treatments also undoubtedly exist in medical care for AIDS, cancer, and heart disease patients. A large part of the emerging field of health services research is, in fact, directed toward discovering waste and inefficiencies in all forms of medical care. Our main conclusion about the relative magnitude of costs between these diseases compared with occupational injuries and illnesses is therefore still valid. It would be inappropriate to second-guess physicians' opinions surrounding treatment for an occupational injury but not surrounding treatment of nonoccupational cancer, AIDS, or cardiovascular conditions (Leigh, Markowitz, and Landrigan 1998).

It could also be that many legitimate claims are denied or, more frequently, never filed. As we saw in chapter 2 (app. A, the NCCI section) WC accounts for only roughly 45 percent of all workplace injuries. The 1 to 2 percent amount of fraud pales in comparison to this 55 percent undercount. Most of the undercount results from institutional factors. Self-employed people, most farmworkers, most household workers, and many workers in small firms are not covered by WC laws. Some of the undercount also involves the nature of the injury. A worker must either be attended to by a medical professional outside the employing firm or disabled from work for at least three days. If the worker is seen in-house by the company nurse and if only one or two days are lost, then the incident may never be recorded as a WC compensable injury.[1] It could also be that the employer would allow a worker a day to recover from a relatively minor injury that would not require medical treatment. Since such minor injuries are more numerous than ones resulting in a medical visit or more than three days of work loss, it is not surprising that the total number of WC cases would underestimate the actual number of cases.

Some employers offer bonuses to employees who do not report injuries. According to a *Wall Street Journal* study, these bonus schemes are especially prevalent in poultry plants — an industry that has experienced rapid growth since consumers have increased their demand for chicken, ironically, for health reasons (Horwitz 1994).

A worker may conceal a job-related injury. Legally, a worker cannot be fired for filing a WC claim. But many workers are afraid of employer reprisal (O'Loughlin 1993; Roy 1992). Biddle et al. (1998) found that at least 55 percent of a sample of ill workers in Michigan who would likely qualify for WC never file. Workers, especially new ones, want to make a good impression. Most employees realize that reliability is highly regarded by employers. Excessive absences for whatever reason can harm the chances for promotions. Most employees, even if they desire to quit, want a strong recommendation from their current employer.[2] Excessive absences would jeopardize that recommendation.

There is also likely to be fraud committed by insurance companies. Fricker (1997) reports on state of California insurance claims audits that show significant numbers of problems caused by insurers. In 45 percent of the cases in which the insurers were supposed to initiate vocational rehabilitation, they never did. In 22 percent of cases, the insurers failed to notify workers of benefits. In 17 percent of cases, workers were never paid money owed by insurers.

There are undoubtedly fraudulent claims filed by workers. We do not rely on the WC count of injuries or illnesses in generating our total estimates.[3] Our view is that there are fraudulent claims, but there are also legitimate claims that are never filed as well as claims, workers, and firms that are not covered by the WC system. We believe that the latter far exceed the number and cost of fraudulent claims. Finally, it is likely that significant fraud is also perpetrated by WC insurers.

II.C. Generous WC Benefits Increase Injuries

Some investigators maintain that generous WC benefits would result in more injuries occurring and greater time away from work. Presumably, workers are aware of the WC benefits they qualify for in the event of an injury. If those benefits are sufficiently generous, some workers may not take fewer precautions at work than if the benefits were stingy. We address this issue in chapter 9. We conclude that, given the relatively low levels of benefits, this moral hazard problem is likely to be small.[4]

II.D. More Injuries Occur at Home Than at Work

The number of injury deaths not job related exceeds job-related injury deaths by roughly 15 to 1 (Rice et al. 1989a; Hensler et al. 1991; Baker, O'Neil, and Ginsburg 1992; National Safety Council 1993). The number of nonfatal injuries away from work exceeds those at work by factors of between 6:1 to 14:1 (Hensler et al. 1991; National Safety Council 1993). These disparities have led some investigators to comment that being at work is much safer than being at home.

These statistics are misleading. There were over 250 million persons living in the United States in 1992 of whom only roughly 120 million held jobs. Moreover, those who work are not a random sample of Americans. People with jobs tend to be 20 to 65 years old and are more likely to be male than female. There is also the "healthy worker effect." A typical employed man age 40 is likely to be healthier than a typical unemployed man age 40. Children and the elderly would not likely be among those who experienced a job-related injury. Finally, most of the time (awake and asleep) of those who work is spent away from work.

To accurately access whether "home" (i.e., not at work) is more dangerous than work, we need to restrict our attention to a group most likely to be employed and express risk as per hour of exposure. Hensler et al. (1991) attempted to make such a comparison for men who held jobs. They did not control for hours of exposure, however. They found that employed men were more likely to be injured on the job than anywhere else and that these injuries were more likely to be serious (i.e., disabling and costly) than any other injuries experienced away from their jobs. Had Hensler et al. controlled for hours of exposure, work hours would have been found to be far more hazardous than home hours. This is true simply because most working people spend less time at work than away from work. Assuming 40 hours a week of work, the ratio of work hours to all hours would be 0.24, or 24 percent (40/168). Thus, for men who work, it is likely that work is more dangerous than "home." A careful study of women has never been conducted, but again, simple comparisons would be inaccurate. Account must be taken of age, employment status, hours at work, and hours away from work.

II.E. WC Medical Costs Exaggerate True
Medical Costs

In the 1980s, WC medical costs were estimated to have increased one and one-half times faster than general medical costs (Nelson 1992).

Some investigators have argued that this evidence suggests that WC pays more than the true medical costs associated with an injury or illness (Baker and Krueger 1995; Leigh and Ward 1997). Hospitals and doctors, for example, may charge a higher price to WC insurers than to all other insurers for the same injury or illness.

There are other reasons for the fast increase in aggregate WC costs. During the 1980s, the economy was contracting in 1981 and 1982 but was expanding in late 1983 through 1989. As the economy expands, more people are put back to work. In the 1970s, WC did not expand as rapidly as other medical costs (Boden and Fleishman 1989), and the economy suffered two serious recessions: 1973–74 and 1979.

As employment expanded, the number of injuries undoubtedly increased for three reasons. First, as a matter of arithmetic, the more people who work, the more the number of injuries. Second, as the economy expands, more workers put in overtime, and each employed worker has greater exposure to hazards. This overtime factor is doubly important because fatigue increases with overtime. Third, many of the newly hired employees were not likely to have much experience at the job. As we indicated in chapter 2, a number of studies suggest that inexperienced workers suffer a disproportionate number of job injuries (Division of Labor Statistics and Research 1985; Chelius 1979).

Another factor pertains to payments. Unlike other insurers in the 1980s, WC insurers paid virtually 100 percent of the medical bill. Neither injured or ill workers nor the firms employing them paid a co-payment or had a deductible. Throughout the 1980s, non-WC insurers rapidly introduced co-payments and deductibles.

In addition, the kinds of injuries and illnesses paid for by WC are not typical when compared to general medical spending. For example, men are more likely than women to receive WC. In addition, roughly 98 percent of WC incidents involve injuries, many requiring ambulance services and emergency care. General medical spending is not so highly concentrated among injuries. Moreover, even within injuries, WC injuries are likely to be more severe than non-WC injuries (Hensler et al. 1991; Marquis 1992; National Safety Council 1993; Miller and Galbraith 1994; Rossman and Miller 1991). As mentioned, the worker faces incentives not to report an injury. If he or she reports and especially if he or she seeks indemnity payment, then the injury or illness must be viewed as serious by people other than the worker and his or her doctor (i.e., the WC board).

Nevertheless, on balance, it is likely that WC medical payments are greater than non-WC payments. We account for this disparity in note 4 of chapter 5 by allowing for roughly a 10 percent differential.

II.F. Full Employment

The largest component of indirect costs is lost wages. But whether lost wages represent a true "opportunity" cost depends upon economic conditions. "Opportunity" costs is the preferred measure of cost in economics. It stresses the importance of the next best available alternative. If there is a substantial amount of unemployment, then the worker sustaining the injury or illness might be easily replaced with someone currently unemployed. Since the unemployed replacement had no wages prior to acquiring the job, the loss to the economy from the injured worker's production may be zero. That is, the next best available alternative — the unemployed worker — had no wage or work production to lose.

The implicit assumption in all prior work on the lost wages component of indirect costs, and the explicit assumption here, is that the economy is operating at full employment. This means that no direct, easy replacement for the injured or ill worker is readily available. The replacement must come from a different sector in the economy, necessitating a drop in output from that sector.

This is a reasonable assumption. It underpins the commonsense idea that people are a valuable resource.[5] If this were not true, then a number of counterintuitive (and incorrect!) conclusions could be drawn about costs in the economy. For example, business groups often complain of the overall costs of environmental OSHA regulations. Businesses must spend more than they otherwise would, for example, on machinery in a cotton mill that reduces the amount of cotton fiber circulating in the plant. These new machines are costly. The manufacturers of the machines must pay people to produce the machines. Presumably, without the added spending on the new machines, these people would have been employed elsewhere in the economy. The fact that they are induced into building new cotton mill machinery presumably means that output elsewhere in the economy must have decreased. But if these workers had been unemployed, then the cost to the economy would be zero. We would have the result that environmental and OSHA standards *create* jobs and therefore do not result in any net loss to the economy.

The implicit assumption behind the argument of the costs of EPA and OSHA regulations is that the economy is operating at full employment. A cleaner environment or safer workplace is not free. It must be paid for. We, therefore, invoke the same full employment assumption used by business groups in our analysis of the costs of lost wages.

II.G. Human Capital Costs and QALYs

We recognize that many U.S. academic economists would prefer WTP over Human Capital estimates. In addition to the justification for the Human Capital approach we provide in chapter 4, there is the point that Human Capital costs, due to the weight given to potential lost earnings, are likely to be strongly correlated with aggregate measures of health such as QALYs (Cutler and Richardson 1997; Murry and Acharya 1997). QALY represents quality-adjusted life years. Two factors are pertinent: age and quality of life. Other things equal, a 20 year old would have more potential QALYs in his or her future than an 80 year old simply because the 20 year old would have more years left to live. This is in contrast to the WTP approach, whereby a wealthy 80 year old may have a higher WTP than a low-income 20 year old. Also, other things equal, a 50 year old with no work-limiting disabilities would be likely to have more QALYs to look forward to than a disabled 50 year old who is not in the workforce. Our Human Capital indirect cost method explicitly accounts for years of working life left and the labor force participation rate; that is, work-disabled people are assigned a zero cost. U.S. academic economists may therefore want to view our Human Capital estimate as well as all other Human Capital disease estimates as indicators of aggregate health (or ill health).

II.H. Other Major Criticisms

Two other major criticisms are mentioned here but were addressed elsewhere. Some economists believe that generous WC benefits increase the numbers of injuries. We address this criticism in section II.C. of chapter 9. When using Human Capital and WTP cost estimates the issue of marginal versus average and total costs is often mentioned. We address this issue in section II.C. of chapter 4.[6]

III. Conclusion

This chapter discusses seven general limitations and criticisms for our study. These include issues surrounding fraudulent WC claims, home versus work injuries, generous WC medical benefits, full employment, and Human Capital costs and QALYs. The chapter also includes two appendixes. In appendix A we detail 31 of the most important assumptions we made. Twenty-five assumptions resulted in our producing estimates that were lower than would be obtained with more generous assumptions. In appendix B we address differences in incidence and prevalence costs.

CHAPTER 11

Conclusion

The summary of our study appears in chapter 1. Here, we simply present our most important estimates in one table.

Table 11.1 summarizes the cost estimates from chapters 5 and 6. Injury data are presented in the first two columns of numbers. Illness data are in the second two columns of numbers. Totals are in the last two columns. Within each pair of columns, the dollar amount and percentage are provided. Direct costs plus indirect costs equal total costs. Within the direct costs, medical only plus medical administration plus indemnity administration equals direct costs. Within the indirect category, lost earnings plus fringe benefits plus home production plus workplace training equals indirect costs.

The grand total for all costs is $155.5 billion dollars for 1992. Of these dollars, roughly $51.8 billion went for direct costs, for a contribution of 33 percent. Roughly $103.7 went for indirect costs, for a contribution of 67 percent. Injuries contributed 85 percent of the grand total of costs, and illnesses contributed 15 percent. Direct costs comprise 29 percent of all injury costs but 59 percent of illness. Indirect costs contributed 71 percent of injury costs but only 41 percent of illness costs. Indemnity administration contributed to 18 percent of direct costs for injuries but only 6 percent for the costs for illnesses. The reason for this last disparity is simple. Workers' compensation insurance administration costs were assumed to be more than double the rate for all other insurance administration, and we assumed no WC indemnity would be paid for illnesses, the vast majority of which would not occur until persons retire.

As we saw in chapter 9, these costs are substantial: five times the costs of AIDS, three times the costs for Alzheimer's disease, more than the costs of arthritis and related disorders, 91 percent of the costs of cancer, and roughly 82 percent of the costs of heart disease and stroke. Yet the scientific and public attention to occupational safety and health pales in comparison to the attention given AIDS, Alzheimer's disease, arthritis, cancer, and heart disease and stroke.

The costs are high because so many people are at risk. One hundred

TABLE 11.1. Total Cost for Injuries and Illnesses (billions of dollars)

			Injuries, Illnesses, and Percentages			
	Injuries	Selected Percentages	Illnesses	Selected Percentages	Total	Selected Percentages
Direct costs	38.380		13.3885	59[b]	51.7687	33[c]
Medical only	25.9825	29[a]	11.0949	83[e]	37.0774	72[f]
Fatalities or mortality	0.1332	68[d]	7.2853		7.4185	
Nonfatalities or morbidity	25.8493		3.8096		29.6589	
Medical administration	5.5017	14[d]	1.5703	12[e]	7.072	14[f]
Fatalities or Mortality	0.0282		1.0311		1.0593	
Nonfatalities or morbidity	5.4735		0.5392		6.0127	
Indemnity administration	6.8296	18[d]	0.7233	6[e]	7.5529	14[f]
Fatalities or mortality	0.0350		0.4749		0.5099	
Nonfatalities or morbidity	6.7946		0.2484		7.0430	
Indirect costs	94.3307	71[a]	9.4040	41[b]	103.7347	67[c]
Lost earnings	67.2604	71[g]	6.8740	73[h]	74.1344	71[i]
Fatalities or mortality	2.6890		4.5130		7.2020	
Nonfatalities or morbidity	64.52114		2.3608		66.8822	

Fringe benefits	15.6600	17[g]	1.6020	17[h]	17.2620	17[i]
Fatalities or mortality	0.6265		1.0520		1.6785	
Nonfatalities or morbidity	15.0335		0.4370		15.4705	
Home production	9.2750	10[g]	0.9280	10[h]	10.2030	10[i]
Fatalities or mortality	0.3710		0.6100		0.9810	
Nonfatalities or morbidity	8.9040		0.3180		9.2220	
Workplace training, restaffing, disruption	2.1853	2[g]	0	0[h]	2.1853	2[i]
Fatalities or mortality	0.0156		0		0.0156	
Nonfatalities or morbidity	2.1697		0		2.1697	
Grand total	132.7109	85[c]	22.7925	15[c]	155.5034	100[c]

Source: Current study.
[a]Percentage of injury total costs.
[b]Percentage of illness total costs.
[c]Percentage of grand total.
[d]Percentage of injury direct costs.
[e]Percentage of illness direct costs.
[f]Percentage of injury and illness direct costs.
[g]Percentage of injury indirect costs.
[h]Percentage of illness indirect costs.
[i]Percentage of injury and illness indirect costs.

twenty million people held jobs in 1992. Any of the 120 million could have experienced a job-related injury or illness.

Whereas the largest share of costs is experienced by the injured or ill workers and their families, all Americans share in these costs. Taxpayers experience them as higher taxes for Medicare, Medicaid, and Social Security. Firms experience them as high premiums for workers' compensation and health insurance and as workplace disruptions. Consumers experience them as higher prices. Healthy, noninjured workers experience them as lower wages.

Finally, we would like to underscore the fact that it took nearly this entire book to justify one number — $155.5 billion. The primary reason for this inordinate effort is that there are so few reliable data sets with information on occupational injuries and illnesses. But with the exception of the Census of Fatal Occupational Injuries, even these proved to be seriously impaired. We were forced to consult far too many secondary sources to justify our assumptions. We have made a number of policy recommendations in chapter 9, but the most important is this: we need better data. The United States needs to develop large, population-based longitudinal data sets to track over time persons who sustain occupational injuries and illnesses. We also need a census that includes not just fatal injuries but nonfatal ones and especially fatal and nonfatal diseases. We need a Census of Occupational Injuries and Illnesses and a price list for each of these injuries and illnesses. Only then will we have a full appreciation of the incidence, prevalence, and costs of occupational injuries and illnesses.

Appendixes

Appendix A for Chapter 2: Descriptions, Problems, and Analyses of Data Sources

1. Census of Fatal Occupational Injuries (CFOI)

According to BLS Report number 891 (U. S. Bureau of Labor Statistics 1995b),

> The Census of Fatal Occupational Injuries (CFOI), developed by the Bureau of Labor Statistics (BLS) in conjunction with participating State agencies, compiles comprehensive and timely information on fatal work injuries occurring in the 50 states and the District of Columbia. The goal of the CFOI program is to collect information on all fatal occupational injuries. To accomplish this, the CFOI uses multiple data sources, such as death certificates, workers' compensation reports and claims, and other Federal and State administrative records. Work relationship is verified for each fatality by using at least two independent source documents. Data compiled by the CFOI program is issued each year, for the previous year (the reference year). The program compiles information on the workers involved and the circumstances surrounding each worker fatality.

The CFOI has become the gold standard on measuring job-related injury deaths. However, as indicated in the text, the "two independent source documents" requirement is a strict test to pass. Deaths among workers in low-paying jobs as well as among African Americans and Hispanics may not be well documented.

The CFOI relied heavily on death certificates to either identify the deaths or corroborate another source. Given the problems associated with death certificates, this heavy reliance suggests a potential problem in the CFOI.

Other sources for the CFOI could have been a special BLS questionnaire sent to employers or another questionnaire sent to employees' next of kin. The questionnaires were sent only if one other source was available for the death. The questionnaire approach entails some problems.

Employers may not be forthcoming about the death, especially if they feel it may trigger an OSHA inspection. Responses from next of kin to questionnaires about dead relatives are also likely to be scattershot.

The CFOI researchers also searched through newspaper obituaries. With over two million Americans dying every year, however, searching through newspaper obituaries is a daunting task.

Another troubling aspect of the CFOI involved the exclusion of 1,361 incidents that were regarded as illnesses. Most of these incidents were recorded as "heart attack while at work" (personal communication with Guy Toscano, May 5, 1994). Many of the "heart attack" cases, in turn, were referred to the CFOI from state WC boards. WC boards have strict guidelines regarding heart failure. In some cases, physician reports and testimony must persuade the WC board that the heart failure was job related. This is easiest to prove when the heart attack occurred immediately after traumatic injury. The injury itself can put so much physiological strain on the heart that the heart fails (Lown 1979). In other cases, certain occupations are assumed to involve so much stress that even a heart attack away from work may automatically qualify the worker for WC benefits. State law in California, for example, requires WC to compensate for all heart attacks experienced by firefighters and police officers even if the attack occurred at home. Leigh and Miller (1998b) analyzed these heart attack data.

The CFOI investigators were aware of the possibility that a heart failure could have resulted from a traumatic event, but unless evidence from one of the sources was presented of such an event precipitating the heart failure, then these cases were excluded. Some of these "heart attack" cases may have been improperly excluded by CFOI investigators, not because of investigators' oversight but because WC records, OSHA reports, police records, and so on, as we have seen, may not always be complete.

The CFOI is the best data set available on injury deaths. Due to the omission of diseases, it is defective in measuring the overall mortality experience of jobs and cannot be used in our analysis of illnesses and diseases. This is not the case in other large data sets we will examine. Heart failures, for example, are regularly included in Supplementary Data System/WC data and the BLS's Annual Survey data.

2. National Traumatic Occupational Fatality Study (NTOF)

According to Fingerhut and Warner (1997, 82), the "NTOF surveillance system is compiled by the NIOSH based on information taken from death certificates. Certificates are collected from 52 vital statistics reporting units (the 50 states, New York City, and D.C.) based on the following criteria: age 16 years or over, an external cause of death (ICD-9, E800–E999), and a positive response to the 'Injury at work?' item. Denominator data were obtained from the BLS's Current Population Surveys (CPSs)."

As indicated in the text discussion of the CFOI and the NTOF, there are several problems associated with exclusively relying on death certificates. Nevertheless, the NTOF contains information on 82,696 deceased workers for the years 1980 through 1993. Despite the drawbacks mentioned previously, the NTOF can be useful for a number of analyses. The one we will consider here is a historical analysis. Whereas the death certificate problem plagues any given overall estimate of total deaths, the problem is probably less severe if we seek to understand trends over time. That is, it is not likely that these counting problems change dramatically over time. It is likely, for example, that a similar percentage undercount applies to 1989 as to 1991.

Figure A2.1 indicates the number of civilian deaths and the death rates in each year. The average number of civilian deaths was around 5,900 per year. The rate was roughly 5.4 per 100,000.

Figure A2.1 shows a provocative downward trend. This trend was apparently real, that is, not due to a statistical quirk or improperly collected data. State of California records on deaths, recorded by WC boards, also show a downward trend from the mid-1960s to 1984 (Division of Labor Statistics and Research 1985). The National Safety Council 1993 estimates of all fatal injuries — on and off the job — also showed a distinct downward trend for death rates in the 1980s and early 1990s. In fact, there has been a downward secular trend for all unintentional injury death rates since at least 1960 (National Safety Council 1993).

Figure A2.1 also shows that the number of deaths is influenced by the business cycle. A higher percentage of people in the labor force are working, and, thus, a higher percentage of people in the labor force are exposed to job hazards when unemployment is low than when unemployment is high. In addition, a falling unemployment rate is generally associated with employment of new and inexperienced employees, who are the most likely of all groups to experience injuries (Division of Labor Statistics and Research 1985). Increases in unemployment may also result in firms laying off accident-prone workers (Leigh 1985a). The economy suffered a recession — the deepest since the Great Depression — from 1980 through mid-1983. Beginning in the summer of 1983, the economy entered a recovery that lasted until the summer of 1990. As evident in the data on numbers of deaths in figure A2.1, the steepest fall occurred from 1980 to 1983. These years combined the downward secular trend with the effect of the rising unemployment rate. The number of

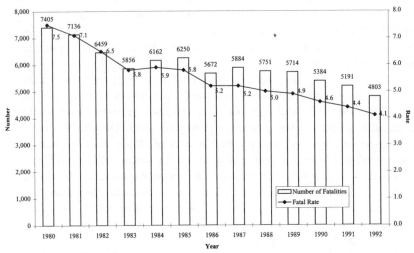

Fig. A2.1.   Distribution and rate of traumatic occupational civilian fatalities by year, United States, 1980–92

deaths actually increased in 1984 and 1985, as the economy expanded. The falling unemployment rate exerted a stronger influence than the secular trend in 1984 and 1985. From 1986 through 1989, the secular downward trend appeared to be evenly matched by the upward pressure on deaths resulting from a falling unemployment rate.

Equations (A2.1) and (A2.2) show the results of linear regressions using the 13 years of NTOF data. The dependent variable was the natural log of the number of deaths (in (A2.1)) and the natural log of the death rate (in (A2.2)). The independent variables were the unemployment rate and years, indicated by integers 1 through 13. The natural log was preferred over simply number of deaths since the log estimates a percentage effect. Percentage changes are more relevant than changes measured in actual numbers of deaths for analyzing data sets that do not have the same number of deaths as the NTOF.

$$\text{Ln(Deaths)} = 9.1642 \qquad - 0.0323 \times \text{unemployment} \qquad \text{(A2.1)}$$
$$(t = 149.016) \qquad (t = -4.647)$$
$$(p < .0001) \qquad (p = .0009)$$

$$- 0.0351 \times \text{years}$$
$$(t = -14.259)$$
$$(p < .0001)$$

$$R^2 = 0.9571 \qquad n = 13,$$

$$\text{Ln(Death Rate)} = 2.1769 \qquad - \quad 0.0187 \times \text{unemployment} \qquad \text{(A2.2)}$$
$$(t = 34.401) \qquad (t = -2.607)$$
$$(p < .0001) \qquad (p = .0262)$$

$$- 0.0497 \times \text{years}$$
$$(t = -19.589)$$
$$(p < .0001)$$

$$R^2 = 0.9804 \qquad n = 13.$$

Consider the coefficient on unemployment in (A2.1): -0.0323. This coefficient suggests that a one-unit increase in unemployment from, say, 5 to 6 percent would be associated with a 3.23 percent reduction in fatalities. The (A2.1) coefficient on years indicates that deaths are falling roughly 3.5 percent per year.

As the t- and p-values (in parentheses) indicate, the unemployment rate and the advancing years are strongly correlated with the number of deaths in the hypothesized direction.

In an earlier version of this study, the 1990 to 1993 years were not available. We constructed a model using the 1980 to 1989 data (Leigh et al. 1996). That model used the same independent variables: unemployment and time. That model predicted a NTOF number of 4,569 in 1992. The actual number was 4,803. Apparently, the unemployment rate and time are reasonably good predictors, at least in the short run.

3. BLS's Annual Survey of Occupational Injuries and Illnesses (Annual Survey)

The OSH Act of 1970 requires that almost all private sector employers with 11 or more employees keep a log of occupational injuries and illnesses and submit the data to the BLS once a year. The BLS surveys roughly 250,000 of these firms and others with fewer than 11 employees. The BLS then assembles the data and publishes the results in its Annual Survey of Occupational Injuries and Illnesses in the U.S. by Industry — what we will refer to as the Annual Survey (U.S. Department of Labor 1992, chap. 14). The Annual Survey contains aggregated data on roughly 250,000 firms. The Annual Survey data suffer a number of weaknesses, as the BLS acknowledges.

The largest limitations are the exclusions of government employees, employees working in small firms, and the self-employed. Roughly 20 percent of the civilian workforce has worked for some form of government in 1992. Small firms (firms with fewer than 100 employees) account for a high percentage (56 percent) of *new* employment in recent years

(Brown, Hamilton, and Medoff 1990). Finally, the self-employed comprise roughly 9 percent of the workforce (Jack and Zak 1993). The limitations involving small firms and the self-employed have resulted in some questionable conclusions drawn from BLS Annual Survey data. For example, Annual Survey data suggest that an inverted U describes the relation between injuries and firm size, with firms employing 100 to 499 persons sustaining the highest injury rates, while the smallest and the largest firms sustain the lowest rates (Leigh 1989a). But the BLS data contradict other studies. Data from death certificates (not the BLS surveys) divided by the appropriate numbers of employees at risk from all firms suggest that the relation is monotonically decreasing (Mendeloff and Kagey 1990). The smallest firms, with one to 10 employees, have the highest injury rates. Using death certificate data from Allegheny County, Pennsylvania, Parkinson et al. (1986) discovered that nearly 80 percent of fatal job-related accidents occurred in firms with fewer than 100 employees, while roughly 50 percent of U.S. private sector employees worked in such firms (Brown, Hamilton, and Medoff 1990). Coal mine accidents and injuries are most frequent in firms with the fewest employees (Bennett and Passmore 1984). Moses and Savage (1994) find a strong negative correlation in firm size and injury rates among trucking firms. McVittie, Baniken, and Brocklebank (1997) find the same pattern in construction. Oleinick, Gluck, and Guire (1995) review the literature showing higher fatality rates in small firms within the mining, construction, manufacturing, and transportation industries. A NIOSH study documents high-risk small business industries (National Institute for Occupational Safety and Health 1999).

Small firms are frequently owned by the self-employed. The Census of Fatal Occupational Injuries (CFOI) data indicated that 20 percent of injury deaths occurred among the self-employed in 1992 (Jack and Zak 1993). The self-employed, however, comprised roughly 9 percent of the workforce in 1992 (Jack and Zak 1993). If employment is hazardous for the boss in small firms, it is likely to be hazardous for the employees as well. Finally, many states exempt small firms from WC coverage; they thus have fewer reasons than larger firms to keep reliable records (Seligman et al. 1988).

We conclude that the wholesale exclusion of the self-employed and the selected exclusion of some small firms as well as possible willful underreporting by small firms are serious. These exclusions and underrreporting more likely explain the inverted U than any suggestion that such firms are safer than medium-sized firms.

In addition to these institutional exclusions involving government workers, small firms, and the self-employed, there are behavioral exclusions; that is, there are economic incentives for firms to underreport. The enforcement arm of the OSH Administration has directly used BLS data. Although BLS has steadfastly refused to let OSHA see its raw data, OSHA has used its own industry log data (OSHA Form 200) to compare a particular firm to the national or industry average. If the firm's injury rate exceeded the average, that firm was sometimes targeted for inspection (Smith 1992; McGarity and Shapiro 1993). In addition, WC insurance companies require some firms to pay high premiums if their injury and illness rates are high (Suruda and Emmett 1988). For both of these reasons, some firms may deliberately underestimate their injuries (Burrough and Lubove 1986).

For nonfatal injuries, there may also be economic incentives for employees not to report. Employees may be fearful that their employers will label them "accident prone" or that they will be laid off if they report too many injuries (O'Loughlin 1993). They may also fear that a WC claim or litigation surrounding a claim (which is public information) may harm their chances of finding a new job. Finally, workers may receive a yearly bonus if none in their work group reports a major WC claim for a year. We are aware of only three studies that attempt to estimate the underreporting carried out by employers and employees and some congressional testimony on the subject.

Nondisabling injuries were undercounted by at least 45 percent. Biddle et al. (1998) found that at least 55 percent of ill workers who would likely qualify for WC never file. Glazner et al. (1998) found substantial underreporting to the BLS from construction firms building the new Denver airport. Disabling injuries appeared to be undercounted by at least 20 percent. Carpal tunnel syndrome (CTS) is addressed in chapter 3. It is nevertheless worth noting that Nelson et al. (1992) found a 60 percent BLS undercount of CTS in the auto industry.

Members of the U.S. House of Representatives have been concerned about underreporting for some time. On March 19, 1987, a subcommittee of the Committee of Government Operations held hearings on underreporting (U.S. Congress, House Subcommittee 1987). A number of people provided testimony, including the BLS's chief of occupational safety and health statistics, William M. Eisenberg. Eisenberg acknowledged that underreporting was substantial and that the BLS Annual Survey's estimated numbers of job-related injuries were roughly half of those in other household surveys.

Lewis Anderson, vice president of the United Food and Commercial Workers International Union, also testified about underreporting by the Iowa Beef Processing Company (IBP) in the Dakota City, Nebraska, plant in a three-month period in 1985. IBP was the nation's largest meatpacking company in 1987. Its chairman in 1985 was Armand Hammer. IBP reported roughly 1,800 incidents to Anderson's union but only 160 to the BLS.

Eisenberg and Anderson were not alone in this opinion. McGarity and Shapiro (1993) point out that in 1988 a congressional Office of Technology Assessment (OTA) review of record-keeping accuracy found "possibly significant injury and illness underreporting to the BLS." In the same vein, although pertaining to diseases, a 1987 study by the National Research Council of the National Academy of Sciences concluded that there was "little doubt that serious underreporting exists for occupational diseases" (National Research Council 1987).

The subcommittee hearings (U.S. Congress Subcommittee 1987) revealed several additional cases of underreporting by employers. Subsequent to these hearings, OSHA began issuing large fines for "willful" underreporting. A number of firms including Caterpillar Tractor, Chrysler, General Dynamics, and Scott Paper have been required to pay substantial fines for "willful" underreporting (Bell and Denmead 1993; Greer 1992).

John Ruser (1994), an economist at the BLS, has published a study on OSHA and BLS data. OSHA began issuing heavy fines for record-keeping violations in April 1986. But these fines were directed only at very large manufacturing companies. OSHA did not target, and has not since targeted, any other group. As a result, from 1985 to 1988, manufacturing plants with more than 2,500 workers increased their reported rates of cases (per 100 employees) from 4.4 to 10.5. This is a 139 percent increase. At the same time, medium-sized and small firms' rates barely moved. National estimates rose from about 8.2 to 8.5, a 4 percent increase. In all likelihood, national rates did not increase much since the great majority of firms did not feel threatened by OSHA's penalty policy aimed at very large manufacturing firms. Subtracting 4 percent from 139 percent yields 135 percent. Although Ruser does not draw any conclusions from those numbers one could argue that this 135 percent indicates the amount of "willful" underreporting. Moreover, this 135 percent estimate ignores any problems involving the exclusion of government workers and the self-employed.

The "willful" underreporting and the exclusion of government workers, the self-employed, and some small firms result in a serious undercount. Evidence in section III.A.3 suggests that the BLS's Annual Survey undercounts the number of injury deaths by 60 percent to 70 percent. The undercount for nonfatal injuries is likely to be even larger than the one for fatal injuries.

Finally, it is unclear whether the Annual Survey fully captures assaults, rapes, and robberies. We know that it greatly underestimates homicides. The National Crime Victimization Survey showed that 3.5 million personal crime victimizations occur annually on the job, including 900,000 assaults and 100,000 rapes and robberies on the job (Backman 1996). In 1994 (the first year available with such numbers) the Annual Survey counted only 20,438 nonfatal assaults resulting in one or more days away from work (U.S. Bureau of Labor Statistics 1996).

Despite the BLS Annual Survey data limitations, they provide the most comprehensive and historically consistent data available on fatal and nonfatal injuries and illnesses. We turn now to analyses of these data.

Diagrams in the National Safety Council's *Accident Facts* and table A2.1 provide some of the trend data available from the BLS. The data in the figure in *Accident Facts* include illnesses. However, illnesses comprised a small percentage of all cases and lost workday cases from 1973 to 1991 (2 percent to 5 percent). This is evident in table A2.1, which contains information on the Annual Survey data on illnesses. The number of illnesses is small when compared to injuries, but their share is rising quickly—from 2.2 percent of the total in 1983 to 5.8 percent in 1991.

Several patterns can be gleaned from historical data on the number of *cases* per 100 employees per year and the lost *workdays* per 100 employees per year. First, the lost *workdays* rate has a secular upward trend. The total *cases* per 100 full-time employees rate, on the other hand, has remained relatively flat, with a slight secular downward trend. Finally, both rates seem to follow the business cycle. We consider each of these in turn.

Consider the trends first. Nelson (1992, 1993) suggests that the rising trend in workdays lost and falling trend in number of injuries can be attributed to an aging workforce. Older workers tend to take longer to recover from any given injury than younger workers. At the same time, older workers have more experience and would probably be more successful than younger, inexperienced workers at avoiding injuries in the first place. Hence, we find fewer injuries per worker but longer recovery times. These longer recovery times are again apparent in table A2.1 under the heading "Average Lost Workdays per Lost Workday Case." The trend is clearly upward from 17 days in 1983 to 21 days in 1991.

The number of nonfatal injuries may also be rising over time since the labor force has been expanding each year and there has been a trend toward workers working more hours during the day and more days during the year (Bluestone and Ross 1997).

There have been other attempts at explaining the secular trends. In Ruser's 1991 and 1993 studies using micro data on manufacturing industries, evidence is presented that the increasing generosity of WC benefits compared to wages over time has resulted in workers staying away from work longer once they become injured. He also finds that the increasing generosity of WC benefits increases the number of injuries per 100 workers regardless of the length of time spent in recovery. The macro (economy-wide) time trend data in our table A2.1 for lost workdays are consistent with Ruser's micro data. The average length of time away from work for any given injury has been increasing. The macro time trend data for the number of cases per 100 employees in our table A2.1, however, are not consistent with Ruser's studies. The rate for numbers of injuries has been decreasing slightly.

Ruser is not alone in investigating the WC payment and recovery time correlation. Cheadle et al. (1994) found that WC benefits did not influence the length of time on WC. They found, instead, that older age, being female, being divorced, being employed in a small firm, and high regional unemployment increased duration.

The second pattern in table A2.1 concerns the business cycle. The number of injuries rises during expansions and falls during contractions. One obvious explanation involves the number of exposed workers. During an expansion, more people are working, and, hence, the total number of job-related injuries would be expected to increase. Other explanations are less obvious. In fact, even after controlling for the number of people employed, that is, by treating the *rate* as the dependent variable (which includes the numbers employed in the denominator), the same pattern emerges. Nonfatal injury rates rise during economic expansions and fall during economic contractions (Smith 1992). Back pain WC claims follow the same pattern: more claims with more employment; fewer claims with less employment (Brooker, Frank, and Tarasuk 1997).

Smith (1990) has discovered two other provocative influences on injury rates involving lies. First, the employer might lie. During the first six Reagan years, OSHA's fines for poor business record keeping on injuries were low. Beginning in 1987, fines became severe primarily for large manufacturing firms. Smith (1992) finds evidence that when fines were low (1981–86), recorded injury rates were low; when fines were high (after 1986), recorded injury rates increased.

Second, the employee might lie. Injuries over the weekend might be attributed to the job on Monday. Opportunistic employees may want to collect WC benefits. Smith (1992) finds that Monday is the most popular day for job-related injuries to be reported. He finds an even higher jump in injuries after three-day weekends. Smith (1992) estimates that perhaps as many as 4 percent of sprains and strains are misrepresented as having occurred at work.

TABLE A2.1. Occupational Nonfatal Injury and Illness Estimates for Private Industry, 1983–92[a]

(1) Year	(2) Number of Nonfatal Injuries	(3) Injury Cases per 100 Full-Time Workers	(4) Number of Lost Workdays for Injuries	(5) Average Lost Workdays per Lost Workday Case	(6) Injury Only Lost Workdays per 100 Full-Time Workers	(7) Number of Nonfatal Illnesses	(8) Illness to Total Cases (%)	(9) Unemployment Rate
1983	4,748,000	7.5	2,140,300	17	57.2	106,100	2.2	9.6
1984	5,294,800	7.8	2,449,700	17	61.8	124,800	2.3	7.5
1985	5,381,700	7.7	2,484,700	18	63.3	125,600	2.3	7.2
1986	5,492,000	7.7	2,532,300	18	63.9	136,900	2.4	7.0
1987	5,845,500	8.0	2,721,300	18	67.3	190,400	3.2	6.2
1988	6,197,700	8.3	2,878,400	19	72.5	240,900	3.8	5.5
1989	6,292,500	8.2	2,955,500	19	74.2	283,700	4.3	5.3
1990	6,421,300	8.3	2,987,300	20	78.3	331,700	4.9	5.5
1991	5,977,400	7.9	2,794,000	21	79.8	368,300	5.8	6.7
1992	6,342,000	8.3						7.4

Source: U.S. Bureau of Labor Statistics, Annual Survey, various years (U.S. Bureau of Labor Statistics 1987, 1989, 1991a, 1992, 1993, 1994b).

[a]The BLS changed their format in 1992. Only information for columns 2, 3, and 9 was available in 1992. Incidence rates are per 100 full-time workers. Data exclude farms with fewer than 11 employees.

But Smith ignores the medical literature on sprains, strains, injuries, and some diseases and deaths. The body adapts to its surroundings. If muscles are not used for a period of time, rapid reuse is likely to result in a sprain or strain. This is the point of stretching before exercising (Schneider et al. 1985). The body can also adapt to chemical surroundings. Symptoms of byssinosis (brown lung) are characteristically at their worse on returning to work Monday morning (Levy and Wegman 1983, 33). That is, over the weekend, the body begins to recover, but with the reintroduction of cotton dust on Monday the symptoms are the most severe. Sleep patterns are also disrupted over the weekend. Mondays are likely to be the most sleep-deprived days of the week. Inadequate sleep is a strong predictor of accidents.

Nitroglycerin workers used to drop dead at work most frequently on Mondays. Their blood vessels would be dilated due to work exposure to nitrates. When the nitrates were not in their environment (on weekends), they would suffer angina away from work. On Monday, with the new introduction of nitrates, their hearts would fail (Levy and Wegman 1983, 33).

These arguments about the reintroduction of a hazard on Monday are especially cogent when vacations are involved. Most people return to work on a Monday after a vacation. Two weeks of vacation away from work provides ample time for the body to lose any resistance that may have been built up while continuously employed.

It is also likely that Mondays are the most popular day for new employees to be introduced to the job. And new employees are much more likely than others to experience an injury. We know, for example, that new employees who are injured are more likely to experience that injury in the first month on the new job than in any other month (Division of Labor Statistics and Research 1985).

An analysis of fatal heart attacks in the CFOI revealed that more attacks occurred on Monday than any other day (Leigh and Miller 1998b). Finally, an OSHA report indicated that construction injury fatalities most often occur on Mondays and Thursdays (Office of Construction and Engineering 1990). While workers might lie about sprains, they could not lie about fatalities.

Because Smith ignores medical reasons for high levels of injury rates on Mondays, he likely overestimates the number of lies by workers.

The associations between injuries on the one hand and unemployment rates, time trends, and the Reagan underenforcement years on the other can be tested in models using 1983–92 data from table A2.1. Two least squares regressions (equations (A2.3) and (A2.4)) were run with the natural log of the number of injuries serving as the dependent variable.

And another two (equations (A2.5) and (A2.6)) were run with the natural log of the nonfatal rate serving as the dependent variable. The number of injuries rather than the rate was preferred as our dependent variable since we wanted to compare our nonfatal injury trend with the NTOF fatal injury trend. Our first nonfatal injury model (equations (A2.3) and (A2.4)) ignores the changing fine patterns. The second model (equations (A2.5) and (A2.6) explicitly accounts for them with a dummy variable equaling one for 1983–86 and zero otherwise. The dummy variable approach was suggested by Smith (1992). Here are the results.

$$\text{Ln (Injuries)} = -23.9563 \quad - 0.0378 \times \text{unemployment} \quad (A2.3)$$
$$(t = -4.570) \quad (t = -6.119)$$
$$(p = .0026) \quad (p = .0005)$$

$$+ 0.0200 \times \text{time}$$
$$(t = 7.624)$$
$$(p < .0001)$$

$$n = 10; \quad R^2 = 0.9690,$$

$$\text{Ln (Injuries)} = -21.009 \quad - 0.0362 \times \text{unemployment} \quad (A2.4)$$
$$(t = -2.392) \quad (t = 4.814)$$
$$(p = .0539) \quad (p = .0030)$$

$$+ 0.0185 \times \text{time} - 0.1028 \times \text{dummy}$$
$$(t = 4.197) \quad (t = -0.434)$$
$$(p = .0057) \quad (p = .6792)$$

$$n = 10; \quad R^2 = .9699,$$

$$\text{Ln (Injury rate)} = 2.1328 \quad - 0.0137 \times \text{unemployment} \quad (A2.5)$$
$$(t = 41.143) \quad (t = -2.219)$$
$$(p < .0001) \quad (p = .0620)$$

$$+ 0.0064 \times \text{time}$$
$$(t = 2.447)$$
$$(p = .0443)$$

$$n = 10; \quad R^2 = .7820,$$

$$\text{Ln (Injury rate)} = 2.1387 \quad - 0.0099 \times \text{unemployment} \quad (A2.6)$$
$$(t = 41.701) \quad (t = -1.429)$$
$$(p < .0001) \quad (p = .2028)$$

$$+ 0.0029 \times \text{years} - 0.0303 \times \text{dummy}$$
$$(t = 0.713) \qquad (t = -1.109)$$
$$(p = .5025) \qquad (p = .3099)$$

$$n = 10 \qquad R^2 = .8190$$
$$t = 1, \ldots, 10.$$

First consider equation (A2.3). The high t-statistics and low p-values on the unemployment rate and on the time trend suggest that these associations are not due to chance. The estimated coefficient on the unemployment rate, -0.0378, suggests that a 1 percent increase in the unemployment rate is associated with a 3.78 percent decrease in the number of injuries. The negative sign on the unemployment rate is consistent with the hypothesis that there should be more injuries in economic expansions and fewer injuries in recessions due to the following factors: (1) the inexperience of newly hired employees; (2) increased fatigue from overtime (Ansbury 1989); and (3) the increase in the number of persons "at risk" as the economy expands. The results are also consistent with those from equation (A2.1) involving fatality data from the NTOF. Increases in unemployment were associated with fewer deaths. The estimated coefficient in the NTOF was -0.0351.

The coefficient on the time trend (0.02) suggests that one more year is associated with 2 percent more nonfatal injuries. This is inconsistent with the result from equation (A2.1) involving NTOF fatality data. Over time, deaths have decreased. These are important findings: while NTOF deaths appear to be falling over time, Annual Survey nonfatal injuries appear to be rising.

Equation (A2.4) confirms the importance of the unemployment rate and the time trend. Both generate relatively large t-statistics and low p-values. The dummy variable for the weak OSHA enforcement years entered with a negative sign, contrary to expectations, and did not garner a big t-statistic or small p-value. When the time trend variable was excluded from the regression, in a separate model (available from the authors), the dummy variable did enter with a positive sign and garnered a big t- and small p-value. Our conclusion is then that Smith's hypothesized weak enforcement years cannot be distinguished from the general secular upward trend in injuries. This conclusion only applies to those data that ignore years prior to 1983 (which Smith includes). Given that considerable evidence demonstrates the enforcement year effects in the Smith 1992 study, we accept Smith's conclusion.

Equations (A2.5) and (A2.6) show the results for regressions of the *rate* on unemployment, time and the dummy. The same general patterns are apparent. The *p*-value on unemployment in equation (A2.5) is .062. This is a two-tailed *p*-value. Given our hypothesis, one could argue that a one-tailed test would be more appropriate; hence the *p* would be .031.

4. National Health Interview Survey (NHIS)

We first consider the advantages and disadvantages of the NHIS. The discussion of disadvantages will involve an analysis of 20 years of NHIS time series data.

The National Health Interview Survey (NHIS) is a

continuing nationwide survey of the U.S. Civilian non-institutionalized population, conducted on households. Each (survey) is a probability sample of household respondents interviewed by trained personnel of the U.S. Bureau of the Census to obtain information about the health and other characteristics of each living member of the sample household. During a year, the sample is composed of 36,000 to 47,000 households including 92,000 to 125,000 persons, depending upon the year. (U.S. Department of Health and Human Services 1992)

The NHIS has been gathering information on injuries "due to an accident" for over 20 years (Adams and Benson 1992). The NHIS injury question asks currently employed respondents 18 years old and up whether the accident resulting in the injury occurred at work or on work time during "the past two weeks." These phrases — "due to an accident" and "during the past two weeks" — as well as the sample restriction that persons must be currently employed need to be emphasized as they apply to job-related injuries.

By using the phrase "due to an accident" the NHIS may unintentionally exclude injuries due to assault, attempted murder, or suicide. The original OSH Act ignored assault and attempted on-the-job murder and suicide. Many OSH researchers continue to ignore them in analyzing job-related injuries (see discussion in Leigh 1995a). Only in the 1990s has NIOSH conducted separate studies on assaults and murders. Only in the late 1990s has OSHA promulgated standards to minimize assault and murder. OSHA recommended that convenience stores train workers on how to behave during a robbery (Vartabedian 1998). It would not be surprising if many NHIS respondents would not regard assault at work as an "accident." It is even less likely that attempted suicide would be regarded as an accident. These omissions would represent a serious bias since Toscano and Windau (1993) found that 20 percent of fatal injuries were due to murders and suicides.

Suicides can be work related, as WC boards recognize. Freedman (1990) reported a WC case involving a construction worker who was permanently and totally disabled from a job-related injury. Prior to the injury, he was very active. After the injury, he had psychological difficulty adapting to his disability. Two years after the accident, he killed himself. Roy (1992) examined cases of psychological disorders following job-related injuries and found many to be severe. Additional suicide cases are discussed in Conroy 1989.

Psychological trauma may also occur. Elisburg (1994) reports that most states will allow WC to pay job-stress claims if the stress followed a job-related injury.

Another related disadvantage of the NHIS is that respondents may also undercount vehicle crashes. As we have seen, self-employed people who experienced a car crash may not have regarded it as an on-the-job injury. There appears to be a general tendency by OSH experts, administrators, police, coroners, and so on, not to regard many vehicle crashes as job related. This bias might also exist among NHIS respondents themselves.

The second phrase, concerning injuries "in the past two weeks," is helpful. Landen and Hendricks (1992) demonstrate that significant recall bias will affect answers to a question asking respondents about injuries that may have occurred during the past 12 months. Another advantage of the two-week interval is that it is more likely that the number of persons injured equals the number of injuries. Over 12 months, persons are more likely to experience more than one injury than over two weeks.

The phrase "in the past two weeks" also needs to be emphasized as it pertains to incidence and prevalence measurements. If the person is still impaired from a job-related accident from, say, 18 months prior to the interview, the NHIS would not include it as an accident. The NHIS data, therefore, are incidence, not prevalence, based.

The last restriction may be the most serious. By restricting attention to those *currently employed* and nonhospitalized, a high percentage of disabling injuries may be ignored. Many serious injuries can result in hospitalizations. More importantly, most permanent disabilities result in exit from the labor force either temporary or permanently.

An advantage of the NHIS is that the definition of an injury is clear and similar to ours and the BLS's Annual Survey definition. For the NHIS to classify an incident as an injury, it either must have been "medically attended," that is, received the attention of a doctor, nurse, or paramedic, or must have resulted in at least one-half day of work loss (since 1983) and one full day of work loss prior to 1983.

Other advantages include the following: (1) the NHIS researchers adjusted the responses for two weeks to reflect annual estimates and rates and (2) the data have been collected in a (relatively) consistent manner since 1970. Recent years of the NHIS have estimated the following annual numbers and rates per 100 workers: 7,806,000, 4.2 (1992); 8,673,000, 7.4 (1991); 7,277,000, 6.2 (1990); 10,947,000, 9.3 (1989); 10,057,000, 8.7 (1988); 9,131,000, 8.1 (1987); and 10,529,000, 9.7 (1986).

Table A2.2 provides information on the NHIS estimates from 1970 through 1991. The first column presents the year. The second, third, and fourth columns present the number of injuries, workdays lost, and bed disability days. The last column presents the national unemployment rate.

TABLE A2.2.   NHIS Estimated Work Injuries, Workdays Lost, Days in Bed, and the National Unemployment Rate

Year	Number of Injuries (in thousands)	Workdays Lost (in thousands)	Bed Disability Days (in thousands)	Unemployment Rate (%)
1970	7,750	110,947	26,798	4.9
1971	9,631	120,384	30,122	5.9
1972	7,938	102,247	24,131	5.6
1973	9,027	124,692	32,212	4.9
1974	9,254	144,191	38,143	5.6
1975	9,841	138,838	36,248	8.5
1976	9,292	140,590	35,272	7.7
1977	11,414	160,533	37,381	7.1
1978	10,511	184,031	42,593	6.1
1979	12,014	176,284	40,707	5.8
1980	10,826	184,636	42,657	7.1
1981	11,291	214,873	43,957	7.6
1982	9,543	130,568	43,540	9.7
1983	8,920	133,060	43,197	9.6
1984	10,634	154,154	45,419	7.5
1985	11,363	165,796	46,940	7.2
1986	10,529	148,351	46,021	7.0
1987	9,131	171,029	52,878	6.2
1988	10,057	178,845	47,625	5.5
1989	10,947	191,544	50,851	5.3
1990	7,277	183,024	48,365	5.5
1991	8,673	233,160	54,187	6.7

Source: National Health Interview Survey, various years.

Given that data are available from 1970 to 1991, we attempted to construct regression models using historical NHIS data. This did not prove to be successful, however, and ultimately led us to question the reliability of the NHIS data. We turn now to examining the regression models.

The data in table A2.2 were used to fit regression equations explaining several dependent variables — injuries, workdays, and bed days, as well as the natural logs of each of these — with independent variables — the unemployment rate and the time trend. These are the same independent variables used for the NTOF and Annual Survey models. In the NTOF and BLS Annual Survey models, both the unemployment rate and time trend were statistically significant predictors. We attempted two sets of regressions on the NHIS. In the first, the dependent variables were entered in their natural units (not logged). In the second, the dependent variables were logged. Here we present only the logged version because both sets yielded similar statistically insignificant results. Moreover, since the results were so similar regardless of the dependent variable, here we discuss all results but present only those for a critical variable: the number of injuries.

$$\text{Ln (Injuries)} = -5.624 \qquad + 0.0184 \times \text{unemployment} \qquad (A2.7)$$
$$(t = 0.6090) \quad (t = 0.9150)$$
$$(p = .5499) \quad (p = .3716)$$

$$+ 0.0017 \times \text{time}$$
$$(t = 0.3710)$$
$$(p = .7148)$$

$$n = 22; \qquad R^2 = 0.0570.$$

The secular upward trend in measures of nonfatal injuries observed in the Annual Survey data is also apparent in these NHIS data: coefficients on the time trend were found to be positive. The time trend in the important injury model, equation (A2.7), does not generate a low p-value.

The statistically significant unemployment patterns observed in the NTOF and Annual Survey models are not found in the NHIS data. None of the unemployment coefficients were statistically significant in any of the six models (available from the authors). Moreover, *positive* associations between unemployment on the one hand and injuries and bed days on the other were observed. *Negative* and statistically significant associations were found in the NTOF and Annual Survey models. These positive associations are not easily explained.

The NHIS slightly changed its definition of injury in 1983, as explained previously. We attempted to account for this change with a dummy variable equaling one for years prior to 1983 and equaling zero after 1983. The same lack of statistical significance and unexpected positive signs on the unemployment rate were obtained, however.

The disparities between the NHIS regression results and the NTOF and Annual Survey results are cause for concern. The unemployment rate has proven itself to be a reliable predictor of job-related injuries using a variety of data sets (Chelius 1977; Brooker, Frank, and Tarasuk 1997; Leigh 1985a; Robinson 1988; Smith 1992). It is unlikely that all of these prior studies together with our NTOF and Annual Survey models data were flawed. Moreover, the explanations of an unemployment-injury correlation are compelling. First, as more people are added to the payroll, there are greater numbers of workers who are at risk of injury. Second, new, "green" employees are more likely to experience an injury than seasoned workers. Third, low unemployment is generally accompanied with overtime, and overtime generates fatigue and hence injuries. It is therefore possible that the NHIS is not producing reliable estimates of job-related injuries and injury rates.

A second problem that plagues the NHIS data, as we saw in section VIII.A.3, is that NHIS job injuries generally show higher rates for whites than African Americans. These results are in conflict with the great volume of research indicating a disproportionately high percentage of African Americans in dangerous jobs.

Given the poor statistical showing of the NHIS data in the preceding models, and the questionable black/white results, we are not confident in using the 1992 NHIS estimate in the text.

5. National Council on Compensation Insurance (NCCI) Ultimate Reports

The NCCI is a private firm that collects data from workers' compensation insurance from 41 states and Washington, DC. Not all WC firms contributed data within each state. Moreover, only WC data are contributed. Here we present a discussion of these data and their advantages and disadvantages.

The NCCI publishes data for an insurance policy year, not a calendar year. We obtained two Ultimate Reports—one from May 1992 and another from May 1993. Sometimes, the policy years began January 1 and ended December 31, but sometimes they did not. For example, for Delaware in the 1992 report, the policy year began in March 1988 and ended in February 1989. In all policy years, however, the 12 consecutive months were covered, and no policy year exceeded 12 months. Consequently, estimates of annual deaths could be made, especially when the two reports were combined and divided by two. Our first NCCI Ultimate Report was completed in May 1992 and covered calendar years 1987, 1988, and 1989, depending upon the state. The second Ultimate Report was completed in May 1993 and covered calendar years 1988, 1989, and 1990.

These Ultimate Reports follow claims originating in one year for at least three years. That is, if an injury/claim occurred in 1989, the Ultimate Report would collect data on that claim at least until December 1992. It could be, for example, that medical expenses were generated in years after the initial year of the injury. The Ultimate Reports would contain that information.

The NCCI also publishes First Year Reports that follow claims for only 18 months. Since some costs accrue beyond 18 months, we determined that the Ultimate Reports would provide us with better information than the First Year Reports.

To generate national estimates based upon the NCCI data, adjustments were made for illnesses, exclusion of some states, exclusion of self-insured firms and some state funds, the well-known WC underestimate, and time and unemployment trends from 1989 to 1992 (Leigh et al. 1996). We estimated 17.21 million nonfatal injuries and 8,306 deaths. Given the number of assumptions required to arrive at these estimates, we do not include them in our estimates of deaths (6,371) or nonfatal injuries (13.34 million). Nevertheless, as we were developing those NCCI-based national estimates an important finding emerged: WC missed at least 55 percent of all job-related injuries. We turn now to a discussion of this provocative 55 percent figure. At least seven studies suggested this 55 percent figure or higher.

(1) As indicated in CFOI data in table 2.1, the traditional state-based WC insurers had records on only roughly 40 percent of all the deaths in the CFOI. If the CFOI itself provides an undercount due to missing African American or Hispanic or poor employees, then this 40 percent figure would shrink further. This implies at least a 60 percent undercount.

(2) Cone et al. (1991) identified 682 job-related deaths in California in 1983. WC insurers had records for only 294, or 43.1 percent. (3) Stout and Bell (1991) estimated that, depending on the state, WC missed from 30 percent to 60 percent of job-related deaths.

The 55 percent or higher undercount extends to nonfatal injuries as well. (4) Parker et al. (1994) studied nonfatal injuries among adolescents in Minnesota. All injuries were serious enough to result in more than three days away from work or in a permanent impairment. Thus, all injuries would have qualified for WC since Minnesota WC requires a three-day waiting period. The Parker et al. 1994 study showed that 67 percent of these serious adolescent work injuries were not reported to Minnesota WC insurers or agencies. An even higher percentage would have been excluded had injuries resulting in only a few hours or one or two days of work loss been included.

(5) As we will explain later in this appendix, the National Health Interview Survey conducted an extensive supplement on occupational health and safety in 1988 (NHIS-OSH). The supplement asked questions regarding WC. Roughly 53 percent of the persons reporting an on-the-job injury to the NHIS interviewers did not file a WC claim (47 percent did file). The missing WC percentage would likely be even higher without the substantial recall bias inherent in the NHIS-OSH (Landen and Hendricks 1992).

(6) The Rand study by Hensler et al. (1991) (discussed in sec. VI.A) also showed a high percentage of injuries missed by WC. On page 77, Hensler et al. presented data on the sources of payment for accident and injury-related hospitalizations. One column pertained to "WC only," while another was "more than one source." The percentage in the WC column was 43.5. The percentage in the "more than one" column was 11.9. Assuming *all* (a conservative assumption) of the "more than one" were also covered by WC, then WC identified roughly 55 percent of all cases. If the "more than one" source never included WC, then WC would identify 43.5 percent of nonfatal injuries requiring hospitalizations. On their following page (78), data on sources of compensation for accident and injury-related outpatient medical care were presented. Several sources were again identified, including "self-pay," "health insurance only," "WC only," "other source," and "more than one source." The percentage in the "WC only" column was 40.4, while the percentage in the "more than one source" column was 8.2. At the most, WC would pay for 48.6 percent. At the least, WC would cover 40.4 percent.

In both of these cases, we favor the lower estimate. Few, if any, WC insurers had deductibles or copayments at the time of the Hensler et al. 1991 study. Once WC was scheduled to pay for medical care, there was no reason for other sources to become involved.

The Rand data therefore suggest that WC was missing 56.5 percent to 59.6 percent of nonfatal, job-related injuries. But Hensler et al. (1991) acknowledge that they undercounted minor injuries due to recall bias. Minor injuries, in turn, are much less likely to be covered by WC. Hence, it is likely that the WC undercount suggested by Hensler et al. (1991) would exceed 60 percent.

(7) Finally, Marquis (1992) adapted the Rand study to analyze costs. Marquis estimated that WC benefits accounted for only 27.5 percent of the total cost of occupational injuries, for a WC omission *cost* estimate of 72.5 percent.

These seven studies suggest a WC undercount of 55 percent or more, on average.

There are a number of reasons for the WC undercount. First, the traditional state-based WC programs do not cover federal employees and sometimes do not cover state and local government employees (the latter are frequently covered under special state-run government employees disability programs).

Second, some household workers, some farmworkers, self-employed people, and some workers in small firms are excluded. While little information exists on the hazardous nature of household work, we know that farmwork is especially dangerous (Jenkins et al. 1993).

Previously we found employees in small firms are at high risks for job-related deaths. But WC frequently does not extend coverage to the smallest employers. WC coverage did not extend to employees in firms with fewer than five employees in Missouri, Tennessee, and Mississippi in 1988. In New Mexico, Arkansas, Alabama, Georgia, Florida, South Carolina, North Carolina, Rhode Island, Virginia, Michigan, and Wisconsin, WC coverage did not extend to firms with fewer than three employees (Nelson 1992).

The Seligman et al. 1988 study supports the argument that even though legal WC coverage extends to some small firms, de facto or actual coverage may not. Seligman et al. found that the OSHA record keeping was the worst (fewest records) for small firms and the best (most records) for the large firms.

Third, there is the possibility that some injuries may go uncompensated or unreported even when they would easily qualify for WC. This is alarming to contemplate especially when considering deaths. It could be argued that of all injuries, deaths would be the most visible and unimpeachable as truly job related. But deaths can be expensive to insurers. They involve indemnity payments to spouses and children. Some insurers may be more inclined to fight a death claim than any other kind of claim.

Fourth, George Rejda, professor of insurance in the Business School at the University of Nebraska, offers an additional reason in his influential book on social insurance (Rejda 1994). Workers often receive advice only from company supervisors or WC insurance agents. The agents also perform the functions of judges in accepting or denying the claim, controlling the payment, and terminating the benefit.

Finally, some investigators will allege that WC overestimates the number of injuries. This view is addressed in chapter 9. We would nevertheless like to point out here that a number of injuries commonly thought to be compensable by WC are, in fact, seldom, if ever, compensable. These include commuting to and from work and injuries that occur after the employee has been drinking (Rejda 1984).

A defect in the NCCI is that WC data combine diseases with injuries. Leigh (1995a) used the SDS/WC data to estimate that roughly 11 percent of all deaths were due to diseases. But the NCCI data in table 2.3 reflect nonfatal cases, and there is evidence that nonfatal cases are more likely to be injuries than fatal cases. In a separate analysis of NCCI claims from 17 states, Rossman, Miller, and Douglas (1991) found that 98.37 percent of WC claims were for an injury. Since the Rossman, Miller, and Douglas estimate applies to disabling claims, not deaths, it is a better estimate than the Leigh 1995a estimate since the latter only applies to deaths. Nelson (1992) finds a 2 percent illness factor in costs for WC, including the costs for fatalities. On the other hand, the BLS's Annual Survey consistently found at least 3 percent of all events were attributed to illnesses during the time of these policy years — 1987 to 1990 (table A2.1). It is likely, therefore, that a 3 percent or less estimate would apply to disease cases. Three percent is not a large figure. Moreover, our use of NCCI data only applies to *relative* comparisons across categories of Permanent Total, Permanent Partial, Temporary Total and Partial, and Medical Only. It is not likely that a disproportionate number of diseases would lie in any of these four categories.

An additional issue surrounding NCCI statistics concerns incidence and prevalence. The NCCI statistics that scientists have studied are incidence, not prevalence, statistics. They do not include cases from prior years that still receive payments.

A final issue concerns the representativeness of the NCCI data in table 2.3. Not all states were included in these data. As the notes to table 2.3 explain, from nine to 12 states were excluded. We are not familiar with any study detailing the numbers or percentage of PTs, PPs, or TTPs for those states excluded or included or for the United States as a whole. However, information from *Employment and Earnings* (U.S. Bureau of Labor Statistics 1991b) is available on the industry divisions of employment. If the industrial mix of employment in the states included in the NCCI is similar to that of the United States as a whole, it is more likely that the data in table 2.3 are similar to PT, PP, and TTP data for the United States as a whole than if the industrial mix is not similar to the industrial mix in the United States. To test the industrial mix hypothesis, we collected employment data on the eight industry divisions for the states and

Washington, DC, included in the NCCI sample and for the United States as a whole. Two NCCI samples were analyzed. In the larger NCCI sample, nine states were excluded as explained in note a of table A2.3. In the smaller NCCI sample, 12 states were excluded.

The first column of numbers in table A2.3 presents employment percentages for the larger NCCI sample. The 0.78 percent indicates that 0.78 percent of all nonsupervisory personnel in the NCCI large sample were employed in mining in 1988 and 1989 (these years were chosen since they correspond to the years for the data in table 2.3). The second column of numbers presents percentages for the smaller NCCI sample. The final column presents percentages for the United States as a whole. These percentages are similar, as reading horizontally across rows will indicate. Chi-square tests were conducted, comparing column 1 with column 3 and column 2 with column 3. These chi-squares and the corresponding p-values appear in the bottom two rows of table A2.3. The p-value in column 2 is a little lower than in column 1, as would be expected since the smaller sample includes a smaller subset of states

TABLE A2.3.   Percentage of Employment, 1988 and 1989

Industry	(1) Includes 41 States and DC[a]	(2) Includes 38 States and DC[b]	(3) U.S. Total
Mining	0.78	0.65	0.69
Construction	5.17	5.24	4.99
Manufacturing	18.81	18.92	18.42
Transportation and public utilities	5.05	5.14	5.26
Wholesale and retail trade	24.07	24.20	23.92
Finance, insurance, and real estate	6.09	6.00	6.30
Services	23.35	23.40	24.01
Government	16.49	16.51	16.40
Chi-square	$\chi_{1,3}^* = 6.140$		$\chi_{2,3}^{**} = 8.347$
Probability of type 1 error	$(p = .512)$		$(p = .308)$

Source: Current study.

[a]The 41 states excluded California, Minnesota, Nevada, New York, North Dakota, Ohio, Washington, West Virginia, and Wyoming.

[b]The 38 states excluded those in note a in addition to Delaware, Pennsylvania, and Texas.

*Chi-square for column 1 with column 3, 7 degrees of freedom.

**Chi-square for column 2 with column 3, 7 degrees of freedom.

included in the larger sample. But neither of the chi-squares generated low *p*-values. We conclude that the columns of percentages are similar, that is, that the industry mix in the NCCI states and Washington, DC, is similar to the industry mix in the United States as a whole. This conclusion is consistent with the idea that the distribution of PTs, PPs, and TTPs in the NCCI data in table 2.3 is similar to the (unobserved) distribution of PTs, PPs, and TTPs in the United States at large.

6. Supplementary Data System (SDS)

The SDS represented a 1980s attempt by the BLS to gather nationwide data on occupational injuries and illnesses and their costs. State WC boards were contacted and asked to participate. Eleven states ultimately provided the most detailed data to the SDS. The SDS effort that collected most of the detailed data ended in 1986. A thorough description of the SDS is available (Leigh 1995a; Leigh and Miller 1998a).

7. National Safety Council (NSC)

A brief discussion of the NSC appears in the text. Here, we examine some NSC data on time trends.

TABLE A2.4.   National Safety Council Estimates of Work Injury Deaths and Death Rates for all Industries, 1973–92

Year	All Work Deaths	Death Rate per 100,000[a]	Motor Vehicle Work Deaths	Government Employee Deaths and Death Rates per 100,000
1973	14,300	17	4,500	—
1975	13,000	15	3,900	—
1980	13,200	13	4,500	—
1985	11,500	11	4,100	1,300 (8)
1986	11,100	10	3,900	1,400 (8)
1987	11,300	10	4,200	1,500 (9)
1988	11,000	10	3,900	1,600 (9)
1989	10,700	9	3,700	1,700 (10)
1990	10,100	9	3,600	1,700 (10)
1991	9,300	8	3,300	1,500 (8)
1992	8,500	7	3,000	1,700 (9)

Source: National Safety Council 1993.
[a]Denominators for death rates include all persons gainfully employed, including owners, managers, other paid employees, the self-employed, and unpaid family workers but excluding private household workers.

The NSC estimated a downward trend in deaths and death rates since 1973, as indicated in table A2.4. From 1980 through 1992, the number of all work deaths (column 2) has fallen roughly 527 per year.

Table A2.4 also presents data on death rates per 100,000 motor vehicle work deaths and deaths among government employees. The last two columns are noteworthy. We are not aware of any other time trend estimates of motor vehicle work deaths or of the number of work deaths among government employees. The latter appears to follow the economy. The economy expanded from 1983 to 1990 but contracted from 1990 through 1992.

The NSC investigators are careful to point out that some of their definitions of injuries and disabilities have changed over time. The NSC explicitly state that their data should not be used for systematic historical analyses. Moreover, the NSC does not collect data from 250,000 firms as does the BLS, nor does the NSC interview over 90,000 people annually as does the NHIS.

Appendix B for Chapter 2

TABLE B2.1. Age Characteristics of Deceased and Nonfatally
Injured Persons

Age	Number	Percentage	Rate per 100,000 Employed
A. CFOI 1992 fatalities			
Total	6,083	100	5.087
Under 20 years	169	3	2.854
20 to 24 years	528	9	4.169
25 to 34 years	1,521	25	4.600
35 to 44 years	1,511	25	4.729
45 to 54 years	1,143	19	5.370
55 to 64 years	751	12	6.664
65 years and over	460	8	13.423
B. NTOF 1980–89 fatalities			
Total	62,218	100	
Under 20	2,630	4.2	3.9
20 to 24 years	7,588	12.2	5.4
25 to 34 years	16,599	26.7	5.2
35 to 44 years	12,434	20.0	5.1
45 to 54 years	10,028	16.1	5.9
55 to 64 years	8,571	13.8	7.4
65 years and over	4,368	7.0	14.6
C. SDS/WC fatalities[a]			
Total[b]	5,338	100	
Under 20 years	244	4.6	
20 to 24 years	456	8.5	
25 to 34 years	940	17.6	
35 to 44 years	867	16.2	
45 to 54 years	1,172	22.0	
55 to 64 years	1,128	21.1	
65 years and over	377	7.1	

TABLE B2.1 — *Continued*

Age	Number	Percentage	Rate per 100,000 Employed

D. BLS's Annual Survey 1992 (BLS 1994a) nonfatal disabling[c] injuries and illnesses[d,e]

Total	2,262,100	100	
Under 20 years	97,300	4.2	
20 to 24 years	346,300	14.9	
25 to 34 years	762,000	32.7	
35 to 44 years	569,300	24.4	
45 to 54 years	318,500	13.7	
55 to 64 years	147,700	6.3	
65 years and over	21,000	0.9	

E. NHIS-OSH 1988 nonfatal injuries

Total	2,211	100	8.1
18 to 29 years	858	38.8	11.1
30 to 44 years	918	41.5	8.0
45 to 64 years	405	18.3	5.7
65 years and over	130	1.4	2.8

Source: See headings for panels A through E.

[a]Denominator data on ages of employed people in the 11 SDS states are not available. We, therefore, do not report rates.

[b]Only decedents with age information were included. One hundred sixty decedents missing ages were excluded.

[c]Disabling: resulting in one or more days away from work

[d]No rate data were published. They would be difficult to estimate given the nonrandom nature of the Annual Survey data.

[e]No separate statistics are available on injuries only. But illnesses comprised roughly 7% of the total in 1992.

TABLE B2.2.　Gender Characteristics of Deceased and Injured Persons

	Number	Percentage	Rate per 100,000 Employed
A.　CFOI 1992 fatalities			
Total	6,083	100	5.087
Female	426	7	0.790
Male	5,657	93	8.675
B.　NTOF 1980–89, fatalities			
Total	62,289	100	7.0
Female	3,737	6	0.8
Male	58,552	94	9.8
C.　SDS/WC 1979–86 fatalities[a]			
Total[b]	5,338	100	
Female	227	4.3	0.28
Male	5,111	95.7	5.0
D.　BLS's Annual Survey 1992 (BLS 1994a) nonfatal disabling[c] injuries and illnesses[d,e]			
Total	2,331,100	100	
Female	764,200	32.8	
Male	1,527,400	65.5	
E.　NHIS-OSH 1988, nonfatal injuries			
Total	2,211	100	8.1
Female	777	35.1	5.6
Male	1,434	64.9	10.5
F.　NHIS 1980–81 (Collins 1985), nonfatal injuries			
Total	11,059,000	100	
Female	2,542,000	30.0	6.0
Male	8,517,000	70.0	14.8

Source: See headings for panels A–F.

[a]Estimated based on national denominator data from *U.S. Statistical Abstract* 1985.

[b]Only decedents with age information were included. One hundred sixty decedents missing ages were excluded.

[c]Resulting in one or more days away from work.

[d]No separate statistics are available on injuries only. But illnesses comprised roughly 7% of the total.

[e]BLS did not calculate rates. They would be difficult to estimate given the nonrandom nature of the BLS Annual Survey data.

TABLE B2.3. Race and Ethnic Characteristics of Deceased and Injured Persons

Employed	Number	Percentage	Rate per 100,000
A. CFOI 1992 fatalities			
Total	6,083	100	5.087
White	5,069	83	4.983
African American	608	10	4.962
Asian or Pacific Islander	166	3	—[a]
Other	240	4	—[a]
Hispanic (of any race)	508	8	5.589
B. NTOF 1980–89, fatalities			
Total	62,218	100	7.0
White	49,837	80	5.8
African American	6,739	11	6.5
Asian or Pacific Islander	919	2	—[b]
Other, Native American	307	5	4.9
Hispanic (of any race)	3,830	6	—[b]
Unknown	659	1	—[b]
C. BLS's Annual Survey 1992 (BLS 1994a), nonfatal disabling[c] injuries and illnesses[d,e]			
Total	2,331,100	100.0	
White, non-Hispanic	1,252,500	53.7	
Black, non-Hispanic	190,600	8.2	
Hispanic	198,000	8.8	
Other	38,900	1.7	
Not reported	651,100	27.9	
D. NHIS-OSH 1988, nonfatal injuries[f]			
Total	2,211	100	
White	1,893	85.6	8.5 per 100
Black	255	11.5	7.7
Hispanic, of any race	132	6.0	8.2
E. NHIS 1980–81 (Collins 1985), nonfatal injuries[g]			
Total (includes all races)	11,059,000	100	11.0
White	9,766,000	88.3	11.1
Black	967,000	8.7	10.4

Source: See headings for panels A through E.
[a]CFOI did not calculate; too few deaths.
[b]NTOF did not calculate.
[c]Resulting in one or more days away from work.
[d]No separate statistics are available on injuries only. But illnesses comprised roughly 7% of the total.
[e]BLS did not calculate rates. They would be difficult to estimate given the nonrandom nature of the BLS Annual Survey data.
[f]Denominator from U.S. Statistical Abstract 1988.
[g]Denominator from U.S. Statistical Abstract 1981.

TABLE B2.4. Number and Percentage Distribution of Fatal Occupational
Injuries by Occupations, 1992, CFOI

	Fatalities			
Occupation[a]	Number	Percentage	Per 100,000 Employed	Rank[b] for the Rate
Total fatalities	6,083	100	5.087	
Managerial and professional specialty	694	11	2.228	20
Technical, sales, and administrative support	814	13	2.211	21
Service occupations	526	9	3.268	18
Protective service	273	4	13.025	11
Farming, forestry, and fishing	931	15	26.939	3
Farming occupations	680	11	20.688	7
Forestry and logging occupations	155	3	14.220	10
Precision production, craft, and repair	1,054	17	8.029	16
Mechanics and repairers	269	4	6.057	17
Construction trades, e.g., carpenters, electricians	578	10	12.067	13
Operators, fabricators, and laborers	1,882	31	11.099	14
Machine operators, assemblers, and inspectors	223	4	2.969	19
Transportation and material moving occupations	1,100	18	22.550	6
Motor vehicle operators	856	14	23.098	5
Truck drivers	685	11	25.427	4
Taxicab drivers and chauffeurs	105	2	49.533	1
Material moving equipment operators	163	3	16.155	8
Handlers, equipment cleaners, helpers, and laborers	559	9	12.270	12
Construction laborers	226	4	34.557	2
Other laborers	170	3	14.444	9
Military occupations Resident armed forces	154[c]	3	9.834	15

Source: U.S. Bureau of Labor Statistics, in cooperation with federal and state agencies, Census of Fatal Occupational Injuries 1992.

Note: Total for major categories may include subcategories not shown separately. Percentages may not add to total because of rounding. There were 28 fatalities for which there was insufficient information to determine an occupational classification.

[a]Based on the 1990 Census of Population Occupational Classification System.

[b]This ranking applies only to the occupations reported in this table. The census has categories for over 500 occupations.

[c]Includes 16 workers not reported as active duty military but reported as working in a military occupation.

TABLE B2.5.   Number and Percentage Distribution of Fatal Occupational
Injuries by Industry, 1992, CFOI

SIC code[a]	Industry	Fatalities			
		Number	Percentage	Per 100,000 Employed	Rank[b] for the Rate
	Total fatalities	6,083	100	5.087	
	Private industry	5,384	89	5.411	
01–02, 07–09	Agriculture, forestry, and fishing	800	13	24.279	2
10–14	Mining	182	3	27.451	1
15–17	Construction	903	15	13.890	3
20–39	Manufacturing	751	12	3.785	7
40–42, 44–49	Transportation and public utilities	884	15	13.220	4
50, 51	Wholesale trade	244	4	5.129	5
52–59	Retail trade	710	12	3.643	8
60–67	Finance, insurance, and real estate	118	2	1.562	13
70–89	Services	725	12	2.361	11
91–97	Government[c]	699	11	3.553	9
	Federal	241	4	4.916	6
	State	112	2	2.349	12
	Local	338	6	3.381	10

Source: U.S. Bureau of Labor Statistics, in cooperation with federal and state agencies, Census of Fatal Occupational Injuries 1992.

Note: Totals for major categories may include subcategories not shown separately. Percentages may not add to total because of rounding. There were 67 fatalities for which there was insufficient information to determine a major industry classification within private industry.

[a]From *Standard Industrial Classification Manual,* 1987.

[b]This ranking applies only to the industries in table 2.18. The SIC has over 200 categories of three-digit industries.

[c]Also includes workers employed by governmental organizations in other SICs. There were eight fatalities to workers employed by foreign or regional governmental agencies.

TABLE B2.6.   Number and Rate of Fatal Injuries by Occupation, 1980–89, NTOF

Occupation	Numbers	Rate per 100,000 Employed	Rank for the Rate
Executive, administration, manager	4,337	3.59	6
Professional	2,297	1.70	9
Technical support	1,713	5.44	5
Sales	3,509	2.81	8
Clerical	1,076	0.62	10
Service	4,206	2.94	7 (tie)
Farming, fishing	7,585	21.28	2
Crafts	12,039	9.30	4
Machine operators	2,387	2.94	7 (tie)
Transport operators	11,578	25.58	1
Laborers	7,934	17.22	3

Source: Data from National Traumatic Occupational Fatality Study.

TABLE B2.7.   Leading Causes of Death within Occupation Divisions, NTOF

Occupation Division	Causes of Death
Executive, administrative, manager	Homicide, motor vehicle crash, machine mishap
Professionals, specialists	Motor vehicle crash, homicide, aircraft crash
Technical support	Aircraft crash, motor vehicle crash, electrocution
Sales workers	Homicide, motor vehicle crash, suicide
Clerks	Motor vehicle crash, homicide, fall
Service workers	Homicide, motor vehicle crash, fall
Farmers, forestry workers, or fishers	Machine mishap, struck by falling object, motor vehicle crash
Craft workers	Fall, electrocution, machine mishap
Machine operators	Machine mishap, homicide, motor vehicle crash, (tie) explosion (tie)
Transport workers	Motor vehicle crash, machine mishap, homicide
Laborers	Motor vehicle crash, machine mishap, fall

Source: National Traumatic Occupational Fatality Study.

241

TABLE B2.8.   Causes of Injury Deaths within Industry Divisions, NTOF

Industry	Causes of Death
Agriculture, forestry, fishing	Machine mishap, motor vehicle crash, struck by falling object
Mining	Machine mishap, motor vehicle crash, struck by falling object
Construction	Fall, electrocution, motor vehicle crash
Manufacturing	Machine mishap, struck by falling object, motor vehicle crash
Transportation, communication, public utility	Motor vehicle crash, aircraft crash, homicide
Wholesale trade	Motor vehicle crash, machine mishap, homicide
Retail trade	Homicide, motor vehicle crash, suicide
Finance, insurance, real estate	Homicide, motor vehicle crash, suicide
Service	Homicide, motor vehicle crash, fall
Public administration	Motor vehicle crash, homicide, aircraft crash

Source: National Traumatic Occupational Fatality Study.

TABLE B2.9.   Four-Digit Industries with the Highest Lost Workday Case Incidence Rates[a] for Injuries Only, Private Industry, 1992, BLS Annual Survey

Industry[b]	SIC Code[c]	Incidence Rate
Household appliances, n.e.c.	3,639	11.3
Raw cane sugar	2,061	10.2
Shipbuilding and ship repairing	3,731	9.5
Cottonseed oil mills	2,074	9.1
Bottled and canned soft drinks	2,086	8.9
Logging	2,411	8.5
Structural wood members, n.e.c.	2,439	8.4
Wood pallets and skids	2,448	8.0
Creamery butter	2,021	7.9
Malt	2,083	7.9
Membership-basis-organization hotels	704	7.9
Trucking terminal facilities	423	7.7
Nursing and personal care facilities	805	7.7
Roofing, siding, and sheet metal work	176	7.6
Prefabricated wood buildings	2,452	7.6
Truck trailers	3,715	7.6
Fluid milk	2,026	7.4
Rice milling	2,044	7.4
Bituminous coal and lignite mining	122	7.3
Interstate and rural bus transportation	413	7.3
Mobile homes	2,451	7.2
Fabricated structural metal	3,441	7.2
Anthracite mining	123	7.0
Masonry, stonework, and plastering	174	7.0
Leather tanning and finishing	3,111	6.9
Asbestos products	3,292	6.9
Steel pipe and tubes	3,317	6.9
Steel foundries, n.e.c.	3,325	6.9
Copper foundries	3,366	6.9
Mattresses and bedsprings	2,515	6.8

Source: U.S. Bureau of Labor Statistics, Annual Survey.

Note: n.e.c. = not elsewhere classified.

[a]The incidence rates represent the number of injuries per 100 full-time workers.

[b]High-rate industries were those having the 20 highest lost workday case incidence rates for injuries only at the most detailed or lowest SIC level at which rates were calculated and published. Based on this comparison, the highest rates were all reported in manufacturing industries, except SIC 478 (miscellaneous transportation services industry). Generally, manufacturing industries were calculated at the four-digit code level based on the *Standard Industrial Classification Manual,* 1987 ed. Agriculture, forestry, and fishing were calculated at the two-digit level; and the remaining industries at the three-digit level.

[c]*Standard Industrial Classification Manual,* 1987 ed.

TABLE B2.10.   Number (not rate) of Nonfatal Occupational Injuries and
Illnesses Involving Days away from Work[a] by Selected Occupations, 1992,
Private Industry,[b] BLS Annual Survey

Occupation	Numbers (in thousands)
Total	2,331.1
Laborers, nonconstruction	152.1
Truck drivers	145.9
Nursing aides, orderlies	111.1
Janitors and cleaners	59.6
Construction laborers	57.1
Assemblers	47.7
Stock handlers and baggers	44.4
Cashiers	41.7
Miscellaneous food preparers	38.5
Cooks	36.1
Carpenters	34.3
Registered nurses	31.4
Maids and housemen	29.4
Welders and cutters	29.4
Supervisors and proprietors, sales	28.4
Shipping and receiving clerks	26.4
Automobile mechanics	25.7
Groundskeepers and gardeners	21.3
Farmworkers	20.8
Kitchen workers	19.5
Waiters and waitresses	19.5
Driver-sales workers	19.2
Electricians	19.2
Sewing machine operators	17.4
Supervisors, production	16.3
Packaging machine operators	15.6
Butchers and meatcutters	15.5
Licensed practical nurses	14.9
Plumbers and pipe fitters	13.9
All other occupations	1,164.4

Source: U.S. Bureau of Labor Statistics, Annual Survey.
Note: Because of rounding, data may not sum to the totals.
[a]Days away from work cases include those that result in days away from work with or without restricted work activity.
[b]Excludes farms with fewer than 11 employees.

TABLE B2.11. Percentage Distribution of Nonfatal Occupational Injuries and Illnesses, Days away from Work[a] by Broad Occupation, 1992, Private Industry,[b] BLS Annual Survey

Characteristic	Percentage
Total (2,331,100 cases)	100.0
Broad occupations	
Operators, fabricators, and laborers	40.8
Service	17.4
Precision production, craft, and repair	17.0
Technical, sales, and administrative support	15.0
Farming, forestry, and fishing	2.7
Managerial and professional	1.5

Source: U.S. Bureau of Labor Statistics, Annual Survey.
Note: Because of rounding, data may not sum to the totals.
[a]Days away from work cases include those that result in days away from work with or without restricted work activity.
[b]Excludes farms with fewer than 11 employees.

TABLE B2.12. Number and Percentage Distribution of Fatal Occupational Injuries by Event or Exposure, 1992, CFOI

Fatalities Event or exposure[a]	Number	Percentage
Total	6,083	100
Transportation accidents	2,441	40
Highway accidents	1,121	18
Farm, industrial vehicle accidents	436	7
Aircraft crashes	350	6
Pedestrians struck by vehicles	342	6
Boating accidents	110	2
Railway accidents	66	1
Assaults and violent acts	2,616	20
Murders	1,004	17
Suicides	183	3
Contacts with objects and equipment	1,001	16
Falls	590	10
Exposure to harmful substances or environments	593	10
Fires and explosions	167	3
Other	75	1

Source: Census of Fatal Occupational Injuries.
[a]Categories are based on the 1992 BLS Occupational Injury and Illness Classification Structures.

TABLE B2.13.   Average Annual Number of Injuries by Class of Accident and Type of Injury, United States, 1985–87, NHIS

| | Class of Injury | | Type of Work Injury | |
| | All Classes | | | |
	Number	Percentage	Number	Percentage
All injuries	64,258	100.0	10,512	100.0
Skull fractures and intracranial injuries	1,931	3.0	164	1.6
Fractures of neck, trunk, and upper limb	4,184	6.5	641	6.1
Fracture of upper limb	3,169	4.9	369	3.5
Fractures of lower limb	2,046	3.2	271	2.6
Dislocations	1,079	1.7	178	1.7
Sprains and strains — total	3,848	6.0	2,925	27.8
Sprains and strains of hip, thigh, knee, and leg	2,210	3.4	436	4.1
Sprains and strains of ankle and foot	3,389	5.3	561	5.3
Sprains and strains of back	4,758	7.4	1,326	12.6
Open wounds and lacerations — total	14,202	22.1	2,496	23.7
Open wounds and lacerations of head, neck, and trunk	4,593	7.1	341	3.2
Open wounds and lacerations of upper limb	5,868	9.1	1,750	16.6
Open wounds and lacerations of shoulder, arm, and hand	2,656	4.1	723	6.9
Open wounds and lacerations of fingers	3,212	5.0	1,027	9.8
Open wounds and lacerations of lower limb	3,740	5.8	406	3.9
Open wounds and lacerations of knee, leg, and ankle	1,878	2.9	264	2.5
Superficial injury	4,279	6.7	661	6.3
Contusion with intact skin surface	9,828	15.3	1,517	14.4
Contusion of face, neck, and scalp	1,328	2.1	53	0.5
Contusion of trunk	1,906	3.0	299	2.8

TABLE B2.13 — *Continued*

| | Class of Injury | | Type of Work Injury | |
| | All Classes | | | |
	Number	Percentage	Number	Percentage
Effects of foreign body				
through orifice	1,056	1.6	454	4.3
Effects of foreign body on				
external eye	837	1.3	433	4.1
Burns	1,753	2.7	393	3.7
Toxic effects — nonmedical	1,323	2.1	—	
All other injuries	8,735	13.6	811	7.7

Source: Data from National Health Interview Survey.

TABLE B2.14.   Part of Body Injured in Nonfatal Incidents, 1991, NSC

	Number of Disabling Injuries	Percentage	Percentage of WC Compensation
Back	800,000	24	31
Legs	440,000	13	14
Arms	370,000	12	10
Fingers	360,000	11	5
Trunk	360,000	11	13
Hands	170,000	5	3
Eyes	140,000	4	1
Feet	130,000	4	2
Head, except eyes	140,000	4	3
Total	3,300,000[a]	100[a]	100[a]

Source: National Safety Council.
[a]Does not sum to 3,300,000 or 100% due to exclusion of "other," "multiple injuries," and "unknown," "neck," "toes," "body systems."

Appendix A for Chapter 10: Assumptions

List of Consequential Assumptions

Chapter 1

1.1. Low. We selected our year of analysis to be 1992, a high unemployment year. Incidence of injuries and illnesses is less in high than in low unemployment years. (This assumption is made throughout the text.)

Chapter 2

2.1. High. We based our incidence-based estimate of injury deaths on prevalence-based death estimates in the CFOI. There is, in fact, a downward secular time trend in injury deaths. Hence, other things equal, incidence deaths should be slightly smaller than prevalence deaths in 1992.

2.2. Low. We chose a 55 percent rather than a 60 percent undercount for WC even though most studies showed a 60 percent undercount.

2.3. Low. We omitted collateral damage to innocent third parties as a result of an accident. For example, when an airplane crashes, the pilot and crew may die. These would be recorded as injury deaths. But 100 or so passengers may also die. Many injury accidents have collateral damage: for example, car and truck crashes; police gun battles in which third parties are wounded; firefighters hosing down blazes; and so on. In an earlier analysis, we estimated these damages to sum to $2.9 billion (Leigh et al. 1996).

2.4. Low. We omitted injuries among military personnel. Toscano and Windau (1993) estimated that military personnel residing in the United States accounted for 2.6 percent of all job-related deaths.

Chapter 3

3.1. Low. Reproductive problems were omitted from our disease and illness calculations (Zhange, Cui, and Lee 1992).

3.2. Low. The full extent of hearing loss was underestimated with BLS Annual Survey data because the losses are gradual and may not become serious until retirement.

3.3. Low. We did not assume any deaths or illnesses resulted from workers who worry about layoffs. As corporate restructuring continues so do feelings of job insecurity that, in turn, could lead to increased colds, flus, cancers, and circulatory disease (Heaney et al. 1993; Marriot, Kirkwood, and Stough 1994). We do not have reliable national estimates for any of these.

3.4. Low. Small proportions (1 percent to 3 percent to 10 percent) were used when we attempted to estimate morbidity and mortality from the major diseases.

3.5. Low. Occupational circulatory morbidity and mortality was limited to events among people less than 65 years old because the extent of the occupational impact on circulatory disease after retirement is uncertain.

3.6. Low. Pneumoconiosis is underdiagnosed.

3.7. Low. No diseases were allowed for persons less than 25 years old. We disallowed any consequences of workers bringing carcinogens home with them (on clothing, for example) and exposing children (Olsham, Taschke, and Baird 1991).

3.8. Unknown bias. Disease deaths were counted as occurring in 1992. However, the exposures leading to the deaths could have occurred 20 or 30 years prior to the death. For example, projected asbestos-related diseases are forecasted to drop considerably after the year 2000 (Center to Protect Worker's Rights 1997) as a result of the standards OSHA required private industry to adopt in the early 1970s. In addition, circulatory disease death rates have been slowly dropping for 20 years. On the other hand, cancer and COPD death rates have been increasing in recent years. Nonfatal illnesses have also displayed time trends. For example, the incidence of carpal tunnel syndrome was rapidly expanding from 1985 through 1992. The point is that the true numbers of disease are moving targets perhaps much more than those for injuries. Our estimates apply only to 1992, and we are uncertain how these total numbers are likely to change in the future.

3.9. Low. We did not allow for a new theory of disease — toxicant-induced loss of tolerance. The theory suggests that exposures to chemicals at low levels, generally regarded as nontoxic, can cause fatigue, memory impairment, headaches, depression, and asthma. These exposures may underlie sick-building syndrome, chronic fatigue syndrome, and chemical sensitivity (Ashford and Miller 1998).

3.10. High. We applied a 59.8 per 10,000 rate (Annual Survey) rather than a 51.9 per 10,000 rate to all workers excluded by the BLS Annual Survey. The 51.9 rate was estimated for federal workers. But no rates were available for all state and local governments or all self-employed workers or farmworkers, all of whom are excluded from the Annual Survey. The self-employed and farmworkers are known to have especially high injury rates. We implicitly assume they have especially high illness rates as well by using this 59.8 rate.

Chapter 5

5.1. Low. We ignored the trend toward longer recovery times for injuries. We used the NCCI cost figures from 1988 to 1990 to create our injury cost figures for 1992. Since average costs per injury will increase with longer recovery times, the use of the 1988–90 average cost data underestimated average costs for 1992.

5.2. Low. Our estimate of hiring and training costs was drawn from a study of low-skilled workers. These cost are likely to be considerably higher for skilled workers.

5.3. Low. In calculating the costs to the firm, we excluded the workplace disruption costs associated with (a) experiencing anxiety with the death of a co-worker and (b) increasing strike frequencies (Leigh 1983), absence, or sabotage rates that are associated with high injury rates.

5.4. Low. We ignored property damage, police and fire services, and time delays. Property damage can result from an injury accident when, for example, the car, truck, van, train, or plane is destroyed. Police and fire services are a municipal government expense when, for example, a truck overturns and kills a driver or a fire burns down a factory. Time delays can result to innocent third parties stuck in a traffic jam caused by a delivery truck explosion. In an earlier version of our study we estimated property damage to be $8.3 billion, police and fire services to be $0.8 billion, and time delays to be $0.07 billion (Leigh et al. 1996).

5.5. Unknown bias. Injury numbers apply only to 1992. If present trends continue, numbers of injuries will continue to decline while average length of time away from work for any given injury will continue to expand.

5.6. Unknown bias. Large self-insured firms, excluded from the NCCI, have average costs similar to those included in the NCCI (Leigh and Fries 1991, 1992; Leigh 1988a, 1993). Nor did we account for low wages as a cause of stress and illness.

Chapters 5 and 6

5 and 6.1. Low. We did not adjust for current employment status in the present value of earnings tables. We merely adjusted for the labor force participation rate (LFPR). In doing so, we undervalued the earnings of those currently employed. That is, those currently employed are not a random sample of all persons in the labor market. Those currently employed probably had better lifetime employment prospects than all persons in the labor force. All persons in the labor force included those persons unemployed.

5 and 6.2. Low. We assumed that fringe benefits were equal to 23.3 percent of the wage. Most studies show fringe benefits above 25 percent.

5 and 6.3. Low. We did not add any damage cost for injuries that would eventually produce arthritis (Krause et al. 1997; Leigh and Fries 1992). Nor did we account for the effect of dull, repetitive work on producing Alzheimer's disease. Adam Smith ([1776] 1976) warned of the deleterious effects of repetitive work on the intellectual capacity of workers. He argued for government intervention to improve working conditions in the *Wealth of Nations,* vol. 2, b. 5, p. 302. We ignored the roles jobs might play in creating mental illness.

5 and 6.4. Unknown bias. We used the same percentage factor to calculate insurance administrative costs for medical costs as for indemnity costs in WC. It is probably the case that more litigation and thus more administrative costs surround indemnity than are associated with medical benefits. We may have overestimated insurance administrative costs for medical care but underestimated them for providing indemnity.

5 and 6.5. Low. We used a 31 percent WC administrative cost estimate using the data from Nelson 1992 and 1993. The Burton 1994 statistics indicated a 38 percent rate.

5 and 6.6. Low. We ignored pain and suffering costs. Lawsuits involving nonfatal injuries almost always involve some payment for pain and suffering. A rule of thumb frequently cited is that pain and suffering equal three times the nonadministrative medical expenses (Ferguson 1995). This would mean adding another roughly $100 billion to our costs. If we assume that the difference between the WTP estimates and the Human Capital estimates is due to pain and suffering, then pain and suffering would add an additional $300 billion to $700 billion.

5 and 6.7. Low. We did not include the costs of family caregivers' time nor the health problems that occur among caregivers. These costs are undoubtedly large but are difficult to estimate (Max, Webber, and Fox 1995; Boaz and Muller 1992). Roy (1992) and McFloyd and Flana-

gan (1993) document the deleterious psychological consequences on spouses.

5 and 6.8. Low. We assumed that once the injured or ill worker was reemployed, no more lost wages would need to be accounted for. However, most permanently impaired workers do not earn their old wage at the new job. They experience permanent wage loss for the rest of their working lives (Abt Associates 1989; Berkowitz 1990; Bound 1989).

5 and 6.9. Low. Children reared in families where one parent is disabled or missing acquire less education and consequently earn less lifetime income than children whose parents are not disabled or are present in the household (Haveman and Wolfe 1994). Children who experience the sudden loss of a parent frequently exhibit lifelong psychological disorders (Black 1998).

Chapter 6

6.1. Low. In estimating days of work loss for diseases, we used the BLS Annual Survey data that were restricted to a 12 month calendar year. But many serious illnesses can generate work loss for much longer than 12 months. Oleinick et al. (1993) showed that the BLS data miss as much as 70 percent of workdays lost.

Remaining Chapters

None of the remaining chapters were used to estimate total injuries, illnesses, or costs. There are limitations and assumptions within chapters 7 through 9, and they are discussed within those chapters.

Appendix B for Chapter 10: Incidence and Prevalence Costs

In chapter 5 we briefly discussed incidence and prevalence as they apply to measuring costs. The concepts are similar to those in epidemiology. Incidence costs indicate costs from, say, 1992 forward. Only new cases of, for example, injuries are counted, and their costs are estimated for 1992 and added to forecasted costs from 1992 onward. ("Incidence" here does not mean "who pays.") Prevalence costs methods look only at cost in 1992 but include injuries that may have originated in prior years.

As a practical matter, our estimates of costs in prior chapters will not be greatly influenced by whether we use incidence or prevalence cost methods.

Nevertheless, some readers may be interested in pursuing the theoretical differences in prevalence and incidence methods. We did discover a difference of opinion in studies of costs. Miller and Galbraith (1994) held that in the steady state, incidence equals prevalence. Hensler et al. (1991) argued that in the steady state, incidence would be smaller than prevalence due to discounting by the real interest rate. We side with Hensler et al. and present the following example to help support our view.

To understand the controversy, it is important to define the steady state. A steady state occurs when the same number and type of injuries and illnesses occur year after year. Before proceeding with our example, we should consider the likelihood of this assumption holding. It is extremely unlikely. Assumptions regarding numbers and types of injuries and illnesses as well as other assumptions regarding direct and indirect costs figure much more prominently in our final estimate of total costs than whether we chose the incidence or prevalence method to calculate costs.

Nevertheless, to explain the difference, consider table B10.1, which describes one possible steady state. In table B10.1, we assume that one injury occurs each year and that the injury lasts two years. In the third year, the worker fully recovers. Six years and five injuries are considered in table B10.1. Years appear down the horizontal side and injuries across the top of table B10.1. We assume only one accident occurs each year. We assume that treatment costs and all costs and prices double every year. This increase in cost is purely inflationary. It does not reflect any improvement in the treatment. (This doubling assumption is an exceptional amount of inflation. We make this assumption because "it is the exceptional case that proves the rule"; that is, it clearly demonstrates whether there is any difference between incidence and prevalence costs.)

The first injury generates a $1 cost in year 1 and a $2 cost in year 2. The total cost for the injury would be $3. But this would not be the present value cost in year 1. Discounting for inflation only in year 1 would require that we divide the year 2 cost by 2. We divide by 2 because we know that inflation doubles prices every year in our example. Hence, the year 1 present value of costs associated with injury number 1 would be 2.

The prevalence cost in year 1 would be $1. Here, the prevalence cost is less than the incidence cost. But year 1 is not the steady state; that is, our exercise begins with year 1, and no prior injuries are allowed into year 1.

Years 2, 3, 4, and 5, on the other hand, are steady state years, that

TABLE B10.1.   Incidence versus Prevalence Costs in the Steady State

			Year			
	1	2	3	4	5	
Year						Prevalence Cost
1	1					1
2	2	2				4
3		4	4			8
4			8	8		16
5				16	16	32
6	—	—	—	—	32	32
(1) Incidence cost: no discount	3	6	12	24	48	
(2) Present value after discounting for inflation	2	4	8	16	32	
(3) Present value after discounting for inflation and after a 4% real interest rate	1.98	3.96	7.92	15.84	31.69	

is, years in which one new injury occurs and one old injury is recovering. Our example ends with year 6, which is not a steady state year, since no new injury is allowed in that year. In the steady state years, prevalence costs and inflation-free (the present value of) incidence costs are identical: 4, 8, 16, 32.

Our inflation-only discounting example suggests that Miller and Galbraith (1994) were right: incidence equals prevalence. But discounting almost always also accounts for a *real* interest rate. In our procedures in chapters 5 and 6, we assumed a 4 percent real discount rate. If we assume a real rate of 0.04, then future dollars should be divided by 2.04, not 2. The dollar totals are seen in the last row. Notice now that in the steady state years (2 through 5) the incidence cost is slightly less than prevalence cost.

Our discounting of future dollars for deaths in chapters 5 and 6 implicitly removes inflation by using earnings data from 1992. We assume persons would have followed the age and gender profiles of earnings displayed by people who were alive in 1992 and in the labor market. We also account for a real interest rate of 4 percent (and a productivity rate of 1 percent). Consequently, in a steady state, our (indirect) incidence costs should be less than our prevalence costs.

But this incidence/prevalence cost analysis is unlikely to explain much of the disparity between, for example, our incidence injury cost estimates and the prevalence injury cost estimate of Hensler et al. (1991). There are simply too many additional assumptions of more consequence that separate the two estimates. For example, Hensler et al. ignore all assaults and murders.

Notes

Chapter 1

1. An early summary of some of our findings was published in the medical literature (Leigh et al. 1997). We received numerous ideas for improvements. As a result, the numbers in the book do not precisely coincide with those in the 1997 study. We prefer our estimates here. These cost estimates are within 10 percent of those from the 1997 summary study. The counts of illnesses and injuries are within 1 percent of those from the 1997 summary paper. The greatest differences between the summary study and this one include these: The summary study included property damage ($9 billion), police and fire protection ($1 billion), and costs to innocent bystanders ($3 billion). None of these are included here.

2. The National Institute for Occupational Safety and Health (NIOSH) receives one of the lowest levels of funding of the nearly 20 National Institutes of Health and related agencies in the Centers for Disease Control. NIOSH research awards sum to roughly one-half of 1 percent of the National Cancer Institute (NCI), less than 1 percent of the National Institute on Aging (NIA), and roughly 7 percent of the National Institute on Dental Research (U.S. Department of Health and Human Services 1992). (There is some overlap between NCI and NIOSH spending. For example, some portion of any NCI spending on bladder cancer would likely have some benefit to a person who developed bladder cancer as a result of job-related exposures. But, in general, the overlap for NCI or NIA or any other institutions is not likely to be large. Among specialists within these fields, few focus on occupational factors. Moreover, if occupation is the focus of a grant proposal to the NIH, reviewers will generally send that grant to NIOSH, regardless of the specific disease being investigated. Finally, 85 percent of our costs arise from injuries, not illnesses.) Moreover, no private charities are available to fund research on occupational injuries and illnesses. By contrast, heart disease has the American Heart Assocation, cancer has the American Cancer Society, AIDS has the Ryan White Institute, and arthritis has the Arthritis Institute.

None of the federal government's flagship health statistics publications *Advanced Data* series on either injury-related data visits (Schapport 1994), or on hospitalizations (Hall and Owings 1994), or on emergency room visits (Burt 1995) include any categories for occupational injuries.

As another example of the lack of resources for occupational injuries and illnesses, it is notable that there are more fish and game inspectors in the United States than OSHA inspectors (McGarity and Shapiro 1993, 213).

Chapter 2

1. We exclude all inmates in prisons and mental hospitals, as well as patients and clients in homes for the aged, infirm, and needy. Employees in these same institutions are included. Finally, we exclude events or exposures that occur to persons commuting to and from work (U.S. Bureau of Labor Statistics 1995b).

2. There are some disadvantages to using these conventional definitions. For example, if the person's job site changes and a longer commute is now required, it seems plausible that any crash injury on the new commute might be viewed as job related. Another example might involve an injury at home that could have resulted from the stress a person feels after being laid off at a job he or she has worked in for, say, 17 years. But it could also be argued that, in the first example, the person could have moved closer to the new job site if the commute was especially burdensome. In the second example, it is difficult to know what percentage of injuries at home are due to stress experienced as the result of recent layoffs. It could also be argued that if a person receives a promotion, the feelings of success might strengthen the immune system, which, in turn, might reduce the recovery time for any given injury. In addition, one could argue that any job is better than no job. Unemployment is stressful (Reynolds 1997). Any job that eliminates unemployment ought to be credited with eliminating stress-related injuries among the unemployed. To properly count job-related injuries we now must subtract injuries that would have occurred at home from those that occur at work. The point is that these broader definitions of job-related injuries rest on some conjecture as well as some merit. They will not be as widely accepted as the conventional definitions. Our first purpose is to generate estimates that comprehensively cover injuries and diseases that are viewed as credible by as many readers as possible. Since no comprehensive estimates have been produced for both injuries and illnesses *using conventional definitions* we feel that our estimates make a contribution. Moreover, we are not familiar with any studies that define job-related injury more broadly than we do. Future researchers may want to broaden these definitions. It will nevertheless be useful to begin with a set of conventional estimates.

3. We say "initially" since in the fall of 1994 the CFOI investigators added an additional 134 deaths that were missed in the initial 1992 study. However, the analysis they conducted on the initial 6,083, including the analysis of table 2.1, was never attempted on the 6,217 (6,083 + 134). We, therefore, rely on the 6,083 as we analyze the CFOI. We use an adjusted CFOI number in our final count. Our adjustments will add the 134 discovered in the fall of 1994 but will exclude 154 military deaths.

4. Copeland (1985) found that blacks contributed to 28 percent of job-related traffic fatalities compared to a 72 percent contribution by whites. Yet, the black percentage in the working population was far less than 28 percent. In

the Baker et al. 1982 study of job-related deaths in Maryland, "non-whites were greatly over-represented, constituting 34% of the deaths and 17% of the employed population." It is likely that the large majority of the nonwhites in the Baker et al. study were black, given that Maryland's Hispanic population is relatively small. In a study using six national data sets and focusing on job exposures to safety and health hazards, Robinson (1991) found African Americans with higher exposure levels than whites in all six data sets. He also found Hispanics with greater hazard exposures than non-Hispanic whites. For all injuries — not just occupational — Baker et al. (1992) found a black rate of 82 per 100,000 and a white rate of 60 per 100,000.

The racial composition of occupational groups presents compelling evidence that further questions the reliability of the 1992 CFOI estimates. African Americans are overrepresented in blue-collar, manual, and unskilled laboring jobs (Gill 1994). Whites are overrepresented in professional and managerial jobs (Gill 1994). But blue-collar, manual, and laboring jobs are more hazardous than white-collar professional jobs. Root and Sebastian (1981) found blue-collar job occupants with four to five times the number of injuries experienced by white-collar jobholders. An April 1994 BLS *News* report based on the Annual Survey confirms this tendency for blue-collar jobs to be much more hazardous than white-collar jobs (U.S. Bureau of Labor Statistics 1994b). Operators, fabricators, and laborers contributed 41 percent of all injuries, yet their employment contribution to the U.S. labor force was less than 15 percent. None of the 30 occupations generating the most injuries in the 1994 U.S. Department of Labor *News* report based on the Annual Survey were professional occupations, and only one — sales supervisors — was a managerial occupation (U.S. Bureau of Labor Statistics 1994b).

5. Several factors could be at work. Some CFOI deaths were identified through newspaper obituaries. It could be that some newspapers omit a higher proportion of black than white deaths from their obituaries. Police reports and death certificates may also be less complete about the circumstances of a black than a white death. Long-standing patterns of bias may, therefore, result in fewer black deaths being counted. The same patterns may result in fewer Hispanic deaths being counted.

6. Our estimated black rate is 20 percent higher than the white rate. This 20 percent figure is drawn from Ruser 1996, using 1993 CFOI data. Our estimated black rate is 5.9256. Assuming roughly 12,252,000 employed blacks in 1992 (Toscano and Windau 1993), then the 5.9256 rate for blacks would result in an estimate of 0.000059256 × 12,252,000, or 726 black deaths as opposed to the 608 deaths recorded in the CFOI for 1992. We believe we are justified in using the male rate since nearly 90 percent of injury deaths were for men.

We assume Robinson's (1984) Hispanic rate (79 percent) is an overestimate but that a 60 percent rate applies, again relying on the 60 percent estimate in Ruser 1996. This would result in a Hispanic rate of 7.9008. Assuming 9,088,000 employed Hispanics in 1992 (Toscano and Windau 1993), this 7.9008 rate would imply 718 deaths, or 210 more Hispanic deaths than recorded in the 1992 CFOI.

All injury death rates with which we are familiar use numbers of workers in the denominator. No adjustment is made for full- or part-time employment. This is because deaths are relatively rare.

7. The 1992 civilian and military deaths number is 6,217, not 6,063, as was originally reported. The inclusion of 154 resident armed forces deaths by the CFOI is commendable. However, as we will see, no other study attempted to include the military. Ideally, we, too, would like to include them. But as a practical matter, so that we can avoid as much interpolation as possible, we will ignore resident armed forces injuries. It is nevertheless worth noting that Toscano and Windau (1993) found that they represented about 3 percent of the total.

8. We are not alone in our belief that the 1992 CFOI underestimated the number of deaths. The CFOI authors themselves, Toscano and Windau (1993), state that as counting methods improve, "fatal work injury counts may increase." They do not suggest that the counts may decrease. In other words, they believe their count is conservative (personal communication with Guy Toscano, May 5, 1994). In fact, 134 errors of omission were discovered in the 1992 counts as the 1993 CFOI counts were being prepared.

9. It could be argued that the prevalence death estimates are too low. Some injuries that occurred in 1992 may not kill the person for some time. Rice et al. (1989a), in their study of all injuries, found that roughly 9 percent of their deaths were attributed to injuries in prior years. Assuming the same percentage would apply to our analysis, roughly 600 more deaths should be added to the CFOI. But, this argument is misleading. The CFOI estimate counts all deaths in 1992 and includes deaths that may have occurred a year or more after the accident. In other words, some 1992 CFOI deaths could have resulted from injuries that occurred in 1991 or perhaps 1990. We therefore assume that the same number of delayed deaths from 1992 into the future *will* occur as *did* occur in prior years up until 1992. Since injury deaths are rarely delayed beyond two years, this appears to be a reasonable assumption.

10. Additional criteria resulted in excluding persons engaged in recreational activities at employer facilities. Activities also excluded, for example, were working for self or nonprofit (e.g., mowing own lawn; repairing own roof; student engaged in school activities; operating commercial vehicle for nonwork purposes; and commuting to or from work).

11. A table footnote in the Annual Survey puts it this way:

> Data conforming to OSHA definitions for employers in the railroad industry and for mining oeprators in coal, metal, and non-metal mining were provided to BLS by the Federal Railroad Administration, U.S. Department of Transportation, and the Mine Safety and Health Administration. Independent mining contractors are excluded from the coal, metal, and non-metal industries (U.S. Bureau of Labor Statistics 1991a).

The last sentence from this Annual Survey suggests that the mine data are incomplete.

12. As testimony to the BLS's dissatisfaction with the surveys, researchers are no longer allowed access to unpublished lists of two- and three-digit industry death rates (Knieser and Leeth 1991). Prior to 1988, the BLS readily made these two- and three-digit industry death rates available to researchers (Leigh 1987b).

13. Macon (1984) estimates 11 percent in the 1980s.

14. A third comparison can be made. The BLS Annual Survey fatality data showed annual declines of roughly 100 in the late 1980s and early 1990s. Assuming another 100 decline, the 1992 number would have been 2,700 subtracting 10 percent due to illnesses results in 2,430. This 2,430 represents roughly 40 percent of the unadjusted and 38.14 percent of the adjusted CFOI numbers (6,063; 6,371).

15. We assume that these 6,371 deaths result from injuries that occurred in 1992. In the language of epidemiology, we assume that 6,371 is an incidence, not a prevalence, number. This assumption will be especially important when we develop our cost estimates. This assumption may be viewed as controversial. After all, the CFOI and NTOF numbers were prevalence based. Some injuries could have occurred prior to 1991 with death not occurring until 1992. Since there is a downward secular trend in injury deaths, one could argue that prevalence exceeds incidence. But there is also an unemployment effect, and unemployment was falling from January through December 1992. There were undoubtedly injuries sustained in November and December 1992 that led to deaths in 1993, but none of these would be counted in the CFOI. Since unemployment was less in November and December 1992 than 1991, we would expect a larger "carryover" from 1992 to 1993 than from 1991 to 1992. But we do not assign numbers to these arguments.

16. These 6.342 million excluded all deaths. BLS investigators deliberately excluded deaths for the first time in 1992. But historical analyses of Annual Survey data including deaths are still meaningful. This is because the number of deaths (2,500 to 2,700 injury deaths) is so small in comparison to the number of nonfatal injuries (roughly 6,000,000,000).

17. We emphasize "at least as great" since it could be argued that deaths are more difficult to ignore than nonfatal injuries (i.e., records for deaths may be more reliable than records for nonfatal injuries). This was the conclusion of some of the scientists who participated in the National Academy's conference on undercounting of occupational injuries and illnesses (National Research Council 1987). It is more clear-cut to identify a *death* as due to an accident at work than a *nonfatal* injury, especially one such as back pain. Moreover, it is probably easier for employers and employees to conceal a nonfatal injury than a fatal one. The 1991 BLS Annual Survey fatality count was 2,800 for injuries and illnesses. In note 14 we estimated 2,430 injuries. This 2,430 would have resulted in a 38 percent undercount of injury deaths.

We can assume that the same percentage undercount applies to 1992 for nonfatal injuries. We can, therefore, divide 6.342 million by 0.3814 to yield an estimate of 16.63 million injuries in 1992.

Alternatively, we could use the undercount statistics from the CFOI in table 2.1. The "OSHA reports" in table 2.1 were the data the BLS Annual Survey relied on for their estimated deaths in the 1980s. The OSHA reports suggest that the BLS Annual Survey would have counted only 32 percent of deaths identified in the CFOI in table 2.1, or 30.6 percent of our 6,371. If the same undercount of deaths by the Annual Survey applied to nonfatal injuries, then we can divide 6.342 million by 0.306 to estimate 20.725 million nonfatal injuries.

18. But 75 percent of total costs are generated among those with 12 or more lost months (Hashemi et al. 1997).

19. The NCCI ratios were 1.5873 for PTs to NCCI deaths; 112.7307 for PPs to NCCI deaths; and 279.4796 for TTPs to NCCI deaths. Multiplying these ratios by our 1992 estimate of deaths (6,371) yields 10,113 for PTs; 718,207 for PPs; and 1,780,695 for TTPs. These sum to 2,508,845. We therefore estimate that 2,508,845 of our injuries would, theoretically, qualify for one of the three WC categories. Thus 50.7 percent (2,508,845/4,950,000) would qualify and 49.3 percent would not, that is, would cause a person to miss at least one but less than three days of work (in some states) and seven days of work (in other states).

20. We are not aware of any studies that count (as opposed to estimate) the number of hospitalizations due to job injuries. Nevertheless, Hensler et al. (1991a) and Miller (1995) provide useful estimates, and the Rice et al. (1985) data can be adjusted to produce an estimate.

Rice et al. (1989a) were concerned with all injuries, whether or not job related. In table 1 of Rice et al. 1989a, estimates are presented for the number and rate of injured persons by gender, age, and class of injury, that is, fatality, and, most importantly, whether the injury resulted in a hospitalization.

We estimate that the percentage of hospitalizations in the Rice et al. 1991a data adjusted for the likely employment status and male/female composition of employment would be 4.2 percent (Leigh et al. 1996).

But, the Rice et al. 1989a data are not the only data that can be used to estimate hospitalizations due to job-related injuries. The Hensler et al. 1991a Rand study, examined previously, estimated a 27 percent hospitalization rate for job-related injuries. This 27 percent figure was their estimate and did not require any adjustment on our part. But the Hensler et al. study, as the authors acknowledge, was much more successful at gathering data on serious than on minor injuries.

The Miller 1995 study (17) estimated a 5.4 percent hospitalization rate for job-related injuries. Again, the 5.4 percent did not require any adjustment on our part. Both Hensler et al. 1991 and Miller 1995 suggest that on-the-job injuries tend to be more serious than off-the-job injuries. Moreover, for job injuries, employees must be able to show employers that the injury was serious enough to seek medical care or temporarily leave the job. No additional third party need attest to the severity of an off-the-job injury.

Hensler et al. (1991a) provide direct estimates of job-related injury hospitalizations. But, the Rice et al. 1989a study is widely cited. Moreover, Miller (1995) uses much of the Rice et al. data in his calculations. We take the middle estimate — 5.4 percent — since this Miller estimate purports to adjust the Rice et al. 1989a data for the widely held belief that job-related injuries are more serious than others.

21. An estimate of the number of individuals affected underestimates the number of injuries since a person can experience more than one injury episode over the course of a year. In Leigh et al. 1996, we constructed our own estimate of the number of injuries using two methods involving the "person-incident" rates estimated by Hensler et al. (1991a) and Marquis (1992). We did not use the seven to 11 million estimate from Marquis 1992. Our first estimate involved a comparison to 1989 NHIS estimates, and our second estimate involved a direct multiplication by the number of civilians employed.

In 1989, Hensler et al. (1991) estimated a 9.1 percent annual injury rate (person-incident rate, i.e., number of incidents, not number of persons) for employed workers 18 years and older. This 9.1 per 100 annual rate compares favorably to the NHIS 9.3 per 100 rate for the same year.

The average of the two estimates, after adjusting for the undercount of assault, was 13.2 million. However, because this 13.2 estimate relied on secondary data and involved a number of assumptions, we do not use it in our estimate. We merely offer it as an example of how a better estimate might be derived from the Rand study.

22. This disparity might arise because of WC treatment of heart disease and stroke. WC authorities will frequently award WC benefits to police officers and firefighters for heart attacks and strokes. Moreover, heart attacks and strokes are far more deadly than most on-the-job injuries; hence illness might have a higher deaths to disabilities ratio than injuries (Leigh and Miller 1998a).

23. It is reassuring that Miller's estimate of the percentage of all injuries resulting in work loss — 46.53 percent — is very close to our own assumption of 45 percent in the BLS Annual Survey data in chapter 2.

24. The first estimate combined the NHIS estimate with the Rice et al. (1989a) estimate of hospitalizations for all injuries. His first estimate was 426,000 hospitalized workplace injuries. The second hospitalized estimate came from Miller's data from the DCI/NCCI data, which suggested that 26.8 percent of *disabling* injuries (using his definition) resulted in hospitalizations. Multiplying the 26.8 percent times Miller's estimated 2,291,000 cases of disabling injuries (Miller's definition) resulted in an estimate of 614,000 hospitalized workplace injuries.

25. The SDS data, which were drawn from WC records, show a higher percentage of decedents aged 45 to 64 than either the CFOI or the NTOF. It could be that this simply reflects WC coverage, not a real age phenomenon. Workers aged 45 to 64 may be in mainstream industries covered by WC while a higher percentage of younger workers are more likely to have jobs in industries not covered by WC.

26. But the bias is not great since illnesses comprised roughly 7 percent of all incidents in 1992. The percentage contribution of illnesses on the Annual Survey continues to rise. In the early 1980s, illnesses contributed to less than 2 percent of all incidents. As we will see in chapter 3, much of this increase from 2 percent to 7 percent was due to the recognition of carpal tunnel syndrome as a work-related illness.

27. The age breakdown conforms to the presentation in the sources so that arbitrary extrapolation could be avoided.

28. The purpose of the NHIS-OSH was to obtain national estimates of the incidence and prevalence of job-related injuries and illnesses. The NHIS-OSH asked close to 100 questions (if all of the branching questions are included). The original objective was to collect data on the leading problems as viewed by NIOSH: lung diseases, musculoskeletal injuries, cancers, traumatic injuries, cardiovascular diseases, disorders of reproduction, neurotoxic disorders, noise-induced loss of hearing, dermatologic conditions, and psychological disorders. But it became evident that information on cancers and neurotoxic conditions could not be obtained through surveys. As a result, attention was focused on back, hand, or neck discomfort; work-related injuries; skin conditions; eyes, nose, and throat irritation; carpal tunnel syndrome; tendinitis; asthma; chronic bronchitis; and deafness. The NHIS-OSH investigators pointed out that there was an "absence of any national data on these leading occupational health problems" (Park et al. 1993, 2).

29. The 12-month recall bias also is important here. Over 12 months, people are more likely to forget injuries that did not cause work loss as opposed to injuries that did cause work loss. Disabling injuries are more likely to receive WC than nondisabling injuries. Again, the 12-month recall bias would likely influence the 52.7 percent rate so that the "true" rate would exceed 52.7. A higher rate would decrease the percentage receiving WC benefits. This information on who filed a WC claim was available in the codebook accompanying the computer tape for NHIS-OSH, page OH-68.

Chapter 3

1. The vigorous debate over how much cancer is ascribed to occupational causes in the early 1980s is an example of such disagreement (Peto and Schneiderman 1981).

2. These considerations determine the type of evidence that would be needed to achieve validity and precision in determining the proportion of categories of diseases due to occupational exposures. Large case control studies including subjects drawn from a nationally representative sample would yield suitable proportionate attributable risk estimates. Such a study for lung cancer was recommended 15 years ago as part of the occupational cancer debate (Doll and Peto 1981). While many smaller lung cancer case control studies in numerous geographic areas have been completed, a truly national study in the United States or elsewhere has not been initiated.

3. See chapter 3 text references associated with note 2.

4. Doll and Peto (1981) ascribed variable proportions to an additional nine sites. They base these proportions on "the crude and unreliable basis of our interpretation of the literature and clinical impression" (1244). More recently, Boffetta (1998), using the proportions proposed by Doll and Peto and adding his own proportions for seven additional sites, attempted to estimate the numbers of occupational cancers occurring in developed and developing countries. Boffetta does not provide references to support his proposed site-specific proportions. In

our view, the body of epidemiologic research available to date is insufficient to allow estimation of the individual site-specific proportions of cancers other than lung, bladder, and pleura.

5. For our analysis, any risk of cardiovascular disease due to physical inactivity of work is excluded for two reasons. First, there is likely to be much disagreement about whether physical inactivity should be considered an occupational risk factor, much less whether it should be viewed in the same manner as other occupational agents. Second, the etiologic fraction assigned to sedentary work is so large that, if used, it would become the greatest determinant of our estimates of the number of cases of CVD due to occupational causes. Given the lack of consensus about sedentary work, it seems reasonable to exclude it in order to maintain the integrity of the proportion of CVD due to other occupational factors.

6. Olsen and Kristensen (1991) use a higher age range of 70.

7. The profile of disease category differed significantly from the profile recorded in the BLS Annual Survey. Two-thirds of the illnesses among New Jersey public employees were skin diseases or respiratory conditions due to toxic agents. Only 3 percent of illness episodes were due to repeated trauma.

8. Data for illnesses among state and local employees are not available for 1992. Since the illness rate in the public sector probably increased in 1992, as it did in the private sector, above 51.9 per 10,000, we feel justified in using the 59.8 per 10,000 figure.

9. With regard to severity of blood lead elevation, 3,199 (28 percent) of the individuals with elevated blood lead levels in 1993 had blood leads greater than or equal to 40 µg/dl, which is the level at which OSHA requires actions to protect workers from lead exposure in the workplace. Roughly 8 percent (906) of the cases reported in the ABLES program had blood lead levels ≥50 µg/dl, which is the level at which OSHA mandates the removal of the individual from lead exposure (Chowdhury et al. 1994).

10. The hospital discharge survey has another obvious liability. Only individuals with disease sufficiently severe to require hospitalization will be included in the database. For many chronic diseases, the majority of patients will not become so ill as to require hospitalization.

11. These are primary and secondary diagnoses. The National Hospital Discharge Survey allows up to seven diagnoses per hospital discharge, including the primary diagnosis. The numbers of discharges with occupationally specific diseases among the secondary diagnoses are considerably higher than those with such diseases constituting the primary diagnoses. This is less true for malignancy of the pleura than for the pneumoconioses, since malignant mesothelioma is highly lethal and can be expected to be the dominating diagnosis on most hospitalizations of patients with this cancer.

12. Since it is likely that virtually all cancers that are identified as occupational by employers would involve lost work time, it is unlikely that many additional cancers would be recorded among the nonserious cases identified in the BLS survey.

Chapter 4

1. The name *Human Capital method* is a misnomer. Certainly the largest element of indirect costs represents lost worker productivity, that is, lost human capital in the traditional sense. But medical costs reflect prices and do not represent lost worker productivity unless one subscribes to Marx's labor theory of value.

2. For example, most studies find that age, especially after 45, income, education, and family size are strongly related to car purchase price (Lave and Train 1979; Manski and Sherman 1980; McCarthy 1990). Manski and Sherman summarized their findings this way: "the influence of price and operating cost varies considerably among socioeconomic and demographic groupings." Manski and Sherman (1980, 359) and Lave and Train (1979) produced evidence of a U-shaped relation between education and price with the cheapest and most expensive cars being owned by those with little education.

But cheap cars tend to be light, lack expensive safety features, and be less crashworthy than large cars (Manski and Sherman 1980; Lave and Train 1979; McCarthy 1990).

In Zlatoper's (1989, 145) extensive review of highway fatality studies, age and income were frequently found to be strongly and inversely related to motor vehicle deaths. Additional risk factors for motor vehicle crash deaths included male sex and employment (Zlatoper 1989). Although not widely researched, education, being married, and number of dependents may be inversely correlated with highway deaths since they have been strongly linked to seat belt use, smoking, and overall health status (Farrell and Fuchs 1982; Leigh 1990; Taubman and Rosen 1982).

Finally, alcohol use is one of the most robust statistically significant covariates of highway fatalities (Zlatoper 1989). In addition, the relation between alcohol abuse and income appears to be U-shaped, with a disproportionate number of heavy drinkers among the poor and rich (Sagan 1987, 163; Manning, Keller, and Newhouse 1988). The poor also have a high and disproportionate number of people who never drink (Sagan 1987; Rubin 1994).

3. Garen (1988) went one step further and argued that holding constant observed personal characteristics was not enough. Workers "self-select" into hazardous and safe jobs, and unobserved personal heterogeneity must be removed to properly estimate the wage-risk relationship.

4. These estimates are especially rough. We are not aware of WTP estimates for occupational disease. We instead substitute WTP estimates for occupational injuries. The extent of the bias resulting from this substitution is not known. One argument would hold that the diseases occur later in life than injuries and that people would be more willing to pay to save their lives if young than if old. But risk aversion seems to grow with age (Leigh 1986c), suggesting just the opposite. Older people might be willing to pay more than younger people. Moreover, we selected a relatively low WTP death estimate at $4 million. The range in the literature goes to $16 million. In any case, the age argument would

not apply to nonfatal diseases and injuries since many nonfatal diseases — skin problems, carpal tunnel syndrome, and so on — can occur early in life.

5. The fact that WTP costs are marginal costs may also explain why they are so much larger than the Human Capital costs. These estimates also indicate the speculative, theoretical nature of the WTP method. If WTP death estimates were applied to the 2.2 million Americans who died in 1992, the total WTP cost for all deaths would exceed GDP by more than two trillion dollars. From a theoretical economic perspective, this high estimate is understandable. Persons' WTP can reflect accumulated wealth that is not measured by GDP. However, for a noneconomist (judge's) perspective, to state that the cost of deaths in any year exceeds the GDP for that year smacks of "junk science."

Chapter 5

1. See appendix A for chapter 2 for discussions of the NCCI and the Ultimate Reports.

2. In most states, WC insurers and insurance commissioners use NCCI data to help develop insurance premiums that WC insurers charge their customers. Rates are established for occupations, trades, and industries based upon their risks.

3. NCCI publishes several reports: First Year, Second Year, Third Year, and up to the Ultimate Report, corresponding to the Fourth Year report. All reports include forecasts of future expenses. The First Year Report covers expenses from policies for the first year after the policy was written. The First Year Report obviously will be limited by lack of information on injuries that occurred at the end of the year or injuries that generate costs for more than a year. The Second Year NCCI Report follows policies for two years and contains more complete data than the First Year Report. The Ultimate Report arguably contains the best data since injuries and policies have been followed for a minimum of three years.

Medical costs are likely to be incurred into the future for Permanent Totals and Partials, beyond the three to five years of data available in the Ultimate Report. The NCCI simply uses the dollar amounts per PT and PP provided by the private insurance company. In a few cases, this is part of a lump sum legal settlement made to the injured worker. In these cases, the insurance company bears no further liability. In most cases, however, these dollars represent payments already made or monies anticipated to be spent. The lump sum payments, as well as the monies anticipated to be spent, reflect the present value forecasts of expected future medical expenditures.

The forecasted costs were developed by the actuarial experts who work for the private insurers. Although mistakes can always be made for forecasted expenditures, it would be presumptuous for us to imagine that we have a better forecast than those experts familiar with each WC claim.

If dollars from the early years are to apply to 1992 they should be inflated. We assumed that, on average, these NCCI dollars were from 1989. Therefore, we multiplied them by the adjustment factor of 1.27328, assuming a 27.328 percent rate of increase in medical costs from 1989 to 1992 (U.S. Bureau of the Census 1993a).

To adjust for the omission of the high cost states, we further inflated the estimate by 1.1445 percent for an adjustment factor of 0.011445 (U.S. Bureau of Labor Statistics, *CPI Detailed Report,* Department of Labor, Washington, DC, January 1993). These adjustment factors together summed to 1.2847.

The 1.2847 was found in the following calculation:

$$(\text{USMedCPI92}/\text{USMedCPI89}) \times [\%\text{MedCPINEW} \times \%\text{POPNYCA}],$$

where

USMedCPI92 = the medical consumer price index for the United States in 1992;
USMedCPI89 = the medical consumer price index for the United States in 1989;
%MedCPINEW = percentage amount by which the average medical consumer price index in the Northeast and the West exceeds those in the South and the Northcentral states;
%POPNYCA = ratio of New York and California populations to the population of the United States minus New York and California.

4. The 89.98 percent figure is drawn from Baker and Krueger 1995. Baker and Krueger present evidence that WC medical payments exceed other insurers' payment for the same procedures, tests, and therapies. One of their most convincing examples involving X rays shows a 10.02 percent difference between WC and all others. Our percentage is, therefore, 100 percent − 10.02 percent = 89.98 percent. There are some problems with the Baker and Krueger study, however (Leigh and Ward 1997).

5. Some readers may question including profit as a cost. But a normal profit is a cost associated with any private firm, as every introductory economics text explains.

6. Reserve expenses would cover the cost associated with accumulating and holding cash reserves, as well as the reserves themselves. Including cash reserves as a cost is appropriate. After all, if no injuries occurred, there would be no need for the cash reserve, and premiums charged to businesses or persons would be zero. The amount of cash reserves is implicitly captured by the premiums that businesses must pay.

7. They do include, however, expenses for injuries that could have occurred in years prior to the years for which costs are calculated.

8. There is a large literature on administrative costs of insurance. We cannot adequately review all of these studies. We instead briefly mention the important studies and suggest a range of reasonable estimates. There is one point all of these studies acknowledge, however: insurance administration costs are significant and cannot be ignored in a cost study of medical care delivery. In our review of these studies, all of our percentages will be expressed in terms of administrative cost per claim or per medical expense, not per dollar spent on all costs including administration.

Cutler (1994) estimated that administration expenses average 15 percent of insurance claims (i.e., 15 percent of medical expenses). Woolhandler and Himmelstein (1991) estimated that the typical private health insurer would generate administrative costs of 24 percent to 33 percent of total benefits. The California Medical Association's (1993) survey of insurers in California indicated an 18 percent rate (out of benefits paid) for purely administrative costs and an additional 6 percent rate for profit (out of benefits paid) in 1992 for a total of 24 percent.

Danzon (1992) estimated a 12 percent rate for private insurers and 49 percent for public insurers. Danzon, however, included the time spent waiting for service by patients for public insurance but not for private insurance. Danzon is unique among analysts for including waiting costs by patients as an administrative cost. Danzon is also unique in arguing for higher administration costs for public than private health insurance. Most published studies show a lower rate in the public sector. Thorpe (1992) estimated a rate of nearly 66 percent for private companies providing insurance for small firms to a little over 2 percent for Medicare. In fact, a lower rate in the public sector is often mentioned in arguments for greater government control of the health insurance market (Woolhandler and Himmelstein 1991; Leigh and Bernstein 1997a, 1997b).

The *U.S. Statistical Abstract* for 1993 in its table 841 shows figures for health insurance companies (U.S. Bureau of the Census 1993a). In 1990, for example, premiums totaled \$118.6 and benefit payments totaled \$97.7 billion. If all dollars over the benefit payments are administrative costs, this would imply a rate of 21.4 percent out of benefits.

It is tempting to use the 21.4 percent figure. However, WC insurance apparently involves a greater administrative cost than the typical insurer. We do not assume 21.4 percent because some portion of non-WC injuries would be lowered by coverage from government agencies and these would likely have administrative costs less than those of the private carriers. Medicare and Medicaid would tend to reduce this non-WC percentage below 21.4, while WC would tend to increase this percentage above 21.4 percent. We therefore assume the 15 percent rate suggested by Cutler (1994).

9. This \$32.2607 billion figure (1992) compares favorably to indemnity benefits for only WC estimated with the Nelson 1992 and 1993 data: \$25.2 billion (1991). Nelson also estimated \$16.8 billion (1991) for only WC medical payments. Again, our medical estimate is \$25.98 billion (1992). We would expect our estimates to be substantially higher than any WC-only estimate because we believe WC misses 55 percent of job-related injuries.

10. To wit: $32.2607 \times 0.47625 \times 0.31 = 4.7629$; $32.2607 \times 0.52275 \times (1 - 0.183) \times 0.15 = 2.0667$; and $4.72539 + 2.0667 = 6.8296$.

11. It is tempting to include the persons in the Permanent Total category as equivalent to the deceased category for the cost calculations. However, the category title — Permanent Total (PT) — is deceptive. Many WC insurers will settle a PT case with a lump sum payment within a year or two after the injury.

12. They found that rates differed across age, gender, time, and states. The WC statutes themselves within each state are an imperfect guide to estimating

replacement rates since the type of injury within any of the categories (i.e., scheduled and unscheduled benefits) can also greatly affect the replacement rate.

13. We do not make any adjustment for out-of-pocket expenses or the lack of indemnity payments. We are estimating lost wages, not lost indemnity benefits.

14. The NCCI Ultimate Report for May 1993 contains indemnity payments on all WC categories—death through Medical Only. For example, the total indemnity payment for Permanent Total injury cases numbered 4,759 and amounted to $1,166,082,099. These cases were from policies originating in either 1988 or 1989 or 1990, depending on the state. Dollars were paid from 1988 to December 1992.

15. In the May 1993 Ultimate Report, most of the cases originated in 1988 or 1989. But these costs could have been incurred anytime from 1988 through 1992. We chose 1990 as our average year. For medical care, we chose 1989. We believe this year difference is justified. Rice et al. (1989a) found 87 percent of direct costs occurred in the first year of the injury. Rice et al. found that 46 percent of morbidity costs occurred in the first year and 54 percent occurred in all the remaining years. Indemnity benefits, on the other hand, can continue indefinitely.

16. Fringe benefits should be included in indirect costs. The purpose of measuring indirect costs is to measure a person's lost contribution to society as measured by his or her production on the job (and at home). Economic theory suggests that the worker's contribution to production for the firm should equal what the firm must pay to attract him or her. Part of the attraction to any job is the value of fringe benefits.

17. Total average compensation per employee was $15.24 per hour in 1992 (U.S. Bureau of the Census 1993a).

18. An alternative method would involve combining old "specific" human capital estimates from Mincer 1962 with data from a nonrandom sample by Flynn (1995). This is carried out in Leigh et al. 1996. Our estimate is $2,986.

19. The $149 and $12 were estimated from table 5.3. We assumed hiring and training costs were proportional to the wage losses of either TTPs or other disabling injuries to PPs.

20. As a corollary to this third limitation, some might argue that a disadvantage is that some portion of WC payments accrue to lawyers who acted on behalf of injured workers. While this point may have some credibility with indemnity payments, it would not with medical payments, since the latter are paid to medical care providers, not to individual injured workers (Berkowitz and Burton 1987). But lawyers can become involved in non-WC cases as when, for example, a worker sues a manufacturer of asbestos. Litigation expenses, unfortunately, are inherent in virtually all foms of our health care system and in the cost of care.

21. The same NSC study found that only 7.4 percent of all claims lost more than two years of work, while 13 percent of back injury claims lost more than two years at work. Other body parts (and their percentage of total costs) generating high costs were multiple parts (15 percent), legs (14 percent), trunk (13

percent), arms (10 percent), fingers (4 percent), head except eyes (3 percent), neck (2 percent), feet (2 percent), body systems (2 percent), eyes (1 percent), and toes (1 percent).

22. Evidence for their undercount of minor injuries lies in the hospitalization rate. Their hospitalization rate for all injuries was 17 percent, whereas Rice et al. (1989a) in an even more widely cited injury study estimated a 4 percent rate for all injuries. Their hospitalization rate for workplace injuries was an astonishing 27 percent. Miller and Galbraith (1994) and Rossman, Miller, and Douglas (1991) estimated workplace injury hospitalization rates of under 8 percent.

23. The Hensler et al. 1991 study also reinforces our view that WC misses a large percentage of all job-related injuries. The Rand interviewers specifically asked respondents whether they attempted to collect WC benefits. They summarized their findings this way.

> Forty-four percent of those who miss more than seven days of work (and so exceed the waiting period in all states) report receiving workers' compensation. (91)

The true percentage of WC undercount is undoubtedly larger than 56 percent (100 − 44) since (1) the great majority of injuries does not result in three or seven days of work loss and thus is less likely to qualify for WC and (2) their survey underrepresents minorities and the poor, who are more likely than other groups to hold jobs that do not qualify for WC (farm labor, domestics).

24. We cite and discuss the Miller and Galbraith 1994 working paper. The published Miller and Galbraith 1995 paper excluded administrative overhead.

25. Miller and Galbraith's $61.8 billion figure was an attempt to account for pain, suffering, and the quality of life. But pain, suffering, and the quality of life are difficult to measure. Miller and Galbraith use Willingness-to-Pay estimates (WTP). Since WTP estimates are designed to capture all of the costs of injuries, and since WTP estimates for fatalities appear to exceed Human Capital costs by factors of 3 to 6 times or more, Miller and Galbraith subtracted the total of their wage loss estimates from the WTP estimates to arrive at the quality of life estimate. This technique results in an unusual blend of the Human Capital method estimates and WTP estimates. WTP advocates would, in general, not want to add any additional cost to a WTP estimate. But Miller and Galbraith add medical cost. WTP estimates, presumably, already capture medical costs. Perhaps Miller and Galbraith reasoned that the person in the WTP experiment would have assumed medical costs would automatically be covered.

26. Workplace disruptions — totaling $10 billion — were calculated differently for each category of injury. A fatal injury was assumed to result in the equivalent of four months of the deceased worker's wages. These four months of wages were assumed to pay for recruitment, retraining, and loss of special skills. A one-month loss was assumed to cover the expense of all bosses and co-workers in the event of a disabling injury that qualified for WC. Disabling injuries not qualifying for WC were assumed to result in two days of lost time

for the supervisor and four days for all co-workers combined. Injuries that resulted in any work loss for the victim but that Miller and Galbraith did not define as disabling were assumed to generate one day lost for the supervisor and one for all co-workers combined. Miller and Galbraith admit that these assumptions were arbitrary. They did not cite any studies to support their assumptions. Our estimate of $2.1853 billion relied on the study by Barron, Black, and Lowenstein (1989).

27. An additional finding merits attention. In comparing their data with Rice et al. 1989a, they find that although workplace injuries accounted for only 20 percent of all injuries, workpalce injuries were more serious than all other injuries. Miller and Galbraith estimated that workplace injuries accounted for 32 percent of the total injury medical costs in Rice et al. 1989a. This reinforces the similar evidence found in Hensler et al. 1991 of the greater severity of workplace injuries when compared to all others.

28. Miller and Galbraith (1994) assert that if the frequencies and types of injuries as well as cost and procedures of medical care do not greatly vary over the years, incidence- and prevalence-based estimates should be roughly equal. This assumption about nonvarying injuries and medical care is referred to as the "steady state" assumption. The Rand researchers (Hensler et al. 1991) argue that discounting would make a difference, so that incidence-based cost measures would be less than prevalence-based measures provided the same number and type of injuries occur each year. The Miller and Galbraith 1994 and Hensler et al. 1991 arguments are at odds. We address this in appendix B for chapter 10. But even theoretical demonstrations of the differences between the prevalence and incidence methods require the additional (unrealistic) assumption of a steady state whereby the number and type of injury and medical care do not change over time.

29. Rice et al. (1989a) did not provide separate cost estimates for job-related injuries. Marquis (1992) and the NSC (1993) do provide these estimates. Marquis estimates 47.3 percent, and the NSC estimates 29 percent; that is, 47.3 percent and 29 percent of total costs for all injuries are accounted for with job-related injuries. These 47.3 percent and 29 percent figures would suggest job-related injury costs of $74.5 billion (Marquis) and $45.7 billion (NSC) in 1985 using the Rice et al. $157.6 billion figure as a base. Assuming an average 41 percent medical and wage inflation from 1985 to 1992 (U.S. Bureau of the Census 1993a), our Rice et al.–based job-related injury costs would be $64.4 billion (NSC) to $105 billion (Marquis 1992) in 1992. We believe both estimates are low. Again, Burton (1993) estimated WC costs alone to be $60 to $73.5 billion in 1992. We believe Rice et al. undercounted injuries by using the NHIS and underestimated costs by ignoring insurance administrative costs.

Chapter 6

1. This approach is to be contrasted with our micro or "bottom-up" approach for injuries in which numbers for given injuries are multiplied by average

prices for those injuries. A micro or "bottom-up" approach is generally preferred by researchers since it relies on fewer assumptions. But the micro approach requires an enormous amount of data; that is, average costs have to be estimated for a variety of diseases. A literature search did not uncover any studies that provided all the average cost figures for all the diseases and conditions we derive estimates for in chapter 3. Some were available, but the methodology varied considerably across these studies, leaving us unsatisfied that a single set of average costs could be relied on in the same way that we relied on average injury costs from the NCCI in chapter 2.

2. We assume that all of our subjects or their survivors will receive some indemnity, most likely from the Social Security Administration.

3. Unlike the injury data the disease data do not indicate whether or not the person was working immediately prior to death. In fact, we implicitly assume many disease deaths occur in retirement years.

4. We did not apply the 31 percent rate to any of the deadly disease estimates since it is unlikely many would be covered by WC.

5. Estimates by disease will vary according to the relationship between direct costs and mortality costs within disease categories. For some diseases such as cancer, using a ratio for morbidity costs that is based on mortality cost, the total estimate of the cause of cancer is slightly lower. This is due to the high relative proportion of direct cost to mortality costs for cancer patients. This relationship is not true for pneumoconioses, which have much higher ratios of mortality costs to direct costs. Therefore, the estimate of total costs for pneumoconioses, using morbidity costs based on mortality costs, is substantially higher than the estimate using morbidity costs based on direct costs. Overall, in the estimates presented, there appears to be a balancing out of these effects, so that the total estimate appears stable.

Chapter 8

1. The word *incidence* has a meaning in this chapter unlike the meaning in epidemiology or in our cost chapters.

2. Nominal costs have also been referred to as "accounting," "legal," or "out-of-pocket" costs in the economics literature. Incidence costs have been referred to as "true" or "actual" costs. The most popular terms are *nominal* and *incidence*.

3. In appendix A for chapter 2, we presented evidence that WC covered only roughly 45 percent of all injuries. WC tends to be a more generous payer than the medical insurance or direct consumers (patients); hence it could be argued that WC covers more than 45 percent of costs. However, WC covers only a small fraction of occupational diseases, especially diseases resulting in death; hence, it could be argued that the 45 percent assumption is too high. Since we are not aware of any studies that resolve these arguments, we continue to assume a 45 to 55 percent split between costs covered by WC and covered by all other carriers and consumers other than WC. It is likely, however, that the

omission of WC coverage for most diseases is greater than the disparity between WC medical cost and all other medical costs.

4. WC programs differ substantially across the states. Three arrangements exist: monopoly state insurers, state-run and private insurers existing side by side, and only private insurers. One monopoly insurer exists in each of six states: Nevada, North Dakota, Ohio, Washington, West Virginia, and Wyoming. State-run insurers coexist with private insurers in Arizona, California, Colorado, Idaho, Maryland, Michigan, Montana, New York, Oklahoma, Oregon, Pennsylvania, and Utah (Redja 1994). Evidence in Nelson 1992 and 1993 demonstrates substantial variation across states in WC premiums and coverage.

5. An interesting test would involve assessing changes in stock market prices following WC premium hikes. If stock prices fall considerably, this would support the idea that some WC premiums reduce profits.

Chapter 9

1. Ashford (1976), Dorman (1996), and Robinson (1991) present a number of thoughtful policy recommendations, including encouraging the development of OSH committees at virtually all places of business and government facilities. Committee members would regularly discuss OSH issues with management.

2. There is a large literature on the effectiveness of OSHA and other safety inspections (Mendeloff 1984; Robertson and Keeve 1983). The Lindell 1997 study of inspections on U.S. Navy shore facilities presents a useful review of these studies.

3. Some preliminary data that would be useful appear in chapter 8 and in Leigh 1995a.

4. A similar lulling phenomenon occurs for police work, in which the highest death rates are observed in small rural towns, not large cities (Weisheit, Falcone, and Wells 1991).

5. Willful underreporting is also present for occupational disease (McCurdy, Schenker, and Samuels 1991).

6. There are three additional points. To the extent that WC serves as an injury tax, it may be creating a disincentive for safety. That is, the WC premium ("tax") is too low, and "the market" will create too many injuries (Lave 1987). Second, the benefit-to-premium ratios have been at extraordinarily low levels in recent years, leading many WC firms to boast that their political efforts to reduce benefits and tighten requirements have led to significant profits industrywide (Hansen 1997). Third, only the large companies that self-insure see a direct economic incentive to reduce their WC claims, however. Non-self-insured firms face only an indirect incentive. Non-self-insured firms are placed in groups with other non-self-insured firms. They are in a pooled risk category. If the injury rate for the group decreases then each non-self-insured firm might be charged a lower premium. But if the non-self-insured firms are small and the group is large, then the non-self-insured firms individually may not have an incentive to reduce accidents. In fact, the opposite may be true. There is little

they can do individually to decrease their premiums, and so they effectively have an incentive to disregard safety. The same phenomenon occurs when eating out with a large group. It is most likely that the bill will be split evenly. Each person then has an incentive to order the most expensive meal at the restaurant.

Some research suggests that self-insured firms are quite responsive to WC premiums (Ruser 1991). As premiums increase, firms make attempts to reduce their injury and illness rates. But these attempts do not always involve expenditures on providing for a safe and healthful workplace. Self-insured firms also appear to be much more disposed to challenging and appealing WC claims than non-self-insured firms (Hyatt and Kralj 1995).

7. In addition to those costs of illness studies mentioned in the text of chapter 9 there are two others worth noting. However, the methodology differed from ours in that both of these added a large cost component for pain and suffering. Johnson and Heler (1983) estimated that years of asbestos exposure will ultimately cost in excess of $326 billion. These costs will be spread from 1967 through the year 2027, for roughly a cost of $5.4 billion per year. This annual estimate is more than five times ours. They estimate that approximately two-thirds of the private costs will be borne by widows. The Environmental Protection Agency has estimated that the annual benefits of clean-air policies are roughly $1.3 trillion, or roughly 22 percent of the gross domestic product (Crandall, Rueter, and Steger 1996). Clearly, as these two studies show, any accounting of pain and suffering adds considerably to overall cost estimates.

An alternative method for calculating cancer costs would be to simply use our estimate from chapter 6 — $10.6 billion — and divide by the percentage of cancer cases we assumed was occupational: 0.0799. This yields $136 billion. This alternative method could also be applied to all circulatory diseases, for an estimate of $392 billion. Whereas the cancer estimate appears reasonable, the circulatory disease estimate does not. This is likely the result of our assumption about excluding persons 65 and over. These persons make up the lion's share of circulatory disease deaths, and their indirect costs are likely to be small compared to those for persons under age 65.

8. Circulatory disease and occupational injuries *and* illnesses overlap by some $3.5 billion. A thorough cost-benefit analysis would compare spending on occupational safety *and* health excluding these $3.5 billion with all circulatory diseases.

9. From this point on we will omit the "(excluding . . .)" qualifying phrase.

10. The examples of biochemists who work on cholesterol-lowering drugs and safety experts are merely illustrative. Biochemists, obviously, need not specialize in cholesterol-lowering drugs.

11. More generally, there should be some balance in the dollars spent between these two activities. Incidentally, cholesterol-lowering drugs are expensive. Moreover, many physicians question their reliability and worry about their side effects.

12. Whereas this is the point of this section, our preference would not be to take any money away from any medical spending. Our preference would be to take away from advertising soda pop.

Chapter 10

1. Such an injury should (but may not!) be recorded for the BLS's Annual Survey, however.

2. There is ample evidence that the great majority of Americans have a strong work ethic. As real wages have declined since 1973, our hours at work have increased (Mishel and Bernstein 1993; Schor 1991).

3. Additional points concerning the WC undercount are discussed in chapter 2, appendix A, in the section on the National Council on Compensation Insurance.

4. Whereas economists are quick to point out the moral hazard for workers, they are slow to point it out for firms. WC coverage is required by law. Any WC insurer can promise coverage, charge low premiums, make high profits, and pay high salaries to upper management in the short term. When bills come due, they can have the state government take over the business. The state governments, that is, taxpayers, guarantee coverage to injured workers. If irresponsible insurers write too many policies with low premiums, taxpayers can end up footing the bill. This financial environment is similar to the environment surrounding the savings and loan debacle in the late 1980s. The WC insurer Golden Eagle from San Diego was charged with precisely this type of financial scam in 1995 (Fricker 1997).

5. One could alternatively argue in addition that the person was engaged in home production of equal value to the economic "at work" production. Typically, economists have put a lower value on home production than "at work" production. This may not be accurate. Divorce laws explicitly value these equally. When a fully employed spouse and a nonworking spouse divorce, the legal assumption is that assets and income should be split evenly.

6. Our attention to total and average costs rather than marginal costs is appropriate. We seek to generate overall cost figures that then may be compared to overall cost figures for other diseases, injuries, and other activities. If our study had been concerned with, for example, evaluating OSH engineering standards, the appropriate cost would be marginal, not average or total. Presumably, few standards eliminate risk altogether. A standard might cut risk by a tenth or a quarter but rarely, if ever, by 100 percent. The total and average cost concepts apply most appropriately to cutting risk by 100 percent. The marginal cost applies to marginal cuts of 5 percent, 10 percent, or 20 percent.

References

Abt Associates. 1989. *Status Report: Persons with Disabilities*. Toronto, ON: Ministry of Citizenship.

Adams, P. F., and Benson, V. National Center for Health Statistics. 1992. *Current Estimates from the National Health Interview Survey, 1991. Vital and Health Statistics*, series 10, no. 184. Hyattsville, MD: Public Health Service.

Alexander, B. H.; Franklin, G. M.; and Wolf, M. F. 1994. The sexual assault of women at work in Washington State, 1980 to 1989. *American Journal of Public Health* 84 (4): 640–42.

American Cancer Society (Department of Epidemiology and Statistics). 1995. Personal communication. Ms. Sheryl Montgomery, March 2.

American Heart Association. 1992. *Heart and Stroke Facts, 1992*. Dallas: American Heart Association Publishers.

———. 1993. *Heart and Stroke Facts and Statistics*. Dallas: American Heart Association Publishers.

———. 1995. *Heart and Stroke Facts: 1995 Statistical Supplement*. Dallas: American Heart Association Publishers.

American Lung Association (Epidemiology and Statistics Unit). 1995. *Trends in Chronic Bronchitis and Emphysema: Morbidity and Mortality*, January. New York: American Lung Association.

American Medical Association. 1992. *Physician Characteristics and Distribution in the U.S., 1992*. Chicago: AMA Publishers.

American National Standards Institute. 1962. *Method of Recording Basic Facts Relating to Nature and Occurrence of Work Injuries*. Z16.2. New York: American National Standards Institute.

Ames, B. N., and Gold, L. S. 1990. Too many rodent carcinogens: Mitogenesis increases mutagenesis. *Science,* August 31 (249): 970–71.

Ansberry, C. 1989. Workplace injuries proliferate as concerns push people to produce. *Wall Street Journal,* July 16, p. A-1.

Arno, P. S.; Levine, C.; and Memmott, M. M. 1999. The economic value of informal caregiving. *Health Affairs* 18 (2): 182–87.

Arnould, R. J., and Nichols, L. M. 1983. Wage-risk premiums and workers' compensation: A refinement of estimates of compensating wage differentials. *Journal of Political Economy* 91:332–40.

Ashford, N. A. 1976. *Crisis in the Workplace*. Cambridge, MA: MIT Press.

Ashford, N. A., and Miller, C. S. 1998. *Chemical Exposures: Low Levels and High Stakes*. New York: John Wiley and Sons.

279

Atkinson, S. E., and Halvorsen, R. 1990. The valuation of risk to life: Evidence from the market for automobiles. *Review of Economics and Statistics* 72 (1): 133–36.

Bachman, R. 1996. Epidemiology of violence and theft in the workplace. *Occupational Medicine: State of the Art Reviews* 111 (2): 237–41.

Baker, L. C., and Krueger, A. B. 1995. Medical costs in workers' compensation insurance. *Journal of Health Economics* 14 (5): 531–49.

Baker, S. P.; O'Neil, B.; Ginsburg, M. J.; and Li, G. 1992. *The Injury Fact Book.* 2d ed. New York: Oxford University Press.

Baker, S. P.; Samkoff, J. S.; Fisher, R. S.; and VanBuren, C. B. 1982. Fatal occupational injuries. *Journal of the American Medical Association* 248: 692–97.

Barron, J. M.; Black, D. A.; and Lowenstein, M. A. 1989. Job matching and on-the-job training. *Journal of Labor Economics* 7 (1): 5–20.

Barry, J. 1985. Women production workers: Low pay and hazardous work. *American Economic Review* 75 (2): 262–65.

Bauman, K. E., and Emmett, S. E. 1994. Tobacco use by black and white adolescents: The validity of self-reports. *American Journal of Public Health* 84 (3): 394–98.

Becker, E. H. 1984. Self-employed workers: An update for 1983. *Monthly Labor Review* 107 (7): 14–18.

Becklake, M. R. 1992. Occupational exposures and airways disease. In *Environmental and Occupational Medicine,* edited by W. Rom, 453–63. Boston: Little, Brown Publishers.

Behrens, V. W., and Brackbill, R. M. 1993. Worker's awareness of exposure: Industries and occupations with low awareness. *Americal Journal of Industrial Medicine* 23:687–701.

Bell, A., and Denmead, E. 1993. OSHRC rules against Caterpillar for record keeping failures. *Cal-OSHA Reporter* 20 (13): 5569–70.

Bell, C. A.; Stout, N. A.; Bender, T. R.; Conroy, C. S.; and Crouse, W. E. 1990. Fatal occupational injuries in the U.S., 1980 through 1985. *Journal of the American Medical Association* 263:3047–50.

Belville, R.; Pollack, S. H.; Godbold, J. H.; and Landrigan, P. J. 1994. Occupational injuries among working adolescents in New York State. *Journal of the American Medical Association* 269 (21): 2754–59.

Benhamou, S.; Benhamou, E.; and Flamant, R. 1988. Occupational risk factors of lung cancer in a French case-control study. *British Journal of Industrial Medicine* 45:231–33.

Bennett, J. D., and Passmore, D. L. 1984. Correlates of coal mine accident and injuries: A literature review. *Accident Analysis and Prevention* 16:37–45.

Benson, V., and Marano, M. A. National Center for Health Statistics. 1994. *Current Estimates from the National Health Interview Survey. Vital and Health Statistics,* series 10, no. 189. Hyattsville, MD: Public Health Service.

Berger, M. C., and Gabriel, P. F. 1991. Risk aversion and the earnings of U.S. immigrants and natives. *Applied Economics* no. 23: 311–18.

Berkowitz, M. 1990. *Returning Injured Workers to Employment: An International Perspective.* Geneva: International Labor Office.

Berkowitz, M., and Burton, J. F. 1987. *Permanent Disability Benefits in Workers' Compensation.* Kalamazoo, MI: W. E. Upjohn Institute.

Biddle, J.; Roberts, K.; Roseman, K. D.; and Welch, E. M. 1998. What percent of workers with work-related illnesses receive workers' compensation benefits? *Journal of Occupational and Environmental Medicine* 40 (4): 325–31.

Black, D. 1998. Coping with loss: Bereavement in childhood. *British Medical Journal* 316:931–33.

Blair, A.; Zahm, S.; and Pearce, N. E., et al. 1992. Clues to cancer etiology from studies of farmers. *Scandinavian Journal of Work and Environmental Health* 18:209–15.

Blanc, P. 1987. Occupational asthma in a national disability survey. *Chest* 92:613–17.

Blincoe, L. J., and Faigin, B. M. 1992. *The Economic Cost of Motor Vehicle Crashes, 1990.* Washington, DC: U.S. Department of Transportation, National Highway Traffic Safety Administration. Report no. DOT-HS-807-876.

Bluestone, B., and Ross, S. 1997. The growth in work time and the implications for macro policy. Working paper no. 204, Jerome Levy Economic Institute at Bard College, New York, October.

Boaz, R. F., and Muller, C. F. 1990. The validity of health limitations as a reason for deciding to retire. *Health Services Research* 25 (2): 361–86.

———. 1992. Paid work and unpaid help by caregivers of the disabled and frail elders. *Medical Care* 30:149–58.

Boden, L. I., and Fleishman, C. R. 1989. *Medical Costs in Workers' Compensation: Trends and Interstate Comparisons.* WC-89-5. Boston: Workers' Compensation Research Institute.

Boffetta, P. 1998. Estimate of the number of cases of cancer attributable to occupational exposures. *Epidemiology* 9 (5): 518–24.

Bosma, H.; Marmot, M. G.; Hemingway, H.; Nicholson, A. C.; Brunner, E.; and Stansfeld, S. 1997. Low job control and risk of coronary heart disease in Whitehall II (prospective cohort) study. *British Medical Journal* 314: 558–65.

Bound, J. 1989. The health and earnings of rejected disability insurance applicants. *American Economic Review* 79 (3): 482–503.

Brand, S., and Hoskin, A. F. 1993. *Allocation Factor Investigation.* Itasca, IL: Statistics Department of National Safety Council.

Bridbord, K.; Decoufle, P.; Fraumeni, J. F.; Hoel, D. G.; Hoover, R. N.; Rall, D. P.; Saffiotti, U.; Schneiderman, M. D.; Upton, A. C.; and Day, N. 1978. Estimates of the fraction of cancer in the United States related to occupational factors. Washington, DC: National Cancer Institute and National Institute for Occupational Safety and Health.

Brodner, P. 1985. *Outrageous Misconduct: The Asbestos Industry on Trial.* New York: Pantheon Books.

Brooker, A. S.; Frank, J. M.; and Tarasuk, V. S. 1997. Back pain claim rates and the business cycle. *Social Science and Medicine* 45 (3): 429–39.

Broome, J. 1985. The economic value of life. *Economica* 52:281–94.

Brown, C.; Hamilton, J.; and Medoff, J. 1990. *Employers Large and Small.* Cambridge, MA: Harvard University Press.

Brown, M. L.; Hodgson, T. A.; and Rice, D. P. 1993. Economic impact of cancer in the United States. In *Cancer Epidemiology and Prevention,* 2d ed., edited by D. Schottenfeld and J. Frauneni. New York: Oxford University Press.

Bryant, R. R. 1990. Job search and information processing in the presence of non-rational behavior. *Journal of Economic Behavior and Organization* 14:249–60.

Burner, S. T., and Waldo, D. R. 1995. National health expenditure projections: 1994–2005. *Health Care Financing Review* 16 (4): 221–42.

Burrough, B., and Lubov, S. H. 1986. Some concerns fudge their safety records to cut insurance costs. *Wall Street Journal,* December 2, p. A1.

Burstein, J. M., and Levy, B. S. 1994. The teaching of occupational health in US medical schools: Little improvement in nine years. *American Journal of Public Health* 84:846–49.

Burton, J. F. 1988. The compensability of workplace stress. *Workers' Compensation Monitor* 1:12.

———. 1993. Workers' compensation costs, 1960–1992: The increases, the causes, and the consequences. *Workers' Compensation Monitor* 6 (2): 1–23.

Burton, J. F., and Schmidle, T. P. 1994. *Workers' Compensation Year Book.* Horsham, PA: LRP Publications.

Burton, J. F.; Yates, E. H.; and Blum, F. 1997. The employers' costs of workers' compensation in the 1990s: The $100 billion gap. *Workers' Compensation Monitor* 10 (2): 1–11.

Castillo, D. N., and Jenkins, E. L. 1994. Industries and occupations at high risk for work-related homicide. *Journal of Occupational Medicine* 36 (2): 125–32.

Castillo, D. N.; Landen, D. D.; and Layne, L. A. 1994. Occupational injury deaths of 16–17 year olds in the U.S. *American Journal of Public Health* 84 (4): 646–49.

Centers for Disease Control. 1992. Surveillance for occupationally acquired HIV infection—U.S., 1981–1992. *Morbidity and Mortality Weekly Report* 41 (43): 823–25.

Center To Protect Workers' Rights. 1997. *Construction Industry Chartbook.* Washington, DC: Center to Protect Workers' Rights.

Cheadle, A.; Franklin, G.; Wolfhagen, C.; Savarino, J.; Liu, P. Y.; Salley, C.; and Weaver, M. 1994. Factors influencing the duration of work-related disability: Population-based study of Washington State workers' compensation. *American Journal of Public Health* 84 (2): 190–96.

Chelius, J. R. 1977. *Workplace Safety and Health: The Role of Workers' Compensation.* Washington, DC: American Enterprise Institute for Public Policy Research.

————. 1979. Economic and demographic aspects of the occupational injury problem. *Quarterly Review of Economics and Business* 19 (2): 65–70.

Chelius, J. R., and Burton, J. F. 1992. Who actually pays for workers' compensation? *Workers' Compensation Monitor* 5 (6): 25–35.

————. 1994. Who actually pays for workers' compensation? The empirical evidence. *Workers' Compensation Monitor* 7 (6): 20–27.

Chowdhury, N. H.; Fowler, C.; and Mycroft, F. J., et al. 1994. Adult blood lead epidemiology and surveillance — United States, 1992–1994. *Morbidity and Mortality Weekly Report* 43:483–85.

Cimini, M. H., and Becker, E. H. 1993. Census of fatal occupational injuries. Results for 32 states, 1991. *Compensation and Working Conditions* 45 (2): 1–13.

Clemmer, D. I., and Diem, J. E. 1995. Major mishaps among mobile offshore drilling units. *International Journal of Epidemiology* 14:106–12.

Collins, J. G. National Center for Health Statistics. 1985. *Persons Injured and Disability Days Due to Injuries. United States, 1980–81. Vital and Health Statistics,* series 10, no. 149, DHHS Pub. no. (PHS) 85–1577. Hyattsville, MD: Public Health Service.

————. National Center for Health Statistics. 1986. *Types of Injuries and Impairments Due to Injuries, United States. Vital and Health Statistics,* series 10, no. 159, DHHS Pub. no. (PHS) 87–1587. Hyattsville, MD: Public Health Service.

————. National Center for Health Statistics. 1990. *Types of Injuries by Selected Characteristics: United States, 1985–87. Vital and Health Statistics,* series 10, no. 175. Hyattsville, MD: Public Health Service. Quoted in C. H. Park, O. K. Wagener, D. M. Winn, and J. P. Pierce. 1993. National Center for Health Statistics. *Health Conditions among the Currently Employed: U.S., 1988. Vital and Health Statistics,* series 19, no. 186. Hyattsville, MD: Public Health Service.

Colorado Department of Health. 1988. *Colorado Population-Based Occupational Injury and Fatality Surveillance System Report, 1982–1984.* Denver: Health Statistics Section, Colorado Department of Health.

Cone, J. E.; Daponte, A.; Makofsky, D.; Reiter, R.; Becker, C.; Harrison, R. J.; and Balmes, J. 1991. Fatal injuries at work in California. *Journal of Occupational Medicine* 33:813–17.

Conroy, C. 1989. Suicide in the workplace: Incidence, victim characteristics, and external cause of death. *Journal of Occupational Medicine* 31 (10): 847–51.

Copeland, A. R. 1985. Fatal occupational accidents — the first year Metro Dade County experience, 1979–1983. *Journal of Forensic Sciences* 30:494–503.

Correa, P.; Pickle, L. W.; and Fontham, E., et al. 1983. The causes of lung cancer in Louisiana. In *Lung Cancer: Causes and Prevention,* edited by M. Mizell and P. Corres, 73–82. Deerfield Beach, FL: Verlag Cheine International.

Cotter, D. M., and Macon, J. A. 1987. Deaths in industry, 1985: BLS survey findings. *Monthly Labor Review* 110 (4): 45–47.

Crandall, R. W.; Rueter, F. H.; and Steger, W. A. 1996. Clearing the air: EPA's self-assessment of clean-air policy. *Regulation* 19 (4): 35–46.

Creech, J. L., and Johnson, M. N. 1974. Angiosarcoma of liver in the manufacture of polyvinyl chloride. *Journal of Occupational Medicine* 16:150.

Cutler, D. M. 1994. A guide to health care reform. *Journal of Economic Perspectives* 8 (3): 13–29.

Cutler, D. M., and Richardson, E. 1997. Measuring the health of the U.S. population. *Brookings Papers on Economic Activity,* 217–82.

Daniell, W. E. 1994. Renal and bladder disorders. In *Textbook of Clinical Occupational and Environmental Medicine,* edited by L. Rosenstock and M. Cullen, 401–22. Philadelphia: Saunders.

Danzon, P. M. 1992. Hidden overhead costs: Is Canada's system really less expensive? *Health Affairs* 11 (1): 21–43.

Davis, H. 1987. Workplace homicides of Texas males. *American Journal of Public Health* 77:1290–93.

———. 1988. The accuracy of industry data from death certificates for workplace homicide victims. *American Journal of Public Health* 78:1579–81.

Davis, H.; Honchar, P. A.; and Suarez, L. 1987. Fatal occupational injuries of women, Texas 1975–84. *American Journal of Public Health* 77 (12): 1521–27.

Demers, P. A.; Checkoway, H.; and Vaughan, T. L., et al. 1994. Cancer incidence among firefighters in Seattle and Tacoma, Washington. *Cancer Causes and Control* 5:129–35.

Demers, P. A.; Heyer, N. J.; and Rosenstock, L. 1992. Mortality among firefighters from three northwestern United States cities. *British Journal of Industrial Medicine* 49:664–70.

DeVol, K. R. 1986. *Income Replacement for Long-Term Disability: The Role of Workers' Compensation and SSDI.* Cambridge, MA: Workers' Compensation Research Institute SP-86-2, December.

Dickens, W. T. 1984. Differences between risk premiums in union and nonunion wages and the case for occupational safety regulation. *American Economic Review* 74 (2): 320–23.

———. 1985. Occupational safety and health and irrational behavior: A preliminary analysis. In *Workers' Compensation Benefits: Adequacy, Equity, and Efficiency,* edited by J. D. Worrall and O. Appel, 19–40. Ithaca, NY: Industrial and Labor Relations Press of Cornell University.

Dieterly, D. L. 1995. Industrial injury cost analysis by occupation in an electric utility. *Human Factors* 37 (3): 591–95.

Dillingham, A. 1985. The influence of risk variable definition on value-of-life estimates. *Economic Injury* 14:277–94.

Division of Labor Statistics and Research. 1985. *California Work Injuries and Illnesses, 1984.* San Francisco: Division of Labor Statistics and Research, State of California, June.

Doll, R., and Peto, R. 1981. *The Causes of Cancer: Quantitative Estimates of Avoidable Risks of Cancer in the United States Today.* New York: Oxford University Press.

Dorman, P. 1996. *Markets and Mortality: Economics, Dangerous Work, and the Value of Human Life.* New York: Cambridge University Press.

Dorman, P., and Hagstrom, P. 1998. Wage compensation for dangerous work revisited. *Industrial and Labor Relations Review* 52 (1): 116–35.

Dorsey, S. 1983. Employment hazards and fringe benefits: Further tests for compensating differentials. In *Safety and the Work Force,* edited by J. D. Worrall. Ithaca, NY: Industrial and Labor Relations Press of Cornell University.

Douglas, J. B.; Kenney, G. M.; and Miller, T. R. 1990. Which estimates of household production are best? *Journal of Forensic Economics* 4 (1): 25–46.

Ehrenberg, R. G., and Smith, R. S. 1991. *Modern Labor Economics: Theory and Policy.* New York: Harper Collins Publishers.

Elisburg, D. 1994. Workplace stress: Legal developments, economic pressures, and violence. *Workers' Compensation Monitor* 7 (6): 12–19.

Ernst, R. L., and Hay, J. 1994. The U.S. economic and social costs of Alzheimers disease revisited. *American Journal of Public Health* 84 (8): 1261–64.

FAA will offer web site on airline-safety data. 1997. *San Jose Mercury News,* January 30, p. 7A.

Fahs, M. C.; Markowitz, S. B.; Fischer, E.; Shapiro, J.; and Landrigan, P. J. 1989. Health costs of occupational disease in New York State. *American Journal of Industrial Medicine* 16:437–49.

Fahs, M. C.; Markowitz, S. B.; Leigh, J. P.; Chin, S.-G.; and Landrigan, P. J. 1998. A national estimate of the costs of occupationally-related disease. *Annals of the New York Academy of Sciences* 837.

Falaris, E. M.; Link, C. R.; and Staten, M. E. 1995. *Causes of Litigation in Workers' Compensation Programs.* Kalamazoo, MI: W. E. Upjohn Institute for Employment Research.

Farer, K. S., and Schieffelbein, C. W. 1987. Respiratory diseases. In *Closing the Gap. The Burden of Unnecessary Illness,* edited by R. W. Amler and H. B. Dull, 115–24. New York: Oxford University Press.

Farnham, P. G. 1995. The economic costs of HIV/AIDS. In *Readings in Public Policy,* edited by J. M. Pogodzinski. Cambridge, MA: Blackwell Publishers.

Farquhar, I.; Sorkin, A.; Corn, M.; and Weir, E. 1998. Occupational cost estimates for diseases. In *Research in Human Capital and Development: Occupational Health,* edited by I. Farquhar and A. Sorkin. Greenwich, CT: JAI Press.

Farrell, P., and Fuchs, V. R. 1982. Schooling and health: The cigarette connection. *Journal of Health Economics* 1:217–30.

Ferguson, T. W. 1995. A triple threat to California's Tort bar. *Wall Street Journal,* April 18, p. A19.

Feurstein, M.; Miller, V. L.; Burrell, L. M.; and Berger, R. 1998. Occupational upper extremity disorders in the federal workforce. *Journal of Occupational and Environmental Medicine* 40 (6): 546–55.

Fine, L. J., and Rosenstock, L. 1994. Cardiovascular disorders. In *Textbook of Clinical Occupational and Environmental Medicine,* edited by L. Rosenstock and M. Cullen, 389–400. Philadelphia: Saunders.

Fingerhut, L. S., and Warner, M. 1997. *Injury Chartbook. Health, United States, 1996–97.* Hyattsville, MD: National Center for Health Statistics.

Fisher, A.; Chestnut, L. G.; and Violette, D. M. 1989. The value of reducing risks of death: A note on new evidence. *Journal of Policy Analysis and Management* 8:8–20.

Flynn, G. 1995. Overall cost per hire is still on the rise. *Personnel Journal* 74 (12): 26.

Fosbroke, D. E.; Kisner, S. M.; and Myers, J. R. 1997. Working lifetime risk of occupational fatal injury. *American Journal of Industrial Medicine* 31:459–67.

Fox, J. A., and Levin, J. 1994. Firing back: The growing threat of workplace homicide. *Annals of the American Academy of Political and Social Science* 536:16–30.

Fox, P.; Gazzaniga, J.; Karter, A.; and Max, W. 1996. The economic costs of cardiovascular disease mortality in California, 1991. Implications for public health policy. *Journal of Public Health Policy* 17 (4): 442–59.

Freedman, W. 1990. *The Law and Occupational Injury, Disease and Death.* Westport, CT: Quorum Books.

French, M. T. 1990. Estimating the full cost of workplace injuries. *American Journal of Public Health* 80 (9): 1118–19.

Fricker, M. 1997. Insult to injury: Workers' compensation costs and consequences. *Santa Rosa Press Democrat,* December 13, p. A1.

Friedman, B. 1994. An act to amend Section 6401.7 of the California Labor Code, relating to employment. Assembly Bill 3230, introduced February 24 to the California Legislature, Sacramento.

Garen, J. 1988. Compensating wage differentials and the endogeneity of job riskiness. *Review of Economics and Statistics* 70 (1): 9–16.

Gill, A. 1994. Incorporating the causes of occupational differences in studies of racial wage differentials. *Journal of Human Resources* 29 (1): 20–41.

Glazner, J. F.; Borgerding, J. A.; Lowery, J. T.; Bondy, J.; Mueller, K. L.; and Kreiss K. 1998. Construction injury rate may exceed national estimates: Evidence from the construction of Denver International airport. *American Journal of Industrial Medicine* 34:105–12.

Goodman, R. A.; Sikes, R. K.; Rogers, D. L.; and Mickey, J. L. 1985. Fatalities associated with farm tractor injuries: An epidemiologic study. *Public Health Reports* 100 (3): 329–33.

Graves, E. J. National Center for Health Statistics. 1994. *Detailed Diagnosis and Procedures National Discharge Survey, 1992. Vital and Health Statistics,* series 13, no. 118. Hyattsville, MD: Public Health Service.

Green, G. P., and Becker, E. H., eds. 1994. *Employment and Earnings.* U.S. Department of Labor, Bureau of Labor Statistics.

Green, H. 1996. Checking up on your doctor. *Health News: Straight Talk on Medical Headlines* 2 (15): 3–5.

Greer, D. F. 1992. *Business, Government and Society.* 3d ed. New York: MacMillan.

Haines, F. 1993. The show must go on: The response to fatalities in multiple employer workplaces. *Social Problems* 40 (4): 547–63.

Hall, J. H., and Owings, J. F. National Center for Health Statistics. 1994. *Hospitalizations For Injury and Poisoning in the U.S., 1991. Advance Data from Vital and Health Statistics*, no. 252. Hyattsville, MD: National Center for Health Statistics.

Hammond, E. C.; Selikoff, I. J.; and Seidman, H. 1979. Asbestos exposure, cigarette smoking and death rates. *Annals of the New York Academy of Sciences* 330:473–90.

Hansen, F. 1997. Who gets hurt, and how much does it cost? *Compensation and Benefits Review* 29 (3): 6–11.

Hartunian, N. S.; Smart, C. N.; and Thompson, M. S. 1981. *The Incidence and Economic Cost of Major Health Impairments.* Lexington, MA: D. C. Heath.

Hashemi, L.; Webster, B. S.; Clancy, E. A.; and Volinn, E. 1997. Length of disability and cost of workers' compsensation low back pain claims. *Journal of Environmental and Occupational Medicine* 39 (10): 937–45.

Haveman, R., and Wolfe, B. 1994. *Succeeding Generations: On the Effects of Investment in Children.* New York: Russell Sage.

Heaney, C. A.; Israel, B. A.; Schurman, S. J.; Baker, E. A.; House, J. S.; and Hugentobler, W. R. 1993. Industrial relations, worksite stress reduction and employee well being. *Journal of Organizational Behavior* 14:498–510.

Hellinger, F. J. 1992. Forecasts of the costs of medical care for persons with HIV: 1992–95. *Inquiry* 29:536–65.

Hensler, D. R., et al. 1991. *Compensation for Accidental Injuries in the United States.* R-3999-HHS-ICJ. Santa Monica: Rand Institute for Civil Justice.

Hibbard, J. H., and Jewett, J. J. 1997. Will quality report cards help consumers? *Health Affairs* 16 (3): 218–28.

Hodgson, T. A., and Meiners, M. 1982. Cost of illness methodology: A guide to current practices and procedures. *Milbank Memorial Fund Quarterly* 60 (3): 429–62.

Honchar, P., and Suarez, L. 1986. Death certificates as a surveillance tool for fatal occupational injuries. Paper presented at the Fifth International Symposium on Epidemiology in Occupational Health, September, Los Angeles.

Horwitz, T. 1994. Nine to nowhere: These jobs are dull, dead-end, sometimes dangerous; they show how 90's trends can make work grimmer for unskilled workers. *Wall Street Journal,* December 1, pp. A1, A10.

Hoskin, A. F.; Allen, J.; and Brand, S., et al. 1993. *Accident Facts, 1993 Edition.* Itasca, IL: National Safety Council.

Huff, J., and Rall, D. P. 1992. Relevance to humans of carcinogenesis results from laboratory animal toxicology studies. In *Macy-Rosenau-Last Public Health and Preventive Medicine*, 13th ed., edited by J. M. Last and R. B. Wallace, 433–40.

Hyatt, D. E., and Kralj, B. 1995. The impact of workers' compensation experience rating on employer appeals activity. *Industrial Relations* 34 (1): 95–106.

International Agency for Research on Cancer (IARC). 1987. *IARC Monographs on the Evaluation of Carcinogenic Risks to Humans.* Overall Evaluations of Carcinogenicity, Supplement 7. Lyon, France: IARC.

Institute of Medicine. 1988. *Role of the Primary Care Physician in Occupational and Environmental Medicine.* Washington, DC: National Academy Press.

Ippolito, P. M., and Mathios, A. D. 1990. Information, advertising, and health choices: A study of the cereal market. *Rand Journal of Economics* 21 (3): 459–80.

Ireland, T. R.; Johnson, W. D.; and Taylor, P. L. 1997. Economic science and hedonic damage analysis in light of Daubert versus Merrell Dow. *Journal of Forensic Economics* 10 (2): 88–96.

Jack, T. A., and Zak, M. T. 1993. Results from the first census of fatal occupational injuries, 1992. *Compensation and Working Conditions* 45 (12): 1–14.

Jacobs, E. E. 1997. *Handbook of U.S. Labor Statistics.* Lanham, MD: Bernan Press.

Jenkins, F. L.; Kisner, S. M.; Fosbroke, D. E.; Layne, L. A.; Stout, N. A.; Castillo, D. N.; Cutlip, P. M.; and Cianfrocco, R. 1993. *Fatal Injuries to Workers in the United States, 1980–1989: A Decade of Surveillance.* Cincinnati: National Institute for Occupational Safety and Health.

Johnson, W. G., and Heler, E. 1983. The cost of asbestos-associated disease and death. *Milbank Memorial Fund Quarterly* 61:210–21.

Kannel, W. B., and Thom, T. J. 1994. Incidence, prevalence and mortality of cardiovascular diseases. Chap. 8 in *The Heart,* 8th ed., edited by W. Hurst. New York: McGraw-Hill.

Karasek, R. A. 1979. Job demands, job decision latitude, and mental strain: Implications for job redesign. *Administrative Science Quarterly* 24:285–308.

Karasek, R., and Theorell, T. 1990. *Healthy Work: Stress, Productivity, and the Reconstruction of Working Life.* New York: Basic Books.

Karlson, T. A., and Baker, S. P. 1978. Fatal occupational injuries associated with motor vehicles. In *Proceedings of the Twenty-Second Conference of the American Association for Automotive Medicine,* vol. 1, 229–41. Arlington Heights, IL: American Association for Automotive Medicine.

Kenkel, D. S. 1991. Health behavior, health knowledge and schooling. *Journal of Political Economy* 99:287–305.

Kilborn, P. T. 1991. Convenience store jobs: High risks alone at night. *New York Times,* April 7, pp. A1, A27.

Kisner, S. M., and Pratt, S. G. 1997. Occupational fatalities among the older workers in the U.S.: 1980–1991. *Journal of Occupational Environmental Medicine* 39 (8): 715–21.

Kjuus, H.; Langard, S.; and Skjeerven, A. 1986. A case-referent study of lung cancer, occupational exposures and smoking. *Scandinavian Journal of Work and Environmental Health* 12:203–9.

Kniesner, T. J., and Leeth, J. D. 1991. Compensating wage differentials for fatal injury risk in Australia, Japan, and the U.S. *Journal of Risk and Uncertainty* 4 (1): 75–90.

Kochanek, K. D., and Hudson, B. L. 1994. Advance report of mortality statistics, 1992. *Monthly Vital Statistics Report* 43 (6, Supplement).

Korn, R. J.; Dockery, D. W.; Speizer, F. E.; Ware, J. H.; and Ferris, B. G. Jr. 1987. Occupational exposures and chronic respiratory symptoms. A population-based study. *American Review of Respiratory Disease* 136:296–304.

Kraus, J. F. 1985. Fatal and non-fatal injuries in occupational settings: A review. *Annual Review of Public Health* 6:403–18.

———. 1987. Homicide while at work: Persons, industries, and occupations at high risk. *American Journal of Public Health* 77 (10): 1285–89.

Kraus, J. F.; Macurda, J.; Sahl, J.; and Anderson, C. 1990. Work-related fatal injuries in older California workers, 1979–1985. *Journal of Occupational Accidents* 12:223–35.

Krause, N.; Lynch, J.; Kaplan, G. A.; Cohen, R. D.; Goldberg, D. F.; and Salonen, J. T. 1997. Predictors of disability retirement. *Scandinavian Journal of Work and Environmental Health* 23:403–13.

Kraut, A. 1994. Estimates of the extent of morbidity and mortality due to occupational diseases in Canada. *American Journal of Industrial Medicine* 25:267–78.

Kristensen, T. S. 1989. Cardiovascular disease in the work environment: A critical review of the epidemiologic literature on chemical factors. *Scandinavian Journal of Work and Environmental Health* 15:245–64.

Landen, D. D., and Hendricks, S. A. 1992. Effect of recall period on reporting of at-work injuries. *Scandinavian Journal of Work and Environmental Health* 18 (Supplement): 18–20.

Landrigan, P. J.; Goyer, R. A.; and Clarkson, T. W., et al. 1984. The work-relatedness of renal disease: Summary of the working group on renal diseases. *Archives of Environmental Health* 39:225.

Landrigan, P. J.; Graham, D. G.; and Thomas, R. D. 1994. Environmental neurotoxic illness: Research for prevention. *Environmental Health Perspectives* 102:117–20.

Landrigan, P. J., and Markowitz, S. B. 1989. Current magnitude of occupational disease in the United States: Estimates from New York State. *Annals of the New York Academy of Sciences* 572:27–45.

Lave, C. A., and Train, K. 1979. A disaggregate model of auto-type choice. *Transportation Research A* 13A:1–9.

Lave, L. B. 1987. Injury as externality: An economic perspective on trauma. *Accident Analysis and Prevention* 19 (1): 29–37.

Layne, L. A.; Castillo, D. N.; Stout, N.; and Cutlip, P. 1994. Adolescent occupational injuries requiring hospital emergency department treatment: A nationally representative sample. *American Journal of Public Health* 84 (4): 657–60.

Lebowitz, M. D. 1977. Occupational exposures in relation to symptomatology and lung function in a community population. *Environmental Research* 14:59–67.

Leigh, J. P. 1981. Compensating wages for occupational injuries and illness. *Social Science Quarterly* 62 (2): 772–78.

———. 1983. Risk preference and the inter-industry propensity to strike. *Industrial and Labor Relations Review* 36 (2): 271–85.

———. 1985a. The effects of unemployment and the business cycle on absentee-ism. *Journal of Economics and Business* 37 (2): 159–70.

———. 1985b. An analysis of workers' compensation using data on individuals. *Industrial Relations* 24 (2): 247–56.

———. 1986a. Hazardous occupations, stress and heart attacks. *Social Science and Medicine* 23 (11): 1181–85.

———. 1986b. Who chooses risky jobs? *Social Science and Medicine* 23 (1): 57–64.

———. 1986c. Accounting for tastes: Correlates of risk and time preference. *Journal of Post-Keynesian Economics* 9 (1): 17–31.

———. 1986d. Individual and job characteristics as predictors of industrial accidents. *Accident Analysis and Prevention* 18 (3): 209–16.

———. 1986e. Compensating wages for risk of death: Comment. *Economic Inquiry* 24 (3): 505–8.

———. 1987a. Estimates of the probability of job-related deaths in 347 occupations. *Journal of Occupational Medicine* 29:510–19.

———. 1987b. Gender, firm size, industry, and estimates of the value of life. *Journal of Health Economics* 6:511–19.

———. 1988a. Occupation and coronary disease: Schooling as a confounder (letter). *Journal of the American Medical Association* 259:157–58.

———. 1988b. Odds ratios of job-related deaths. *British Journal of Industrial Medicine* 45:158–66.

———. 1989a. Firm size and injury rates in manufacturing industries. *Journal of Community Health* 14 (1): 44–52.

———. 1989b. Specific illnesses and working conditions which contribute to absenteeism. *Journal of Occupational Medicine* 31 (9): 793–97.

———. 1990. Schooling and use of seat belts. *Southern Economic Journal* 57:195–207.

———. 1991a. No evidence on compensating wages for occupational fatalities. *Industrial Relations* 30 (3): 382–95.

———. 1991b. A ranking of jobs based upon the blood pressures of incumbents. *Journal of Occupational Medicine* 33 (8): 853–61.

———. 1991c. Employee and job attributes as predictors of absenteeism in a national sample of workers. *Social Science and Medicine* 33 (2): 127.

———. 1993. Multidisciplinary findings on socioeconomic status and health (letter). *American Journal of Public Health* 83 (2): 289–90.

———. 1995a. *Causes of Death in the Workplace.* Westport, CT: Quorum.

———. 1995b. Compensating wages, value of a statistical life, and inter-industry differentials. *Journal of Environmental Economics and Management* 28: 83–97.

———. 1995c. Dangerous jobs and heavy alcohol use in two national probability samples. *Alcohol and Alcoholism* 30 (1): 71–86.

———. 1996. Occupations, cigarette smoking, and lung cancer. *Bulletin of the New York Academy of Medicine* 73 (2): 370–97.

———. 1998. A report card for occupational injuries and illnesses. *American Journal of Industrial Medicine* 33 (4): 422–24.

Leigh, J. P., and Bernstein, J. 1997a. Public and private workers' compensation insurance. *Journal of Occupational and Environmental Medicine* 39 (2): 119–21.

———. 1997b. The authors' reply. *Journal of Occupational and Environmental Medicine* 39 (9): 819–20.

Leigh, J. P., and Folsom, R. N. 1984. Estimates of the values of accident avoidance at the job depend on the concavity of the equalizing differences curve. *Quarterly Review of Economics and Business* 24:55–66.

Leigh, J. P., and Fries, J. F. 1991. Occupation, income, and education as independent covariates of arthritis in four national probability samples. *Arthritis and Rheumatism* 34:984–95.

———. 1992. Disability in occupations in a national sample. *American Journal of Public Health* 82 (11): 1517–24.

Leigh, J. P., and Gill, A. 1991. Do women receive compensating wages for job-related death? *Social Science Quarterly* 72 (4): 727–37.

Leigh, J. P., and Jiang, W. Y. 1993. Liver cirrhosis deaths within occupations and industries in the California occupational mortality study. *Addiction* 88 (6): 767–79.

Leigh, J. P.; Lubeck, D. P.; Farnham, P. G.; and Fries, J. F. 1995. Hours of work and employment status among HIV patients *AIDS* 9 (1): 81–88.

Leigh, J. P., Markowitz, S. B.; Fahs, M.; Shin, C.-G.; and Landrigan, P. J. 1996. Costs of occupational injuries and illnesses, 1992. Final Report for Cooperative Agreement with E.R.C. Inc. U60/CCU902886. Atlanta, GA: NIOSH.

———. 1997. Occupational injury and illness: Estimates of costs, mortality and morbidity. *Archives of Internal Medicine* 157:1557–68.

Leigh, J. P.; Markowitz, S. B.; and Landrigan, P. J. 1998. In reply. *Archives of Internal Medicine* 158:196–97.

Leigh, J. P., and Miller, T. R. 1997. Ranking occupations based upon the costs of job-related injuries and illnesses. *Journal of Occupational and Environmental Medicine* 39 (12): 1170–82.

———. 1998a. Job-related diseases and occupations within a large workers' compensation data set. *American Journal of Industrial Medicine* 33 (3): 197–211.

———. 1998b. Occupational illness within two national data sets. *International Journal of Occupational and Environmental Health* 4 (2): 99–113.

———. 1998c. Ranking industries based upon the costs of job-related injuries and illnesses. In *Research in Human Capital and Development: Economic and Social Aspects of Occupational and Environmental Health*, vol. 12, edited by I. Farquhar and A. Sorkin. Stamford, CT: JAI Press.

Leigh, J. P., and Ward, M. 1997. Medical costs in workers' compensation insurance: Comment. *Journal of Health Economics* 16:121–24.

Lemen, R. A.; Mazzuckelli, L. F.; Niemeir, R. W.; and Ahlers, H. W. 1989. Occupational safety and health standards. *Annals of the New York Academy of Sciences* 572:100–106.

Lerchen, M. L.; Wiggins, C. L.; and Samet, J. M. 1987. Lung cancer and occupation in New Mexico. *Journal of the National Cancer Institute* 79: 639–45.

Levin, L. I.; Zheng, W.; and Blot, W. J., et al. 1988. Occupation and lung cancer in Shanghai: A case-control study. *British Journal of Industrial Medicine* 45:450–58.

Levit, K. R.; Lazenby, H. C.; Sivarajan, L.; Stewart, M. W.; Braden, B. R.; and Cowan, C. A. 1996. National health expenditures, 1999. *Health Care Financing Review* 17 (3): 205–42.

Levit, K. R.; Cowan, C. A.; Lazenby, H. C.; McDonnell, C. R.; Sensenig, A. L.; Stiller, J. M.; and Won, O. K. 1994. National health care spending trends, 1960–1993. *Health Affairs* 13 (5): 14–31.

Levy, B. S., and Wegman, D. H. 1983. Recognizing occupational diseases. In *Occupational Health*, edited by B. S. Levy and D. H. Wegman. Boston: Little, Brown.

Lindell, M. K. 1997. Occupational safety and health inspection scores predict rates of workers' lost-time injuries. *Accident Analysis and Prevention* 29 (5): 563–71.

Low, S. A., and McPheters, L. R. 1983. Wage differentials and risk of deaths: An empirical analysis. *Economic Inquiry* 21 (2): 271–80.

Lown, B. 1979. Sudden cardiac death. *Circulation* 60:1593–1602.

Lynch, J.; Krause, N.; Kaplan, G. A.; Tuomilehto, J.; and Salonen, J. T. 1997a. Workplace conditions, socioeconomic status, and the risk of mortality and acute myocardial infarction: The Kuopio ischemic heart disease risk factor study. *American Journal of Public Health* 87:617–22.

Lynch, J.; Krause, N.; Kaplan, G. A.; Salonen, R.; and Salonen, J. T. 1997b. Workplace demands, economic reward, and progression of carotid atherosclerosis. *Circulation* 96:302–7.

Macon, J. A. 1984. BLS' 1982 survey of work-related deaths. *Monthly Labor Review* 107 (3): 43–45.

Manning, W.; Keeler, E.; and Newhouse, J. 1988. The taxes of sin: Do smokers and drinkers pay their way? *Journal of the American Medical Association* 261:1604–9.

Manning, W. G.; Keeler, E. B.; Newhouse, J. P.; Sloss, E. M.; and Wasserman, J. 1991. *The Costs of Poor Health Habits.* Cambridge, MA: Harvard University Press.

Manski, C. F., and Sherman, L. 1980. An empirical analysis of household choice among motor vehicles. *Transportation Research A* 14A:349–66.

Marine, W. M.; Garrett, C.; Keefer, S. M.; Vancil, R.; Hoffman, R.; and McKenzie, L. 1990. Occupational injury deaths in Colorado, 1982–1987. Denver: Colorado Department of Health.

Markowitz, S. B.; Fischer, E.; Fahs, M. C.; Shapiro, J.; and Landrigan, P. J. 1989a. Occupational disease in New York State: A comprehensive examination. *American Journal of Industrial Medicine* 16:417–35.

Markowitz, S. B.; Landrigan, P. J.; Fahs, M.; Garibaldi, K.; and Gleaton, K.

1989b. *Occupational Disease in New Jersey.* Report to the New Jersey Department of Health, December.

Markowitz, S. B.; Morabia, A.; Lilis, R.; Miller, A.; Nicholson, W. J.; and Levin, S. L. 1997. Clinical predictors of mortality from asbestosis in the North American insulator cohort, 1981 to 1991. *American Journal of Respiratory Critical Care Medicine* 156:101–8.

Marmot, M. G.; Bosma, H.; Hemingway, H.; Brunner, E.; and Stansfeld, S. 1997. Contribution of job control and other risk factors to social variations in coronary heart disease incidence. *Lancet* 350:235–39.

Marquis, M. S. 1992. *Economic Consequences of Work-Related Injuries.* Report no. CT-103. Santa Monica: Rand Institute of Civil Justice.

Marriott, D.; Kirkwood, B. J.; and Stough, C. 1994. Immunological effects of unemployment. *Lancet* 344 (8916): 269–70.

Marsh, B. 1994. Workers at risk: Chance of getting hurt is generally far higher at smaller companies. *Wall Street Journal,* February 3, pp. A1, A8.

Max, W., and Rice, D. P. 1993. Shooting in the dark: Estimating the cost of firearm injuries. *Health Affairs* 12:171–85.

Max, W.; Rice, D. P.; and MacKenzie, E. J. 1990. The lifetime cost of injury. *Inquiry* 27 (4): 332–43.

Max, W.; Webber, P.; and Fox, P. 1995. Alzheimer's disease: The unpaid burden of caring. *Journal of Aging and Health* 7 (2): 179–99.

McCarthy, P. S. 1990. Consumer demand for vehicle safety: An empirical study. *Economic Inquiry* 28 (3): 530–43.

McCurdy, S. A.; Schenker, M. B.; and Samuels, S. J. 1991. Reporting occupational injury and illness in the semiconductor manufacturing industry. *American Journal of Public Health* 81 (1): 85–89.

McFloyd, V. C., and Flanagan, C. A. 1993. *Economic Stress: Effects on Family Life and Child Development.* San Francisco: Jossey-Bass.

McGarity, T. D., and Shapiro, S. A. 1993. *Workers at Risk: The Failed Promise of the Occupational Safety and Health Administration.* Westport, CT: Praeger.

McVittie, D.; Baniken, H.; and Brocklebank, W. 1997. The effects of firm size on injury frequency in construction. *Safety Science* 27 (1): 19–23.

Mendeloff, J. M. 1984. The role of OSHA violations in serious workplace accidents. *Journal of Occupational Medicine* 26:353–60.

Mendeloff, J. M., and Kagey, B. T. 1990. Using occupational safety and health administration accident investigation to study patterns in work fatalities. *Journal of Occupational Medicine* 32 (11): 1117–23.

Meng, R. 1991. How dangerous is work in Canada? Estimates of job-related fatalities in 482 occupations. *Journal of Occupational Medicine* 33:1084–91.

Mennemeyer, S. T.; Morrisey, M. S.; and Howard, L. Z. 1997. Death and reputation: How consumers acted upon HCFA mortality information. *Inquiry* 34 (2): 117–29.

Mensch, B. S., and Kandel, D. B. 1988. Under-reporting of substance use in a longitudinal youth cohort, individual and interviewer effects. *Public Opinion Quarterly* 52:100–124.

Miller, T. R. 1990. The plausible range for the value-of-life: Red herrings among the mackeral. *Journal of Forensic Economics* 13:17–40.

———. 1995. Injuries to workers and their dependents. *Journal of Safety Research* 26 (2): 75–86.

Miller, T. R., and Blincoe, L. J. 1994. Incidence and cost of alcohol-involved crashes in the U.S. *Accident Analysis and Prevention* 26 (5): 583–92.

Miller, T. R., and Galbraith, M. 1994. Estimating the costs of occupational injuries in the U.S. Working paper, NPSRI.

———. 1995. Estimating the costs of occupational injuries in the United States. *Accident Analysis and Prevention* 20 (6): 741–47.

Mincer, J. 1962. On-the-job training: Costs, returns, and some implications. *Journal of Political Economy* 70 (Supplement): 50–79.

Minter, S. G. 1993. When is suicide compensable? *Occupational Hazards* (February): 57.

Mishel, L., and Bernstein, J. 1993. *The State of Working America 1992–1993*. Economic Policy Institute Series. Armonk, NY: M. E. Sharpe.

Mitchell, O. S. 1988. The relation of age to workplace injuries. *Monthly Labor Review* 111:8–13.

Moore, M. J., and Viscusi, W. K. 1988. Doubling the estimated value of life: Results using new occupational fatality data. *Journal of Policy Analysis and Management* 7 (3): 476–90.

Morabia, A.; Markowitz, S.; Garibaldi, K.; and Wynder, E. L. 1992. Lung cancer and occupation: Results of a multicentre case-control study. *British Journal of Industrial Medicine* 49:721–27.

Morgan, M. G.; Bostrom, A.; Gillespie, T. D., et al. 1996. *Shopping for Safety: Providing Consumer Automobile Safety Information*. National Research Council, Transportation Research Board. Washington, DC: National Academy Press.

Moses, L. N., and Savage, I. 1994. The effect of firm characteristics on truck accidents. *Accident Analysis and Prevention* 26 (2): 173–79.

Murphy, D. J.; Seltzer, B. L.; and Yesalis, C. E. 1990. Comparison of two methodologies to measure agricultural occupational fatalities. *American Journal of Public Health* 80:198–200.

Murphy, L. R. 1991. Job dimensions associated with severe disability due to cardiovascular disease. *Journal of Clinical Epidemiology* 44 (2): 155–66.

Murry, C. J. L., and Acharya, A. K. 1997. Understanding QALYs. *Journal of Health Economics* 16:703–30.

National Center for Health Statistics. 1985. *Persons Injured and Disability Days Due to Injuries, United States 1980–1981. Vital and Health Statistics*, series 510, no. 149. Hyattsville, MD: Public Health Service.

———. 1993a. *Health, United States 1992*. Hyattsville, MD: Public Health Service.

———. 1993b. *Advance Report of Final Mortality Statistics, 1991. Monthly Vital Statistics Report*, series 42, no. 2, supplement. Hyattsville, MD: Public Health Service.

————. 1994. *Health, United States, 1993.* Washington, DC: U.S. Government Printing Office.

————. 1996. *Vital Statistics of the U.S., 1991.* Vol. 2, *Mortality,* part A. Washington, DC: Public Health Service.

National Council on Compensation Insurance (NCCI). 1992. *Workers' Compensation Experience—Countrywide—Ultimate Report Basis Exhibit 5B.* Boca Raton, FL, May.

————. 1993. *Workers' Compensation Experience—Countrywide—Ultimate Report Basis Exhibit 5B.* Boca Raton, FL, May.

National Hospital Discharge Survey database. 1991.

National Institute for Occupational Safety and Health. 1999. Identifying High-Risk Small Business Industries. DHHS (NIOSH) Publication 99–107. Cincinnati: Public Health Service, May.

National Research Council. 1984. *Toxicity Testing Strategies to Determine Needs and Priorities.* Washington, DC: National Academy Press.

National Research Council. National Academy of Sciences. 1987. *Counting Injuries and Illnesses in the Workplace: Proposals for a Better System,* Washington, DC: National Academy Press.

National Research Council (Committee on Neurotoxicity and Models for Assessing Risk). 1992. *Environmental Neurotoxicology.* Washington, DC: National Academy Press.

National Safety Council. 1992. *Accidents Facts, 1992 Edition.* Itasca, IL.

————. 1993. *Accidents Facts, 1993 Edition.* Itasca, IL.

National Toxicology Program. 1998. *Eighth Annual Report on Carcinogens. Summary* Research Triangle Park, NC: U.S. Department of Health and Human Services.

Nelson, N. A.; Park, R. M.; Silverstein, M. A.; and Mirer, F. E. 1992. Cumulative trauma disorders of hand and wrist in the auto industry. *American Journal of Public Health* 82:1550–52.

Nelson, W. J. 1992. Workers' compensation: 1984–88 benchmark revisions. *Social Security Bulletin* 55 (3): 41–58.

————. 1993. Workers' compensation: Coverage, benefits, and costs, 1989. *Social Security Bulletin* 56 (35): 68–74.

Neumark, D.; Johnson, R. W.; Bresnitz, E. A.; Frumkin, H.; Hodgson, M.; and Needleman, C. 1991. Costs of occupational injury and illness in Pennsylvania. *Journal of Occupational Medicine* 33 (9): 971–76.

New York Workers' Compensation Board. 1993. *Compensated Cases Closed, 1988.* New York: Office of Research and Statistics.

Occupational Health Working Group. 1990. *Occupational Disease in Connecticut, 1989: An Assessment of the Magnitude of Occupational Disease.* Hartford, CT: Workers Compensation Commission Statistical Division, February.

Office of Construction and Engineering. 1990. *Analysis of Construction Fatalities—The OSHA Data Base 1985–1989.* U.S. Department of Labor, Occupational Safety and Health Administration, November.

Office of Technology Assessment. 1985. *Preventing Illness and Injury in the Work-place.* U.S. Congress, Office of Technology Assessment OTA-H-256. Washington, DC.

Office of Technology Assessment (Congress of the United States). 1990. *Neurotoxicity. Identifying and Controlling Poisons of the Nervous System.* Washington, DC: U.S. Government Printing Office, April.

Oi, W. 1962. Labor as a quasi-fixed factor. *Journal of Political Economy* 70: 738–55.

Oleinick, A., and Gluck, J. V. 1992. Critique of Neumark's estimate of costs of occupational injury and illness. *Journal of Occupational Medicine* 34 (10): 969, 972–74.

Oleinick, A.; Gluck, J. V.; and Guire, K. E. 1995. Establishment size and risk of occupational injury. *American Journal of Industrial Medicine* 28:1–21.

Oleinick, A.; Guire, K. E.; and Hawthorne, V. M., et al. 1993. Current methods of estimating severity for occupational injuries and illnesses: Data from the 1986 Michigan comprehensive compensable injury and illness database. *American Journal of Industrial Medicine* 23:231–52.

O'Loughlin, M. 1993. Are your employees afraid to report injuries? *Safety and Health* 148 (6): 50–52.

Olsen, O., and Kristensen, T. S. 1991. Impact of work environment or cardiovascular diseases in Denmark. *Journal of Epidemiology and Community Health* 45:4–10.

Olsham, A. F.; Taschke, K.; and Baird, P. A. 1991. Paternal occupation and congenital anomalies in offspring. *American Journal of Industrial Medicine* 20:447–75.

Oxenburgh, M. 1991. *Increasing Productivity and Profit through Health and Safety.* Chicago: CCH International.

Oxman, A. D.; Muir, D.; and Shannon, S., et al. 1993. Occupational dust exposure and chronic obstructive pulmonary disease. A systematic overview of the evidence. *American Review of Respiratory Disease* 148:38–48.

Park, C. H.; Wagener, O. K.; Winn, D. M.; and Pierce, J. P. 1993. National Center for Health Statistics. *Health Conditions among the Currently Employed: U.S., 1988. Vital and Health Statistics,* series 19, no. 186. Hyattsville, MD: Public Health Service.

Parker, D. L.; Carl, W. R.; French, L. R.; and Martin, F. B. 1994. Characteristics of adolescent work injuries reported to the Minnesota Department of Labor and Industry. *American Journal of Public Health* 84 (4): 606–11.

Parkinson, D. K.; Gauss, W. F.; Perper, J. A.; and Elliot, S. A. 1986. Traumatic workplace deaths in Allegheny County, Pennsylvania, 1983 and 1984. *Journal of Occupational Medicine* 28 (2): 100–102.

Pastorino, U.; Berrubi, F.; and Gervasio, A., et al. 1984. Proportion of lung cancers due to occupational exposure. *International Journal of Cancer* 33:231–337.

Pearce, N., and Reif, J. S. 1990. Epidemiologic studies of cancer in agricultural workers. *American Journal of Industrial Medicine* 18:133–48.

Pennsylvania Department of Health. 1990. *Occupational Disease and Injury in Pennsylvania.* Harrisburg, PA: Pennsylvania Division of Environmental Health, June.

Personick, M. E. 1992a. Injury and illness experience in logging. *Compensation and Working Conditions* 44 (8): 1–3.

―――. 1992b. Safety and health conditions in poultry plants. *Compensation and Working Conditions* 44 (10): 1–3.

―――. 1992c. Safety and health risks of airline employees. *Compensation and Working Conditions* 44 (5): 1–2.

―――. 1992d. Work injuries in oil and gas field services. *Compensation and Working Conditions* 44 (6): 1–2.

Peto, R., and Schneiderman, M. 1981. *Quantification of Occupational Cancer.* Banbury Report no. 9. Cold Spring Harbor Laboratory.

Pollack, E. S., and Keimig, D. G., eds. 1987. Counting injuries and illnesses in the workplace: Proposals for a better system. Committee on National Statistics, National Research Council. Washington, DC: National Academy Press.

President's Report on Occupational Safety and Health. 1972. Washington, DC: U.S. Government Printing Office.

Purschwitz, M. A., and Field, W. E. 1985. Scope and magnitude of injuries in the agricultural workplace. *American Journal of Industrial Medicine* 18: 179–92.

Rall, D. P.; Hogan, M. D.; Huff, J. E.; Schwetz, A.; and Tennant, R. W. 1987. Alternatives to using human experience in assessing health risks. *Annual Review of Public Health* 8:355–85.

Rejda, G. E. 1984. *Social Insurance and Economic Security.* Englewood Cliffs, NJ: Prentice-Hall.

Reynolds, J. R. 1997. The effects of industrial employment conditions on job-related distress. *Journal of Health and Social Behavior* 38 (3): 105–15.

Rice, D. P. 1966. *Estimating the Cost of Illness.* Health Economic Series. Washington, DC: U.S. Department of Health Education and Welfare. PHS Pub. no. 974–6. Public Health Service, no. 6.

Rice, D. P.; Hodgson, T. A.; and Kopstein, A. N. 1985. The economic costs of illness: A replication and update. *Health Care Financing Review* 7 (1): 61–80.

Rice, D. P.; MacKenzie, E. J.; and associates. 1989a. *Cost of Injury in the United States: A Report to Congress.* San Francisco: Institute for Health and Aging, University of California, and Injury Prevention Center, Johns Hopkins University.

Rice, D. P.; Hodgson, T. A.; and Capell, F. 1989b. The economic burden of cancer, 1985: United States and California. Chap. 3 in *Cancer Care and Cost. DRGs and Beyond,* edited by R. M. Scheffler and N. C. Andrews, 39–59. Ann Arbor, MI: Health Administration Press Perspectives.

Richardson, S. 1993. Workplace homicides in Texas, 1990–91. In *Fatal Workplace Injuries in 1991: A Collection of Data and Analysis,* 39–44. U.S. Department of Labor, Bureau of Labor Statistics. Report no. 845, April.

Robertson, L. S., and Keeve, J. P. 1983. Worker injuries: The effects of workers' compensation and OSHA inspections. *Journal of Health, Politics, Policy and the Law* 8:581–97.

Robinson, J. C. 1984. Racial inequality and the probability of occupation-related injury and illness. *Milbank Memorial Fund Quarterly* 62:567–90.

———. 1986. Philosophical origins of the economic value of life. *Milbank Memorial Fund Quarterly* 64:133–55.

———. 1988. The rising long-term trend in occupational injury rates. *American Journal of Public Health* 78:276–81.

———. 1991. *Toil and Toxins: Workplace Struggles and Political Strategies for Occupational Health.* Berkeley: University of California Press.

Roche, L. M. 1993. Use of employer illness reports for occupational disease surveillance among public employees in New Jersey. *American Journal of Industrial Medicine* 35:581–86.

———. 1995. Economic costs of occupational injury fatalities in New Jersey in 1992. *Compensation and Working Conditions* 47 (3): 1–5.

Rogot, E.; Sorlie, P. D.; and Johnson, N. J. 1992. Life expectancy by employment status, income, and education in the National Longitudinal Mortality Survey. *Public Health Reports* 107 (4): 457–60.

Rolle, L. 1993. Using improved data on work-related vehicle fatalities in Washington State. In *Fatal Workplace Injuries in 1991: A Collection of Data and Analysis.* U.S. Department of Labor, Bureau of Labor Statistics. Report no. 845, April, 25–29.

Ronco, G., Ciccone, G., and Mirabelli, D., et al. 1988. Occupation and lung cancer in two industrialized areas of Northern Italy. *International Journal of Cancer* 41:354–58.

Root, N., and Sebastian, D. 1981. BLS develops measure of job risk by occupation. *Monthly Labor Review* 104 (10): 26–30.

Rosenman, K. D.; Trimbath, L.; and Stanbury, M. 1990. Surveillance of occupational lung disease: Comparison of hospital discharge data to physician reporting. *American Journal of Public Health* 80:1257–58.

Rosenstock, L. 1981. Occupational medicine: Too long neglected. *Annals of Internal Medicine* 95:664.

Rossignol, A. M.; Locke, J. A.; Boyle, C. M.; and Burke, J. F. 1986. Epidemiology of work-related burn injuries in Massachusetts requiring hospitalization. *Journal of Trauma* 26:1097–1101.

Rossignol, M., and Pineault, M. 1993. Fatal occupational injury rates: Quebec, 1981 through 1988. *American Journal of Public Health* 83 (11): 1563–66.

Rossman, S. B.; Miller, T. R.; and Douglas, J. B. 1991. *The Costs of Occupational Traumatic and Cumulative Injuries.* Research report supported by the NIOSH and CDS (CDC Grant no. R49/CCR 303675–02), (NTIS PB92–141399), March.

Rothstein, M. A., and Cooper, S. P. 1993. *Occupational Injury and Illness in Texas.* Report to the Texas Legislature. University of Houston Health Law and Policy Institute, March.

Roy, R. 1992. *The Social Context of the Chronic Pain Sufferer.* Toronto: University of Toronto Press.

Rubin, L. B. 1994. *Families on the Fault Line: America's Working Class Speaks about the Family, the Economy, Race, and Ethnicity.* New York: Harper Collins.

Ruble, R. 1993. An evaluation of certificates of death as a source of data on fatal work injuries: The Indiana experience. In *Fatal Workplace Injuries in 1991: A Collection of Data and Analysis,* 30–33. Department of Labor, Bureau of Labor Statistics. Report no. 845, April.

Runyan, C. W., Loomis, D.; and Butts, J. 1994. Practices of county medical examiners in classifying deaths as on the job. *Journal of Occupational Medicine* 36 (1): 36–41.

Ruser, J. W. 1991. Workers' compensation and occupational injuries and illnesses. *Journal of Labor Economics* 19 (4): 325–50.

———. 1993. Workers' compensation and the distribution of occupational injuries. *Journal of Human Resources* 28 (3): 593–617.

———. 1994. Safety and health in the workplace. Chap. 3 in *Report on the American Workforce.* U.S. Department of Labor. Washington, DC: U.S. Government Printing Office.

———. 1996. Demographic correlations of workplace safety and health risk. Working paper, Bureau of Labor Statistics, Washington, DC, April.

Russell, J., and Conroy, C. 1991. Representativeness of deaths identified through the injury-at-work item on the death certificate: Implications for surveillance. *American Journal of Public Health* 81:1613–18.

Sagan, L. A. 1987. *The Health of Nations.* New York: Basic Books.

Schnall, P. L.; Landsbergis, P. A.; and Baker, D. 1994. Job strain and cardiovascular disease. *Annual Review of Public Health* 15:381–411.

Schneider, R. C.; Kennedy, J. C.; Plant, M. L.; Fowler, P. J.; Hoff, J. T.; and Matthews, L. S. 1985. *Sports Injuries: Mechanisms, Prevention, and Treatment.* Baltimore, MD: Williams and Wilkins.

Schoenberg, J. B.; Sternhagen, A.; Mason, T. J., et al. 1987. Occupation and lung cancer risk among New Jersey white males. *Journal of the National Cancer Institute* 79:13–21.

Schor, J. 1991. *The Overworked American.* Cambridge, MA: Harvard University Press.

Schroeder, E., and Shapiro, S. 1984. Responses to occupational disease: The role of markets, regulation, and information. *Georgetown Law Journal* 72:1265–66.

Seeman, M.; Seeman, A. Z.; and Bardoz, A. 1988. Powerlessness, work, and community: A longitudinal study of alienation and alcohol use. *Journal of Health and Social Behavior* 29:185–98.

Sehgal, E. 1984. Occupational mobility and job tenure in 1983. *Monthly Labor Review* 107 (10): 18–23.

Seligman, P. J., Newman, S. C.; Timbrook, L. L.; and Halperin, W. E. 1987. Sexual assault of women at work. *American Journal of Industrial Medicine* 12:445–50.

Seligman, P. J.; Sieber, W. K.; Pederson, D. H.; Sundin, D. S.; and Frazier, T. M. 1988. Compliance with OSHA record-keeping requirements. *American Journal of Public Health* 78 (9): 1218–19.

Selikoff, I. J.; Churg, J.; and Hammond, E. C. 1964. Asbestos exposure and neoplasia. *Journal of the American Medical Association* 188:22.

Selikoff, I. J., and Lee, D. 1978. *Asbestos and Disease.* Orlando, FL: Academic Press.

Selikoff, I. J., and Seidman, H. 1991. Asbestos-associated deaths among insulation workers in the United States and Canada, 1967–1987. *Annals of the New York Academy of Science* 643:1–14.

Sellers, C., and Markowitz, S. 1992. Reevaluating the carcinogenicity of ortho-Toluidine: A new conclusion and its implications. *Review of Toxicology and Pharmacology* 16:301–17.

Shillings, S., and Brackbill, R. M. 1987. Occupational health and safety risks and potential health consequences perceived by U.S. workers, 1985. *Public Health Reports* 102 (1): 36–48.

Silverman, D. T.; Levin, L. I.; Hoover, R. H.; and Harge, P. 1989a. Occupational risks of bladder cancer in the United States: I. White men. *Journal of the National Cancer Institute* 81:1472–80.

———. 1989b. Occupational risks of bladder cancer in the United States: II. Nonwhite men. *Journal of the National Cancer Institute* 81:1480–83.

Slovic, P. 1978. The psychology of protective behavior. *Journal of Safety Research* 10 (2): 58–68.

Smart, B. D. 1987. Progressive approaches for hiring the best people. *Training and Development Journal* 41 (9): 46, 53.

Smith, A. [1776] 1976. *An Inquiry in to the Nature and Causes of the Wealth of Nations.* Vol. 2, bk. 5. Reprint, Chicago: University of Chicago Press.

Smith, R. B. 1995. In other news. *Occupational Health and Safety* 64 (6): 21.

Smith, R. S. 1974. The feasibility of an injury tax approach to occupational safety. *Law and Contemporary Problems* 38 (4): 730–44.

———. 1990. Mostly on Mondays: Is workers' compensation covering off-the-job injuries? In *Benefits, Costs, and Cycles in Workers' Compensation,* edited by P. S. Borba and D. Appel, 115–28. Boston: Kluwer Academic Publishers.

———. 1992. Have OSHA and workers' compensation made the workplace safer? In *Research Frontiers in Industrial Relations and Human Resources,* edited by D. Levin, O. S. Mitchell, and P. D. Sherer. Madison: Industrial Relations Research Association, University of Wisconsin.

Staller, J. M.; Sullivan, B. P.; and Friedman, E. A. 1994. Value of life estimates—too imprecise for courtroom use: A note. *Journal of Forensic Economics* 7 (2): 215–19.

Stallones, R. A., and Downs, T. A. 1978. *A Critical Review of Estimates of the Fraction of Cancer in the United States. Related to Occupational Factors.* Prepared by Research Statistics, Inc., under contract from the American Industrial Health Council, Houston, TX, and B. F. Goodrich Company.

Steenland, K.; Johnson, J.; and Nowlin, S. 1997. A follow-up study of job strain and heart disease among males in the NHANES1 population. *American Journal of Industrial Medicine* 31:256–60.

Steenland, K.; Loomis, D.; Shy, C.; and Simonsen, N. 1996. Review of occupational lung carcinogens. *American Journal of Industrial Medicine* 29: 474–90.

Stern, R. K.; Peterson, M. A.; Pefille, R. T.; and Vaiana, M. E. 1997. *Findings and Recommendations on California's Permanent Partial Disability System.* Santa Monica: Rand Institute for Social Justice.

Stout, N., and Bell, C. 1991. Effectiveness of source documents for identifying fatal occupational injuries: A synthesis of studies. *American Journal of Public Health* 81 (6): 725–28.

Suruda, A., and Emmett, E. A. 1988. Counting recognized occupational deaths in the U.S. *Journal of Occupational Medicine* 30 (11): 868–72.

Talbott, E. D. 1988. Noise-induced hearing loss and high blood pressure. In *NIOSH Grants, Research and Demonstration Projects: 1987 Annual Report,* edited by J. D. Millar. Atlanta: CDC.

Tanaka, S.; Seligman, P.; and Halperin, W., et al. 1988. Use of workers' compensation claims data for surveillance of cumulative trauma disorders. *Journal of Occupational Medicine* 30 (6): 488–92.

Tanaka, S.; Wild, D. K.; Seligman, P. J.; Halperin, W. E.; Behrens, V. J.; and Putz-Anderson, V. 1995. Prevalence and work-relatedness of self-reported carpal tunnel syndrome among U.S. workers — analysis of the occupational health supplement data of 1988 National Health Interview Survey. *American Journal of Industrial Medicine* 27:451–70.

Taubman, P., and Rosen, S. 1982. Healthiness, education, and marital status. *Economic Aspects of Health,* edited by V. R. Fuchs. Chicago: University of Chicago Press.

Thaler, R., and Rosen, S. 1976. The value of saving a life — evidence from the labor market. *Household Production and Consumption,* edited by N. Terleckyj. New York: National Bureau of Economic Research and Columbia University.

Thorpe, K. E. 1992. Inside the black box of administrative costs. *Health Affairs* 11 (2): 42–55.

Toscano, G. A. 1996. National Census of Fatal Occupational Injuries, 1995. *News Release.* Washington, DC: Bureau of Labor Statistics, U.S. Department of Labor, August 8.

———. 1997. Dangerous jobs. *Compensation and Working Conditions* 49 (2): 57–60.

Toscano, G. A.; Derstine, B.; Jack, T.; Kenestat, A.; Windau, J.; and Zak, M. 1995. *Fatal Workplace Injuries in 1993: A Collection of Data and Analysis.* Report no. 891. Washington, DC: U.S. Department of Labor, Bureau of Labor Statistics, June.

Toscano, G. A., and Windau, J. 1993. Fatal work injuries: Results from the 1992 national census. *Monthly Labor Review* 116 (10): 39–48.

———. 1994. The changing character of fatal work injuries. *Monthly Labor Review* 117 (10, November): 17–28.

U.S. Bureau of the Census. 1992. *Statistical Abstract for the U.S., 1992.* 112th ed. Washington, DC.

———. 1993a. *Statistical Abstract for the U.S., 1993.* 113th ed. Washington, DC.

———. 1993b. Current Population Reports, Series P60-184. *Money Income of Households, Families and Persons in the U.S. in 1992.* Washington, DC: U.S. Government Printing Office.

———. 1995. *Statistical Abstract for the U.S., 1995.* 115th ed. Washington, DC.

U.S. Bureau of Labor Statistics. 1985. *Employment and Earnings.* U.S. Department of Labor. Washington, DC: U.S. Government Printing Office.

———. 1986. *Employment and Earnings.* U.S. Department of Labor. Washington, DC: U.S. Government Printing Office.

———. 1987. *Occupational Injuries and Illnesses in the U.S. by Industry, 1985.* Bulletin no. 2278. U.S. Department of Labor. Washington, DC: U.S. Government Printing Office, May.

———. 1989. *Occupational Injuries and Illnesses in the U.S. by Industry, 1987.* Bulletin no. 2424. U.S. Department of Labor. Washington, DC: U.S. Government Printing Office, May.

———. 1991a. *Occupational Injuries and Illnesses in the U.S. by Industry, 1989.* Bulletin no. 2379. U.S. Department of Labor. Washington, DC: U.S. Government Printing Office, April.

———. 1991b. Bulletin no. 2370, Supplement to *Employment and Earnings,* July.

———. 1992. *Occupational Injuries and Illnesses in the U.S. by Industry, 1990.* Bulletin no. 2399. U.S. Department of Labor. Washington, DC: U.S. Government Printing Office, April.

———. 1993. *Occupational Injuries and Illnesses in the U.S. by Industry, 1991.* Bulletin no. 2328. U.S. Department of Labor. Washington, DC: U.S. Government Printing Office, May.

———. 1994a. *News: Work Injuries and Illnesses by Selected Characteristics, 1992.* USDL-94-213. U.S. Department of Labor, April 26.

———. 1994b. *Occupational Injuries and Illnesses in the U.S. by Industry, 1992.* Summary 94–3. U.S. Department of Labor. Washington DC: U.S. Government Printing Office, May.

———. 1994c. *News: The Employment Situation, June 1994.* USDL 94-326. Washington, DC: U.S. Department of Labor, July 8.

———. 1995a. *Occupational Injuries and Illnesses; Counts, Rates, and Characteristics, 1992.* Bulletin no. 2455. U.S. Department of Labor. Washington, DC: U.S. Government Printing Office, April.

———. 1995b. *Fatal Workplace Injuries in 1993: A Collection of Data and Analysis.* Report no. 891. Washington, DC, June.

———. 1996. *News: Characteristics of Injuries and Illnesses Resulting in Absence from Work, 1994.* USDL-96-163. Washington, DC: U.S. Department of Labor, May 8.

U.S. Chamber of Commerce. 1980–92. *Analysis of Workers' Compensation Laws.* Washington, DC: U.S. Chamber of Commerce.

———. 1993. Table 4. *Employee Benefits, 1992.* Washington, DC: U.S. Chamber of Commerce.

U.S. Congress. 1987. House Subcommittee of Committee on Government Operations chaired by Tom Lantes. *Hearings on Underreporting of Occupational Injuries and Its Impact on Workers' Safety,* pt. 1, 100th Cong., 1st sess., March 19.

U.S. Department of Commerce. 1993. Bureau of the Census. Current Population Reports Series P-60. *Money Income of Households, Families, and Persons in the U.S., 1992.* Washington, DC: U.S. Government Printing Office.

U.S. Department of Health and Human Services. 1985. *The Health Consequences of Smoking, Cancer and Chronic Lung Disease in the Workplace. A Report of the Surgeon General.* Rockville, MD: U.S. Public Health Service, Office on Smoking and Health.

———. 1991. *Vital and Health Statistics: Detailed Diagnoses and Procedures.* Hyattsville, MD: National Hospital Discharge Survey, NCHS.

———. 1992. *Catalog of Electronic Data Products.* DHHS Pub. (PHS) 92–1213. Hyattsville, MD: National Centers for Health Statistics, July.

———. 1993a. *Morbidity and Mortality Weekly Report* 42 (39): 757–72.

———. 1993b. *Vital and Health Statistics: Health Conditions among the Currently Employed: United States, 1988.* Series 10, no. 198, July.

———. 1993c. National Center for Health Statistics. *Work Table 1. Death from Each Cause by 5-Year Age Groups, Race and Sex: United States, 1991.* Vital Statistics of the U.S., annual and unpublished data, Washington, DC.

———. 1994. National Center for Health Statistics. *Life Tables, Vital Statistics of the U.S., 1990.* Vol. 2, sec. 6, pub. no. 94–1104. Washington, DC.

U.S. Department of Labor. 1992. Occupational Safety and Health Statistics, Chap. 14 in *BLS Handbook of Methods.* Bureau of Labor Statistics, Bulletin no. 2414. Washington, DC: U.S. Government Printing Office, September.

Vartabedian, R. 1998. Retail clerks get safety boost. *San Jose Mercury News,* April 28, p. C1.

Vena, J. E., and Fiedler, R. C. 1987. Mortality of a municipal-worker cohort: IV. Fire fighters. *American Journal of Industrial Medicine* 11:671–84.

Viegi, G.; Prediletto, R.; and Paoletti, P., et al. 1991. Respiratory effects of occupational exposure in a general population sample in North Italy. *American Review of Respiratory Disease* 143:510–15.

Vineis, P., and Simonato, L. 1991. Proportion of lung and bladder cancers in males resulting from occupation: A systematic approach. *Archives of Environmental Health* 46 (1, January/February): 6–15.

Vineis, P.; Thomas, T.; and Hayes, R. B., et al. 1988. Proportion of lung cancers in males, due to occupation, in different areas of the USA. *International Journal of Cancer* 42:851–56.

Vingard, E.; Alfredson, L.; Goldie, I.; and Hogstedt, C. 1991. Occupation and osteoarthritis of the hip and knee: A register based cohort study. *International Journal of Epidemiology* 30:1025–31.

Viscusi, W. K. 1979. *Employment Hazards: An Investigtion of Market Perfor-mance.* Cambridge, MA: Harvard University Press.

———. 1992. *Fatal Tradeoffs: Public and Private Responsibilities for Risk.* New York: Oxford University Press.

———. 1993. The value of risks to life and health. *Journal of Economic Litera-ture* 31 (4): 1912–46.

———. 1998. *Rational Risk Policy.* New York: Oxford University Press.

Viscusi, W. K., and Moore, M. J. 1988. The quality-adjusted value of life. *Economic Inquiry* 26:369–88.

Ward, E. 1995. Overview of preventable industrial causes of occupational can-cer. *Environmental Health Perspectives* 103 (Supplement 8, November): 197–203.

Ward, W.; Carpenter, A.; Markowitz, S.; Roberts, D.; and Halperin, W. 1991. Excess number of bladder cancers in workers exposed to ortho-toluidine and aniline. *Journal of the National Cancer Institute* 83:501–6.

Weisheit, R.; Falcone, D. N.; and Wells, L. E. 1996. *Crime and Policing in Rural and Urban America.* Prospect Heights, IL: Waveland Press.

Wildarsky, A. 1980. Richer is safer. *Public Interest* 60:23–29.

Windau, J.; Rosenman, K.; Anderson, H.; Hanrahan, M.; Rudolph, L.; Stanbury, M.; and Stark, A. 1990. The identification of occupational lung disease from hospital discharge data. *Journal of Occupational Medicine* 33:1060–66.

Windau, J., and Goodrich, D. 1990. Testing a census approach to compiling data on fatal work injuries. *Monthly Labor Review* 113 (12): 47–49.

Wong, O.; Whorton, M. D.; Foliart, D. E.; and Ragland, D. 1991. An industry-wide epidemiologic study of vinyl chloride workers, 1942–1982. *American Journal of Industrial Medicine* 20:317–34.

Woolhandler, S., and Himmelstein, D. U. 1991. The deteriorating administra-tive efficiency of the U.S. health care system. *New England Journal of Medicine* 324 (18): 1535–38.

Xu, S.; Christiani, D. C.; Dockery, D. W.; and Wang, L. 1992. Exposure-response relationships between occupational exposures and chronic respira-tory illness: A community-based study. *American Review of Respiratory Disease* 145:413–18.

Yelin, E., and Callahan, L. E. 1995. The economic cost, social and psychologi-cal impact of musculoskeletal conditions. *Arthritis and Rheumatism* 38: 1351–67.

Zhange, J.; Cui, W. W.; and Lee, D. J. 1992. Occupational hazards and preg-nancy outcomes. *American Journal of Industrial Medicine* 21:397–408.

Zlatoper, T. J. 1989. Models explaining motor vehicle death rates in the United States. *Accident Analysis and Prevention* 21:125–54.

Zwerling, C.; Sprince, N. L.; Ryan, J.; and Jones, M. P. 1993. Occupational injuries: Comparing the rates of male and female postal workers. *American Journal of Epidemiology* 138 (1): 46–55.

Index

nervous system disorders, 6, 7, 10, 60, 87, 89, 135, 143, 146, 154
Neumark, D., 90, 101, 107, 122, 126–28, 135, 139, 149, 154, 155
New Jersey, 55, 59, 76, 77, 83, 118, 128, 129, 154, 267
New York, 21, 22, 24, 25, 30, 49, 55, 59, 77, 83, 97, 99, 101, 108, 121, 128, 129, 154, 158, 211, 232, 270, 276
nominal payment (nominal costs), 11, 170, 171, 173, 179, 180, 275
nondisabling, 2, 4, 5, 17, 27, 28, 32, 52, 105, 108, 109, 113, 114, 125, 134, 157, 215, 266
nonfatal injuries, 1–6, 13–18, 20, 23–29, 31–33, 36, 39–42, 51, 54, 98, 105, 106, 112, 119, 124, 126, 127, 131, 132, 135, 157, 168, 198, 215–17, 219, 222, 226, 228, 229, 236–38, 252, 263, 264
North Carolina, 25, 129, 158, 230

Occupational Safety and Health Administration (OSHA), 18, 19, 21, 23, 26, 27, 44, 45, 55, 58, 68, 95, 133, 182–88, 192, 201, 210, 214–16, 220, 222, 223, 230, 250
Oleinick, A., 44, 154, 155, 214, 253
Olsen, O., 64, 65, 267
overtime, 124, 126, 133, 200, 222, 226

pain and suffering, 3, 8, 93, 104, 105, 134, 252, 277
Pennsylvania, 30, 44, 49, 59, 77, 101, 121, 126–28, 154, 155, 214, 232, 276
Permanent Partial, 4, 9, 25, 29, 30, 32, 53, 108, 112–14, 119, 157–59, 231
Permanent Total, 4, 9, 25, 29, 30, 32, 53, 108, 109, 112–14, 118, 119, 157–59, 231, 269, 271, 272
Peto, R., 58, 60, 61, 266
pilots, 49, 92, 98, 100, 166, 168, 169
plumbers, 94, 162, 165, 244

pneumoconioses, 6, 10, 12, 66, 67, 75, 81, 82, 85–87, 89, 141, 143, 146, 148, 149, 154, 267, 275
police officers, 11, 46, 92, 100, 210, 265
present value, 8, 9, 10, 107, 111–13, 115–18, 120, 136, 138, 139, 252, 256, 257, 269
prevalence, 1, 17, 20, 21, 26, 28, 29, 34, 61, 73, 74, 79, 80, 81, 85, 108, 110, 123, 125, 126, 128, 135, 136, 154, 189, 194, 202, 206, 224, 231, 249, 255, 256, 257, 262, 263, 266, 274
prison guards (correctional officers), 2, 46, 163, 165
production helpers, 10, 11, 71, 162, 164, 165
proportional attributable risk, 58, 78, 83, 87, 88

race, 19, 20–23, 39, 43, 44, 74, 92, 238
rape, 29, 34, 54, 216, 217
renal disorders, 7, 10, 60, 87, 135, 146, 148
replacement rate or rates, 113, 138, 143, 187
Rice, D. P., 17, 35, 90, 91, 107, 108, 116, 118, 121, 122, 130–32, 136, 139, 143, 145, 146, 148, 155, 156, 189, 190, 199, 262, 264, 265, 272–74
Robertson, L. S., 276
Robinson, J. C., 20, 43–45, 90, 91, 97, 102, 226, 261, 276
roofers, 48, 167, 169
Rosenstock, L., 13, 64
Rossignol, A. M., 44, 50
Ruser, J. W., 20, 27, 187, 216–18, 261, 277

Schnall, P. L., 64
self-employed, 2, 5, 7, 21, 23, 26, 27, 35, 37, 44, 76–79, 149, 157, 187, 197, 213, 214, 216, 224, 229, 233, 251
Selikoff, I. J., 56, 67
Seligman, P. J., 43, 45, 214, 230